Contents

Authors

Peter Stimpson
Hurtwood House, Surrey

David Dyer
Director of Cambridge Business Studies Trust

Ian Dorton
United World College, Singapore

David Grainger
Coleraine Boys' Secondary School, Northern Ireland

Preface

This book has been written specifically for the AS level Business Studies specification of the OCR examination board. The second edition includes new material that fully meets the requirements of the redrafted 2002 specification and assessment methods. It is the only book that is endorsed by the OCR for use by centres and students following this specification. It will meet the needs of those who intend to complete the AS qualification and provide a firm foundation for those who intend to study the subject beyond AS level. The first edition was also widely used by students following other examination specifications and it proved useful to students on courses requiring a business background.

The second edition builds upon the strengths of the first. It also adds further questions and case studies and guidance for candidates in preparing for the new AS unit examinations. There are also specimen papers for all three AS units and Chapter 19 provides a valuable insight into what examiners will be looking for from students' answers in these examinations.

The book contains features designed to support teachers and students in the successful completion of the AS course and prepare them effectively to continue into A2. The book is divided into two distinct parts:

◆ Part 1 (Chapters 1–7) covers the course for 'Businesses: their objectives and environment'.
◆ Part 2 (Chapters 8–18) fulfils the requirement for 'Business decisions' and 'Business behaviour' – the two final teaching modules of the AS course.

Each chapter contains:

◆ A clear statement of objectives.
◆ Student friendly text that continually highlights key issues and vital subject vocabulary.
◆ Many activities that reinforce the learning process. Most of these are specifically designed to encourage group learning.
◆ Case studies designed to enrich understanding of the subject by giving an insight into real business problems.
◆ Test activities that allow students to check their progress against AS level type case studies and questions. Mark allocations and suggested time limits are also given.
◆ An 'over-to-you' section at the end of each chapter which contains a wide variety of short test questions, AS case study questions and group 'discover and learn' activities.
◆ A summary of the main learning points covered in the chapter.
◆ A list of key words that are defined in the extensive glossary on pp.269–280.

The key aim of this book is to bring the business world into the classroom in a way that encourages learning and provides an awareness of business studies as a dynamic process that reflects what is happening in the wider community. The book is written on the assumption that students are observant and curious. The authors hope that students will bring their perceptions of what is happening at a local and national level into their studies. There is also the expectation that students will update their knowledge through the continuous use of libraries, the business press and the internet.

From a student point of view the existence of examinations is a challenge. They need to both understand the process of examinations and know how to prepare for them. Chapter 19 provides this support. It should be read in preparation for every case study examination – pre-issued and unseen – and not just at the end of the year. It suggests the most effective ways of preparing for examinations and helps students avoid the most common ways of losing marks.

The companion book – *Business strategy for A2* (ISBN 0521003652) provides essential support for those preparing for the A2 core examinations.

Peter Stimpson
Hurtwood House, Surrey
David Dyer
Cambridge Business Studies Project

v

Part 1

Businesses: their objectives and environment

1 Introduction

On completion of this chapter you should be able to:

➤ understand the nature and structure of this book and the ways in which it has been directed specifically at the OCR Business Studies AS specification

➤ understand the ways in which each chapter has been made interactive so as to ensure that reading is combined with active study

➤ understand the importance of the local community and the way it works as a central part of your studies

➤ appreciate the need to learn and use the language and concepts of the subject

➤ develop your awareness of the extent to which businesses have to work in a highly developed network of constraints and supports

➤ begin to develop an understanding of what is required of you in the examinations that are to come, and of ways in which you can make success more likely

About this book

The OCR A level in Business Studies is taken in two distinct stages. The first stage is **AS level** and this book is solely concerned with that stage. You may take AS on its own or continue the course through A2 to complete the full advanced level qualification.

In this book you will find:

◆ Part 1: Chapters 1–7 designed to support your studies for teaching module 1 called 'Businesses: their objectives and environment'.

◆ Part 2: Chapters 8–18 designed to cover teaching module 2 which is assessed by two examination units. Each covers the whole of the specification for teaching module 2. The first is called 'Business decisions' and the second 'Business behaviour'.

These three examination units are all compulsory and make up the examination for the AS qualification.

The final chapter (Chapter 19) offers help, advice and examples which will assist you in preparing for each of the AS examinations. You would be wise to read and use it before the first examination and then again before the other two.

When you have completed the AS course you will need the second book in this series to carry on your studies to complete the full A level – it is called *Business Strategy* for A2.

The format of each chapter

Each chapter is intended to be treated as a workshop and not just as a reading source. You will lose a lot of the benefit of the book if you do nothing more than read it. The activities and case studies are there to support you in your studies, use them as you work your way through each chapter.

Objectives

Objectives are right at the heart of all decisions that are made. Look at the decision-making model in Figure 1.1 – objectives are at the centre of this model. If objectives are unclear or too ambitious they often lead to failure. If they are too easy, they may be reached but without a feeling of achievement or satisfaction.

Setting objectives has three important benefits:

◆ they help in the setting of strategies to achieve these aims;

◆ they can motivate and give focus to our actions;

◆ actual achievement can be compared with them – and strategies changed if necessary.

Objectives in this book

The objectives we have set for each chapter are written in terms of what we want you to achieve using that section. Please read them – they will give you clues as to what examiners are going to expect. We can see that

Clear	Unclear	Too ambitious?
To break even in the first year	To make a profit	To double profit each year
To increase turnover by 5% this year	To increase sales	To triple sales next year
To get a Grade B in A level Business Studies	To pass A level Business Studies	To get 100% in Business Studies A level
To take a degree in Business Studies at UMIST	To go to university	
To become an accountant	To get a job	

Table 1.1 Objectives

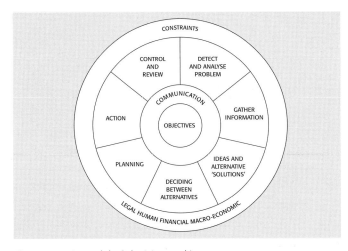

Figure 1.1 A model of decision making

On completion of this section you should be able to:
- understand the nature, variety and pattern of business activity through the businesses found in your area
- understand how businesses must meet the needs of both consumers and other stakeholders if they are to be successful
- explain the nature of production as added value
- appreciate problems associated with waste and its disposal and with various kinds of pollution
- understand the departments into which businesses divide as they grow
- appreciate some of the problems associated with the setting up of new businesses and their first year of operation

Table 1.2 Objectives for Chapter 2

from the objectives of Chapter 2 shown in Table 1.2. These objectives give you a good idea of the contents of the chapter and the purpose of reading it, but they are worth further study and will tell you much more.

The first objective should tell you how important to your studies is an understanding of the things that are happening in business in the area in which you live. Business is not just about what you read; it is also about what you see and what you do. Almost all aspects of the subject can be seen in your community. You will benefit from the understanding that careful observation and use of local business activity can give you.

Begin with a bird's eye view of your community. Learn from each other, your teacher and your family, some of the most important business-related features of where you live. You will find your local newspaper is an endless source of very useful information. Local television news is also very helpful from time to time. But above all keep your eyes open.

Some of the major features of a small market town could be:
- There is a very good railway service, which is quite unusual for small towns. What a student of Business Studies has to ask is why? The answer lies in two facts: the railway links several large towns and cities and makes the town a very good commuter town. The result is that the line is well used. There is a good demand for the service. The second is that there are few good East–West links in this railway system. So a combination of freight traffic and high passenger numbers not only keeps the service open, but has led to its improvement.
- There are a large number of estate agents in the town. Why? Partly because it is a good commuter area, partly because the local authority wants to concentrate new development in the towns rather than in the villages and partly because five public schools in the area have attracted people to live there.
- There are many fast food shops in the small town. The explanation for this is that, because of the building of a very large lake, tourists, coach parties, bird watchers, anglers and sailors are all attracted to the area.

These are but three examples of business in action. There are countless others. You must find out what is at the business heart of your community and

Aerial view of small town, showing railway, market, shops, housing and businesses — everything that makes up a typical community
Source: Aerofilms Ltd.

use it to help you with your studies. See Activity 1 on page 6.

The second objective for Chapter 2 gets to the very heart of our subject. If you are going to be in business, you have to meet people's needs. If you do not do that in a way that satisfies them and provides a profit for you, the business will fail. There are many examples of this in small communities. You will be able to find new businesses that open and existing ones that close. Don't just observe these things happening. Keep your eyes open, read articles in the newspapers, talk to people and find out why things happen. This will tell you an enormous amount about why businesses start up, where they do and the problems they face in trying to survive. See Activity 2 on page 6.

The fourth objective reminds you that businesses

do not just exist on their own, doing as they please. They have to rely on others and to operate within the wishes of the community, the law of the land, the safety of customers and employees and many other constraints, which we consider throughout the book. Not all constraints stop organisations doing things. Some protect or provide opportunities for success. In one issue of a local newspaper there were about 25 items (events/news issues) which could affect local businesses in positive or negative ways. The top five of these were:

◆ The planning of a new large air show for the local RAF station. This will make the area known, will increase trade and will attract tourist business. It may be noisy, it may congest some of the roads. It will employ several people.

◆ A decision that the by-pass for the town, first considered in the 1960s, will now be built. Again, there will be more trade and income whilst it is being built, considerable temporary employment and greater freedom to travel through, park and shop in the town, once the by-pass is open. There may be some loss of passing trade and one garage may decide to re-locate.

◆ Plans for a new housing development and an industrial park on the site of an old brewery. Again, this will bring many opportunities for more trade and a larger market for local traders. It will also make the village in which the brewery was situated much larger. It may enable one or more of the shops in the village to survive. It may prevent the closure of the village primary school. It may alleviate the unemployment that was caused by the closure of the brewery.

◆ Planning application by a transport and distribution firm is turned down. Here a firm wished to locate in the town and would have brought business and employment. Permission has been refused by the local authority. This is a good example of one of the duties local authorities have on behalf of the community. The fear is that noise, traffic congestion and possible traffic dangers will be costs that are greater, between them, than the benefits.

◆ A medium-sized business in the town is to close. This will cause unemployment, and therefore a general loss of business in the town. It will also improve the environment because noxious smells are involved with the product this company makes.

To explore this further, see Activity 3 on page 6.

The fifth objective for Chapter 2 really underlines the idea that to be efficient we need to plan and to organise and that this organisation needs to grow in importance as an organisation, e.g. a firm gets bigger. See Activity 4 on page 6.

Use these objectives to check, at the end of each chapter, whether or not you think you have learnt the things they say. If not, read some bits again, do some more of the work associated with the chapter, discuss it with your classmates and with your teacher, research in *Business Review*, on the Internet or in other written material.

Activities in each chapter

All the chapters are meant to be frameworks for working and developing your understanding. Throughout each one, there is opportunity to show what you have learned. The Activity given as an example below asks you to think about an important idea in the subject. You are not meant to attempt it now.

Activity (example)

Think about each of the following from the point of view of the organisation producing them:

◆ a pop concert;
◆ a music centre;
◆ a web site on the Internet;
◆ a second-hand car.

How is value added in each case?

At the centre of this task is an important concept called 'added value'. It is necessary that you read and understand that concept and that you prove to yourself that you understand by writing about it, write some examples and in discussions with your classmates. This book is based upon the idea that you will work together and learn from each other. It is not important that you do precisely the things we ask about, but it is essential that you try it with some products. You will also find some Test Activities throughout, which are designed to help you with your revision and are the kind of questions you will experience in your examinations.

Activities

1 Your community

Work in groups of four. Discuss your community:

(a) What are the most striking aspects of business activity in your area?

(b) Why do you think this is?

(c) Have you seen or are you seeing any significant changes?

2 Hello and goodbye

Work in groups of four:

(a) Two of you find a business that is closing down. Find out why it is closing and comment on what you discover.

(b) Two of you find a business that is preparing to open up and find out why the owner thinks the business will be successful. Comment on what you discover.

3 Good news/bad news in your area

Take your local newspaper. Cut out all the articles you think will produce some good or bad effects for organisations or people in your community. Put them all into a pot and then draw one each out of it. Using the report you have selected:

(a) Write a short memo on ways in which you think organisations in your town, and the people who live there, may be positively or negatively affected by the situation you have chosen.

(b) Swap your comments with someone else.

◆ See if you agree with what was written by your classmate.

◆ Add to it or say why you agree/disagree with what is written.

4 Organisers please

Select one of the four activities below and discuss in your group the way it should be organised and planned. Discuss the steps you would take to ensure its success:

◆ a disco for your year;

◆ a school/college trip;

◆ the provision or improvement of a senior common room;

◆ fund raising for a school/college minibus.

Case studies in each chapter

Where it is useful to stop and pull ideas together you will find case studies in the chapters. Some of these will simply tell a story and act as good examples for you to use. The first case study from Chapter 2 is a good example at this point.

The point of this case is that a firm has to know what business it is in if it is to be successful. The business here is not associated with the product, as perhaps a car dealership or a railway station might be. It is associated with a more general class of needs and what is being sold is not as important as meeting those needs. The customer wants general light reading, not a specific book, wants something to keep the child happy on the beach, not a specific toy, a snack and a drink, not a meal. Most of the products sold must be very reasonably

Case Study – The shop on the beach

On the sea front above the beach there is a shop. Today it is busy. It sells books, but is not a bookshop; it sells buckets and spades, but is not a garden centre. In it you can buy sandwiches, tea and coffee, but it is not a restaurant. You can buy balls, comics, newspapers, swimwear and many other things. The shop is satisfying two groups of needs, those of people trying to enjoy (children) or to endure (parents) the beach and the facilities and opportunities of the seaside. At high tide and when it rains there is no business. In the evening and in winter the shop is closed.

priced because they will probably be broken, lost or forgotten once the customers leave the beach.

You can learn general messages about business from these cases studies and learn how to find your own examples. Some case studies suggest work for you to do and form part of the Activities or Test Activities. All of your written examinations will be in case study form and you will need to get used to answering questions on them.

Things that are important in every chapter
Working together

Many of the cases and Activities the book offers you suggest that you work in groups. This makes learning more complete because each one of you has different ideas, strengths and weaknesses. What you do not understand from listening or working in class or from the text you may understand from discussing it. Equally important, what you do understand you can share with others. Working together is also useful because work can be broken down into separate tasks for everyone, so that you can get much more done and broaden the area of learning. It is much more fun in any case. Whatever you do will be more successful if you can find ways of enjoying it. Teamwork of this kind is a skill in itself and you may like to bear this in mind when you are developing your key skills portfolio. However, it also carries with it responsibility as well as benefits. Your group will be contributing to your learning, but they will also be relying on you to do your bit well.

The idea that learning should be fun may seem strange, but it might do no harm to realise that a major objective for all Richard Branson's Virgin network of businesses is that those who work for them should have fun.

Language

Business Studies has its own language and every chapter gives you opportunity both to learn it and use it. We expect you to:

◆ know what terms mean.

At the moment you probably do not know the business studies meaning of words like **random**, **productivity**

and **segment**. At this point that does not matter, but in an examination it could make the difference between a good grade and failure. You should, therefore, be able to:

◆ define them;
◆ explain them clearly, correctly and concisely;
◆ respond accurately to them if they are used in questions;
◆ appreciate the importance of the context in which a word or phrase is used and show this in the ways you discuss meaning and relevance in any question asked;
◆ use business words and phrases in your own answers correctly, confidently and as a matter of habit. The use of the right language in a correct and appropriate way not only helps to convince a reader or a listener that you know what you are saying, but it also makes the answer more to the point and usually of a higher standard.

When you come across a new word or phrase with a special meaning:

◆ make sure you know what it means;
◆ have a vocabulary book and write it up in your own words;
◆ check that meaning with a good dictionary of the subject and/or with your teacher, or you will find it in the glossary on page 269;
◆ add in an example or a way of measuring the idea.

Examples

1 For **Working capital** you might write:
'Working capital is that part of the capital of a business that is used in day-to-day transactions.'
You might draw the sketch shown here to remind you. You might show how it is calculated with the formula:

Working capital = Current assets − Current liabilities

2 For **Market segmentation** you might write: 'Market segmentation is dividing a whole market up into small sections which have their own characteristics.'
Methods of dividing could be by sex, by age, by occupation or by region, among others.
You could use the diagram here to remind you.

◆ Keep looking at these words and keep the vocabulary book up to date.

◆ Use the words you have in there regularly in your written work.

◆ When you are reading and you are doubtful about the meaning of a word, check it out, try to find out the meaning for yourself first and then ask.

Always remember that a word or phrase may mean something slightly but importantly different in the context in which it is used. Examiners are most often interested in the contextual meaning and relevance of the things they ask you about. We give examples of this contextual meaning throughout the book but here is an example to make the point:

Location
(a) 'The location of the business will be of prime importance. We must find a site in the centre of a large town.'
(b) 'The location of the office is 34 Bridge Street. It is clearly marked on the map.'
(c) 'I cannot locate the mineral deposits you say are there.'

All these statements are concerned with the placing of something but the differences are:
In (a) it is about where the business might be.
In (b) it is about where the business is.
In (c) it is about not knowing where the deposits are.
There is both a **glossary** and an **index** at the end of this book. They will help you to research things you are uncertain about or need to find out about.

Concepts

In its simplest form a concept is an idea. Many new products start their lives as concepts in the minds of those who invent or develop them. However, we often need a word or phrase that sums up large areas of the subject in ways that will be understood by students. Mathematics and accounting are full of concepts that help to make what is happening understandable and certain.

A triangle and an equation are concepts. They help us to visualise, in the first case, any three-sided figure and, in the second, any statement that makes two things balance. See Figure 1.2.

(a) Triangles

(b) Equations:

$5x = 3y$ (A simple equation)

$y = mx + c$ (The equation of a straight line)

Total cost = Fixed costs + Variable costs

Figure 1.2 Examples of (a) triangles and (b) equations

Sometimes we have to use a word to explain a more general idea for which there is no simple or certain definition, for example:

1 It is likely that no two writers would totally agree about the meaning of the word **Motivation** and there are several different ways in which people think it should be measured. Nevertheless, the word sums up a certain group of ideas for us and enables us to think fairly consistently about them.

2 **Efficiency.** This word provides a yardstick by which we might measure the performance of a machine, a worker or a team.

In contrast, there are some concepts that are capable of precise definition:

1 A phrase like **Working capital** is an example. Go back to our earlier example and read the definition suggested for the vocabulary book.

2 **Fixed cost.** Costs that, in the short run, do not vary with output. An example of such a cost might be the cost of premises and insurance.

Summary

Each chapter has a summary. Its purpose is to remind you of what has been developed in that chapter. It will help with location of ideas you are seeking to read about and be a useful reminder. It will never be a substitute for reading and use of the main ideas.

Studying business

What most of us see as a business is a result of a host of activities too numerous to count in many cases and involving all kinds of activity. We tend to study businesses as if they were isolated units. We look at their structure, their objectives, their internal organisation and the ways in which they work to achieve the results they want. We realise that there is a context that involves many other people and organisations, but the focus is still on a particular business or organisation for much of the time. We do much the same with the activities in the business and this is evident in Part 2, where there are sections on marketing, accounting, people and operations management. Before we break down the subject in this way we need to see the whole picture.

The picture we need to see is to be found in your community and careful study of it will tell you all you need to know about how businesses have to be aware of each other and the environment in which they work. Good management is about looking outwards and responding to, or even anticipating, changes and the ways in which they will affect business behaviour and success. Business managers must be aware of and correctly respond to the large number of influences which come from other businesses, all the stakeholders in the business and the State. The influence of the State is at three levels, that of the local authority, that of the nation and increasingly that of the European Union.

Over-to-you

The ability to answer questions should come from a combination of classroom learning, reading and practice. It could be said that the over-to-you tasks are the reason the chapters are written. They certainly explain why each chapter has been made deliberately interactive, with things for you to do all the way

through. Over-to-you tasks are likely to be used by teachers to test your understanding and skills, but they should also be used by you to ensure you are ready to go forward. There are three parts to the over-to-you tasks at the end of most chapters. If you get low marks for your efforts don't just shrug your shoulders, find out why and find the time to do a better job. We all learn from experience.

Test revision questions These are designed to test your knowledge but also to enable you to learn to give full and accurate answers very concisely. Answers gain 2 or 3 marks on average and that means 2 or 3 minutes to give a full-mark answer. This kind of question will be common in your examinations for Units 1 and 2. If you become skilled in answering them, you will do well. As you carry on with your studies they will still be very important in checking your subject language and subject knowledge, but will be of less importance in the examination.

Discover and learn It should already be clear that to be good at business studies you must be able to look away from the text books and out into the business community. This section will suggest some ways of doing that and of developing the quality and breadth of your knowledge. These exercises are also best done as a member of a group rather than on your own. In your groups you should learn to divide these tasks up and to rely on each other. This will help you to develop your skills of enquiry, observation and discussion. It will also begin to set the foundation for the coursework you may do later on.

Case studies The objective of each case study is as an example of what you have been learning. Mostly they are an opportunity to use the learning derived from the chapter. But they also provide the opportunity to demonstrate your ability to use the information gained from the start of the course. The cases should be very similar to those you will get in the examination, and you will see that for some, marks and a time have been given. For others it might be best to work in groups, using group discussion and research as a basis for your own answers.

Over-to-you

Case study
Decision making in action

Let's take a closer look at the decision-making model. We are going to use it to help a fellow student decide on whether to go to University or not – and, if yes, which course to consider taking.

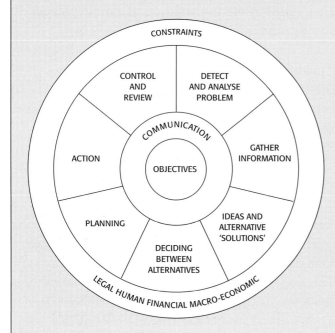

A model of decision making

Stage 1: Objectives. Our friend's aim is to become a qualified accountant – and to earn as high a salary as possible!

Stage 2: Detect and analyse problem. The problem is how best to become an accountant in order to be able to earn high salaries as quickly as possible.

Stage 3: Gather information. She will need to contact a careers office or the accountancy professional bodies. Is a degree essential? Can it be in any subject? If the degree is in accounting, will this lead to quicker qualification? If no degree is taken, how many years of work experience will be needed and how long do the professional examinations take to pass? What A level grades will she need? These are just some of the questions she needs answers to.

Stage 4: Ideas and alternatives. In the light of this information, make a list of the options available.

Stage 5: Decide between alternatives. This decision will probably have to be taken in Year 13. A detailed analysis of the advantages and disadvantages of all of the options will be needed.

Stage 6: Planning. Assume that the decision has been taken to study for a Business Studies degree with a Finance option. This may give one year's remission from Accountancy examinations. Plan to visit the University (ies) chosen. Plan student finances and accommodation.

Stage 7: Go to University!

Stage 8: Control and review the decision. At University, is it the right course for her? How is she doing? Is she achieving the right standard to get the Upper Second she is aiming for? If all is going to plan, then the initial objective should be reached. If not – then further action will be needed.

(a) Using the same model and the same approach, discuss in groups of four the information that will be needed and the possible actions that could be required at each stage for the following situation:
Neschoc Ltd. are concerned about their share of the chocolate confectionery market. It is 15% but was 20% three years ago. They aim to increase it to 25% in two years.

(b) Compare the actions and decisions taken by different groups.

(c) In 2002 Nestlé launched 'Double Cream' chocolate bar. It was a great success and increased their market share. How do you think that using the decision-making model helped the firm's managers to take the 'right decision'?

2 The nature of business

Business activity

In primitive societies there is an immense amount of work as individuals and families struggle to survive by meeting all their own needs. As society grows, the value of specialising and sharing emerges and the need to exchange things becomes apparent. Through exchange of either the skills we develop or the fruits of those skills, business activity gradually emerges.

The photograph below is of a typical town market, which is a hive of activity on Wednesdays and Saturdays. A range of businesses in addition to the market can also be found in the town. Typical businesses might include:

A gift shop This is owned and run by a family and is typical of many businesses in the town. It sells memorabilia of the town and the area. It tells us the town is a tourist town. The shop is well located since coaches unload in the market square. It does not have a high turnover but each item it sells will have a high mark-up.

A small café Seasonal trade, especially busy in the summer and on market days. Business is largely between morning coffee and afternoon tea. The opening hours and the menu tell us this. A small business that relies on a single female owner and on part-time employees including students.

An estate agent A small office. It is one of many in the town and this suggests there is a good market for buying and selling property. A drive around would show seven large private housing estates and many villages in which there are houses for sale. A more careful study would explain why estate agents are very busy.

A small hotel Part of a national chain. The hotel can accommodate 58 people, has a restaurant with a good reputation and two bars. Trade is seasonal and the hotel barely breaks even in winter. A large hall is being built on the back. The manager sees the conference business as a good source of winter profits. The choice is either grow and prosper or close down.

A typical town market which attracts many people to the town centre

Activity

Analyse your community (or a part of it) in this way. Find out what businesses there are and what customer needs they satisfy.

Consumer needs

Businesses are started up because the owners think they have found something to produce which **consumers** will want. They will stay in business if they are satisfying those needs sufficiently well to make a profit (see case studies opposite and below).

Case study – The shop on the beach

On the front above the beach there is a shop. Today it is busy. It sells books, but is not a bookshop; it sells buckets and spades, but is not a garden centre. In it you can buy sandwiches, tea and coffee, but it is not a restaurant. You can buy balls, comics, newspapers, swimming trunks and many other things. The shop is satisfying two groups of needs, those of people trying to enjoy (children) or to endure (parents) the beach and the facilities and opportunities of the seaside. At high tide and when it rains there is no business. In the evening and in winter the shop is closed.

Case study – Selling televisions

Do customers just want a television set? Will any set do? If the answers to these questions are 'Yes' then the shop will offer little choice for a straight sale. Think of three different customers:

Sharon has never had a television set. She can't afford to spend much but is wary of second-hand sets and needs helpful advice.

Simon and Kate They have been married ten years and already have two colour sets. They have a high disposable income and watch television a lot. They have no children. Why do you think they are buying together? How will this influence the attempt to sell? What might they be looking for?

Mary Mary is a Head of Business Studies and is looking for three sets for classroom use. What might Mary be seeking?

There are no right answers and the purpose is only to set you thinking about consumers satisfying needs rather than just buying products. Products like television sets are sold as packages. The simplest package is a basic set for cash, taken away by the customer. More complex packages include insurance, delivery, aerials, rent or buy decisions, HP or cash decisions, and add-on products like video recorders, digital receivers and teletext. Mary might even want a discount. Selling televisions is much more than stocking a range of them in the shop. What the customer needs must be anticipated. It would be a mistake to assume that customer needs are all product orientated or that the business which offers a host of different packages will necessarily be successful.

Think of these two situations:

The dead hotel A potential customer needing a room for the night rang a hotel he had often stayed at. No reply. He tried again. No reply. He phoned another hotel and made the booking.

The missing product Customer: 'I need two pairs of shoes. You only seem to have up to size 11 on the shelf.' Assistant: 'Yeah! We don't bother with larger sizes. We can't sell them.'

In both cases the business has lost a sale and probably a customer. In both cases the customer's dissatisfaction may be spread to other potential customers. Part of satisfying customer needs is to give good and helpful service.

The needs of owners

Being in business is a two-way process. To succeed, the business must satisfy sufficient customers and persuade them that they want to come back. To stay in business, it must satisfy the needs of the owners. The cost of setting up most small businesses is very high and commonly requires reliance on other people's money. These people may be family and friends or there may be a loan from the bank. In almost all cases there is very little left and the risk that the owner and others may have taken is often high. All borrowed money has to be returned, usually by agreed dates, and it has to be paid for in the form of interest. Even using your own money has a cost since it could be earning interest in a safe investment. The business owner has to earn enough to make these payments regularly, to earn a wage on which to live and to earn some profit that makes the risks taken worthwhile. In fact, ownership normally implies several **stakeholders** and the interest in the success of the business that each of them will have. Do not confuse stakeholders with **shareholders**. The distinction is as follows:

Shareholders The term implies that the business is a public or private limited company and that ownership has been divided into shares owned by a few or by many owners of shares.

Stakeholders People who have an interest in the organisation. Clearly owners, whether they be shareholders or not, will have an interest, but lenders, employees, customers are among those who have a stake of some kind in the business and so are stakeholders.

Owners do not expect to make good profits, or even to earn good wages, immediately; they do not expect to pay off all borrowed money by the end of year one, but they realise the importance of **cash flow** and the need to pay bills as they come in. Many of the businesses that fail do so because their forward planning and market research has not been good enough; because they have not anticipated the ease with which cash will flow outwards at the start or the sluggishness with which it flows inwards.

Even profitable young businesses have failed because they could not compete with cash-flow problems.

Adding value

From a producer's point of view **value added** is the difference between the cost of inputs and the price consumers are prepared to pay for the finished product. It is this added value that creates the surplus from which wages and other costs can be paid.

Example:
Selling price (£10) − cost of bought in materials (£3.50) = value added (£6.50). This value added might then be distributed as follows:

- ◆ Wages and salaries £3
- ◆ Overhead costs   £2
- ◆ Profit   £1.50

Clearly, the greater the value added, the greater will be the surplus to pay for other costs and to give a profit. All businesses are striving to increase value added. This might be done in a number of ways. A jewellery shop might use lavish displays and interior designs to convince customers that its high prices are justified. A well-known branded good, such as Coca-Cola, can charge more than its competitors as consumers have confidence in the brand name and product quality.

Test Activities

(40 marks, 40 minutes)

1 Consider each of the following from the point of view of the organisation producing each of them:

   (a) a pop concert;   (c) a web site on the Internet;   (b) a music centre;   (d) a second-hand car.

   What inputs were probably used to produce these for you? Which ones may have been most important? How might value added be increased in each case? (20)

2 Read the following case study and then, working in small groups, discuss value from the point of view of both the producers and the purchasers of the desks. (20)

Case study – Value for money?

Anna and Dyfed both need a desk. Anna is a busy computer analyst and has a very full social and sporting life. She sees this as a simple problem, goes to a furniture shop with a reasonable choice and selects a desk she likes. The firm agrees to deliver and the cost to Anna is £780. Anna would have been prepared to spend £850. Dyfed is a young teacher in Newport, South Wales and his budget for the desk is £350. He looks in several shopping catalogues and on the Internet and eventually selects one that will be delivered at a total cost to him of £290. When it comes it is a flat pack with instructions for assembly, which Dyfed cannot understand. He seeks the help of three young friends and eventually the desk is assembled and everything seems to be in the right place.

Other firms will try to reduce material costs, whilst keeping their selling prices the same.

◆ From the consumer's point of view value added is measured by the difference between the price charged and the price the consumer would have been prepared to pay. Many consumers – but by no means all – will try to maximise this value added by finding the cheapest source of the products they wish to buy.

Inputs All businesses start with a range of **inputs**. Typically these will be:

Natural resources These include resources such as land, coal, oil, fish, and there is concern that many of these are being exhausted. Buildings and machinery are physical assets.

Test Activity

Read the case study below and then tackle the exercises that follow.

Case study – Value added at James the Jewellers

James sells a wide variety of rings, earrings, other jewellery and watches from his shop. It is located some way from the high street, but it has a good customer base as James established a good reputation for value for money. Although sales increased, year-by-year profits did not. James does not believe that he could realistically cut costs and decides to look into ways in which he could increase revenue. Last year the shop's turnover was £50,000 from the sale of bought-in jewellery and watches costing £15,000. A friend who was an accountant had told him that the key to success was to 'increase value added'. He explained to James how he might do this and this set James thinking.

(20 marks, 25 minutes)
(a) Calculate the value added by James' shop last year. (2)
(b) Explain to James why value added is so important to the success of his business. (6)
(c) Outline three ways in which James could try to increase the value added from his business. (6)
(d) Select one of the methods outlined in (c). Evaluate the problems James could experience in using it to increase added value successfully. (6)

Capital The assets through which business is done or the cash that makes it possible. All businesses need capital. For a shop, needs are small compared with those required to build and run an oil refinery.

People Often said to be the most important asset of a business. People think and act for themselves. This can be a great strength or a source of weakness. Some people provide unskilled work in situations where the machines do most of the producing; others, skilled work where training, experience and care are vital; and some craft work, where a particular talent is paramount.

What is produced?

Some businesses produce only goods, e.g. farming, mining, construction and manufacture, although services will be associated with them. Others are service providers and people often think that there is no production in a bus ride or in borrowing money. Of course there is, since the term production includes all activity that adds value. The kinds of goods you might find on a shopping expedition include:

Single-use goods All food, drink, football matches, one-day business studies conferences and many other products can only be used once. Some you use regularly, others are infrequently used; some may be recycled.

Multiple-use goods Not normally consumed in one go but not expected to last for any length of time. These include a box of matches, a packet of sweets, a weekly season ticket.

Durable consumer goods Expected to last a long time and often the subject of guarantees and maintenance agreements to ensure that they do. Cars, domestic appliances, carpets and houses are examples.

Investment goods All organisations have to buy things in order to work effectively. Investment goods are so called because of the way they are used and not for what they are. Businesses will buy machinery to make things and vans or lorries to deliver. They will also buy the goods consumers buy, but for investment purposes. You may buy grapes to eat, while the vintner will buy them to make wine. For home use you may buy sugar, but the bakery will buy it to make bread and cakes. You will buy peas for the home but the factory will buy them straight from the farmer to can, freeze or dry.

Services These are produced for both the consumer and the producer and have become important in our economy. We want utilities like gas and electricity, government-provided services like defence and law and order, convenience services like the delivery of newspapers, the post and milk, communication services like the telephone, fax, email and the Internet. Most of these services are also available to business and industry. Services like the police, roads, libraries and transport are public, but many services are private and personal. Services are a specifically produced good requiring providers to use inputs, to add value and to market them to potential buyers. They are not to be confused with 'service', which is an essential ingredient in providing any good or service to any buyer.

Unwanted production

Not everything that is produced is valuable. Less desirable 'productions' include:

Waste materials Whilst every effort can and should be made to recycle these materials, this is not always possible. The production of waste has led to laws designed to protect the community and to require socially acceptable practices from producers. Waste has given rise to many businesses that make their profits from the collection, recycling or disposal of waste.

Waste products These arise from some defect in the production process or from over-ordering, which leaves products which are past their sell-by date.

Noise There is some protection from noise within businesses through the Health and Safety at Work Act. Noise often affects the community. Planning permission is required for firms that emit excessive noise. They need careful location.

Activity

Working in pairs or groups, analyse the service provision in your locality and decide:
- (a) What services seem to be over-provided?
- (b) Can you think of an explanation for this?
- (c) What services seem to be unavailable or in short supply?
- (d) Can you think of an explanation for this?

Pollution The law attempts to control pollution, but emissions from buses and lorries are often difficult to control. Sometimes the pollution is a smell, e.g. from a glue factory or from an abattoir. Sometimes objections are to things like the smell from a fish and chip shop or to the litter such shops are thought to cause.

All of these external factors are considered in greater depth in Chapter 6.

Business on the inside

The smallest business has no employees and there are many like that, particularly in service industries such as plumbing, gardening and window cleaning. In such businesses there is no scope for specialisation, although owners may well organise and plan to be as effective as possible. Often there is hidden support in the unpaid help the family give. A window cleaner may have his wife answering the telephone, taking bookings and doing the VAT returns. Remarkably, he will not think of her as part of the business, just as 'giving him a hand'.

Activities

1 Look around your local community. How might waste and pollution be a problem in your area? What steps are taken to control them?
2 Read the case study below and then tackle the exercises that follow.

Case study – Corridge plc

Corridge plc is a rapidly growing waste disposal firm.

It has applied for permission to set up a waste disposal site in a disused quarry 6 miles from your town and 2 miles from a small village. The site would also be a depot from which 40 lorries would operate. No toxic or nuclear waste would be disposed of on the site, but the waste would be exclusively industrial. When fully operational the firm would employ 90 people, most of whom would be recruited locally.

(a) Why should the firm have to apply for planning permission and why should the local authority be able to say no?
(b) Discuss the issues involved and consult local opinion. Make it clear that this is not an actual proposal. Decide whether the firm should be given permission.

There is much help of this kind that supports many businesses. Once a business grows beyond this point there is scope for **specialisation**:

◆ A team of two who decorate houses divide the tasks into lower work done by the older man and 'up the ladder work' done by the younger person.

◆ A small gardening company devoted to garden makeovers, works with a team of three. Primarily, one of them plans and directs, one does the water features and the third does all the other construction work.

Specialisation isolates particular types of work and seeks to ensure that these are undertaken by the worker with the greatest skill in completing them. In the example of the windowcleaner the unpaid wife is really doing all of the 'office work'. In fact, the windowcleaner now employs two other people, has taken on more rounds and each of the three has their own round. Specialisation in large firms tends to occur first by operations within a function. An example of this is when law partners divide the work so that one partner does all the conveyancing, one all the work associated with wills, one all the other civil work and one all the criminal work. Once a firm gets bigger, it tends to organise by function and a common pattern is:

Personnel Some personnel departments are quite small, while others are large and subdivide even further into recruitment, training, payments and training functions.

Not everyone thinks a specialist department is necessary. In some organisations each department does its own personnel work. This makes implementing common policies and practices for the whole organisation rather difficult.

Marketing Marketing has become increasingly important. It can no longer be assumed that a good product will market itself. Markets have to be found, targeted and then served. This is a continuous process as new uses for products and new products come on to the market and as consumers seek to satisfy a widening range of needs. For an increasing range of goods the market is worldwide. Although ecommerce has yet to make a real impact, it will not be long before many goods and services are sold over the Internet. Marketing also has its specialist divisions to meet these changing needs.

Production This used to be considered the core of the firm. Now most firms must produce what they can sell and must be flexible. They must become more efficient in a fast-moving world, where modern technology can be crucial to success. In effect, the modern production department has a much greater market focus. The approach is increasingly set on such targets as continuous improvement (Kaizan), just-in-time stockholding policies, total quality management and lean production. Lean production is an attitude of mind, which changes approaches to all aspects of production.

Finance and accounts First, the department must order all information about costs and revenues that concern the firm. This will be used to inform and to report to the stakeholders. Second, it must control. The department usually produces the plans (budgets) and assists in allocation. It is also expected to control practices and procedures and to ensure that they are common throughout the firm. The money the firm uses and collects is not its own. It belongs to the stakeholders and it must be properly and honestly accounted for. Finally, the department is at the centre of planning and forecasting. In general, things will not be done unless the firm can see that the benefits of an action will outweigh its costs. Many of the factors (but not all of them) will involve the inflow or outflow of money.

All of these functions exist in any organisation, whether or not there is a specialist person or department. The two case studies in the Activity demonstrate this.

Activity

Read the case studies below and then tackle the exercises that follow.

Case study – Redgate College

Personnel 50 full-time teachers and ten part time. One principal and one assistant principal. Twenty support staff – all but three are part time. The Principal is the equivalent of a managing director. He has considerable independence, although, in the final analysis, he is answerable to the Board of Governors.

Marketing There is a promotion budget of £20,000. Much of this is spent advertising the two open days in the regional press. The remainder goes towards the glossy Prospectus, which attracts some advertising from local firms. *Production* Education is obviously a service activity. The services provided are the wide range of courses that attract 16–19-year old students from a wide ability range. Successful 'production' is measured by the number of students who enroll, the proportion who complete their courses and the examination success rate. 'Value added' is measured by comparing the GCSE results student have on entry with the results they gain at College.

Finance The College receives funding directly from central government. The amount received depends on a complicated formula. This includes numbers of students, the number and range of courses and the number of students who finish and pass their courses. In addition, some adult students pay tuition fees. Full-time 16–19-year old students cannot be charged fees according to current government policy. The College also has the power to borrow funds for capital spending projects, such as new buildings. These tend to attract even more students – a virtuous circle as long as the College does not over-borrow.

Case study – Home Farm

This is a local business, which changed its focus dramatically over the ten-year period (Table 2.1). The owners have been forced by the Common Agricultural Policy of the EU and by the changing fortunes of agriculture to seek other markets, to service the markets in more cost-effective ways and to organise what they do in a very much more 'managed' way.

Personnel The farm was a family partnership until it broadened its market base by converting its outbuildings into holiday accommodation in 1998. At that time it formed a private limited company. This was partly to raise more capital, but largely to obtain limited liability status. The six members of the family are on the Board, together with two other directors. It employs eight others full time. One of these runs the Home Farm office. It also employs additional casual labour at lambing and harvest times and for the holiday months. These are usually students. It has a 'pick your own' approach to the marketing of fruit and some vegetables. Family members are salaried and workers are paid an hourly wage.

Marketing There is a varied approach to marketing, which depends on the products concerned. With arable and meat products most marketing is by contract with an industrial user. With fruit and vegetables some marketing is through 'pick your own' and some through the farm shop. These are

1990	Four members of the family worked on a mixed farm. No other activities.
1992	A farm shop was opened to sell farm-produced fruit, vegetables and eggs. As the shop grew, a wider range of produce was bought in.
1993	A camping and caravan site was developed using some under-used hectares close to the road. This has been extended and developed each year since.
1994	Beef farming was discontinued and pig and poultry farming increased. New, local markets were found for an increasing volume of produce.
1996	'Pick your own' developed for soft and hard fruit and for some vegetables.
1998	Four outbuildings were converted for bed and breakfast and holiday cottage lets. Staff were taken on to run these and the camping and caravan site. Marketing was through a national holiday-cottage chain.
2002	Camping and caravan site extended. All animal husbandry except poultry and pigs discontinued. Both of these converted to free range and vegetable production to organic methods. Regular attendance at a farmers' market.

Table 2.1 Home Farm: calendar of change

advertised on local radio, in local papers and through on-site promotion. Some marketing is through a local 'farmers' market' established recently. A registered camp and caravan site is marketed through the specialist press and bed-and-breakfast facilities through the Regional Tourist Board. Milk is collected daily. The holiday part of the business has been carried out through an agency agreement with 'Country Holidays', a holiday letting firm. However, they now get a large number of regular returners and have decided that this and word of mouth promotion will be sufficient from now on.

Production Most of the staff work on the traditional farm products, but there are three people who work on the holiday side. One is full time and the other two work only between April and October. Farming activities are capital intensive, but holiday activities are labour intensive. The directors are considering the potential for moving into organic

---

food production, but this will be a long-term objective since it takes about five years to ensure that the land is free of non-organic substances.

Finance The farming and the holiday accounts are kept separate through the formation of a private limited company, which manages the tourist business and the farm business as separate units. Financial control is difficult because of the seasonal aspect of most of the work. Only chicken, egg and milk production are continuous, all the rest have a seasonal cycle. Most of the revenue comes in from May to September. Good management is necessary to avoid cash-flow problems in the winter months. The farm relies heavily on bank finance during this period. In the last ten years most of the profits have been ploughed back into the changes which have taken place. The capital of the firm was increased by the company formation and there is no long-term borrowing.

(a) Choose a large retail business and a manufacturing business known to you and analyse them in the same way.

(b) Find a business in your area that is either (i) relocating or (ii) closing down and try to discover why this is happening.

(c) Analyse the advantages and possible drawbacks to Home Farm of the diversification strategy it has adopted.

Business start-up

What persuades people to set up in business? Most start small and many because of the personal ambitions of the sole owner who wants to be the boss. What has deterred many has been lack of capital and many businesses can be traced to winnings, inheritances and redundancy payments. All that the 'entrepreneurs' lacked was finance. Something like 400,000 new businesses are started every year and every major bank has extensive literature and service and support departments devoted to business start-up.

The difficulties of small businesses

Suppose you want to set up a small business. You have been a well-respected chef for some years and you think you can go it alone. What are the issues you must face if you are to have a hope of being successful?

- Is there a market sufficient to sustain the business and provide a reasonable living for the owner? Many businesses are not researched well and people are satisfied by a few positive indications from well-meaning friends. Without real evidence it is impossible to plan. Without a plan it is difficult to persuade those whose financial support you need.
- Under what conditions will the potential consumers actually buy? What is your unique selling point (USP)? What is going to be different about your menu and your venue?
- Is there likely to be a long-term market? Will your restaurant survive beyond the curiosity visits?

- What kind of business ought you to start? Most start as sole owners or as partnerships. The risks of unlimited liability can be massive. Is it wiser to be a private limited company? It is often thought that a limited company is more creditworthy than a sole trader or a partnership.
- Are you going to buy an existing restaurant or set up a new one?
- The business name is a vital marketing tool and your own name may not have the impact of a more imaginative approach. Names like 'The Happy Eater' carry an initial marketing boost, because of the goodwill attached to the name. You may have a unique selling point that can be summed up in the name or its associated logo. Names like 'Kwik Save', 'Prontoprint' and 'Rapid Results' were all designed to promote a feature of the business. One owner chose the name 'Alpha' because it would come high in an alphabetical list of businesses in the same trade.
- You are in business. You could not afford a High Street location so nobody knows about you. You have to get the message across and almost certainly on a limited budget. Which market are you going to be in? The lunch trade is a different market from the evening trade. How can it be targeted? You must target it as well and as often as you can. Many businesses have failed because their owners thought they could not afford to advertise.
- Setting the right prices is crucial. Many have failed because they set low prices to attract custom and then lost it all when prices had to rise. Giving value

for money is much more important than being cheap. In the restaurant business quality of service, range of menu, comfort and environment are often more important.

◆ Choosing an effective location. A sandwich bar will need to be convenient; a speciality restaurant can be almost anywhere; car-parking facilities may be necessary.

◆ What are your objectives? If these are too ambitious or if you have not really worked any out and are just going to drift along, the business risks

will be far greater and you are more likely to fail.

◆ Finance. It is difficult for organisations to acquire credit support before a trading reputation has been established. Inadequate financing, cash-flow problems, failure to keep good records and to plan for cash needs are, between them, major reasons for failure.

◆ Market research. It can be too expensive for small firms to commission their own *primary* research. You may therefore be dependent on secondary sources of data.

Case study – New businesses

Discover the new businesses that have set up in your area in the last two years. Try to discover why the owners began the business.

Among the reasons you may discover are:

◆ An opportunity to turn a hobby into a business. In one town there is a motor cycle shop and workshop started by a speedway rider after he retired from the sport.

◆ To develop a market for a product. One of our shops is a bakery specialising in making and decorating speciality cakes. The owner had been doing this from home for years but demand grew and premises were needed.

◆ The wish has always been there and now the capital is available. The common source is redundancy payments because the owner of the capital is also unemployed. This often happens with older workers for whom job prospects are bleak. The electrician, the windowcleaner and the plumber in one area all came from redundancy when the local steel works rationalised and greatly reduced its workforce.

◆ Belief in greater rewards from self-employment. Often, people doing this do not understand the management aspects or the risks of being self-employed and their businesses are short lived. Two take-away food businesses and one florist in one locality failed for these reasons, within a year of starting.

◆ The desire for independence. There comes a time in most people's careers when they are fed up with taking orders. They want to be their own boss. One of these now runs a very successful small café, having previously driven a mobile ice cream van. He was fed up with driving around all day and being under pressure to achieve high weekly targets.

◆ The desire to leave something for the family. Many sole-owner shops are really family businesses because every one in the family plays some part in their success. They often close when family individuals no longer want to be so closely tied or do not want to carry on the business.

Over-to-you

1 A friend of yours, a qualified car mechanic, is planning to leave his job with a large garage. He asks for your advice. He is uncertain whether to establish his own business 'from scratch' or to buy out a small garage that is currently for sale. Discuss the advantages and disadvantages of buying the existing business. Would you advise him to set up his own firm, or to buy the existing garage?

2 After much thought, he decides to set up his own firm.

Make a checklist of ten decisions that he will need to make. Explain briefly the importance of each one to the success of his business.

Test revision questions (60 marks, 1 hour)

1 What is meant by the term 'stakeholder'? Give two examples of internal and two examples of external stakeholders. (5)

2 Mary (see the Case study about selling television sets)

is seeking a 'discount'. Explain what this is and why Mary thinks she is entitled to a discount. (3)

3 Explain why the trader might be prepared to give Mary a trade discount. (3)

4 Explain the process of 'adding value'. How would you measure added value if you ran:
   (a) a fish and chip shop?
   (b) a bus service? (4)

5 Outline two ways in which the owner of a fish and chip shop might increase her value added. (4)

6 Explain what is meant by the term 'capital' in the context of owning a business. (2)

7 Explain why it is that the same good may be either a consumer good or an investment good. (3)

8 Explain what the activities of (a) a personnel department and (b) a finance department might be. (6)

9 Explain what is meant by the term 'unique selling point' (USP) and give an example of one for either a business or a product known to you. (3)

10 Outline three problems that are commonly faced by new businesses. (6)

11 Briefly explain how a new hairdressing business might tackle the three problems identified above. (6)

12 Outline three factors that you consider would be necessary for a new retail business to succeed. (6)

13 Suggest three possible reasons why someone might set up their own business. (3)

14 Why might production lead to 'unwanted products'? (2)

15 Why might some firms be very concerned to reduce the quantity of 'unwanted goods' that they produce? (4)

Discover and learn

1 Choose a consumer durable good priced at more than £100. Discover where, in your locality, it can be bought and how many ways there are of buying it. Think about the associated services and consumer advantages. Decide where you would buy it and explain why.

2 What have you learnt about the importance of identifying and satisfying consumer needs from the exercise in the previous question?

Mini case study – Railway preservation society looks to the future

A railway preservation society has been running a small section of track, which passes from one major town to another and through three rural stations. The members of the society have worked as amateurs for many years, raising enough from summer holiday rides and from memorabilia to keep their hobby going. They think that now is the time to turn the hobby into a business. Some members are prepared to give up their existing jobs. They know that substantially more income will have to be created and that the summer tourists and gift shop sales will be nothing like enough. They are in the initial stages of planning for setting up their business.

Source: Bodmin and Wenford Railway.

3 Read the case study above and then tackle these questions:
(24 marks, 25 minutes)
   (a) Outline two reasons why some members are so keen to establish their own business. (6)
   (b) Discuss four problems they might face in turning their hobby into a successful business. (12)
   (c) Suggest and explain two market opportunities that the members could investigate to make the business pay. (6)

Summary

In this chapter we have recognised that:

- Business activity has a particular nature and various features.

- Your locality can be used to understand the great variety of organisational activity and what these organisations contribute in context.

- Good business satisfies consumer needs and also meets the needs of its stakeholders.

- All businesses seek to add value and, because they succeed in this, they are producers, regardless of whether they produce a good or a service, or of whether their market is a consumer good or an industrial one.

- To achieve this they must use resources effectively. Consumers are constantly looking for value for money, which is a complex of many things.

- The production process leads to many different kinds of waste and pollution. Society must find ways of dealing with this problem.

- All businesses must be organised and, as they grow, the organisation becomes more complex with the opportunity for specialisation.

- Work is departmentalised to keep it focused and controlled.

- All businesses have to start somewhere and will face problems and difficulties, particularly in the first year.

Key words

Definitions of Key words can be found in the Glossary on page 269

capital	noise
cash flow	production
consumers	services
finance and accounts	shareholders
inputs	specialisation
investment goods	stakeholders
marketing	value added
natural resources	waste

3 Classification of businesses

On completion of this chapter you should be able to:

➤ explain the ways in which businesses within the economy are classified

➤ classify any business appropriately

➤ consider ways in which the size of a business can be measured and difficulties in doing this

➤ explain the different ways in which a business may be legally structured

➤ explain the advantages and disadvantages of different legal forms

➤ distinguish between public and private ownership

➤ discuss the issues arising from public and private ownership

Introduction

Classifying things helps us to understand them but classifications are rarely discrete and this is certainly true when we think of businesses. In this chapter we look at some ways of classifying business but realise that many businesses do so many things and in such a variety of different ways that they make classification very difficult.

Classification by nature of activity

Business is possible because one group of people has the skills and resources to make things and make them available to others. This would be a waste of time if nobody actually wanted them. Here we can see two groups that are essential to business activity:

♦ those who grow the food, build the furniture, provide the power, make the cars;

♦ those who seek to buy the products because they have the ability and willingness to do so.

You want your newspapers and post delivered and you want a whole range of other services, such as hairdressing, banking and legal services. Business and industry want services too, including financial support, delivery services, maintenance and repair. Most of these services we want as individuals, but there is another group that we want collectively. These include road and transport links, education, defence and law and order. This produces two more groups:

♦ those who provide the personal and private services that individual businesses and individual people need;

♦ those who provide the public services we all need.

The government itself provides some of the latter through organisations that it develops and creates, e.g. the armed forces and the police force. Others it contracts out to private firms, e.g. road building. Some are jointly provided by state and private organisations, e.g. education. Firms which provide our essential services, such as water, telephone and electricity, are called utilities and are run by private business but are subject to firm control by public bodies, such as OFWAT which oversees the supply of water.

This classification is not very helpful but it does serve to remind us of two things:

♦ that production without likely consumers is a waste of time;

♦ that the services we use are as much production as the goods we buy.

Classification by level of activity

Within the economy there are three levels of activity, each of which takes businesses closer to the consumer.

22

Primary activity Takes all the natural resources and makes them more useful to consumers. In Chapter 2 we called this process adding value. Fish are of little (economic) value in the sea and timber is not available until the trees are cut down. Little of food value would grow without agriculture and the mineral resources we need have to be mined. All of these are primary activities using the resources that nature provides.

Secondary activity Takes the materials provided by primary industry and processes them so that some of the more complex needs of society are met. Food is processed both to give variety and to provide more effective storage. Minerals are processed to provide energy or to enable construction. It is through these manufacturing activities that cars and computers come on the market.

Tertiary activity Provides all the services private, personal and public, that industry and consumers demand.

Again these are not completely separate categories. There is much that is manufactured found in modern agricultural and fishing methods. There are many firms operating at all three levels of activity. However, the classification is a useful one and changes in the relative importance of each type of activity tell us much about the way the economy is changing.

Classification by size

In the Activity opposite you will classify the businesses by size. You could use the terms large, medium and small. How did you decide what a particular firm was? If we consider the three businesses in Table 3.1, which one is the biggest? How can we decide?

In this example we see the problem of defining size. Hotelier C has the greatest number of hotels but they

Factor	Hotelier A	Hotelier B	Hotelier C
Number of hotels	1	10	15
Capacity	700 rooms	600 rooms	600 rooms
	900 people	1,000 people	1,100 people
Employees	350	140	90
Turnover per annum	£2 million	£1.5 million	£1.5 million
Net profit	£100,000	£200,000	£400,000
Capital employed	£14 million	£7 million	£6 million

Table 3.1 Problem of defining size

Activity

Go to the map of economic activity in your area that you built up in working through Chapter 2. From that information classify the businesses in your area in accordance with Table 3.2. To qualify for entry into your table there must be a firm, or a branch of it, located in your area. For example, every office and most houses will have a telephone, but that does not qualify unless there is a telephone company in your area. On the other hand, a railway station would qualify.

Level of activity	Example	Number/Size
Primary agriculture	Farming	
Primary/Others	Forestry/Fishing	
Secondary/Construction	Builders	
Secondary/Others	Manufacture	
Tertiary private services	Banks/Doctors	
Tertiary public	Gas/Water/Electricity	
Total		

Table 3.2 Example of levels of activity in your local area

(a) What do you conclude about the nature of economic activity in your area?
(b) Has it changed significantly in the last five years?

are quite small. Firm A has only one hotel, but has more rooms than either of the others. Firm A has by far the largest capital employed but makes a much smaller net profit. With all these problems how can we measure size?

At the extremes there are no problems. We all accept that a multinational is a very large business, even though its establishment in a particular area may be quite small. We also know that the majority of businesses are very small. This is probably true of your area. It is also true that most businesses start small and then grow.

Potential measures of size
Number of workers

This is the simplest measure and it is clear that shops with just the owner or the family are small. Perhaps it is more obvious that a firm employing many people is large since labour is not a cheap resource. But there are problems. How do you measure part-time employment? How about firms in which the labour force is self-employed? How about the firms that employ few people because they are very highly capitalised?

Example There are two breweries in the same town. One is traditional, making 200,000 gallons of beer a week and employing 88 people in the processes involved. The other is totally automated, produces 1,000,000 gallons a week and employs eight people.

Capital employed

Where this is high the firm is likely to be large, provided the capital is being used efficiently, but it may not be large for the industry it is in. There are, of course, many industries where the scope for capital intensity is low and the measure would not be a helpful one. This is true of many of the personal service industries.

Turnover

In most instances, if turnover is large the firm is large. However, there are businesses in which small scale is associated with high turnover. Financial services and working precious stones and precious metals are examples.

Balance sheet values

One of the values shown in a balance sheet is the capital employed of the business and this may well be a good measure of size. This, too, may be misleading with some industries in which quite small-scale activity is associated with a high net capital employed such as a specialised printing firm.

Market share

Market share is a relative term. If a firm has a high market share, then it must be among the leaders in its field and hence comparatively large. However, when total markets are small, the measure will not indicate a particularly large firm.

Share values

Firms with large shareholdings are almost certainly large. The problem lies in the potential for organisations that are not companies to be large. In the days when most of our utilities were in public hands they were large, but had no shareholders at all. The Post Office is still like that, although attempts have been made to privatise it. Many government bodies are very large.

National networks

There are many businesses in which the size of the technical unit can be small but which, overall, are large. In the hotel business, there are many chains with small or moderate-sized hotels and the same is true with retail chains. The business here is not the individual outlet but the whole network. What is large by this criterion? Each unit may be so small that it cannot really enjoy economies of scale. How many of them should there be to qualify as large – 10, 15, 25?

Unit costs

The value of being large is related to the unit costs at which the firm can produce. If a firm has low unit costs, it is certainly efficient but is it large?

Impact on the community

In many small towns one or perhaps two employers dominate. When those firms go through difficult times, so does the town, its people and its businesses, which all rely on the prosperity of the dominating business for their livelihood. A current example is Tiverton with John Heathcote and another example used to be Corby with British Steel. In both instances these firms are considered large on other measures.

How to measure

We are really no nearer a conclusion and the best way to make the choice is probably to test a firm on more than one of the above criteria and accept that it is large or small if three criteria point to the same conclusion. The Bolton Commission, established in 1968 to consider this problem, recommended two criteria should be sufficient to determine size.

Legal structure
Sole traders

This is the most common form of business, although many only last a short period of time and others grow and change their structure. Sole traders, however, account for a relatively small proportion of annual business turnover. All sole traders have **unlimited liability**, which means that the owner's personal possessions and property can be taken to pay the debts of the business. They also run, in most instances, on limited capital and find it difficult to acquire more and to grow. Examples of this type of business are small construction, retailing, farming, personal services, finance and catering. Advantages and disadvantages of this business structure are given in Table 3.3.

Advantages	Disadvantages
Less legal restriction	Unlimited liability
Personal; complete control	Poor profits often
Keeps profits	Long hours
Choose work patterns	No scope for specialisation
Relationships more personal	Difficult to raise additional capital
	Lack of continuity

Table 3.3 Sole traders

Partnerships

Most commonly found in professional services, retailing, small construction, and in catering and financial services. A partnership is an agreement between two or more people to work together. At least one of the partners, and it can be all of them, must take unlimited liability for the business. Partners who do not do this can only offer their money to the business and can take no part in decision making or management. For this reason they are called limited partners. Partnership requires mutual trust to work, since one partner can bind all the others by action taken. Advantages and disadvantages of this business structure are given in Table 3.4.

Advantages	Disadvantages
Possible to specialise	Unlimited liability
Shared decision making	Shared profits
Increased capital	No continuity
Greater market opportunity	Bound by actions of the partner(s)
Tight control	Capital not easy to raise

Table 3.4 Partnerships

The dangers of unlimited liability

Business is about taking risks and, if the risk of failure is high or the cost of failure may be financial ruin, few will take those risks. Yet, change and development come because people are prepared to take risks. Partnerships and sole traders will rarely grow to a great size if liability remains unlimited. An economy that wishes to grow and develop needs a form of business structure in which there is a limit to the risk taken and in which the business begins to take responsibility, rather than the people who own it. The other big business risk that sole traders and partnerships face is that the business has no life beyond that of the people involved; there is a lack of continuity. Finding a way out of this problem required the development of three legal principles:

- **legal personality**;
- **limited liability**;
- **continuity**.

Legal personality

You are a person and as one you have all kinds of legal rights. Those rights grow as you reach certain ages and are complete by the age of 18 unless you are subjected to legal restrictions by circumstances such as being an alien (i.e. not a citizen of the country in which you live), not being of sound mind or being in prison. You can make contracts and you can take responsibility for the credit you receive. You can enter into business agreements and it is to you personally that people will come if they seek redress. You can use the law against people who break their agreements and in turn the law can be used against you. Nobody else is responsible for you. All of this, of course, assumes that you are 18.

How much easier it would be if a business had these rights and responsibilities. Provided the business becomes a company, registers as a co-operative or is a public corporation, it does achieve these rights. It acquires **legal personality**. This means that in all possible ways the business is treated as if it were a person and all transactions and agreements are pursued in its name. This does not take all responsibility away from those who are its owners or managers. They must still act responsibly and in accordance with the approved objectives of the business, and within the law.

Limited liability

The ownership of companies is divided up into small units (shares), usually but not always of one pound (£1) in face value. People can buy these shares and hence become part owners of the business. In the main these shares are owned in blocks and in some instances one person or organisation has absolute control by virtue of owning more than 50% of the shares. People who own large blocks often become directors of the business.

The only liability a shareholder has is for the amount paid for the shares. Nobody can make any further claim against shareholders. **Liability** is **limited** to the shareholding. Thus people are prepared to provide the necessary finance for very much larger firms.

Continuity

When sole owners die or when partners leave a business, the business ceases to exist. For a sole owner the value of the business passes into their estate and may well continue in the family if it can be inherited intact and the beneficiary wishes it to continue. A partnership can regroup around different people, but continuity is not guaranteed. In a company all that happens is that ownership, through the inheritance of shares, carries on and there is no break.

Private limited companies

The protection that comes from being a company is, therefore, substantial and it can be obtained by small firms, the owner(s) of which will create a **private limited company**. It is the word 'Limited' or 'Ltd' that tells us that a business has adopted this form. It has limited liability for its owners, legal personality and continuity, but the shareholders own their shares privately, meaning that they cannot sell them or advertise them publicly and can only sell them at all with the agreement of the other shareholders. Usually these shares are owned by family, friends or employees. They know each other and often the previous sole owner still has a controlling interest. The structure is adopted for its protection and for the possibilities of further capital for growth that are opened up. The capital to which the company has access is still small but significantly greater than that for unincorporated firms. The shares are usually owned by a small number of people and someone, usually the original owner, has

overall control. Since the capital is owned in shares, the firm has continuity and the shares can be passed down from one generation to the next. The fact of incorporation does impose certain legal formalities. These are primarily designed to protect various stakeholders because the liability of the shareholders is limited. Examples of this type of business are found in retailing, computer services, financial services, small and medium manufacture and small construction. The advantages and disadvantages are given in Table 3.5.

Advantages	Disadvantages
Limited liability	Capital acquisition limited
Legal personality	Legal constraints
Continuity	Difficult to sell shares
Tight control	
Easier capital acquisition	
Greater status	

Table 3.5 Private limited (Ltd) company

Many of the Activities and cases in the sections on accounting and finance focus on this issue of small private limited companies, looking at whether they should change their structure to pursue a new objective. Any one of these will help in understanding the issues involved in company structure.

Public limited companies (plc)

These are not always large but virtually all the giants of the business world have adopted this form. They can be recognised by plc or inc. at the end of their business name. They have all the advantages of private status plus the quotation of their share values and the public marketing of them through the Stock Exchange. Because ownership is more divided and because it is divorced from control, the law, through the Companies Acts, places even more detailed controls on the way a plc must be run and on the matters that must be reported to the shareholders. Examples are highly capitalised industries, multinationals and high-risk developments. Advantages and disadvantages of this business structure are given in Table 3.6.

Advantages	Disadvantages
Limited liability	Legal formalities
Legal personality	Cost of incorporation
Continuity	Share prices subject to fluctuation
Ease of share buying and selling	Legal requirements
Ease of capital acquisition	Subject to possible takeover battles

Table 3.6 Public limited companies (plc) or (inc.)

Activity

Give yourselves a present of £1,000 (or more if you wish) and discuss the share values you see in the financial sections of a daily newspaper. Select a range of them at the prices quoted. Monitor the prices on a weekly basis and decide when to sell and buy something else. Keep this exercise going for six months. Discuss and try to find reasons for your results at the end.

Alternatively, there are several national competitions, one of which is 'Beat The Boss'. This competition has a much broader business base than simply buying shares.

The formalities of incorporating

As soon as you form a company, ownership and control is divided and risk is shared with those who become stakeholders in the business. For these reasons, companies, like people, need birth certificates and the State needs a device through which it can protect the weaker parties in this situation. The documents the directors must complete are:

Memorandum of Association This shows the agreement to form a company and the objectives it will pursue. It also indicates the maximum share capital the company seeks authorisation for and registers a head office through which the business can be contacted.
Articles of Association The day-to-day constitution of the company, which covers the firm's operating arrangements in relationships with its stakeholders, for example the way meetings will be conducted and how voting will be carried out. The document is a more

sophisticated form of the kind of formal document that a cricket or tennis club would call its constitution.

As is always the case, there are fees attached to this procedure and when all is in order a Certificate of Incorporation is issued. Private companies can be open for business from this point on but public ones need to show they can raise the capital first and from that point they are issued with a certificate to commence business.

Some interesting exceptions

For some people the risks of business are large and they will incorporate purely to limit liability. A number of 'pop groups' have done this because their business is not just music but, if they are successful, all the memorabilia and spin-off trading that takes place.

Individual people can do this and become known as **corporations sole**. For example, in the church, a Diocese must always have a Bishop to lead it, but would lack continuity every time a Bishop died or retired. This problem is solved by incorporation, which makes each Bishop a corporation sole.

Some small non-trading organisations also need a means to ensure that the finances of the organisation will not dry up with nobody responsible. They can incorporate by guarantee. This means that, in the event of difficulty, the directors and shareholders guarantee a certain sum of money. They do not buy any shares at the time of incorporation. A local cricket club may have this kind of structure.

All three of these types of organisation have one thing in common. They need the security or continuity given to them by company status, but they do not need capital.

Co-operative societies

Whenever this term is used, the local retail co-operative probably comes to mind. To most people that is just another supermarket, but its legal structure is different. Its purpose is to serve the interest of the members and its profits are shared with them. The organisation does have shares but there is little purpose, for ordinary members, in having more than one share since all members have equal voting rights. In the older form all members participated in the running of the business, but in the modern form the business is managed professionally.

In fact co-operation is much more common than that. It sometimes happens through special contracts

Test Activity

Read the case study below and then tackle the exercises that follow.

Case study – Hobson's Garage

Ron Hobson has been in business for many years owning a small garage in a Devon village. He has two sons and a daughter and they want to be involved in his business. It isn't big enough to support more than one family and all Ron's children are married, living elsewhere in the village. Many of the village car owners buy fuel from Ron but there is little return in that and specialist garages are taking more and more of Ron's repair work. Ron is thinking of several ways of expanding:

◆ Philip, one of his sons, is licensed to drive buses and taxis. So Ron thinks there might be prospects in providing a taxi service.

◆ The local bus service has been withdrawn and workers who need to get to Tiverton, Exeter or Crediton now find it difficult. There is a possibility of running services or of tendering for contracts for special factory and school journeys.

◆ The village has only had one shop for many years and now this is closing down. The garage is in the centre of town and there is plenty of space and one spare building. Ron wonders about the possibility of opening a shop and knows that his daughter Stephanie and her husband Iain would be interested in running it.

Ron knows that, unless he takes some action, his present business will not survive. He also wants to retain control of his business and pass it on to his children. He has very little money saved and each of the possible ways of expanding will require capital. Early in his life Ron had real difficulties over debts in his family and under no circumstances will he consider borrowing.

(24 marks – 30 minutes)

(a) Ron currently runs his business as a sole trader. Explain the advantages and drawbacks to converting the business into a partnership with his children. (8)

(b) An alternative is to set up a private limited company. Would you advise Ron to do this? Explain your answer. (8)

(c) Suppose that Ron can only afford one of the possible ways of expanding. Explain four pieces of information about these options that he needs to help him decide which one to choose. (8)

---

between the members and is called a **joint venture**. A good example of this was the production of *Concorde*. Joint ventures are often set up by farmers, who co-operate to buy and use expensive farm machinery, such as combined harvesters. In buy-out situations, particularly where the new owners are the members of the workforce, the resulting structure is often a co-operative.

There are many examples of housing associations that work on this principle. They permit people who wish to own their own homes, but do not have enough capital, to come into the property market.

MG Rover/China Brilliance. MG Rover has signed a joint venture deal with China Brilliance to produce a new medium-sized car. Risks and fixed costs will be equally shared.

Public corporations

The two uses of the word 'public' often cause confusion, but public corporations are very different from public companies. Public corporations are owned by institutions such as insurance companies and pension funds and also by private individuals through the shares they buy. Each public corporation is subject to the provisions of its own Act of Parliament and its modes of management determined within the Act. Responsibility for the running of the corporation lies with a government minister. There used to be many public corporations, but the majority have now been privatised. Examples that still exist are the BBC, ITV and the Post Office.

The importance of classifying businesses

There is a mass of detail associated with the way firms are classified and this is specially true when they are classified by legal structure. It is not this detail that is of interest to us in Business Studies. We are interested in what firms want to do (their objectives), the context in which they do it (their environment) and the efficiency with which the activities are undertaken. It is in each of these senses that the features of a business may be of importance.

A firm may well start small, it may be locked into one limited form of business activity and, in most instances, it will be a sole trader. Many of the successful ones will want to grow. Some will do so by increasing activity gradually over time, some will do so by acquisition and merger, some will do so by moving into other, usually related, fields of activity. All will need more capital for these purposes and few will gain it entirely from their own resources or from the profits of the business. They will need to seek another structure. Here is where our real interest lies. How do firms change from one structure to another, how do they decide what form will be best suited to their environment and their needs?

Over-to-you

Table 3.7 shows the statistics for a small town:

(a) Calculate the actual and percentage unemployed for each year.

(b) Which level has declined most in recent years? Explain your answer.

(c) What might have been the effect of such a decline?

(d) How has the relative position of the three sectors changed over time?

(e) How might these changes be explained?

(f) Compare the changes you have noticed in this case with ones that have occurred in your area.

Year	1998	1999	2000	2001
Total population available for work	34,500	34,650	35,700	33,600
Percentage in: Primary employment	3.0	3.0	2.9	2.5
Secondary employment	37.0	35.0	33.0	27.6
Tertiary employment	56.3	57.2	59.6	60.4
Unemployed (actual)				
Unemployed (percentage)				

Table 3.7 Statistics for a small town

Test revision questions (60 marks, 1 hour)

1 Into what three levels of activity may businesses be divided? (3)

2 Distinguish between private and public consumer services. (3)

3 Why do some owners wish to keep their businesses small? (6)

4 Distinguish between ownership and control. (3)

5 Why is this distinction important? (4)

6 Limited liability seems unfair. Why is it necessary? (4)

7 Explain how legal personality and continuity help businesses to operate efficiently. (4)

8 Why do you think Manchester United is a plc? (4)

9 Explain what is meant by privatisation. (4)

10 Explain why there is no point in owning more than one share in a retail co-operative. (2)

11 Outline two reasons why the owners of a private limited company may not wish to convert the company into a plc. (6)

12 Why might some partners wish to remain in partnership rather than forming a private limited company? (3)

13 Which sector of industry is Marks and Spencer in? Explain your answer. (4)

14 Why might a car manufacturer planning to export to China set up a joint venture with a Chinese distributor? (4)

15 A business analyst is comparing the size of two companies – a retailer and a chemical manufacturer. Suggest two appropriate forms of measurement that could be used. Explain your answer. (6)

Discover and learn

1 Using the classification primary, secondary and tertiary, analyse business in your area.
   (a) How important is each level relative to the others?
   (b) What changes have been noticed in the last ten years?
   (c) What explanations can you offer for these changes?

2 Select one large firm in your area:
   (a) Has it grown or declined in recent years?
   (b) How do you explain the change or the fact that there has not been one?
   (c) Comment on its legal structure.
   (d) What might be the impact on the community if it closed down?

3 Explain the structure and ownership of each of the following in your area:
   (a) the local hospital;
   (b) the library;
   (c) the bus service;
   (d) a charity shop;
   (e) a supermarket.

4 Read the case study below and then tackle the exercises that follow.

Case study – When it pays to stay private

Source: Paul Barker/UNP.

Hugh Facey has an uncomplimentary view of the institutional investors that put money into public companies. 'They're all short-term profiteers' he says.

This negative stance explains why Mr Facey, founder and chairman of Gripple, which makes small metal wiring connectors for the agriculture and building industries, is determined to keep his company private. 'Public investors are not interested in growing companies, but in churning money,' he says. Even those who disagree with his view would find it hard not to admire his achievement in turning Gripple into a business with expected sales this year of £11m, 80 per cent exported, and expanding much faster than comparable engineering companies.

The company is based on selling ingeniously designed small metal grippers that sell for 50p and are turned out by Gripple at 1m a month using high-speed assembly machines.

Mr Facey says keeping the company private has several advantages. Since he is the majority owner, with 62 per cent of the company, he can control its strategic direction, and take decisions over such matters as development spending and setting up overseas sales offices, without concerning himself too much with other shareholders' views. Other owners include Gripple employees, with 28 per cent between them and the 3i venture capitalists with 10 per cent. Because he is firmly in charge financially, Mr Facey can operate more informally than if his business were quoted. For instance, he prepares a formal set of accounts just eight times a year, instead of the more normal 12. 'This saves a lot of time and money,' says Mr Facey. He also points out that, with expected after-tax profits this year of £1.5m, Gripple does not have to go public to raise funds for expansion. The company funds its growth plans largely through debt; it is fairly heavily geared, with borrowings of about £1.5m compared with physical assets of £3m. A public listing could be used to reduce debt. Gripple also has an overdraft facility of £2.5m. 'The bank has been very supportive,' says Mr Facey. Sales have risen from £7m in 2000. Mr Facey is projecting £14m next year and £30m by 2006.

One secret behind this growth, he says, is putting significant sums of money – some 6 per cent of Gripple's sales – into developing technical ideas. Indeed, a number of new products are under wraps at the moment.

In the past three years Gripple has also moved into grippers for holding together the metal wire that keeps in place equipment suspended from ceilings, including air conditioners or lighting. This range should account for almost half of Gripple's sales this year. The company has spent £1m since 1988 on filing and maintaining 12 key patents that protect its inventions. 'If you can't patent your products, there's no point in making them,' says Mr Facey.

Another key strategy is to focus on exports. 'Britain is only a small part of the world economy, and this should be reflected in a manufacturing company's sales,' says Mr Facey. Of Gripple's agriculture products, 94 per cent are exported, while the newer building products side of the company sells about 50 per cent of its output overseas. Mr Facey believes the key to exporting is to set up wholly owned sales subsidiaries. 'I say to our salesmen, get in there (to other countries) and push the product,' says Mr Facey.

Mr Facey says that in roughly half of the 50 or so other countries where Gripple sells its products, the company has conventional distributors that sell them on. In the other half, Gripple has formed more formal partnerships with local companies that sometimes incorporate them in their products so lifting the possibilities of increasing the UK business's sales.

By continuing with the twin focus on innovation and exports, Mr Facey thinks Gripple can continue to increase sales by 30 per cent a year, well above what most other makers of more conventional metal goods can manage.

As for the company staying private, at 56, he says he has no plans to retire, nor to sell the company.

Source: Financial Times, 24 October 2002.

(45 marks – 45 minutes)

(a) Outline three differences between private limited and public limited companies. (6)

(b) Explain three of the advantages given by Gripple's chairman for keeping the business a private limited company. (9)

(c) Examine the benefits to Gripple and its shareholders of 'going public'. (9)

(d) What are the potential benefits of encouraging workers to become shareholders? (5)

(e) Why does the Chairman consider that exporting is so important to his business? (4)

(f) Do you agree with him when he says: 'If you can't patent your products, there's no point in making them'? Explain your answer. (6)

(g) Calculate the total annual sales revenue from 'small metal grippers'. (3)

(h) Total sales revenue from all products is forecast to be £14m next year. If sales increase by 30%, what will be the new level of sales in the following year? (3)

Summary

In this chapter we have recognised that:

● There is no perfect way of classifying business but it helps to try so that the pattern of business is clearer. We can learn much about our own local area from the patterns of business it contains.

● We can classify businesses on various different bases.

● The classification can be based on the nature of the activity, e.g. consuming and producing.

● It can be based on the level of activity from primary through to secondary.

● It can be based on the the size of the business, from the micro business through to the very large and the public company.

● It can be based on the legal structure, from sole trader through to public limited company.

● It can be based on the distinction between private and public enterprise.

● There are other classifications largely based on the financial and capital structure of the firm. These measures will be discussed further in Chapters 10 to 13 where finance and accounting are considered.

Key words

Definitions of Key words can be found in the Glossary on page 269.

articles of association
co-operatives
corporation sole
joint ventures
legal personality
limited liability
memorandum of
    association

partnerships
primary activity
private limited companies
public limited companies
secondary activity
sole traders
tertiary activity
unlimited liability

4 Organisations and their objectives

On completion of this chapter you should be able to:

➤ understand the nature and purpose of objectives

➤ state, explain and comment on the objectives an organisation is likely to have

➤ understand the patterns of objectives an organisation may develop and show awareness of ways in which priorities may change and conflicts may develop

➤ show understanding of the elements of SWOT analysis and how this technique may be used in diagnosis

➤ understand how objectives influence business behaviour and business decisions

➤ name and explain the role of different stakeholders in business and comment upon the objectives they may have and the way these are likely to influence business behaviour and decisions

➤ comment upon the objectives of an organisation in a given situation

Introduction

Every activity in which we take part has an outcome. When that outcome is planned and worked for we can see an objective, a strategy to achieve it and a result.

Objective To attend a meeting in Scarborough tomorrow at 9.30 a.m.

Research Check on times of trains from home. This reveals that you cannot arrive in Scarborough before 10.15.

Strategy Find and book a hotel room for tonight, so as to arrive at the meeting place in plenty of time. Catch train this evening.

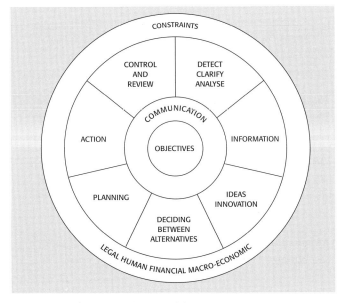

Figure 4.1 A decision-making model

Not everything we do is planned. Some things happen by accident, some are a surprise and some things we do on impulse, but the most important things are carefully thought about and, for each, we begin by deciding the objective.

The objectives of an organisation

Objectives are right at the centre of everything a business does (see Figure 4.1). This is a decision wheel that emphasises the fact that the process of making decisions and putting them into practice is a continuous one. Two things are right at the centre and influence every stage. At the heart is objectives and surrounding it communication.

Three objectives are commonly associated with all organisations:

♦ **survival;**
♦ **profit;**
♦ **growth.**

Survival

Surviving only becomes important as an objective when an organisation is threatened. The rest of the time it will be an objective that makes people a little cautious and prevents them doing things that are likely to put the business in danger. Not all organisations look for long-term survival. Many committees are formed to complete

Activities

1 Explain what your objective might be in each of the following situations:

   (a) You have to decide what to do after A levels are over.

   (b) It is your birthday and you have £500 to spend.

   (c) You have been asked to organise a disco at the end of term.

   For each of these outcomes you could have several potential objectives; decide between them explaining the basis of your decision.

2 Read the case study below and then answer the questions that follow.

Case study – Tea time

When two friends decided to open a teashop last year, they thought that the increasing number of visitors to town, and the greater frequency with which coach excursions were stopping in the town for short breaks, would provide a ready market for their 'home-made' produce. In a way they were right and business seemed brisk on most days of the week, although dependence on the weather was obviously a problem. Neither had any business experience and they had not undertaken any research to back up their belief in a favourable outcome. Pricing had been based on what they thought people would pay and had erred on the side of 'not being too expensive'. Many of their bills over the first six months were a surprise to them and within eight months, with the lower income of the winter, they had an overdraft and no real prospect of reducing it for three months or so.

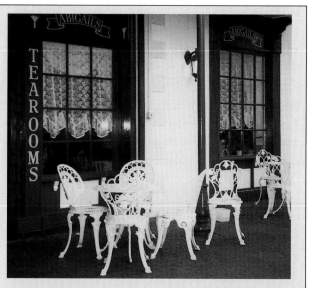

This teashop serves traditional cream teas as well as a range of light meals, cakes and ice cream

   (a) How would some careful thinking about objectives, before they started on the venture, have helped them to work more efficiently?

   (b) What should their objectives be from this point on and how might they pursue them?

a given task, such as organising a school disco or researching a new market segment. Newly formed businesses are likely to be more concerned with survival than any other objective. Failure rates are high with new firms. Some people find it difficult to take risks, although survival is vital for an organisation some risks need to be taken.

Profit

Profit is a word we must always use precisely. Get into the habit of putting an adjective in front of the word profit. On its own the word means very little. You should be familiar with the definitions in Table 4.1.

   Most organisations must make a profit. Some, like local authorities and leisure centres, seek only to break even, whilst others seek to maximise profits. In between

Gross profit The profit from the firm's activity before any of the expenses and provisions involved in running the business have been deducted.

Net profit Profit after provisions and expenses have been deducted. Net profit may be considered before or after tax and interest on money borrowed have been deducted.

Disposable profit That part of the profit of the firm which is available to distribute to owners. The amount disposed of to sole traders and partners is called drawings and that given out to shareholders is called dividends.

Retained profit That part of the profit which is retained in the business to provide necessary additional capital.

Table 4.1 Definitions of types of profit

these two extremes are organisations in which the aim is to make enough profit. A profit objective is often expressed in terms of a target return on capital employed. This is an idea we shall return to when considering balance sheets. Sufficient profit will provide:

◆ the working capital with which the activities of the organisation can continue;

◆ finance for growth and development which reduces the need for external funding;

◆ a reward for the owners without which the risks of business would not be accepted by anyone.

Suppose a new venture requires the investment of £30,000 and the firm expects a return on capital employed of 20%. Then the net profit on the venture must be at least £6,000.

Owners of small firms are very often content to make a reasonable profit. Their real objective is more the satisfaction of working for themselves than with making the largest possible profit. As firms get bigger there are more stakeholders in their success and more interests to satisfy. The urge for bigger profits often comes from this.

Growth

It is possible to grow in one or more of many measurable ways. Some organisations see growth as desirable. After all isn't a bigger business better than a smaller one? Isn't Tesco more successful than a small local shop? Others see growth as necessary, arguing that, unless a business grows, it will decline and that it is impossible to stand still.

Is growth always the right objective? Can a business or an organisation get too big? Are there not situations in which small is not only beautiful but is also more efficient and more successful?

◆ What might happen in your school/college if growth continued for too long?

◆ Do you think you would be as well taught in a class of over 50?

◆ Might there be greater cost than benefit if the number of students doubled?

◆ Would the speed of growth make any difference?

◆ Would the nature or direction of the growth matter?

In one school the head master pledges that A-level classes will be no larger than 12 students and lower-school classes no larger than 25. Think of the marketing aspect of this. For many, growth is an objective, but it has to be pursued with care. Too-rapid growth can threaten survival. Growth attempts that are badly timed can lead to disaster. Look around your community; you will see examples of very successful growth and you will see examples of businesses that flourished for a little while and then were either absorbed or closed.

Test Activity

Read the case study below and then tackle the exercises that follow.

Case study – The ambitious son

John Hinman used to run a small butcher's shop and made a satisfactory living for many years. He had been a cautious business manager, never borrowing finance to fund expansion of his business. He had always wanted time to devote to his family and hobbies as well as running the shop. When he was 60 he retired and handed over his shop to his son, Andrew. He had been working in the shop for several years but had been rather frustrated by his father's approach to business. Andrew was very ambitious and he was determined to make the business 'more successful'. Within 6 months he had opened another branch in a town 12 miles away. Most of the capital was borrowed. Two further branches followed soon afterwards. Total sales grew by 40% for each of the next two years but then stagnated. Andrew found that he was spending much of his time on management issues such as recruiting staff and keeping financial records. He spent less time serving customers. By the end of the third year the business had a very large overdraft. It also owed money to its suppliers. The attempt to expand the business seemed to threaten its survival. Andrew's father helped him out of the difficulty but on condition that the three new branches were closed. Now Andrew runs a successful single branch shop.

(25 marks, 25 minutes)

(a) Contrast the apparent business objectives of John with those of his son. (8)

(b) Using the case as a starting point, analyse the problems of running an expanding business. (8)

(c) Discuss how Andrew might have expanded his business without risking its survival. (9)

Other objectives

The three objectives we have considered are thought to be the most important objectives of most organisations. However, those who manage or control organisations often have other objectives. These may be long or short term. Some examples follow:

◆ An important objective of all organisations in the public sector is to operate in the interests of the consumer. The Inland Revenue and the Benefits Office seek to ensure that people make the claims to which they are entitled.

◆ Charity organisations and shops seek to maximise profits, but only so that the causes they support receive greater benefits.

◆ Increasingly, businesses are showing concern for the environment and adopting codes of practice that follow 'ethical' lines. However, many have argued that this is because such behaviour is now profitable. There is really nothing new about this approach. Many of the industrialists of the nineteenth century showed far greater concern for the welfare of their workers than conventional practice of the time required.

◆ Owners of small businesses are often more interested in their business as a way of life than they are in profit or growth. The ability to hand over a successful business to the next generation may be more important than annual net profit.

The importance of a business culture in setting objectives

Think about groups to which you belong. Within your school or college there may be many: the place itself, the classes you are in, the activities, organisations or informal groups of which you are a member. The people involved in each of these groups will have attitudes to what they do as members. There will be rules, expected patterns of behaviour, expectations of each other, past experiences and perceptions. Someone will be leading the group and will have a particular style of doing so. Your feelings about that leadership style may be positive or negative. All of these things, and many more, make up the culture of the group and it is within this culture that objectives will be set.

The same is true of organisations. The culture of the whole business will influence the objectives set, the plans that are worked out to achieve them and whether they are achieved. For example:

◆ A skilled craftworker may be most concerned with the quality and beauty of the work done. The result may be that the product is very costly and has to be sold at a price that nobody is prepared to pay. The worker has to learn to produce at the level of quality that the market is prepared to pay for. The objective here was to make something good and beautiful. It should have been to make something the consumer is prepared to buy.

◆ The business you work for has set an objective to achieve a 30% return on capital employed. This is thought to be a realistic objective, but the leadership style of your boss is poor, the work of people in your group is poor and the target is not reached.

To have set objectives is not enough; they have to be realistic and possible within the culture of the organisation. As the second example shows, the culture may well prevent achievement of a realistic objective.

Conflicts between objectives

There is no constant order in which objectives are considered and pursued. The priority that an organisation attaches to a given objective will vary from one situation to another. In the first year of business a firm will be most anxious to survive, will have no ideas of growth and may be happy to aim for break-even. But, in most cases, break-even cannot be a long-term objective. As a firm becomes more successful, attention may well turn to greater profit and even to growth.

Businesses change their objectives over time. Indeed, those refusing to do so often go out of business. Reasons to change might include:

◆ Circumstances have changed.
◆ The original objective was not well thought out or was too ambitious.
◆ A new opportunity has arisen.
◆ Competition has endangered survival.
◆ Consumer attitudes, needs, perceptions or buying habits have changed.

Objectives can only be changed if the culture of the organisation permits it. Continuous change is no more desirable than being inflexible. To anticipate the need for change and to be able to make successful changes, organisations must monitor what is happening and have an agreed procedure for making changes so that people will accept them, understand them and make them work.

Communicating objectives

Go back and have another look at Figure 4.1. Surrounding the objectives that are at the hub of the wheel is the word 'communication'. To communicate objectives is essential. How does anyone know what is to be done unless someone has explained? But it is not enough to tell people about the objectives. Suppose you were working as a member of one of several production teams and one of the messages you were given said: 'We must reach a net profit target of 30% on capital employed.' That might well be the target and it may well be achievable, but what does it mean? The chances are that you will ignore it because you do not understand it. It is certain that achieving the objective is important and that you are expected to play your part in making that possible, but what is your part, what do you have to do? Obviously the objective has to be communicated in a better way. What might that better way be?

Figure 4.2 illustrates one way in which an objective may be translated as it goes down the hierarchy of a business so that it is understood and can be acted upon at all levels. Now you and your team know what you must do – produce 20 units per shift/per hour. You may

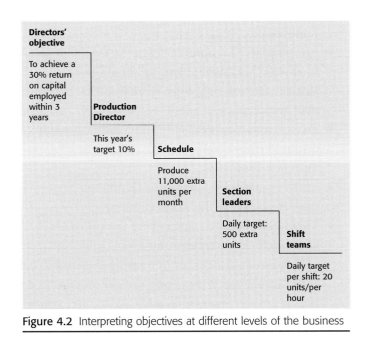

Figure 4.2 Interpreting objectives at different levels of the business

not want to do it; you may not think it is possible, but you know what is expected. This suggests another aspect of good communication. The business needs your team to produce 20 units per shift/per day. It must find a way of ensuring that you do. Good communication does not just tell you about things in ways you understand; it gets from you the response that is needed.

Objectives and time

Time span is a vital element of many objectives. A management team may know that its ultimate goal is market leadership but that may be too far into the future to be an objective for the present. The planning has to be broken down into a series of objectives which will reach that goal. It is difficult to respond to something which must be achieved in five or even ten years time but wise to plan towards it.

Example

Objective: Market leadership in a stated segment of the market.

This is far too vague, distant and unattainable but the following might be achieved:

Year One: To penetrate the market and establish sales of 10,000.
Year Two: To achieve a 10% market share.
Year Three: To ensure growth in market share to 25%.
Year Four: To become market leader.

These more precise and directed targets are likely to be more feasible and each year there is a specified objective against which to measure progress. Strategy and/or tactics can then be modified to keep the firm on course for its overall four-year objectives. In establishing these objectives a firm may well work backwards from the eventual goal to establish the intermediate ones. To know where you want to be and then to work backwards towards the steps that must be taken to get to the ultimate goal is sensible planning. This kind of time span planning is often necessary within the strategy to achieve a short-term objective. Table 4.2 (page 38) shows an example from *Business Review*: it works backwards from the known publication date and hence sets firm targets for all those involved.

Activity

Apply this kind of analysis to your own life and the long- or medium-term objectives that you may have. This could well begin with a stated objective to achieve a good AS grade in Business Studies.

Objectives and strategy

In effect what Table 4.2 shows is a strategy to ensure the achievement of an objective. *Business Review* is published four times a year and the stages of planning to ensure publication on the date specified and the availability of the magazine to you, are more detailed than the stages shown. The whole process will begin with a planning meeting, probably annually, at which the editors review the recent issues and decide on the kind of material which would be appropriate for the next volume of four issues. This must be balanced so that each issue comes fresh and worth reading. There will be some features which are common to every issue and others which are part of a series for one volume. The magazine will then be filled with individual articles which the editors think you will benefit from. For some of these the authors will be known and for others authors may have to be commissioned. Occasionally the editors will receive articles from writers who would like to be given space in the magazine and these will be carefully considered and a decision made.

The magazine has a defined market and the editors must ensure that this market is satisfied. If the known market is not given value for money then the magazine will fail. Editorial policy establishes what the magazine should look like and contain in order to meet the needs of the market, and careful editing will ensure the required standards are reached.

In due course the editor will have put together the features and articles needed for the coming issue. The following ideas will have been part of the strategic thinking to this point:

- Have I ensured that all the articles are edited in a way which reflects the objectives and style of the magazine and that they represent a balanced coverage of issues to which the readers will respond positively?
- Have I ensured that the ideas in the articles are clearly expressed and likely to be of interest and value to most of the readers?
- Have I ensured that the issues are accurately expressed in terms of the specifications for which they are written?
- Does the issue provide a reasonable balance of articles?

These are just some of the strategic ideas which underpin success and there will be similar ones which determine the way in which the magazine is illustrated, the design of the cover and the order in which it is put together. These are the responsibility of the publishing editor.

From the above you can see the ways in which objectives are planned for, and reached, and you should gather that the following things are true of successful strategy:

- It is designed to achieve a stated objective. Any elements which do not do this must be removed.
- It is necessary to monitor it wherever possible so as to ensure that the objective will be achieved. Remedial action or reconsideration of the objective may be necessary.
- To ensure success flexibility and planned ways of dealing with problems should, as far as possible, be built into the system.
- In the majority of cases time will play an important part in the whole process.
- There must be some elements of the approach which define the strategy and which will be adhered to. In the case of our example there will be general publication decisions, such as four issues a year at known times, and editorial decisions which form the policy.

Publication date	September	10th
Copies complete	August	12th
Film to printer	August	1st
Final corrections	July	3rd
Page proofs to editor	June	25th
Galley corrections	May	27th
Galleys to editor	May	12th
Copy at publishers	April	1st
Copy to editor	March	1st

Table 4.2 *Business Review* publishing schedule for an issue

- Several groups of people are normally involved. In a business these will usually be the managers and the departments of the organisation. In our example they are the original authors, the editors, the publishing team, the printers and the distributors.
- At the end of it all the position will be reviewed. Much of this will be on the basis of 'in house' information, but if the strategy was designed to produce a product or a service the response of the market, largely judged by its buying behaviour, will be crucial evidence.
- The result of the review will possibly be some modifications to the way things are done next time. We all learn from experience and the successful business puts this learning to good effect.

There is a very close link between the objectives of an organisation and the strategies it adopts. Indeed the starting point of all strategy is the objective. Without a known, clear and measurable objective no coherent strategy is possible. Without an effective and well-executed strategy any objective, however good, is unlikely to be achieved.

Objectives around the firm

The setting of the objectives we have been considering takes place at the top. For larger firms, objectives must then be set for all the various areas of operation. The absolute requirement is that objectives set for a section of an organisation will not conflict either with those of other sections or with those of the organisation as a whole.

Marketing objectives

For a business, success means that consumer needs have been identified, targeted and satisfied at a profit. Initially a firm will be satisfied to break into a market and the objective will be a successful launch. Thereafter, the objective will change to one expressed in terms of volume of sales, sales revenue or market share. Over a period the firm will seek at least to maintain its position or to obtain a steady growth. Before realistic objectives can be set, the firm must know where it is (**market standing**) and what the possibilities are (**market potential**) Then the objective set must be a specific target in relation to time and to segment(s) of the market. Next, it can be translated into targets for each member of the sales team. In setting such an objective the marketing department should be aware of the quantities and qualities the production department is capable of delivering and intends to deliver.

A firm could be product orientated. If it is, it is simply producing at the most efficient levels of production and leaving it to the marketing department to maximise revenue from that product.

The danger in this situation is that the product does not meet the needs of the consumer and the goods cannot be sold in sufficient quantity or will produce too low a level of profit. It is wiser for modern business to be market orientated. With this approach the firm first identifies all the characteristics of consumer needs and then produces to satisfy them. The attitude changes from 'sell what you have produced' to 'produce what you know you can sell'.

Activities

1 Think about the part-time job that you have or about one you might have taken on. What might be the best way of communicating to you what you need to do to help achieve a return on capital employed of 25%.
2 Read the case study below and then answer the questions that follow.

Case study – Confused negotiation at Broland Plastics plc

Broland is a small company located on an industrial estate outside a city in the north west of England. The following conversation took place between a union representative (UR) and the managing director (MD). Tuesday afternoon. 2.30 p.m. (The union representative had been waiting since 1.30 p.m., the agreed time of the meeting.)

MD We must get down to detailed discussion of our production plans right away.
UR Certainly, there is no time to waste. We have worked things out and I know what our objectives are. If you know your objectives, perhaps we can get somewhere.

MD Our new plant is larger than we intended at first. The market is growing and we think we can sell enough to keep the plant going at 90% capacity. That gives us some room for growth. I will have targets for each shift for you by tomorrow and we should be able to put them into operation from Monday.

UR Just a minute! We should take things one at a time. Conditions of work are not good enough to make a start possible on Monday. I came to discuss pay and conditions, hours of work and training.

MD Look! It's very important to get production started.

UR All the more reason for you to state what your intentions are and what you are going to offer. We must come to a working agreement; the workers are not going to be ignored.

MD You do realise that without products to sell we can't pay or employ anyone. We can make improvements in time.

UR We certainly expect that. The heating and lighting are poor and dangerous. The sanitary facilities are below standard, especially for the women. Health

and safety procedures are not always followed and there are no canteen facilities. It is impossible to reach any targets in these conditions.

MD I guarantee that these problems will be sorted within three months of working for the new targets.

UR Now what about rates of pay? Our figures are based on a 40-hour week, differentials for night-shift working, keeping to national agreements and bonuses for exceeding the targets.

MD National agreements, of course, and we have a bonus scheme to propose but we expect a 44-hour week.

UR We expect that every employee will be trained or re-trained as an insurance against change.

MD It's not that simple.

UR Are you implying you will not fulfil your obligations to train, as required by law?

MD The Act is not really appropriate for small firms like us.

UR So! No training, poor or illegal facilities and a 44-hour week. I don't think we are talking the same language... (walks out)

(a) What do you think were the objectives of:
   ◆ the managing director?
   ◆ the union representative?

(b) What do you think has been achieved by this meeting?

(c) How would you suggest the situation might be saved?

Test Activity

Read the case study below and then answer the questions that follow.

Case study – Wrigley puts £5m into first 'non-gum'

Wrigley, the world's biggest chewing and bubble gum maker, has broken with tradition after 111 years and launched its first non-gum sweet in the UK. It is spending £5m on promoting Extra Thin Ice, a pack of 24 micro-thin transluscent strips of peppermint-flavoured candy. There will be a TV campaign, press ads and free samples. The Marketing Director is reported as saying that: 'Sales of

Wrigley are expanding faster than any other confectionery item but we always need to consider diversifying into other types of sweet'. Last month the company launched a bid for Hershey Foods – if this goes through it will lead to even further growth and diversification.

Sources: Various

(25 marks, 25 minutes)

(a) Outline Wrigley's objectives in launching this new non-gum sweet. (6)

(b) Before using this new product strategy, the firm undertook a great deal of market research. Analyse why this was thought to be necessary. (7)

(c) Discuss four factors that could determine whether Wrigley's successfully achieve their objectives for Extra Thin Ice. (12)

Research and development

This is not just about new products, or even new ways of producing them. Satisfying consumer needs is much wider than that. In Chapter 2 we discussed the idea that consumers buy different packages of services that surround the product. Research and development may be about the characteristics of the market or about all the consumer services that might make a sale more likely and build regular buying habits around the product. Change is a rapid and continuous fact in the business environment. Good and constant research and development is the lifeblood of adapting successfully to that change.

Human resource management

Annual reports to shareholders commonly stress that people are a firm's most important resource. Modern approaches to personnel management see people less as individuals and more as members of a team empowered to take responsibility and make significant contributions to achievements. The culture of the business is centred much more on people and on their integration into all stages of business activity. This being so, objectives relating to recruitment, induction, training and human resource management now assume an importance they did not have in the past. The law plays an active part in ensuring that personnel objectives are set. It requires businesses to adopt equal opportunity policies and to make provision for the effective employment of people who are disadvantaged. It requires an approach to all aspects of employment and this protects the interests of the employees. Central to all of the objectives that might be set is an overall workforce plan.

To provide a consistently excellent standard of service forms the basis of this company motto
Source: Select Appointments plc.

Social responsibility

Businesses have responsibility to their stakeholders. How much wider than that does social responsibility go? In many of the things a firm does, particularly if it is a large one, it produces good and bad effects for groups not really considered its stakeholders:

◆ A firm that produces waste may dump it far away from the community in which it is located or may spill into the sea or a river.

◆ A firm that makes people redundant will reduce disposable income throughout the community and be likely to cause further unemployment.

◆ Some firms cause problems of noise and air pollution.

◆ Some firms tend to cause litter.

◆ Some firms have little regard for the environment, whilst others make a point of emphasising their environmental concerns and policies.

◆ Some firms behave in ways that would be considered unethical whilst others have a strictly applied code of ethical conduct.

What firms will do about issues like this depends upon a number of things, many of which are part of their culture. Among those things are:

◆ the beliefs and opinions of the management and the leadership style they adopt;

◆ the social conditions prevailing at the time and in the locality;

◆ the costs and benefits the firm associates with a given line of action;

◆ the strength of pressure groups and pressure organisations;

◆ political decisions and procedures put in place by government;

◆ the prevailing law at local, national and EU level.

Stakeholders and their objectives

The larger a business gets, the more stakeholders it has. All of them have at least one vital relationship with the business and objectives that will not always be in harmony with the objectives of the firm. This often changes the firm's priorities or creates conflicts with which the firm must deal.

Owners

At its simplest level ownership involves one person, who is probably the sole or major decision-maker within the firm. Ownership and control are fully integrated. This should mean that there are no conflicts, but this is not necessarily true. Sole owners often have ambitions to grow, about which they are impatient or for which they have insufficient evidence. Pursuit of growth can then lead to failure to survive. In the early years they often lack the expertise to pursue a realistic objective. The case study concerning the ambitious son earlier in this section is a good example of these problems.

A first step in growth may be to find a partner. While the liability is still unlimited, there is now another interest in the business and its success. The partner may not have the same objectives as the original sole owner but will have the authority to commit the firm. Here there is a clear need for organisation and planning to ensure that both or all partners are pulling in the same direction for the same or very similar reasons.

It is when a firm moves into limited liability status that **ownership** and **control** begin to move apart. Ownership is divided into small units called shares and it is the shareholders who own the business collectively. In a private limited (Ltd) company this is less of a break. The owners are often the controllers because shares are divided between members of a family or between a group who work together in managing the business. Control is usually firm in that one of the owners has a controlling interest. Where this is not the case, scope for conflict exists between the managing group, who wish to pursue business-centred objectives, and the owning group, who wish to see a good dividend. The directors may want to plough profits back into the business, whilst the owners may want a better return. The directors may see a need to raise more capital externally, whilst the owners may be anxious to maintain their position.

When the firm has reached public company (plc) status, ownership and control are effectively divided. Apart from those who own large blocks of shares and are probably directors, shareholders have a very weak voice. Their interests are still the same, but they have less power to defend them. The group is a widespread one and, even collectively, the shareholders find it difficult to have an influence on the firm's activities. Unlike shareholders in a private limited company, who must seek the approval of their fellow owners, they can attempt to sell their shares and invest elsewhere. The objectives of the Board are always certain to be different from those of some of the shareholders and the only meeting to discuss these issues is the general one. At this meeting, if sufficient support is there, one or more of the directors can be voted off the Board. Collective opinion may convince the Board to change its objectives or its priorities or to find different methods of pursuing them.

The State intervenes to protect the interests of shareholders by requiring a registration procedure before a company can commence business. This also includes a 'constitution', which sets out the objectives of the company (Memorandum of Association) and the rules under which it will work (Articles of Association). Audited annual accounts are required and there are regulations as to what these must contain. If directors operate outside this framework, shareholders can use the courts to bring them back in line.

Most of our national utility services were owned by the State, but have now been privatised. To keep them under control and following appropriate objectives in the interest of the consumer, the State has set up monitoring groups, which can and do intervene. Keep your eye on the newspapers to see what OFTEL and OFWAT are saying to British Telecom and the private water authorities.

The State uses the same kind of controlling body in dealing with organisations it controls and most of you will have come face to face with members of OFSTED, who try to ensure standards in education.

Where an organisation is either part of State provision or is still in State control, it will have different objectives from those common in private business and different priorities in pursuing them. There are strong reasons for retaining some activities within the control of the State. These are usually related to the need for such industries to be large and potentially monopolistic or to ensure that the interests of either the nation as a whole (air traffic control) or the interests of all consumers (the Post Office) are maintained. Such industries are still expected to break even in the long run. Beyond that, consumer and public interests should be the main objective. The State tries to promote this approach even within industries that are now in private hands:

- Many rural bus services are run by the bus companies, but are heavily subsidised by the local authorities whose communities are served by the buses.
- Even in large city areas like Manchester and the West Midlands, some rail services are supported by the local authorities.
- Many dramatic societies are given support by local authorities to enable small communities to receive their services.
- Many of the country's great orchestras are in financial difficulty and have been given additional support, provided they pursue objectives including musical education.

Employees

The people who are employed by an organisation will have very different objectives. Some may simply be working for the money they earn. This is generally true of student employees working at weekends and some evenings. Some will have a much broader interest in the job and see themselves as seeking promotion within it. Some may have an interest in the profits of the business through productivity bonuses or through shares they hold. Some may have found objectives through things other than the work. This could be working for the union or just a friendship group. Some will have managerial responsibility and through that a wide range of objectives.

In some instances a person's overwhelming objective may be to keep a job that they believe is under threat. In many instances employees will unite to protect their interests and to pursue their own objectives. This is the purpose of unions and the Broland Plastics case (page 39) illustrates this. Have another look at the objectives of workers, which are being represented by the union representative in that situation. The objectives of employees are so diverse, particularly in some instances those of management and other workers, that collective action is difficult. Those who often find themselves in a very difficult position are workers who are not members of a union that is in dispute with the management.

Some time ago, the drivers and conductors of Devon General (a bus company) were in dispute with the management over one-person operation. A student working there was recommended to join a union if he wished to keep his holiday job with the firm. Now he could not be required to join, but relations with workmates would not be very good if he did not join.

Customers

Here you have to think about those who *might* be customers as well as those who are. It is the aim of every business to create customers, i.e. people who come back to purchase on a reasonably regular basis. Most business is done through regular customers. The objective of a customer is to get value for money. Most often the customer knows what he or she wants and where to get it and recent history has shown that the customer has power. This power has been exercised positively in ensuring recycling, the provision of organic foods, better provision for vegetarians and better labelling. It has led to Sunday opening and to 24-hour shopping. Negatively, it has led to goods being withdrawn from sale; the ban by some supermarkets on French goods during the beef crisis was a typical example. Collectively, consumers have more power through specialist agencies like the Consumers' Association and through consumer programmes like 'We Can Work It Out' and 'Watchdog'. In highly competitive fields, such as food and general sales in supermarkets, consumers have, by their actions, led to the closure of many small shops and led supermarkets to fight for their custom. Every day brings a new way in which this fight is pursued:

- *Price wars*: low-price strategies at Asda; price match promises by John Lewis; 'two for the price of one' offers by Somerfield.
- *Loyalty Cards*: Tesco linked with cheaper in-store purchasing; Co-op linked with dividend on selected purchases, Somerfield linked with Argos purchases and Sainsburys linked with Air Miles.
- *Delivery services*: in one area both of local supermarkets have introduced them.
- *Increased facilities*: bag-packing services, more tills, a restaurant, a mother and baby room.
- *Longer opening hours*: 24-hour opening or late night opening; Sunday opening.

The State offers considerable support to the consumer through the law and such acts as the Consumer Credit Act, the Fair Trading Act and the Food Safety Act. This is usually enforced through local agencies such as the Trading Standards Office. Much depends on what the consumer wants. Using the rights conveyed by law will often put things right but without much benefit to the consumer. An individual, whose goodwill is too precious to lose, might get a better result by direct contact with the firm. However, in this country, when things go wrong, most customers seem to take their custom elsewhere for a while and grumble to their friends. This may, of course, have a powerful effect; bad news often travels fast.

Suppliers

The main interests among this group are to retain or increase the business, to make a satisfactory profit on the business and to be paid as promptly as possible. Their views of the purchaser will be in pursuit of these objectives. They tend to avoid giving credit to unknown organisations or those with poor financial reputations. Sometimes, particularly when sources of supply are easy to find, suppliers have to put up with long credit periods in order to retain the business. Sometimes the supplier can dictate terms, because there are few reliable sources of supply or it is costly to change from one supplier to another. There are certain brands that customers expect to see on the shelves and if they are absent the store may lose business. Suppliers sometimes negotiate contracts that ensure further business.

If the suppliers of, for example, a photocopier, sells the customer a maintenance contract, this will ensure that, at least in three years, the customer will have the machine repaired by them and will buy paper and toner from them. On the other hand, many supermarkets have contracts with suppliers that specify the day and time when goods will be delivered, often as strictly as 9.00 a.m. on Thursday morning.

Lenders and creditors

A creditor of an organisation is owed money for goods or services supplied. His/her objectives are to protect their own cash-flow position, to ensure they get their money in full as quickly as possible and to keep the customers' subsequent business. It is often a difficult position to be in. Often they may not want to give credit, but have to do so in order to get business. Often they would like to push for payment, but this may risk losing later business. Cash-and-carry businesses avoid

this issue by not giving credit, while most businesses minimise the risk by requiring credit references or making credit enquiries. Some, particularly those who finance on hire purchase, franchise the debt to specialist finance houses; some give inducements like 5% off for prompt payment. Creditors who feel that the position of a firm is precarious and fear they will not get their money back can often exert pressure and may even force a firm into liquidation or a sole trader into bankruptcy. However, they do not always get their money back.

Loans may be short or long term. Business relies heavily on borrowing and the objectives of the lender are to carry on doing business of that kind, to get the sum lent back when it is due and to receive the interest when that is due. In most cases these objectives will not conflict with those of the business, but, when they do, lenders may enforce the agreement and this too can lead to the closure of the business.

Community

A community develops objectives in relation to the activities of a firm when it sees cost or benefit to the locality resulting from the intentions of the business. Sometimes these objectives are focused through the local authority, as when business and industrial parks are developed and incentives offered to move to an area. It is also through local authorities that firms and intending firms must apply both for change of use permission and for planning permission. Sometimes the community will be organised by a single individual and pressure groups will develop to make a point. In one locality in recent years pressure groups have attempted to influence:

- the construction of a reservoir;
- the path of a by-pass round the town;
- parking charges;
- the building and location of a new supermarket;
- the retention and development of railway services;
- the location and waste disposal activity of a local business;
- a proposal to close the local hospital.

On some of these issues the community, with the aid of the media, has won, on others some concessions have been granted. For example, the local hospital has not been closed, but its maternity facilities have been withdrawn. The railway services have been retained and significantly improved. Even when the objectives of the community are not achieved, the fact of pursuing them reminds both the local authority and firms intending to take action that there is an interest in what they do. Those interests may have to be built into an action taken or into the way of doing it.

Table 4.3 gives a summary of stakeholder objectives.

Changing objectives

An organisation must continually review its objectives and progress towards their achievement if it is to retain or improve its position in a dynamic business world. The actions of competitors, changes in technology, actions by government and the changing pattern of consumer tastes and preferences are among the many things that may change and influence the objectives that a business can and should pursue. Every day is really a new starting position and ongoing analysis of where the organisation is and where it can go is essential. Tesco have responded positively to ecommerce by ensuring that 90% of its UK customer base will be able to shop on the internet by the end of the year 2000.

SWOT analysis

SWOT is an acronym for Strengths, Weaknesses, Opportunities and Threats (see Table 4.4) and is normally associated with marketing, but it can be used to analyse any aspects of business activity by reflecting on the internal and external factors relating to it. It is an audit of the position now:

Internally It discovers and analyses the strengths and weaknesses of the organisation with a view to using the strengths to greater effect and minimising the negative effects that weaknesses might have.

Externally It identifies the opportunities that may be grasped and ways of grasping them. It also identifies the threats posed by the variables outside the firm. These must be anticipated and action taken to avoid damage.

Table 4.4 (page 46) shows an example of a SWOT analysis for one firm.

The uses of SWOT

SWOT is not a decision-making technique. Managers are not able to refer to a SWOT analysis and identify immediately what action is required to enable the business to perform better in the future. What use is it

Stakeholder	Objectives	Power
Sole owner	Survival, profit, independence	Very limited
Partner	Survival, profit, growth	Limited, depends on agreement
Shareholder in private limited company	Survival, independence, return on capital	Limited but one may have overall control
Shareholder in plc	Continued good dividends	Can sell but little power unless holding is large enough
Employees	Job security, job satisfaction, good wages, promotion	Little unless skilled, except through unions and the law
Customers	Satisfaction of needs, good service, convenience	Through pressure groups and the law
Suppliers	To retain customer, to be paid on time	Varies with market conditions
Lenders	To be paid on time, continue business, receive interest	Depends on amount and nature of the lender
Creditors	To retain business, to be paid in full on time	Often depends on size and the relationship with debtor
Community	To maintain quality of life; objectives often vary within the community	Through pressure group or the law; can be strong
The State, local authorities, the national government, the EU	To maintain the economy, act in the interest of various groups	Very powerful but often act through persuasion and support; action at one level must not conflict with that at a higher one
	To pursue its own priorities through constraints upon and support for business decision and activities	Direct action, fiscal and monetary policy and the enactment and enforcement of new laws are the normal methods. Much is done through financial support. The Directives of the EU are increasingly important, and the devolved governing bodies of London, Scotland, Wales and Northern Ireland will increasingly have an impact.

Table 4.3 A summary of stakeholder objectives

Strengths Internal	Weaknesses Internal
Good efficient equipment	Equipment is old and there is more sophisticated equipment available
Good well-trained workforce	All three workers are soon to retire
Steady market	Market is loyal but very few new customers in last 18 months
Location well known	Poor location
Good reputation for high-quality work	Prices are not competitive
No cash-flow problems	Sole trader. No scope for further finance
Threats External	**Opportunities External**
Larger firms with lower unit costs and improved technology	Overall demand is rising
Many more potential customers providing their own facilities	Quality segment increasing very rapidly
Rising unit costs if costs continue to rise and customer base declines	Potential for entry into the repair and maintenance market
Compulsory purchase	Agency work for larger firms
Failure to survive in the long term	Entry into the market for consumables
New and expensive technology in a field change is rapid and replacement expensive. Continuous training needs are also difficult to meet	Possibility of merger with a local firm. This could enable a larger technical unit and therefore economies of scale which would decrease unit costs, broaden the range of services and make the firm more competitive.

Table 4.4 Norton Photocopiers – a SWOT analysis

then? A SWOT analysis has two main benefits:

(a) It forces managers to take a wide view of where the business currently is in terms of its external environment (in the fullest sense) and its own internal operations. It is too easy for directors and other managers to become so tied up in their own work that they fail to see the 'big picture' and how their business fits into it.

(b) It helps to diagnose potential problem areas – and potential areas for growth. As a 'diagnostic' technique it identifies the main forces that might prevent the firm from achieving its objectives. In addition, there will almost certainly be opportunities that the firm could exploit – and strengths that could be built upon.

Such a diagnostic analysis of the business will throw up some ways in which the performance of the business could be improved. The decision on which options to go ahead with – if any – can only be made after careful analysis of quantitative and qualitative data. SWOT alone cannot make this decision.

Test Activity

Read the case study below and then tackle the exercises on the facing page.

Case study – Tesco widens net for direct sales: impact on stakeholders

Tesco is to treble the number of stores from which it runs Internet shopping. This strategy is aiming to achieve the firm's objectives of raising Internet sales of grocery to £300 m by the end of the year. Terry Leahy, chief executive, yesterday said that 90% of the UK population would have access to this service. The expansion will create around 300 new jobs. The scale of the programme of expansion is much larger than the City expected – Tesco shares jumped 6% yesterday on the news. The company has now set up Tesco.com as a separate, wholly owned company in which it will invest £35 million, taken from profits, next year. Tesco said that Tesco.com could eventually be floated as a separate company and existing shareholders could benefit from this.

Source: Adapted from *The Times*, 12 April 2000.

(a) Outline the benefits of Tesco's decision on three stakeholder groups. (9)

(b) Why might some shareholders prefer that £35 million from profits was NOT invested in this project? (3)

(c) Explain briefly four reasons why this Internet selling strategy might prove to be unprofitable. (8)

Over-to-you

1 Taking into account all or most of the points outlined in Table 4.4, analyse the present position of Norton Photocopiers and suggest:

   (a) what its short-term objectives should be;

   (b) what its long-term objectives should be.

2 Read the case study below and then tackle the exercises that follow.

Case study – Middletown High School

Middletown High School is a school for 1,000 pupils aged 11–19. It is due to accept its first pupils in a year's time. The Governing Body, the Head and the senior staff have been appointed and they have a year to plan so that the school will operate effectively. The Head wants to set out the objectives of the school as a framework for how the school should work. Some of his colleagues think this is an impractical waste of time, but he produces his ideas for the second meeting of the group. His paper began with what he called a **mission statement**, which was:

'To search for excellence, to provide for maximum development of the individual and to equip all students for the world of to-morrow'

The Deputy Head argued that objectives should now be set in four areas and that she considered these to be:

◆ The operational structure of the school. By this she meant divisions of the school into upper, middle and lower, into year groups and into classes, the subjects that would be offered and how these should be grouped.

◆ New ideas. By this she meant the extent to which the school should venture beyond the traditional subject areas. For example, the school's catchment area is multicultural so what languages should be taught and what social and religious education should be offered? Which of the 'modern' subjects should be offered in the Upper School and what examinations should be possible?

◆ Staffing. What should be the number of teaching staff, support staff and others. What should the job descriptions and the roles be?

◆ Administration. What support systems should be in place to ensure the effective marketing of the school and its efficient relationships with staff, students, parents and the community? How should relationships with feeder schools, with business and industry and with higher education be developed?

The Deputy Head stressed that the ideas she presented merely scratched at the surface of the things that needed to be done. She suggested that four groups be formed and that in each group there should be at least one member of the Governing Body and at least one senior teacher. Each group should develop the objectives and outline a strategy for one of the four areas. The Head accepted this and suggested that they should all meet again in a fortnight.

(a) Summarise the advantages to be gained from setting out objectives for the school in this way.

(b) Using your school or college as a basis for comparison, comment upon any areas of school activity that you think may be:

   ◆ under-provided for; or

   ◆ under-provided for in the above framework.

(c) Choose any one of the four areas and comment on the objectives from the point of view of:

   ◆ a prospective student;

   ◆ a prospective parent;

   ◆ a potential employer of students from the school.

Test revision questions

(60 marks, 1 hour)

1 Explain why objectives are an essential part of running an effective business. (4)

2 What do you understand by the term 'culture of an organization'. (4)

3 What part does culture play in setting business objectives? (4)

4 Give examples to show how conflict between business objectives is likely to occur. (4)

5 In what ways would you expect the objectives of a state-owned and operated business to differ from those of a typical private business. (4)

6 List five stakeholders of Marks and Spencer and outline what their objectives are. (10)

7 Do you think that a firm should take notice of the objectives of the local community and show social responsibility? Explain your answer. (4)

8 Explain the main stages of SWOT analysis. (4)

9 Undertake a SWOT analysis for either:
   ◆ Your school or college,
   ◆ Vodaphone mobile phones. (8)

10 Explain why the principal objectives of a business might change over time. (4)

11 Why should departmental objectives (e.g. marketing or production) be based on the overall business objective? (4)

12 Explain the concept of 'divorce between ownership and control' in public limited companies and consider the different objectives that might exist as a result. (6)

Discover and learn

1 Consider your own objectives.
   (a) How well are they formed?
   (b) In what ways do they influence what you do?
   (c) Are they realistic?
   (d) What are you doing in order to achieve them?
   (e) How might a modification of your actions improve the position?

2 Choose any one of the local public services (Police, Fire Service, Ambulance). Discover what their objectives are. How have those objectives changed in recent years?

3 Choose any sole trader, discover what the owner's objectives are and the extent to which he or she thinks they have been achieved.

4 In a group undertake a SWOT analysis of McDonalds restaurants. Present your findings to the rest of the class.

Summary

In this chapter we have recognised that:

● The objectives of a business are central to all its activities.

● The main ones will be survival, profit and growth but priorities between these will depend on the situation.

● The culture of the organisation will play a big part in the formulation of objectives.

● A business will establish objectives for all departments that are in harmony with the overall objectives.

● Stakeholders will have their objectives and these may sometimes conflict with the interests of the firm.

● No firm can afford to ignore the objectives of its stakeholders.

● Business is in a dynamic environment and must constantly review its position.

● SWOT analysis is one technique which might be helpful in this context.

Key words

Definitions of Key words can be found in the Glossary on page 269.

growth	profit
human resource management	research and development
lenders	social responsibility
market potential	suppliers
market standing	SWOT analysis

5 Responding to external economic influences

On completion of this chapter you should be able to:

➤ understand the nature of a market and its role in influencing business behaviour
➤ show how demand and supply interact in the market and how business might respond
➤ show how the market allocates resources
➤ discuss the effects of competition on business behaviour
➤ understand the importance of the rate of interest
➤ understand the influences of exchange rates on business behaviour
➤ show how changes in interest rates and exchange rates may influence business behaviour
➤ understand the nature of taxation, both direct and indirect, and show its influences on business behaviour
➤ show how, and consider possible reasons why, the level of business and economic activity changes
➤ show understanding of all economic influences on business behaviour

Introduction

No matter how small or how large a business might be it is impossible for it to be independent of 'external constraints'. These are factors that limit a firm's ability to achieve its objectives that are external to the business. Here are some examples of potential external constraints for the Nestlé confectionery company:

◆ The actions of competitors, e.g. a fall in the price of Cadbury's Dairy Milk.
◆ Consumer tastes – a medical report detailing health problems experienced by regular chocolate eaters would not exactly lead to an increase in demand!
◆ The exchange rate, especially as all cocoa is imported.
◆ Government tax policy – if the government increased value added tax on confectionery items that would be a negative constraint for the Nestlé objective of further growth.
◆ New health and safety laws demand that all chocolate sold in shops has a 'sell by date' no more than 14 days after manufacture.

Figure 5.1 might help to illustrate just how many external influences there are on business decision makers, such as the directors of Nestlé.

This diagram shows the general framework within which firms operate. It is a framework which is unpredictable and some changes can occur suddenly. It is an environment in which continual awareness and flexibility are essential requirements for successful business operations.

These external influences are dealt with in this book in two chapters. This chapter considers the nature and impact of external *economic* constraints whereas Chapter 6 analyses all other external influences on business behaviour.

Our view of economic influences on business activity is not that of an economist. This chapter uses economic concepts and ideas but it is not about theoretical economics. We are concerned with how the economic environment and changes in it will impact on business performance and decisions. This chapter is about a washing machine manufacturer in Nottingham, a travel agent in Newcastle, a farmer in Norfolk and an importer in Cardiff. All are trying to decide what action they need to take in the light of current and expected economic events.

Figure 5.1 The environment of business

Test Activity

Here are some recent newspaper headlines. Read them carefully and then answer the questions that follow.

'Inflation set to rise as wage increases exceed 5%'

'The Government today announced an increase in National Insurance charges on business – an additional 1% of all staff wages and salaries must be paid in through this tax'

'The German economy is on the brink of a recession'

'The next move in UK interest rates could be upwards'

(24 marks, 30 minutes)

(a) Explain how a labour-intensive firm – such as the Post Office – will be affected by the economic changes in the first two headlines. (4)

(b) Examine two ways in which this firm might react to this news. (4)

(c) Explain how a business exporting luxury goods – such as Bentley – might be affected by the news contained in the third headline. (4)

(d) Examine two ways in which the firm might react to the third headline. (4)

(e) Explain how a UK housebuilding firm – such as Wimpey – might be affected by the news reported in the fourth headline. (4)

(f) Examine two ways in which the firm might react to this news. (4)

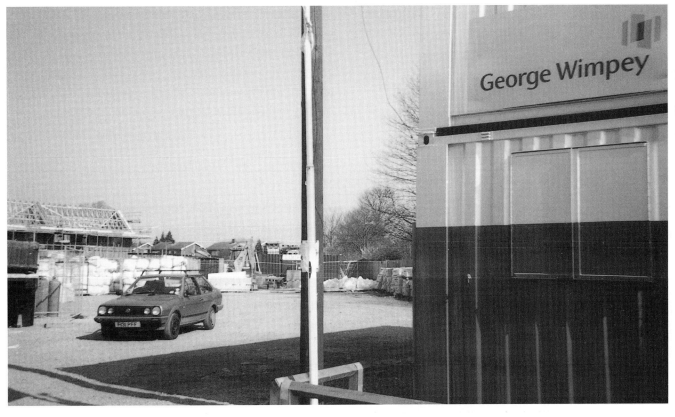

Mortgage interest rates have an impact on demand for new houses.

External economic influences
1 The market

To be successful, a business must identify a market or a market segment, satisfy the needs of the consumers in that market and do so at a reasonable profit. This will happen in a context where competitors are always juggling for market share, the state is intervening and the consumer is constantly making different decisions about what is wanted. Meanwhile, ways of producing things will be changing and new or better products will be continually entering the market.

The term 'market' simply means the coming together of buyers and sellers. This is often a place like the local markets at which many consumer goods can be bought. Some of these, like the market in Leicester, are world famous and large, while some are small, local markets open only on one or two days of the week. However, many marketing activities take place without a particular place and this kind of market is increasing rapidly with the development of e-commerce on the Internet. Here buyer and seller never meet, the seller provides, while the buyer surfs the net and makes a decision. Some markets, like that for shipping, for precious metals and for shares, are specialist; others like local supermarkets will sell anything they think will provide a profit. The two aspects of the market are:

Supply Sellers making goods and services available on the market and trying to persuade people to buy. When there is too much on the market there is a **glut** and when there is too little there is a **shortage**.

Demand The quantity to which people are prepared to buy at different prices. Being a buyer means having sufficient disposable income available, or the preparedness to buy on credit, and being prepared to buy when a product or service is offered and at the price asked.

Factors that determine supply
Price

The object of making things available for purchase is usually profit. Most goods offered for sale have already been produced and the cost of producing them is known. It follows that, the higher the available price, the more people will offer for sale. A supply schedule might look something like Table 5.1.

We can express the reaction to price in the form of a graph (Figure 5.2). This shows that more supply is brought to the market if the price is raised. Less is supplied if the price is lowered.

Costs of producing

The lower the total cost of producing a unit of a product, the lower the price at which a firm can enter the market. If a farmer can produce potatoes at 10p a kilo, the market can be entered at the lowest price shown in the schedule. The higher the actual price, the greater will be the producer's profit margin. Any action that can lower costs of production without reducing quality will persuade suppliers to enter the market.

Activity

Read the case study below and then answer the questions that follow.

Case study – Who are Petra's competitors?

Petra runs a very successful catering business in central London. She works from two premises she bought near Russell Square in London. In one she provides for those who need breakfasts, light lunches and snacks and also has a very busy sandwich bar. Petra opens for business at 6.00 a.m. and closes at 5.00 p.m.

In the premises next door she opens at 6.00 p.m. and closes at about 12.30 a.m. Here you can have a superb evening meal with a speciality range of Italian dishes to supplement the English menu. She also caters well and imaginatively for vegetarian customers.

She employs a staff of 23 to run the business. Six of these are in the common kitchen, which services both parts of the business; two are managers who are in charge when Petra is not there; two are wine waiters; two are cleaners; two are kitchen assistants; the rest are waiters and counter workers.

(a) Why has Petra separated off the two sides of her business?

(b) With whom does Petra compete?

Price per kilo	Quantity on offer (1,000 kilos)
12p	200
13p	220
14p	260
15p	320
16p	500

Table 5.1 A supply schedule: potatoes

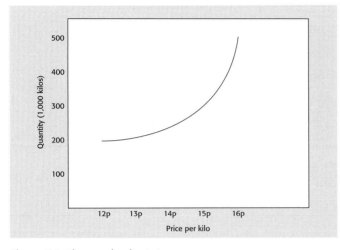

Figure 5.2 The supply of potatoes

The new Aston Martin DB7 – market conditions – both supply and demand – explain why this model is so expensive.

Supermarkets can buy at much lower costs per unit than small shops; hence their stock is much more extensive and their prices lower. New technology often lowers costs of production and makes supply at a lower price possible.

Production methods

To produce a car to customer specifications and without mass production methods is very costly. This can be seen in the cost of producing Aston Martin cars. It is the application of mass production methods to standard designs that makes cars available to most consumers.

Product flexibility

Where it is possible to respond easily to changes in the market, such a change will occur. For example, a change in the price of many publicly quoted shares will often produce an immediate response from sellers. Other responses take longer. In agriculture a fall in the demand for sweetcorn might persuade farmers to switch to another product, but it will take a full season for the change to be felt. On the other hand, a news-vendor on the streets of London can vary the number of papers available on a daily basis.

Government action

The biggest supply shift would come as a result of a government ban on a product. This might not take the product out of the market, but it would remove it from the local market. Quotas placed on milk production and on fish catches are examples. A government may subsidise in order to increase supply, as it does with branch railway lines. A government may interfere, through organisations like OFWAT and OFTEL, in the prices that water companies and telephone service providers can charge

Legislation is also a government weapon. Through laws like the Sale of Goods Act the State ensures that goods are fit for the purpose for which they sold. Through health and safety legislation it governs the conditions in which goods can be produced. This may well affect the quantity of goods that can be produced and the cost of each unit. The budgetary policy of the government may also affect costs of production and the prices of goods. Increases in the rate of interest may reduce investment, whilst an increase in VAT is likely to be passed on to the consumer.

Political decisions may also influence supply. A good example is the EU ban on British beef, our own ban on beef on the bone and, even after the EU had lifted the ban, the refusal of the French to accept the beef.

Regulations controlling the conditions under which motor fuel can be sold to the public have closed down a number of small rural petrol stations.

The weather

The weather has its most noticeable effects on supply in the transport industry and in agriculture, but extreme forms of weather can close down any source of supply.

The climate and seasonality influence the supply of many products. Several coastal hotels in the UK close down in the winter season, whereas in parts of Europe winter conditions have the opposite effect.

Forecasts

Supply is often managed so as to get the best return. Agriculture is a good example. Suppliers try to ensure that there is a steady supply of fruit and vegetables from around the world. The producers on the Scilly Isles try to get spring flowers on to the market as early as possible in the spring and all producers of flowers focus supply on special occasions like Mother's Day and Easter. The greetings card industry does its best to develop reasons for buying cards, but its main push is Christmas. The toy industry has a similar focus on the Christmas market. Forecast demand for millennium entertainment persuaded providers to inflate their prices, but many consumers rebelled against that and stayed at home.

The objectives of the firm

Most businesses try to increase the return from their efforts. This sometimes leads to marketing and promotional campaigns that temporarily increase the amount supplied. Early in the marketing of new products supply may be kept at a minimum in order to ensure the enjoyment of higher prices by the producer. In the production of novels, the issue of paperback versions is deliberately delayed to ensure a good market for the hardback versions. The world markets for diamonds and gold are carefully controlled by the suppliers to maintain prices.

The nature of demand

For consumers to demand a product it is not sufficient merely to want a good; we must also be able and willing to buy it at the price asked. We defined a supply

schedule for potatoes in Table 5.1. In Table 5.2 a demand schedule has been added. It is, as you would expect, showing that as price falls there is a demand for more potatoes. Supply and demand are the two forces in the market that have to be equal if we are to avoid either glut or shortage. In this simplified schedule you can see **equilibrium** at a glance, when the price is 14p per kilo. This we can plot on a graph, as shown in Figure 5.3.

Price per kilo	Supply (1,000 kilos)	Demand (1,000 kilos)
12p	200	500
13p	220	320
14p	260	260
15p	320	220
16p	500	200

Table 5.2 Demand and supply schedules

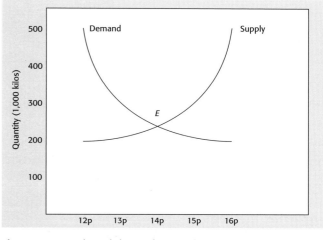

Figure 5.3 Supply and demand curves for potatoes

Factors that affect demand
Price

Are there any things that you would buy without even considering price? Maybe some 'one off' good or activity that you have been determined to be involved in or to purchase. Even in that case you would spend so much of your disposable income that something else you normally buy would have to be given up. Prices affect the likelihood of buying a particular good, the amount of it we purchase in a given time and/or the pattern of our demand. If someone wants to see England play Australia in a test match at Lords, or would like to enjoy an expensive holiday abroad or to purchase their own house, they may be able to spread the expenditure through some form of credit or borrowing, but the effect is always the same: if they cannot command more income, they will have to change their pattern of spending so that the expensive item can be paid for.

Changes in prices of other goods

There are different situations here:

- Changes in prices of goods that we are committed to consume. These might be electricity, gas or water. An increase may lead to personal economy drives to try and keep the amount paid the same, even though the price has gone up, or it will lead to a decrease in disposable income and a change in the pattern of our expenditure or saving.

- Changes in the prices of brands of goods that we buy. For most products brand loyalty is not very great and most people will switch to a cheaper brand for as long as that is possible.

- Changes in the prices of close substitutes. One general magazine may be much like another; you may be equally content with tea or coffee or with one kind of soft drink rather than another. You may be prepared to desert your favourite fast food shop for another where prices have not gone up.

- Complementary goods are those that tend to be bought together and therefore changes in the price of one may cause a change in the demand for the other. If the price of cars goes up sufficiently to deter demand, then the consumption of petrol or diesel will fall. For many, if the price of bacon went up it might cause a fall in the demand for eggs or a rise in the demand for sausages. A rise in the price of any computer hardware will cause a fall in the consumption of associated software.

Activity

Identify and explain how the following factors are likely to affect the supply of washing machines to the UK market:

(a) An increase in the price of essential components used by UK manufacturers in washing machines;

(b) An improvement in labour productivity resulting from better production methods in the same factories;

(c) Increased imports from a manufacturer based in the Czech Republic.

Income

We have to look at income in several different ways. It usually comes from work and the total amount earned is **gross income**. From this must come some unavoidable deductions, such as national insurance payments and taxation. These are usually taken away by the employer and leave us with **net income**. As we get older, we tend to acquire more and more commitments that use up our income and must be paid for regularly. These would include, for example, rent or a mortgage on the place we live in; electricity, gas and other regular bills; and items bought on credit. For some people this list is long and for others quite short. After all these payments have been accounted for, we arrive at **disposable income**. This is the income that can freely be used, but much of this may still be required for habitual expenditures such as food and clothing for ourselves and a family. The greater the real disposable income is, the more freedom there is to choose. Some people might choose to save some or all of this or might take the opportunity to buy the things they could not otherwise afford. Changes in ordinary income tend to come in small amounts so they lead to gradual changes in lifestyle, but windfall changes like winning the lottery or receiving an inheritance of some value may have substantial effects. Few of us know what we would really do with a sudden change in income and experience shows that the often stated, 'it won't change my life' just isn't true.

Some changes in disposable income are outside our control. Here are some examples, there are many more:

- for home buyers with a mortgage a change in the rate of interest or for those who rent their home an increase or decrease in the rent they have to pay;

- a change in either national (income) tax or in local tax (council tax);

- an increase in pay or an unexpected promotion;

- redundancy, sickness or injury.

Some of these we can provide for by savings or by insurance. If we do insure ourselves well or save significant amounts, we are reducing our present disposable income to provide for the future.

Activity

Identify and explain how the following factors are likely to affect the demand for DVD players in the UK:

(a) a fall in unemployment and rising consumer incomes;

(b) a rise in interest rates;

(c) a fall in the price of cable TV subscriptions;

(d) Increased advertising of the players by manufacturers.

Tastes, fashions and customs

In the marketing of some goods and services, these factors are crucial. The two obvious examples are the fashion industry and the pop music industry, but there are other examples. A new toy, for adults or children, tends to have a short hectic life and then often disappears from use. Cinema attendances dropped with the advent of television, but attendances are growing again now. The mobile phone has become a product that some hate and everyone else wants because of the convenience it offers. Customs tend to affect the availability of products and their prices at different times of the year. Cards at Christmas, fireworks before 5 November and flowers for Mothering Sunday are all examples. The custom of giving presents on religious festivals and on birthdays and anniversaries adds to the demand for a wide range of products.

Population changes

Our population changes in several different ways, all of which affect the pattern of demand.

The age distribution What people need depends on their age. We have an ageing population, so demand for health care, for social services and other products chiefly associated with the elderly may be expected to rise. Over recent years the demand for school places has fallen, but this is now changing again.

The ethnic pattern of the population Race and culture affect demand patterns. This is most evident in food provision, clothing requirements, religious observance and education. In some areas, such as parts of London, Leicester and Bradford, we can see the way retailers and schools have both reacted to changing needs.

Other population characteristics What shops stock is a very good indicator of what people need. The range

of clothing found in predominantly rural areas, such as Devon and Norfolk, is significantly different from what will be found in Oxford Street, London. Many people require specific things for work and, in areas where a particular kind of occupation predominates or particular pursuits are evident, there are features of this in the demand and therefore in the supply. A small market town will not necessarily have a good bookshop but you would expect more than one in a university town. A country town near the moors is likely to provoke more demand for climbing, walking and camping equipment, a tourist town is likely to mean greater demand for catering facilities and a seaside town more demand for holiday accommodation. A large city will mean more demand for taxis and entertainment. The demand for a car is almost universal now, but the need is probably greater in remote areas.

Changes in lifestyle

Many changes in lifestyle have come about over the past few decades. For example, because of reduced grants, most students look for part-time jobs. Many more women seek work outside the home. Lifestyle changes bring about changes in patterns of demand, some of which are as a result of increased purchasing power; for example more people take at least one holiday a year, sometimes abroad. This is reflected in the increased number of travel agents and holiday brochures. The tendency for people to own their own home is greater than ever, particularly in Britain.

Promotion and the focus on unique selling points (USP)

Firms can work hard to persuade customers to make a purchase and to distinguish their products from those of competitors.

People will not buy things that do not satisfy a need. The art of being successful includes that of correctly predicting what consumers will want and how and when they will want it. Failure to forecast accurately can be very costly, as when McDonalds made a two for the price of one offer and totally failed to appreciate how much this would increase the demand for the product.

Advertising

That advertising affects our choices is undeniable. It will probably rarely persuade us to buy things we really do not need, but it is instrumental in promoting new products and new services, and it may well affect our brand choices and our purchase decisions between close alternatives. It may well influence where and when we buy things. Similarly, promotion within a shop may well persuade us to buy the occasional product on impulse.

The law

The law has an impact on our behaviour in various ways. For example most people probably wear motor cycle helmets only because the law requires it. Most cyclists do not wear them. The law imposes age limits on the sale of alcohol, on cigarettes; an age limit applies to a driving licence; a passport and sometimes a visa are necessary for foreign travel.

Activity

Think of three unusual things that you or a relative have bought recently:

(a) Try to analyse the factors that led to the purchasing of those goods or services.

(b) What conclusions, if any, do you draw about influences on your buying patterns?

The interaction of supply and demand

Let us consider Figure 5.3 again. The graph shows the interaction of supply and demand and one point E at which supply and demand are equal. Here everyone who wants to buy at that price can do so and everyone who wants to supply will do so. This is the **equilibrium point** and is unlikely to be reached. A large number of suppliers all making independent decisions about what to supply and a larger number of customers all deciding to purchase are unlikely to bring about such a precise position. What matters is what happens if the position is different.

Situation 1 Demand is greater than supply (Figure 5.4). There will be a shortage, so some people will be prepared to pay more (P_1) and the price will rise until enough people have withdrawn from the market in the **short term**. In the longer term the higher price will bring more supplies onto the market and this will bring the price back down.

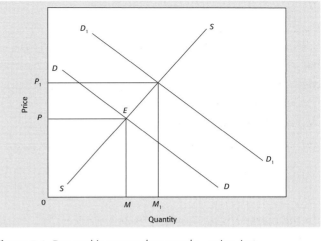

Figure 5.4 Demand is greater than supply – price rises

Situation 2 Supply is greater than demand. If supplies can be withdrawn from the market and stored then that is what will happen. If not, there is a **glut** and suppliers will reduce prices (P_1) until the product is sold. This may lead to greater demand and force the price back up towards equilibrium (Figure 5.5).

In other words, equilibrium is the market position around which activity and price tend to fluctuate. These natural market forces come into play when the market is able to operate freely, but this is not always the case. Some reasons for the market not operating freely are considered in the following sections.

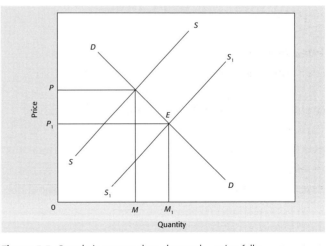

Figure 5.5 Supply is greater than demand – price falls

Supply fixed

There are only a limited number of tickets for a concert or a football match. If the number wanting to go is less than this, there are no problems, except for the organisers whose income is lower than they might have expected. But if demand is higher, the price will rise unless it is fixed. If it is fixed, as it usually is, it will lead to an unofficial **black market** in tickets (Figure 5.6).

When pop concerts are held at Wembley tickets are hard to get and must be bought well in advance. A ticket costing £24 can sometimes be sold outside the grounds for over £100.

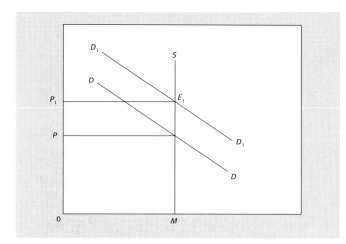

Figure 5.6 Fixed supply, but demand increases. Tickets will exchange on the 'black market' at P_1

Demand fixed

For a concert at Wembley, tickets were limited to two per person. This can happen through rationing. In times of great shortage, rationing is applied to a wide range of essential goods. Your grandparents will remember ration books. Time sharing is an increasingly common way of going on holiday, but if at any time you want to exchange your holiday for one of the popular resorts you can find yourself waiting up to four years.

Legislation

The EU banned British beef and this led to demands that Britain should retaliate. The effect on suppliers and on customer choice was significant. From time to time we make laws that restrict demand. For example, a restriction on credit purchasing would substantially cut the demand for durable consumer goods. However, there is little evidence to suggest that the ban on TV cigarette advertising has reduced smoking.

Unexpected factors

In the case of food products this could include the weather, which often creates shortages of basic foods. Strikes may make either production or distribution difficult and political action in other parts of the world

may restrict choice. One of our major problems in the world economy is the inability to find effective distribution methods so that we have food 'mountains' and 'lakes' in the EU and desperate shortages in other parts of the world.

Allocation of resources

There are times when the free market system does not work very well and we have to find means like the law or price control or government provision to try to ensure that distribution is as fair as it can be and that things do not simply go to those with very high disposable incomes.

This is not just a matter of ensuring a fair distribution of consumer goods, but of guaranteeing the most efficient distribution of all our resources. In the labour market we need to find ways of ensuring that there are sufficient supplies of the skilled and trained personnel we need. In part this is a matter of general education, e.g. ensuring that we are computer literate and have all the key skills needed. In part it is a matter of attracting into specific careers those we need with the skills we need. We must have efficient and imaginative management, good teachers in sufficient numbers, enough people in the health service and enough craft persons and skilled engineers. Getting this right is not easy and it is unlikely to happen unless we can control market forces or make an input into them that will have the desired effect.

This is not simply wages and salaries; it is often things like suitable remuneration in long training processes, conditions of work, status in society and prospects for promotion. In all of these situations, clear objectives have to be set and followed through and we have to decide that the costs of meeting the objective will be met.

2 The impact of competition

What is competition? It is other sources of supply of the same good or service to which a potential consumer can go, but it is more than that. Think of the case study of Petra's cafe on which you spent some time earlier in this section. With whom does Petra compete? Petra is satisfying a range of needs. We can examine some of them.

Activity

Explain how the following changes in supply and demand are likely to affect a producer in the following markets (you should consider the possible effect on price and output):

  (a) a house builder following a reduction in mortgage interest rates making it easier for people to buy houses;

  (b) a Kenyan coffee grower following a heavy frost that destroys the coffee crop in Brazil;

  (c) an insurance company after serious floods make house owners keen to increase the insurance cover on their properties;

  (d) a car manufacturer in the EU after the EU decides to put import restrictions on imports of Japanese cars.

Attempt to illustrate your answer with a supply and demand diagram in each case.

Severe flooding will increase demand for house insurance
Source: Popperfoto/Reuters.

- In providing breakfast Petra is competing with many other cafes doing the same in a fairly small local area, with breakfasts brought from or eaten at home, with catering businesses on the way to work or on the train and with a decision by potential customers to forget breakfast altogether. To gain business Petra will need to be good in terms of what and how she cooks, to offer this at reasonable prices and to give good service, because time is short.

- In providing take-away sandwiches Petra is competing with many of the same buying opportunities, with business canteens, with pubs and with other quick sources of a meal at lunch time. To compete successfully she has to use good-quality materials, provide a wide range of sandwiches or baguettes, pack them well and give speedy friendly service.

- In the evenings Petra caters to an entirely different market. Here the needs that are being satisfied are much broader. There are many ways in which people can spend the disposable income that a meal in the restaurant will take. Now, Petra is competing with all ways of using that amount of income. A night at a disco or in the pub, a trip to the cinema or the theatre, eating at home and saving the money for something else and many other uses. The consumer is looking for a good meal, probably one that would not be cooked at home, a good atmosphere, attentive service, additional things like wine and a good night out.

So, deciding who our competitors really are and devising a good strategy is not as easy as it seems. The first step is to analyse the needs that are being satisfied and the relative importance of each of them in attracting customers. Like most businesses, Petra is not in one market but in several.

Competition and its effects

You may think that the obvious way to compete is to cut prices, but this is not always possible because firms need a sufficient margin on the things they sell in order to survive. Sometimes cutting prices would have the opposite effect. If the suppliers of Aston Martin or Rolls Royce cars tried to compete through price, people would think the cars were less desirable, that lower prices meant either loss of status or that inferior materials were being used.

If small shops tried to compete with supermarkets through price, they would make losses rather than profits. The smaller a business is, the greater the number of competing products in the market, while the closer alternative suppliers are to each other, the more difficult price competition is. Firms try to improve their chances of competing through price by differentiating their products, by trying to find **unique selling points** (**USPs**) for their products and by various point-of-sale promotion strategies.

Test Activity

Read the case study below and then tackle the exercises that follow.

Case study – Tablet Computers Ltd

Tablet Computers assemble a wide range of computers for both home and business use. All major components are imported but smaller items are supplied by local specialist firms. The prices of the imported supplies vary with the £ exchange rate. The managing director has always believed that it is important to sell to both domestic and industrial customers. She recognises that competition is increasing in both markets. She is always encouraging her research and development team to come up with innovative products that could make Tablet Computers seem different from the many other products available.

One computer model – the 'Playmaker' – is specifically designed for use with the latest computer games. It is marketed heavily to customers with children. Another model – the 'Organiser' - is loaded with powerful business software and has proven popular with small firms.

The computer market is highly competitive. Price is a major factor in customers' buying decisions. However, Tablet find it difficult to compete on price alone and emphasise reliable machines and excellent customer support. Competition is also encouraging more computer manufacturers to offer similar support and other customer packages, such as extended gurarantees. Total computer sales in the UK were static last year – the market is mature and many potential customers were cautious due to rumours of interest rate increases.

(30 marks, 30 minutes)

(a) Identify and explain four external factors that might impact on the future success of Tablet Computers. (8)

(b) Why do you think that it is important for Tablet Computers to:
  ◆ invest in research and development and
  ◆ produce more than one model of computer and sell in different markets? (12)

(c) Discuss how Tablet Computers might compete effectively in the future. (10)

Activity

Read the case study below and then tackle the exercises that follow.

Case Study – Competition

Non-price competition is simply any way of competing with other firms that does not involve price. A visit to a superstore will give you a good idea of what these methods might be. They range from customer services through additional services to loyalty cards. Competition among providers of holiday packages is very keen at the moment and this is reflected in:

- facilities in the packages to allow holidaymakers to arrive at the end of their journey by coach, rail or air;
- feeder services from as many points as possible;
- tour packages within the holiday itself;
- services provided on the coach;
- extension packages for second weeks;
- free insurance or free child places;
- tempting discounts for second, third and fourth holidays a year.

Competition is a fact of business life for most producers. The need to find ways of survival is there, even for the very large. This is well demonstrated by:

- the fight between the big superstores for market share;
- the number of small businessess that fail because they cannot compete;
- small businesses that succeed because they find a small market niche which they can satisfy but which does not tempt the bigger organisations;
- many small shops, which survive because of where they are, i.e. on an outlying housing estate or in a small village;
- businesses that are prepared to go to the customer; we buy our milk, newspapers, fish and fresh vegetables from suppliers who are prepared to come to us;
- businesses that cut out stages in the process of distribution, e.g. farmers who sell at the farm gate, go to farmers' markets or sell through 'pick your own' are doing this;
- businesses that deliberately appeal to consumers who have high disposable incomes, e.g. the elite car market, the five-star hotel and shops like Harrods;.
- businesses that go to the other end of the market, e.g. market stalls where products can be cheap because there are fewer overheads, shops like Kwik Save and others where all the frills are cut out so as to sell a limited range of goods at much lower prices.

Where there is no, or little, competition, there is the danger of much higher prices. There is the possibility that customers will be exploited. This is one of the arguments for keeping industries like the utilities and the transport suppliers under state control. At the moment we have a halfway situation, where these goods and services are privately provided but the State appoints watchdogs to act on behalf of consumer interests.

Competition does vary and the extent of competition is a major factor influencing business behaviour. Competition is said to be in the interest of the consumer, but if its effect is to close businesses and to reduce choice that is not necessarily good. There are many villages without shops, post offices and other amenities because those who would provide them cannot survive.

Working in groups of four to six, choose one advertisement. Look at it or watch it closely.

(a) What part of the market is the firm aiming at? Make sure you have evidence for your view on this.

(b) What do the advertisement designers think is the USP that this product has?

(c) Make a collective and supported judgement of the success of the advertisements.

3 The level of economic activity

Several references are made in this chapter to the level of economic activity, to dampening it down and to stimulating it, to the role of the government in controlling or manipulating it. No economy stands still; nor does it grow steadily. It is rather like a roller coaster with movements up and down, which are sometimes sudden and violent, as they are in periods of great depression followed by growth out of it. The objective of government is to keep fluctuations as small as possible so as to provide an environment in which it is easy to plan and to forecast, easy to take risks and effectively manage them. Figure 5.7 shows the cyclic pattern that economies tend to follow.

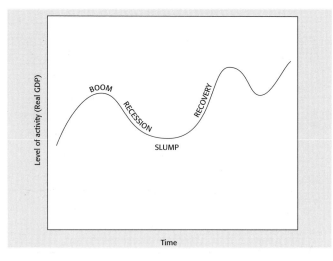

Figure 5.7 The business cycle

The level of economic activity is measured by the total value of a country's annual output (GDP) Gross Domestic Product. In times of **recession** we would expect to see that:

- The number of new businesses is smaller.
- The failure rate of businesses has increased.
- The disposable income of many people is lower.
- Unemployment is high and rising.
- Investment by business is falling.
- The profit margins of most businesses are falling.
- Merger and takeover activity is rising.
- There is government and Bank of England action to stimulate the economy.
- There is concentration on survival and a reduction of risk-taking activity.
- Firms and consumers are stretching credit to the limit.
- Firms are increasing credit control and debt recovery activity.
- There is increased reliance on short-term financing.
- There are reductions in stock levels.
- There is increased competitive activity.
- Profit margins are reduced.
- Firms will be searching for other markets.
- Firms will be cutting back and keeping to safe market segments.

- There are continuous searches for cost-reducing methods.

In times of economic growth we would expect to see:

- a rise in consumer spending;
- a fall in unemployment;
- greater activity in the housing market;
- new businesses starting up;
- government action to manage growth;
- increases in reported profits;
- greater activity in the holiday and leisure industries.

There are firms such as pawnbrokers and money lenders that tend to thrive in times of low growth, but firms in general tend to suffer. In times of steady growth we can expect to see changes such as the following:

- The atmosphere in which activity takes place gradually changes from one of uncertainty and a concentration on survival to one of optimism and confidence. Regular reporters from both sides of industry, from government and from economic agencies will be making positive predictions.
- Consumer spending will broaden out into the non-essential purchases, which have been neglected for a while. The quantity of goods bought on credit will begin to rise and people will again be seeking to buy houses.
- Demand can only rise if suppliers can make the goods available. Businesses will see the opportunity for greater profits and will increase supply as much as is possible in the short term. In the longer term they will invest in new machinery, in technology and in research and development, all of which provide stimulus to further growth.
- Some firms will seize the opportunity to expand. This could require more staff or more overtime, relocation and greater capitalisation, all of which will stimulate further activity.
- Business is about taking carefully controlled risks and, in an atmosphere of growth and confidence, risk taking will seem more attractive.

But economic growth that threatens to become an uncontrolled boom could:

- If some of the risks are unwise, it will produce failure and this can flatten growth.
- If the speed of growth is too rapid, it will simply raise prices and therefore discourage investment and reduce disposable income.

- If the government sees growth to be too rapid, it will take action to control it and dampen activity down, perhaps by raising the rate of interest.
- In an atmosphere of confidence and greater prosperity organised labour can be expected to seek better rewards. If these remain within increased productivity there will be no problem, but if they rise above that level they will raise unit costs and therefore prices.

4 The rate of interest

The rate of interest is a cost. It is the cost we pay for using other people's money. For individuals it is a drain on their disposable income and for businesses it is a cost to them of investing. Without interest charges, borrowing, which is essential to our culture and its development, would not happen and growth and development would be very much slower. The market today is flooded with offers to borrow money. An individual may get two or three offers to take out loans ranging from £500 to £30,000, every week. Some of the rates of interest are very high indeed and only the desperate will borrow at those rates. On the other hand, you can also find offers to sell on credit at either delayed interest or at no interest at all. These offers are common in the furniture and the new-car market. The base rate for borrowing money is set by the Monetary Policy Committee (MPC) of the Bank of England. Borrowing at that rate is unlikely and all other rates are usually higher. Given that the rate is an expense, we can usually live with once it has become a part of expenditure. The problem comes with changes in that rate. The MPL reduced the rate in February 2003. This was in response to fears that the UK economy was on the verge of a recession.

Why should the rate change?

In some circumstances a fixed rate can be negotiated and this would be common for short-term borrowing or for long-term borrowing like debentures (read Chapter 2 if you are not sure what debentures are). In other instances, interest rates rise and fall in response to changes in the base rate. Base-rate changes are usually small and may be supposed to have little effect. However, changes are as important for the impression they convey as they are for the difference they make.

A rise in rates

Suppose your mortgage rate goes up by 0.5% and therefore your monthly mortgage payment by £30, then you have £30 less to spend per month than you had before. If similar interest payments occur for credit cards, bank charges and other flexible-interest loans, then disposable income could fall by a total of £50 or more per month. This will cause a fall in savings or a cutback in demand for goods. This kind of effect will hit different people to variable extents, but the overall fall in the level of purchases will be considerable, just because the money is not there. The effect is increased because anyone who was thinking of buying a car, a washing machine or any other durable consumer good on credit may well decide to delay that purchase and anyone who was thinking of buying a house is even more likely to delay purchase. The level of business activity will fall significantly.

A business will be conscious of two things when this interest rise occurs. The first will be that its own cost of borrowing, particularly on bank loans and overdrafts, is going to rise. The decision makers will be more inclined to push debtors to pay and yet to delay their own payments if they can. They will be less inclined to invest, partly because the cost of doing so will have risen and partly because they anticipate that demand for goods and services may fall off. So investment activity will also fall off. The combined increase in costs and expectation of a fall in demand will lead to attempts to reduce the wage bill, through cutting out overtime, reducing hours of work or even redundancies. All of these will reduce disposable income and this begins to have further effects on the level of activity. For those with larger disposable incomes it is likely that the rewards for savings will rise and they may be persuaded to save a larger proportion of their income rather than spend it. This too may reduce the level of activity.

Businesses will seek other outlets for their products to maintain turnover, employment and profits. This could be in markets overseas. They may also sell on

Activity

Trace the likely effects of a fall in interest rates on a business arising from:
  (a) changes in its costs and potential costs;
  (b) changes in consumer buying decisions.

lower margins rather than lose sales. Bargains may tempt consumers not to delay purchasing certain items.

It is probable that the rise in the rate was originally designed to bring about precisely this effect, because the projection is that the economy is starting to run too fast and needs to be slowed down. This is the sense in which the level of interest is a tool in managing the economy.

A fall in rates

When interest rates fall the general movement downwards tends to be less speedy and any positive change in attitude is often more difficult to bring about, but otherwise the changes are the opposite of the ones outlined above.

Exchange rates

If you want to trade with French customers they will want to pay in Euros and you may want sterling. This requires currency exchange. The rate at which one currency exchanges against another depends on world trade in each one. Suppose you are trading with a customer in France and that customer is paying in Euros.

You agree to sell 100 units to the customer at	£25 a unit
Total cost in sterling	£2,500
The rate of exchange is	1 Euro = £0.58
Cost to French customer	4.310.3 Euros
But suppose the Euro depreciates against sterling to	1 Euro = £0.50
Cost to the French customer now	5,000 Euros
You gain 690 Euros which is	£345

Activities

1 Calculate the loss to you if you had agreed to be paid in Euros and at the time the rate of exchange was 1 Euro = £0.50 but before payment was due the Euro appreciated against sterling to 1 Euro is £0.65

2 Use the results of your calculations to explain why many exporters are in difficulty when the pound is strong in foreign markets.

3 Explain the likely effects if the price of holidays taken in Germany by British nationals was to increase by 25% whilst the price of holidays taken by Germans in the UK remain unchanged.

Exchange rates and the rate of interest

If the rate of interest is higher in the UK than it is in other countries lenders will move their money towards the UK. This will reduce the general supply of sterling and cause its price in terms of other currencies to rise. Large fluctuations can cause real problems.

The government can and does intervene to influence the external value of sterling. When the international value of sterling is too low the government will buy other currencies thus releasing sterling and causing its value to fall. They work the other way when the value is too high. Individual movements will go on all the time as a result of trading, tourism and buying and selling in currencies. What matters is the overall effect at any one time.

Further effects of exchange rate changes on business

When the value of sterling falls (i.e. pound depreciates):
- Imports become more expensive.
- Overseas holidays are more expensive and may be reduced whilst the overseas tourist is more attracted to the UK.
- If demand for overseas products remains high disposable income will be reduced and demand for other products will fall.
- Demand for UK holiday accommodation is likely to rise.
- Manufacturers will look for cheaper, possibly home-produced, raw materials.
- If they cannot find them the prices of many home-produced goods are likely to rise.
- Many exports will fall in price and producers may be attracted to sell abroad.

The effects of a rise in the value of sterling will be the opposite of this. But these are probabilities rather than certainties. Factors other than price will always be taken into account. There will be contracts which the parties to them will have to honour and there will be loyalties which may not change. Governments will want to avoid instability because of the uncertainty it brings and to do this they may well use interest rates as a weapon.

The government budget

The government does generate some income from the things that it does but most of what it needs comes

In the UK the Monetary Policy Committee of the Bank of England has the responsibility of keeping inflation below 2.5% per annum by making interest rate changes as necessary
Source: Popperfoto.

- to manage the economy towards the achievement of a stated objective;
- to keep the economy under control and to minimise or reverse any unwanted changes;
- to send signals to business, industry, consumers, overseas governments and traders, intended to influence their attitudes and behaviour.

It has become common practice to signal some changes so that they are announced in one budget and are put into effect in the next. This is because it is sometimes necessary and often wise to take time over some changes and to give warning that they are to be made. Recently signalled changes were to remove the TV licence fee for those over 75, to maintain the winter heating allowance at £100 and to allocate taxes in cigarettes and tobacco to the National Health Service. You should listen to the budget when it is given in the Spring and discuss the effects of the changes it makes.

through the budget which is normally introduced once a year in April. First they must decide how they need to spend money in the coming year and then how it is to be raised. This takes money out of the pockets of consumers and businesses (or puts it in) and thus affects what we do. Governments have many purposes including:

- to raise the money needed for the year;
- to affect the balance of disposable income by determining who it is taken from and in what ways;
- to decide who will benefit from expenditure, to what extent and in what ways;

Taxation

For people the two main taxes are **Income tax** and **VAT**. We all make significant additional contributions through things like National Health contributions and TV licences. Table 5.3 lists some of our payments and the way in which we pay them.

For most people who have a regular job, income tax is calculated on a monthly or weekly basis and deducted straight from earnings before we receive them. National Insurance is dealt with in the same way. Each income earner tells the Inland Revenue about earnings and about allowances which are claimed on an annual tax return. The deductions and the code number on which they are based can be seen on a payslip. If you have one study it carefully and make sure that you know what each statement on it is telling you.

Type of payment	Frequency	How	Fixed or variable
Car licence	Year or half year	From take home pay	Fixed annually
TV licence	Year	From take home pay	Fixed annually
National insurance	Per week/month	From gross pay	Varies with gross pay
Income tax	Per week/month/year	From gross pay	Varies with gross pay
VAT	Most things we buy	Through purchases	Fixed at 17.5%
Customs duty	On imports	At port or airport	Fixed
Excise duty	On car fuel/tobacco	Through purchases	Fixed annually

Table 5.3 Examples of taxes paid to government

The effects of taxation on business

Corporation tax or profits tax

This is levied on profits and hence reduces the dividend or drawings that owners can take out of the business or the profit that can be retained for use in the business. Either way an increase has the potential to reduce the level of activity because consumer spending power or business investing capability has been reduced. The extent to which activity reduces will depend also on the effect the reductions have on the attitude of the business and the income earners. The same tax change will occur for all businesses unless the Chancellor is selective in terms of applying it. Many consumers will have their buying power reduced. Some firms, particularly those that sell non-essential goods, may have their earnings reduced.

Import duties

The objective in imposing these duties or increasing them is to change buying habits. Purchasers are discouraged from buying the taxed goods and encouraged to buy cheaper alternatives. These may still come from abroad or they may be either made by the supplying firm or bought in from home producers. If the firm continues buying what are now more expensive imports, this will increase costs and either increase the price or decrease profits.

Excise duties

The major duty of this kind is on alcohol and tobacco products. In most budgets there is an increase in these duties, which make a substantial contribution to government revenue. A change usually deters expenditure in the short term, but the long-term effect is very much less. Businesses must decide the extent to which they will bear the burden of this tax themselves or pass it on in price rises to the consumer. To the extent that it dampens down trade it reduces business incomes and profits. If there was little competition in the market, consumers would bear the whole burden of tax increases. However, if competition is very fierce, decisions about margins are often revised to gain a competitive edge.

Value Added Tax (VAT)

This is the major tax on purchasing and, for most products, is fixed at 17.5% This is subject to change in the annual budget. From the consumer's point of view an increase raises prices and discourages expenditure. Once it is imposed and if it remains unchanged for some time, consumers get used to it and its effect is noticed less. There is no real incentive to change purchasing behaviour if the rate is common to all goods. Governments can decide the goods upon which it is levied, such as no VAT on food and on children's clothing. Firms must pay the tax to the State, but do not have to pass it on to the customer.

Income tax

This is generally thought of as the major tax we all pay because it comes in a significant lump sum from income. In practice, most of us are likely to spend more on VAT than we pay in income tax. There are three ways in which the State can influence the effect of income tax and direct it at or away from defined groups of people:
Allowances and reliefs In calculating taxable income we have to deduct income that is not subject to tax because we have been able to claim allowances.
Levels of income below which tax is not paid Below a certain level of income (depending on how many allowances you can claim) you will not have to pay income tax. If the government raises the tax threshold more people will not have to pay income tax.

By changing taxation bands and other variables the State influences the disposable income we have.

Activities

1 Obtain a copy of the most recent statement of taxation bands, rates and allowances. Using them calculate the amount a single person earning £38,000 a year and entitled only to the personal allowance might expect to pay in a year.

2 Explain, for the benefit of someone who does not understand, why these taxes are raised and why different people will pay different amounts.

The overall effect of changes in income tax on business comes through the resulting changes in disposable income. However, it is not a simple effect because it depends on who bears the burden. If an increase in income tax falls on those with high incomes (i.e. through the higher rate or through moving that threshold downwards), then the effect may be small.

This is partly because those who earn sufficient to pay the top rates are not a very large number and partly because they are less inclined to change their expenditure habits unless the change is very substantial. If the change releases or removes income from people having average or below-average incomes, the effect is normally more substantial and more immediate. When these incomes are reduced, the greatest changes will be found in businesses selling durable consumer goods and non-essential goods, the purchase of which can be delayed. Sales of cars, washing machines and holidays may be affected. There will, of course, also be a reduction in the tendency to invest in those industries and employment may be reduced. In effect, the economy will be slowed down.

But this is only one side of the story. What happens will also be influenced by the things that the Chancellor does with the additional income collected. There will be a reduction in income from VAT and there may be increased unemployment and social security costs, so it will not all be a gain for the Treasury. The increased revenue can be used positively (i.e. put back into the economy through pensions, benefits and investment programmes) and, in as far as it is, it will create employment and expenditure. The net effect will be to dampen down some industries and to stimulate others. There may be other effects which influence the balance of payments and the rate of exchange. For example, there may be a greater tendency to take holidays or short breaks in this country rather than go abroad.

There is no certainty about these changes. If there were, the Chancellor's job would be much simpler. What examiners look for is your ability to think about these things and produce well-argued, logical responses.

Over-to-you

Test revision questions

(60 marks, 1 hour)

1 Define what is meant by 'an external constraint'. (3)
2 Identify a local business in your area and list three external constraints that it faces. (3)
3 Explain how an equilibrium price might be obtained in a free market for a good. Use a diagram to help you. (4)
4 Explain three factors that could lead to an increase in demand for sports shoes over the next 12 months (excluding price changes). (6)
5 Explain one way in which market forces tend to fail. (3)
6 How might you expect a restaurant owner to respond following the opening of another restaurant in the same road? (3)
7 Examine one of your answers to 6 and evaluate why it might or might not be a good response. (6)
8 Use a diagram to help explain what is meant by the business cycle. (4)
9 By referring to the diagram, comment on the main stages in the business cycle. (6)
10 Identify a firm that might benefit from economic growth – and explain why. (4)
11 Identify a firm that could lose from a period of rapid economic growth – explain why. (4)
12 Distinguish between gross, net and disposable incomes. (6)
13 Explain why a strong pound (a high exchange rate for the pound £) may be disadvantageous for UK business. (4)
14 Outline two ways in which a car manufacturer with high debts will lose from an increase in interest rates. (4)

Discover and learn

1 Go into any supermarket and discover the ways in which they compete.
  (a) Discover which of those ways are known to customers.
  (b) Discover how consumers react to them.
  (c) On the basis of your research, what advice would you offer to the managing team?
2 Find out how small shops are trying to compete.
3 Choose one firm in each case and find out how each of the following have influenced its activities and decision making:
  (a) The Sale of Goods Act;
  (b) The Food Safety Act;
  (c) The Health and Safety at Work Act;
  (d) Employment legislation.
4 Choose any one firm and find out how the following affect the running and success of the business:
  (a) exchange rates;
  (b) interest rates;
  (c) taxation.
5 Discover from the local council:

(a) If it has a business or industrial estate and why the estate is there. If the council does not have such an estate, why is that?

(b) Examples of ways in which it:
◆ supports business in its area;
◆ constrains business in its area.

(c) What part it plays directly in the local economy.

(d) Goods and services it supplies for consumers.

6 Look around your area. Find examples of ways in which membership of the EU is influencing business activity in the area.

7 Look around your area, using the indicators given in this section and any others you think are useful. Decide whether, on local evidence alone, we are in a period of growth or a period of decline. Provide and analyse sufficient evidence to support your case. Compare your findings with those of others.

8 Read the case study and data below and then tackle the exercises that follow.

Case study

Recent changes in the UK economy have had different impacts on different industries. Recent reductions in UK interest rates have proven to be a real bonus for Britain's housebuilders as house prices are rising by 20% a year. On the other hand, the slow down in economic activity has been at the expense of some manufacturing firms which have actually reduced their output levels. These firms have cut employment and this has reduced some consumers' disposable incomes. The reduction in interest rates in the USA of half of 1% this week has contributed to a fall in the exchange rate of the dollar. UK firms were hoping for an announcement by the Bank of England that interest rates would be brought down, but they were disappointed.

The announcement by the Chancellor next month is also eagerly awaited. The fear is that with government tax revenues lower than expected he will take the opportunity in his next budget speech to raise tax rates – possibly on income tax or VAT.

Sources: Various from the week ending 8 November 2002.

UK: BANK OF ENGLAND HOLDS RATES

(30 marks, 35 minutes)

(a) Outline the trend in UK interest rates since 1999. (3)

(b) Does there appear to be a link between changes in interest rates and the level of economic activity (GDP growth)? Explain your answer. (4)

(c) Analyse why housebuilders benefit from reduction in UK interest rates. (8)

(d) Examine the impact on a lower $ exchange rate for:
◆ a UK exporter to the USA;
◆ an importer of US goods into the UK. (6)

(e) To what extent might a UK car manufacturer be affected by the changes in UK taxes suggested in the article? (9)

Summary

In this chapter we have recognised that:

- Businesses operate in a dynamic and often uncertain environment and the stage on which they perform is now the world.

- Most markets are worldwide and changes wherever they occur will have effects on what businesses can do and how they should do them.

- Market forces determine much of what happens, but they are not always the best way of distributing resources or of ensuring fairness and stability. These are among the reasons why the State intervenes to manage and control the economy using the main weapons of the Budget, the legal system and the rate of interest.

- Despite the intervention of government at local, national and EU level, the level of activity changes in a cyclic fashion, significantly changing the ways in which businesses behave.

- In all of this the 'feel good factor' is often as important as any changes which occur. If consumers or businesses are not confident, little can be done that will have any assurance of success.

- On the other hand, if the stakeholders in our economy are too confident and want to move too quickly, this can overheat the economy and send the cycle downwards again.

- Both exchange rates, and the budgetary decisions made by the government, have significant effects on personal and business decisions.

Key words

Definitions of Key words can be found in the Glossary on page 269.

black economy	import duties
competition	income tax
corporation tax	industrial marketing
creditors	insolvency
debtors	net income
demand	shortage
disposable income	supply
equilibrium point	taxation
exchange rates	unique selling point (USP)
excise duties	value added tax (VAT)
gross income	

6 Responding to other external influences

On completion of this chapter you should be able to:

➤ exemplify and explain social and cultural factors that constrain business

➤ demonstrate understanding of the ways in which stakeholder interests may combine or conflict in influencing business decisions

➤ show how businesses try to balance the needs of all stakeholders

➤ explain the purpose and impact of the laws which constrain decisions in the main aspects of business behaviour

➤ explain how moral and ethical restraints can influence the way business decisions are taken

➤ understand the impact of environmental issues on business

➤ show how the political relationships and activities of the state influence business actions

➤ explain the role of technology and the opportunities and threats it creates in different business situations, explain how business reacts to all the constraints within which it must work

Introduction

In Chapter 5 we looked at the ways in which economic constraints might influence business behaviour and at the ways in which businesses might react to them. In this section we extend the discussion to consider the constraints shown in Table 6.1.

◆ Social constraints:	The effects people have
◆ Legal constraints:	The State working through the law
◆ Environmental:	Our world and its changing nature
◆ Ethical constraints:	The moral code by which we live
◆ Political constraints:	The effects of government behaviour
◆ Technological:	The change we create

Table 6.1 New economic external constraints on business behaviour

The conflicting pressures and influences that make up the business environment are bound to offer opportunities to some firms and pose threats for others. In some cases they will support and in others they will frustrate or prevent. Effective response is therefore a key to success. The business management cannot afford to ignore what is happening; in fact, most of the time managers must reach out, discover and interpret. Only by doing this can they plan ahead or modify existing plans in the light of changing circumstances.

The working population

Figures on the UK population are collected every ten years in the census. Every household is legally bound to return the census form correctly completed. The first year of each decade is chosen. The main features suggested by the last census that would be of significance in business have been updated by the publication of other data collected from a variety of sources.

Mid-term estimates by the local council in one area make it clear that the population has risen by about 17.4% since the last census. This is a big change and by far the greatest contributor to this increase is people who have moved into the area from big towns. From *Social Trends*, which is an annual publication to be found in all public reference libraries, we can gather the general features of changes that will affect the labour market and the pattern of demand.

Table 6.2 shows that approximately 75% of people of working age are economically active. The economically inactive include those who have retired early, those who choose not to work outside the home and those who are unable to work. Working patterns have changed considerably in the period. One of the biggest changes has been in part-time employment, which has increased by 30.95% in the period.

	1986	1998
Full time	16.6	17.4
Part time	4.2	5.5
Self-employed	2.7	3.1
Other[1]	0.4	0.3
Total	23.9	26.2
Unemployed	3.1	1.7
Economically active[2]	27.0	27.9
Inactive[3]	7.5	7.9
Working population	34.5	35.8

Table 6.2 UK population of working age by employment (figures in millions)
Notes: 1. Examples: Government training schemes, unpaid family workers. 2. Includes the unemployed available for work. 3. Those who could but do not seek work.
Source: Office for National Statistics.

Activities

1 What other changes in the pattern of work can you see in Table 6.2?
2 Comment on the significance of this evidence.
3 Compare your findings with those of other groups in the class.
4 Use either the Internet or the reference library as a source and obtain the most recent figures you can. Comment on any significant changes you see and try to explain them.

One of the features of change concerns the role of women and this is shown in Table 6.3, together with a forecast of the positions expected in 2001 and 2011. One of the things we can see from Table 6.3 is that the role of women is changing. The number of women in work or actively seeking it has risen by 2.4% between 1991 and 1997 and is projected to rise by a further 11% on the 1997 figure. The number of economically active men has declined, probably as a result of the increasingly common practice of early retirement, between 1991 and 1997. However, this trend is projected to reverse between 2000 and 2011. This is because we have an increasingly ageing population.

The pattern for young people entering the labour market is also changing. The ageing population is partly a consequence of falling birth rates and hence there are

fewer teenagers available to enter the labour market. This fall is made greater by an increasing number who are continuing full-time education after the age of 16. The larger number of younger women in the labour market reflects the tendency for women to postpone their families until later in life.

		Age 16-24	25-44	45-54	55-59	60-64	65+
1991	M	3.1	8.1	3.0	1.1	0.8	0.3
1991	F	2.6	6.1	2.4	0.8	0.3	0.2
1997	M	2.4	8.1	3.4	1.1	0.7	0.3
1997	F	2.0	6.4	2.9	0.8	0.4	0.2
2001	M	2.4	8.2	3.4	1.3	0.7	0.3
2001	F	2.1	6.4	3.0	0.9	0.4	0.2
2011	M	2.8	7.3	3.9	1.3	0.9	0.3
2011	F	2.3	6.2	3.6	1.0	0.7	0.2

Table 6.3 UK labour force by gender and age (figures in millions)

The *Family and Working Life Survey* (1994–1995, Office of National Statistics) offers a range of reasons why part-time employment is rising and why women tend to seek it more than men. These include:

◆ Only a quarter of men working part time do not want a full-time job, whilst more than three-quarters of the women only wanted part-time employment.
◆ The main reasons for women in part-time employment were child related. Women said that either they wished to be with their children or they regarded their children as too young to permit a return to full-time work.
◆ A significant number have more than one part-time job. More women than men have second jobs.
◆ More than half of those who have second jobs are putting together two or more part-time jobs.

Some effects on business of patterns of work

The effects of part-time working, job sharing and early retirement are that many people have more time for leisure and this is seen in increased activity in the leisure industry and in the holiday industry. The holiday industry in particular now targets those it calls the 'empty nesters', older people whose children have now left home, and the 54+ group, which includes many who have retired early and who seek more regular holidays and short breaks. The success of SAGA is an indicator of this. Part-time working, particularly among students, increases disposable income and there is now a significant sector of business that targets the income they earn. Among the leaders are fast-food shops, music retailers, fashion clothing shops and the holiday and leisure industry.

The effects of women showing a greater tendency to seek employment include:

◆ a much greater tendency for firms to meet the requirements of the equal opportunity legislation and to offer employment to women;
◆ a considerable increase in families with two or more cars;
◆ the building of houses either with parking space for more than one car or with double garages;
◆ an increase in child-care facilities and in the numbers employed in the child-care industry;
◆ an increase in the tendency for firms and educational institutions to provide child-care and crèche facilities;
◆ an increase in the disposable income of many families and therefore changing patterns of demand;
◆ significant changes in shopping habits; consumers now want 24-hour shopping, convenience foods, pre-packed foods and one-stop shopping;
◆ an increase in the number of people working in the domestic services industry;
◆ an increase in sales of domestic electric appliances.

Time spent at work is also changing. In part this will be a reaction to the EU Working Time Directive. This Directive requires employers to ensure that employees do not work more than an average of 48 hours a week against their will. Nevertheless, more than 30% of all men are at work for more than 48 hours, as are 7% of women. The Directive is not universally applicable and owners and self-employed people are excluded. It is not a requirement and still permits willing overtime. Nevertheless, the trend is towards longer working hours. Table 6.4 illustrates that trend.

	Hours worked per week
1986	42.6
1990	43.7
1998	44.0
2002	44.8

Table 6.4 Increasing average working hours per week (UK)
Source: Labour Force Survey. Office for National Statistics.

Occupational patterns

The kinds of things people do have also changed over the years. The comparison given in Table 6.5 represents a trend that has been going on for some years.

Occupation	Males 1991	1998	Females 1991	1998
Managers and administrators	16	19	8	11
Professional	10	11	8	9
Associate professional and technical	8	9	10	11
Clerical and secretarial	8	8	29	26
Craft and related	21	17	4	2
Personal and protective services	7	8	14	17
Selling	6	5	12	12
Plant and machinery operatives	15	15	5	4
Other occupations	8	8	10	8
All employees (millions)	11.8	12.2	10.1	10.6

Table 6.5 UK employees by gender and occupation (percentages)

Activities

1 Use the table to comment on the main changes in occupational structure.
2 Compare your findings with those of other groups and discuss possible reasons and effects.
3 Obtain more recent information of the same kind and try to explain any differences you observe.

The environment of work

The **environment** in which businesses work has changed. Among the changes are:

◆ the continuing decline in Britain's manufacturing activities;

- the increasing role of the tertiary sector;
- the change, due to technology, in the nature of many tasks both on the shop floor and in the office; in the years to come the Internet will have as big an impact;
- the development of the EU, which has meant that the focus of both work and the marketplace is now the whole of Europe and in some instances the world;
- an increasing body of Euro-law to which British businesses are subject.

Table 6.5 still shows gender differences. Women are far more likely than men to be engaged in clerical and secretarial jobs and in nursing. The craft jobs, although they are rapidly declining, are still largely the preserve of men. The progress of women towards management roles is significant, with a 10% increase from 30% to 33%.

Other evidence shows that the number of males engaged in manufacture between 1981 and 1998 fell from a third to a quarter, whilst the percentage in distribution rose from 16% to 20% and that in financial services from 10% to 16%. Self-employment has increased in significance. Table 6.6 shows the top five self-employment areas for both men and women in 1998.

Male	Percentage employed	Female	Percentage employed
Construction	27	Distribution	23
Distribution	18	Public administration	22
Financial services	18	Financial services	17
Manufacturing	8	Manufacturing	8
Transport	8	Agriculture and fishing	5
Agriculture and fishing	8		

Table 6.6 Self-employment 1998

Notes: Distribution includes hotels and restaurants; 21% of all women work in 'other services', as compared with 8% of men. The total number of self-employed people is 3.3 million, of whom 2.4 million are male.

Legal influences

The law intervenes in what business does more and more. There is much more legislation from Westminster and, additionally, there is more direction from Europe.

You do not have to know the detail of this body of law or even the names and dates of Acts of Parliament. In effect what is needed is:

- an understanding of why the law intervenes;
- an ability to explain where intervention takes place;
- the effects on business decisions of complying with the law;
- the consequences for the various stakeholders.

Why does government intervene?

All business activity has at least two parties involved and interested in or affected by the outcome of that activity. In most situations one of the parties is much stronger than the other and the law intervenes to protect the weaker party. Thus:

- In the raising of finance, shareholders who are not directors are in a much weaker position than those who are, particularly where one or two shareholders have a controlling interest.
- In recruitment the applicant is usually in a much weaker position than the employer.
- In employment the employee is usually in a much weaker position than the manager or the owner.
- The customer is in a much weaker position than the supplier in most cases.

In all of these situations there is a law to protect the weaker party:

- Once an organisation incorporates and becomes a private or public limited company, accounts must be audited and specific information must be publicly available. There has to be an annual general meeting and the Memorandum of Association prevents the company from acting outside its declared objectives.
- In recruitment most organisations must be equal-opportunity employers at all stages of the recruitment, selection and training process. This relates to discrimination in respect of age, sex, race, creed, culture and disability.
- In employment the law protects the employee from unfair dismissal and provides a procedure through which employees can go to protect their rights. In the work situation the employee is also protected with respect to health and safety. It is the responsibility of the employer to provide a safe place of work and healthy conditions of work. This protection also applies to people visiting the place of work.

◆ The general principle of buying things is that you are presumed to want to buy what you do in fact buy. However, there is a large body of legislation that protects consumers in certain situations.

How does the law work?

Interesting as legal principles and practices are, they are not part of this syllabus. However, it does help to know where the law comes from.

UK government

Most of our law comes from Acts of Parliament and is administered through either a specialist body of people created for the purpose or through the courts. Much of the law that applies to business is **civil**. That means that it lays down what the rights and responsibilities of the parties to a situation are and leaves it to them to take an issue to the courts or to a tribunal if one of the parties wishes to do so. In civil law we are not dealing with crimes but with a breakdown in a relationship and an attempt either to put things right or to obtain compensation for one of the parties.

Some law is administered through specially created bodies given the right to intervene in what businesses do. The utility services like gas, water, electricity and the telephone services are constrained by 'watchdog bodies' called OFTEL, OFWAT and so on. They have intervened to ensure improved quality of services and to control prices. OFSTED may well be better known to you since they have the duty to ensure standards in education. Some bodies like this operate at local level. The trading standards officer is particularly concerned about matters relating to the sale of goods and the conditions within which goods and services are offered. That officer operates at local-authority level. The local authority itself is responsible for the general control of business activity in its area. On the one hand, it may offer support and develop business parks; on the other, it may give or refuse planning permission for new business developments in its area. Finally, the local authority has duties of its own, which it must perform in the community. It can franchise these to private businesses if it wants to. It can run activities itself: education, libraries and transport are examples. It can give direct support to business that is considered necessary for the welfare of the community. It is on this basis that many local bus and train services are run.

Activities

1 Find out what your local authority is called and where its offices are.
2 Find out what officials it has who control what businesses do and protect your interests.
3 Find out what planning permission is. You may find that bank or local-authority literature will help with this.
4 Find out what your local authority does directly in the community.

The State now shares some of its responsibilities and controls with a wide range of organisations. These include:

◆ the European Union;
◆ treaty arrangements and international agreements like the World Trade Organisation (WTO).

The one with greatest effect on us is the European Union, which continues to grow rapidly. There is almost endless controversy about the role of the EU, the euro currency and our membership of it. The situation changes almost daily and you will need to keep up with the changes as they occur. Increasingly, the EU is important to us as a market, as a competitor within our markets and as a law-making body whose directives apply to our businesses. Businesses such as farming and fishing are particularly tightly controlled by EU directives, but the rest of business and industry is also subject to an increasing number of directives, particularly ones that affect the rights of workers.

Some law, like place of work legislation, has been a concern of government for centuries. Nowadays, it is far more complete. Health and safety provisions apply not only to the obvious working situations but also to institutions like schools and churches, as well as to leisure and entertainment complexes. What happens in the marketplace has also been a long-standing concern, with consumer protection extending to goods that are fit for the purpose for which they are bought and to circumstances in which consumers buy on credit. Other law has arisen in response to changing circumstances and to emerging concerns. The Food Safety Act is a case in point. It controls the manufacture of all things that relate to food, the processing of food and its sale. In any café or restaurant now you will see at least one certificate of food hygiene displayed and you will see the extensive use of protective clothing. At both European and state levels, directives and legislation about the sale of beef and beef products are only just being reconsidered and removed. These things show that government bodies can react quickly to worrying situations and also have long-standing areas of concern for particular situations. The protection of shareholders is contained within the Companies Acts and attempts to ensure a framework of true, fair and public reporting is in place.

Some legal changes are in pursuit of government objectives. The best example is the annual Finance Act, which sets out the framework of taxation for each year. It contains all the changes that the Chancellor has made in the Budget. The Act usually contains measures of support either for all business or for selected ones. It affects decisions like investment and business growth or decline. The changes that are directed at individuals will affect disposable income and often the price of goods on which different taxes have been levied. An objective of government in 1999 was to establish a minimum wage, which was established at that time at £3.60 an hour.

The State takes the view that some situations are of very great social importance and cannot be left simply to the parties themselves. The implications of some behaviour are so extensive that the criminal law is involved. Businesses cannot be permitted to defraud customers, employees or shareholders. Practices that would expose people to injury or real danger and situations in which things are done with reckless negligence must all have a penalty under the law. It is important to prevent these situations and to ensure that there is a general awareness of social disapproval.

Two sides to rights

Most people remember their rights. In fact, when examiners ask about rights and responsibilities at work, they find that answers are long on rights but very short on responsibilities. An employee has rights at work but also has a duty to give a fair day's work, to keep the secrets of the employer in so far as they relate to the business, to work safely and to wear and use all safety clothing and equipment. Every right that anyone has can only be ensured because that right is someone else's responsibility. We shall return to this when we consider ethics.

Law in action

In this sub-section, through examples of situations involving the law we will see how it influences business behaviour. These examples show the extent and operation of the law. You can think of many of your own examples, especially where you are involved in buying something, going on a journey or doing a part-time job. Even at school or college the law has a lot to say about what goes on.

Activity

Read the case study below and tackle the exercises that follow.

Case study – Branstead Components plc

Philip Branstead set up a small light engineering business on a business park run by the local authority outside a small town in Devon. After three years he went into partnership with another small business and they relocated to Somerset. The business has grown and a public limited company was formed in 1998.

The business produces components for the domestic electric appliance industry and, apart from some small business for self-employed repair people, there are only seven large customers.

The firm needs to expand on site and to extend the factory into an adjoining field. This was discussed at a recent Board meeting. The following points were made:
- There are some concerns relating to finding the right staff.
- The layout of the factory does not give much scope for expansion.
- Additional capital will be needed. A share issue may be necessary.

75

- The coming budget will increase taxes.
- Employment prospects are good since unemployment is high and wages could be kept low. The difficulty will be finding skilled labour.
- Increasing the numbers employed might make it necessary to provide for refreshments and possibly lunches.
- Transport will need to be supplied for many new workers.
- There is a dispute with two workers sacked last week and one of the charge hands is leaving to have a baby.

The discussion continued...

This is only an extract but it provides an example of how understanding of the effect of the law on business decisions can be worked out. Within the case there are many examples of situations where what the firm does is covered by the law. Consider some of them.

1 *Branstead Components plc*. The firm started as a sole ownership business. Philip was supported by a local authority business park. Here, the authority is fulfilling a duty to act in the best interest of the community and its economy. If Philip had set up elsewhere he would have needed planning permission. In the early days Philip would have been running the risks of unlimited liability. Later he formed first a partnership, and then a plc. A partnership still has unlimited liability and there has to be an agreement between the partners. Forming a plc really brought the law into operation. The company had to have a memorandum and articles of association; it had to state clear objectives and keep to them; in getting the finance a prospectus had to show a true and fair view of the prospects of the business. Properly audited accounts had be made public.

2 *Finding the right staff*. Here there are implications that the recruitment and selection processes will be conducted fairly with equal opportunity for all. It is not sufficient that the interviews are fair since it is possible to exclude people by what is said in advertisements and by where and when they are displayed.

3 *The layout of the factory*. The intention is that the firm is going to grow and therefore there is the possible danger of overcrowding and lack of space, which could contravene the provisions of the health and safety legislation, and could cause accidents. It could make movement around the factory floor difficult and hence increase the risks to personnel.

4 *The coming budget will increase taxes*. This would happen through the Finance Act. If taxes on businesses are increased, this could reduce the profits of the business. This would mean less to pay out in dividends and less available to plough back into the business. It might lead to a greater amount borrowed or to increased prices. If VAT is increased, this would increase prices, or it might be absorbed by the business, increasing their costs and reducing profits. If the increase is in personal taxation, this will reduce disposable income. The firm makes components for domestic electric appliances, which are consumer durables. Buying this kind of good is often delayed when disposable income falls. The overall effect of such changes might be to convince the firm that now is not a good time to expand the business. The firm might react to a falling home market by seeking new markets overseas.

(a) Some of the features of the above case that involve the law have not been considered in the examples. Trace the legal point involved and the possible effects in each of the following:
- raising additional capital by share issue;
- keeping wages low;
- providing refreshments and possibly lunches;
- providing transport for many of our new workers;
- resolving a dispute with two workers sacked last week;
- replacing the charge hand who is leaving to have a baby.

(b) Work in groups. Each member of the group should choose another case or a business article from a newspaper. Go through it identifying the legal issues involved.
- Exchange your article and list with one of the group and work through the one you now have.
- Do you agree with the issues selected or do you want to cut some out or add some in?
- Now comment on the issues and their possible effects on business or personal behaviour.

Ethical issues

These are very close to the legal ones we have been discussing. It could be said that law is about the things that society has decided we must do but might try not to do, whilst ethics is about those things we ought to do in the opinion of society generally. People may differ about what they think is ethical, but would normally recognise behaviour that they considered unethical. Some examples may help.

For employers

- It is unethical to sell goods that are known to be faulty. In some situations the law would take over, e.g. goods past their sell-by date and those known to have been stolen.
- It is unethical to let someone work for so long without rest that they may no longer be able to do a job, e.g. doctors and nurses in hospital. Again, through the Working Hours Directive the EU has stepped in to limit this. However the Directive does not apply to every situation and would not apply if the worker was willing.
- It is unethical to run the business in ways that damage the environment. The law does demand environmentally friendly behaviour in many instances. Businesses can ignore the law and pay the price.

For employees

- Employees are paid to give a fair day's work. Ethics would suggest that they should not be deliberately absent without good reason. It could be argued it is less unethical to be absent from work if you are then not paid than if you are paid a salary and would still be paid.
- It is unethical to use the employer's time and resources for your own private purposes unless this has been agreed. If this amounted to stealing from the employer, there would be redress through the courts or by dismissal.
- It is unethical to steal the employer's clients and do business with them on your own private account. An example might be a garage mechanic who worked for customers he had persuaded away from his employer.

For customers

- If you are given more change than you are entitled to at the checkout, on the bus or anywhere else, technically this is stealing. Since the change giver does not know it has happened, it is your responsibility to give it back.
- If you jump the queue at the checkout or anywhere else, you could argue that it is up to other people to make sure that you don't queue jump. However, this is deliberately relying on other people to let you bully them.
- Here is a more difficult one. If you know that something wrong is taking place, should you speak out? There is a growing belief that you should.
- You could simply take a dangerous toy, or a contaminated pie, back to the shop and probably benefit from the shop's goodwill. But what if that same business continues to sell the dangerous toy or the contaminated pie? Someone could be injured or die.
- If you don't tell your employer that a worker is smoking in a dangerous situation in which smoking is banned lives, jobs and valuable equipment and products could be lost.

Business and ethics

Ethical behaviour is not always easy. One of the responsibilities of business managers is to make a profit, either to plough back into further growth or to distribute to the owners. Without that profit, owners would not have taken the risks involved in business. How far, then, should they pursue the ethical interests of others if doing so means that profits are lower than they would otherwise be? It could be that money spent on ethical behaviour would so reduce the profitability of business that jobs were lost.

All this is not to suggest that businesses should not behave ethically, but only to demonstrate that the conflicting needs of stakeholders do not make the decision clear cut. However, there is increasing evidence that more and more businesses are concerned about ethics and want to behave ethically. Examples include:

- Not trading with others whose practices appear to be unethical. Not trading with firms that supply arms is an example.

- Not stocking goods of which there is disapproval.
- Stocking products that are healthier, that are recycled or that show a greater concern for human welfare.
- Only investing in firms that have a good ethical or environmental reputation.
- Engaging in business practices that show concern for the environment, keep the streets clean and free of litter, etc.

This is likely to develop further if the benefits to a business of behaving ethically become more obvious and become greater than the costs. The law does much to ensure certain minimum standards and the test of an ethical business is that it is not behaving in a socially responsible way because the law says so, but takes that responsibility beyond the extent and letter of the law. The benefits of doing so might include the following:

- Recruitment of staff may be easier. A firm that has a reputation for ethical behaviour is likely to attract people with high ideals.
- For the same reasons, there will be greater likelihood of retaining staff. We would expect to see lower labour turnover, which reduces costs.
- If employees want to work for a firm, they are already a long way towards being motivated to work well.
- Sales may grow. There is increasing evidence that, where there is a genuine choice for them, consumers are more likely to patronise and be loyal to firms that behave ethically. The success of Body Shop is based on this belief.

Environmental issues

The environment in which a business operates will impact on its operations in many different ways. This is not just the physical environment, but everything that influences decisions and actions. Some pressures we

Test Activitiy

Read the case study below and then tackle the exercises that follow.

Case study – Tibet protesters target BP over PetroChina stake

The oil giant BP Amoco will face renewed action next week from Tibetan pressure groups to withdraw from PetroChina, the state-run Chinese oil company which is building a gas pipeline through ethnic Tibetan areas.

Tibetan activists will coordinate a worldwide series of protests starting next Thursday while the Free Tibet Campaign is planning to disrupt BP's AGM in April. It has tabled a resolution calling on BP to dispose of its PetroChina stake on the grounds that it contravenes the company's ethical policy on human rights and the environment.

A government minister admitted

to reporters in Beijing that BP and PetroChina would face a public relations 'disaster' if the resolution is passed.

Human rights groups view the pipeline project as a main policy of Beijing's 'economic colonisation' of the Tibetan people. BP, which paid $578m for its 2.2 per cent stake in PetroChina a year ago, said there was nothing it could do about the pipeline. 'Our investment in PetroChina is a passive one. We have no influence with the PetroChina management and no interest in the Tibetan pipeline.'

Source: Callum McClean and Michael Harrison, *Independent*, 7 February 2001.

(20 marks, 25 minutes)

(a) What change in BP's strategy is the Tibetan pressure group attempting to bring about? (3)

(b) What do you understand by the term 'ethical policy'? (3)

(c) Explain what impact a 'public relations disaster' could have on BP. (6)

(d) Evaluate the factors that will determine whether this pressure group's campaign is successful. (8)

have already considered in this section and in Chapter 5. Among those we have not considered are:

◆ government objectives;
◆ the level of employment;
◆ global activity;
◆ business and the physical environment.

Government objectives

We have seen how important objectives are in all aspects of business discussed so far. It is also clear from Chapter 5 and this section that government has a central role in how the economy is managed and the support and constraint of businesses within that economy. It should not be surprising, then, that governments have objectives. Here we are concerned with the objectives that all governments may be expected to have rather than with those that have a party-political purpose. It is in pursuit of its objectives that the State takes the action it does. Chief among them are:

Economic growth This is what determines the extent to which standards of living can at least remain stable and possibly rise. Too rapid growth will lead to inflation and to other problems. The State will be looking for steady and balanced growth. Even the economy of this small country does not grow in a balanced way. We have seen good growth in London and the South East, often balanced by poor growth or even decline in the regions. Growth always means change and it is not possible for every firm or every industry to grow. There has been considerable growth in the tertiary sector and decline in manufacture and primary industry. Governments may deliberately seek to foster growth in some areas of our economy and to dampen it in others.

Price stability In the modern world this means keeping a curb on inflation and this has been a major issue of policy. In order to make the objective more stable and to make work towards it both long term and free of party politics, in 1998 control over the rate of interest was passed from the Treasury to a Monetary Policy Committee chaired by the Governor of the Bank of England. He has been given a target of 2.5% inflation.

Stable exchange rates The rate at which our currency exchanges against the major currencies of the world is crucial to the success of British firms in the world markets. In 1999 and early 2000 our currency has been too strong in foreign markets, which makes it difficult for our firms to export, although this has advantages for

importers and for everybody taking holidays abroad.

Reducing the level of unemployment A high level of unemployment means that there is a big burden on the social services as well as a reputation of poor performance for the government. Increasing employment is largely associated with growth, but much modern growth is not labour intensive and does not solve the problem. Job sharing, increasing part-time work and the growth of the tertiary sector all help with reduction in unemployment. The level of unemployment varies enormously from one region to another and governments often implement policies that attempt to attract industry to the unemployment black spots.

Greater equality of income It is neither possible nor wise to aim for absolute equality of income, but there are some major imbalances. Governments often use income-tax levels and allowances to promote greater equality. One such measure was the introduction of a minimum wage, which applies to most but not all wage earners.

Managing the economy Market forces do not always operate efficiently or smoothly. The result is that the State has to intervene to keep the economy on course. It does so through the Budget, through monetary policy changes and through direct intervention measures. The danger of this intervention is that timing may be poor or that the adjustment may be too little or too much. The only evidence available is forecasts and they are often inaccurate.

The level of employment

The number of people in work varies substantially and is difficult to measure with any degree of accuracy. The occupation and unemployment statistics were shown in Table 6.2, which is repeated on page 80.

There are several reasons why people may be unemployed:

Inactive People are not seeking work, in many instances because they cannot through disabilities of one kind or another. There is a small group who could seek work but have no intention of doing so. The biggest element in this group is housewives who have no desire or intention to work outside the home in gainful employment.

Seasonally unemployed There are more jobs on the market at different seasons of the year. In the summer

	1986	2001
Full time	16.6	18.2
Part time	4.2	5.6
Self-employed	2.7	3.2
Other[1]	0.4	0.4
Total	23.9	27.4
Unemployed	3.1	1.3
Economically active[2]	27.0	28.7
Inactive[3]	7.5	8.0
Working population	34.5	36.7

Table 6.2 Population of working age by employment (figures in millions)
Notes: 1. Examples: Government training schemes, unpaid family workers. 2. Includes the unemployed available for work. 3. Those who could but do not seek work.
Source: Office for National Statistics.

this includes substantially greater employment in the leisure and tourist industries and in agriculture. In the winter there are small pockets of increase, like that associated with Christmas

Unemployment associated with change This happens when people move and is more acute when families move from situations in which all are employed to places elsewhere in the country where only one person is employed. Because the others will be actively seeking work, this kind of unemployment is often short term. Improved communication of job vacancies would reduce this problem.

Structural unemployment This comes about because of the demands of the economy for labour change. In this country fewer workers are now needed in mining, in heavy manufacture and in farming. This kind of change often produces balancing increases elsewhere. Examples would be in financial services, computer technology and in the personal service industries. But much of the change in this country has led to high unemployment in the regions and a steady increase in jobs in London and the South East.

Technological unemployment This has been one of the most dramatic creators of unemployment and has particularly affected middle management as computers have replaced people and chains of command in business have become much flatter. Certain manufacturing industries have also been affected in this way as computer-aided design and computer-aided

manufacturing have become more common.

Demand-related unemployment This is often called cyclical unemployment and comes about because the level of economic activity changes. This is maximised right at the bottom of the business cycle. Extreme periods of depression are rare now, but the economy does fluctuate. It is a central objective of government to so manage the economy that extreme fluctuations do not occur. As can be seen from Figure 6.1 some governments are more successful than others in achieving this objective.

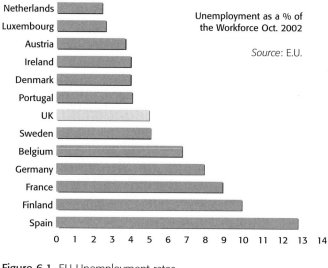

Figure 6.1 EU Unemployment rates

Business and unemployment

There are firms that lose and firms that benefit in any situation. There are benefits for business in unemployment, but on balance it reduces the level of activity and drives many businesses out of existence. The real damage of unemployment comes from:

Falling sales The obvious effect of unemployment is that disposable income falls and the greatest effect is on non-essential products and services. Firms producing leisure goods, durable consumer goods and non-essential services suffer most.

Falling profits These come partly from falling sales and partly from cuts in margins in an attempt to maintain sales.

Search for new markets This may be a broader product range in the home market, but it is more likely to be new markets abroad where disposable income may be higher.

Increased unemployment One of the highest costs for most businesses is labour costs. Firms will lay off staff or reduce hours in order to cut this cost when revenue is falling.

Lower investment Times of high unemployment are not the best for growth and development, so firms will be less inclined to take investment opportunities.

Personnel People who leave are less likely to be replaced and this may require greater flexibility of retained staff and some new training so that they can take on the responsibilities and skills of leavers.

Creditors Businesses will try to extend their own payments to firms that supply them with services and resources.

Debtors Businesses will try to be more careful in taking on new debtors and will be pushing existing ones for payment or selling the debt to factors in a search to maintain cash flow. Debts from both business and industry are likely to be more difficult to collect and may have to be 'written off'.

Increased costs These may include retraining, greater marketing costs and redundancy payments.

Bankruptcies and liquidations These could be because of falling trade or extreme cash-flow problems. They could occur because creditors have 'pulled the plug'. Many businesses operate on a very thin line between failure and survival and the failure rate can be very high at these times.

Activity

What happens when a country recovers from a slump is very much a mirror image of the above changes. Outline the likely effects on businesses as a recovery develops.

Global activity

Increasingly, in response to improvements in transport, carriage conditions and quality packing, through the medium of such communication devices as the telephone, fax machine and Internet, the world has become a very small place and almost a single market. Large firms have become multinationals and have the ability to produce and sell worldwide. Brand names like McDonalds, Coca-Cola and many others are recognised and marketed the world over. This has not only brought about an escalation in the volume of international trade, but has also created worldwide businesses for which marketing strategy focuses on the world rather than on small segments of a market. The car industry is a good

example. A car may now be assembled from parts that have been made in several countries and car makers from all over the world site their manufacturing plants closer to their markets. Japanese and American cars are now sold to countries in Europe from manufacturing plants within Europe. The rapid development of these changes is largely owing to:

- ◆ Technological change: the computer first and then the spin-offs from it.
- ◆ Communication changes: the fax machine, the Internet.
- ◆ Transport: cheaper, faster and a more complete network.
- ◆ Privatisation: throughout the world governments have relinquished control of business and industry and private companies now merge on a global basis.
- ◆ World trade is freer than it was. This is largely the result of international agreements and bodies such as the World Trade Organisation.
- ◆ Consumers are less nationalistic in their trends. This has spread to a wide range of products, but can be noticed easily in our supermarkets and restaurants. It can also be seen on our roads where there is a wide variety of foreign cars.
- ◆ The industrialisation of many of the developing countries of the world. This was probably first noticed in the so-called 'tiger economies' of Asia. Although some of them have suffered a setback, the overall direction is forward.

For many businesses the effect has of this movement has been an increase in the markets they serve and hence an increase in the size of the technical unit. Many more businesses have been able to reap internal economies of scale and in many industries the smaller firm has found it difficult to survive except in genuine niche markets – Aston Martin is an example – and as feeder firms producing for the larger ones.

Business and the physical environment

In one area there are all the following:

- ◆ In one part of the country there are large areas of quarried land from iron ore workings. They are all exhausted but remain as scars on the landscape; some have been recycled. There are two active RAF camps, which when they are in full swing constitute a significant noise pollution.

There is a cement factory that belches out pollutants into the atmosphere and offers the majority of its workers appallingly hot working conditions. The owners, however, have done a good job of shielding the site from all angles.

In the main street of the town, an endless stream of heavy lorries pollutes the atmosphere and makes the town dangerous for pedestrians to use.

Test Activity

Read the case study below and then tackle the exercises that follow.

Case study – Petrobras bids to clean up dismal safety and environment record

Oil company is having to change more than finances in its culture

Petrobras, the Brazilian state-run oil company, has had much to celebrate in recent years.

Oil output as well as productivity has increased significantly and profits last year reached an all-time record.

Yet last week's devastating explosion on an offshore oil platform, which killed 10 people and yesterday caused the $450m rig to sink to the bottom of the sea, revealed what may be the company's biggest challenge yet: overcoming a dismal safety and environmental record.

The fatal explosion brings the death toll for work-related accidents in the oil industry to 91 over three years. Last year, there were 22 oil or fuel spills, two of them very large.

Henri Philippe Reichstul, chief executive, admits that some of the company's installations and equipment are outdated, considerable industrial waste goes untreated and the attitude of many employees towards environment and operational safety is inadequate.

The company has stepped up inspections, overhauled safety regulations and is obtaining international safety certifications for its installations, from refineries to ports.

Yet judging by the accidents, the company has a long way to go before reaching its goal of environmental and safety excellence.

Critics argue that accidents such as last week's explosion may have been the result of Petrobras pushing too hard to meet its production targets.

One oil engineer said the four-month test phase of the oil platform was only half as long as normal.

Working, and particularly living, conditions on several platforms are said to be inadequate. 'We sleep on a chair in the television room because the bedrooms are over-crowded,' said a worker on one platform.

Union leaders argue that employees of contracted companies, who account for 54 per cent of a total workforce of 75,000 are under-qualified. 'Some of these companies exist only for the duration of their contract and have no interest in their workers,' says Elio Luiz Seidel, from the federation of oil workers (FUP).

Petrobras used to train all personnel but recently either transferred that responsibility to contractors or is charging them for training. Some contractors, in turn, are now said to be taking the cost of training out of employees' pay checks.

Management has reassured investors that the platform was insured and that financial damages were limited to no more than $450m this year.

Source: Raymond Colitt, *Financial Times*, 21 March 2001.

Source: Popperfoto.

(30 marks, 35 minutes)

(a) What evidence is there for the claim that Petrobas is putting the interests of investors before those of other stakeholder groups? (6)

(b) Analyse the likely factors contributing to the recent accidents at Petrobas sites. (6)

(c) The company is now taking steps to improve its safety and environmental records. Explain the likely reasons for this policy. (8)

(d) Discuss whether Petrobas should be more concerned with the environment and worker safety. (10)

Three children hold oil-covered Scater ducks shortly after rescuing them off the coast of Pendine. Thousands of birds and fish were put at risk after the oil tanker the *Sea Empress* ran aground off the coast of Wales losing over half its cargo in February 1996.
Source: Shawn Baldwan, Popperfoto/Reuter.

External costs of business activity

Not all external costs are related to what businesses do. External costs are those costs that are not paid for by the consumers or producers involved in it. Some result from the activities of private individuals or groups; some result from the activities of government. Nevertheless, there is growing concern for the damage that many business practices are doing to the environment and to the quality of life. Among those damages are:

Noise pollution There are many sufferers of this in areas close to our major airports but many of the causes are smaller and more local. Someone living next to a busy railway station finds the noise of constant announcements a significant burden.

Air pollution This is evident in any busy street, particularly where traffic is often at a standstill. Many factories pollute the atmosphere and many processing firms do also.

Congestion Congestion may pollute but it also has other substantial costs. The greatest cost of congestion is probably the London 'rush hour' or the M6 around Birmingham. Costs from this are in terms of valuable time and accidents as people get more and more frustrated. There will have been additional costs on a daily basis in terms of missed appointments and cancelled activities.

Physical destruction The raw materials of the world cannot be mined without destruction, There are dangers that agricultural land can be over-used and our food is polluted if chemicals are used to improve the growth of produce. Paper cannot be made in the quantities we need without felling trees. People cannot be housed without taking more and more hectares of the countryside. The list is almost endless and still growing.

Water pollution There are many rivers in which fish cannot live and people dare not swim. Industrial waste of all kinds is daily poured into our rivers and into the sea. Some of that pollution is accidental rather than planned. Agriculture uses a range of chemicals on the land and there is no way they can be prevented from seeping into streams and rivers. The sea is a massive dump for waste from ships and incidents of large oil slicks from accidents at sea are common. Significant land waste is dumped in the sea and most of our beaches cannot be maintained to an acceptable standard.

Waste Modern ways of selling products in pre-packed form create an enormous amount of waste that cannot be recycled. Many production methods also create by-products or residues that cannot be used. Some of our customs create waste and litter: the daily and evening newspaper; the habit of eating in the street and on trains. An estimate of the litter left on trains in Kings Cross runs into several tons a day. As commuters come out of London at night, the waste is increased by the habit of buying evening newspapers, which are left when the passengers get off. At least paper can be recycled, but many waste products, especially those of chemical production and nuclear activity, cannot be recycled and special disposal sites have to be found.

Waste is sometimes created by inefficient systems. We waste a very large amount of water every year, partly because we are not good enough at capturing it and storing it and partly because it seeps away from our reservoirs and pipes. However, the major wastage of water is the overuse of it in many homes and businesses.

Minimising external costs

It is easy to recognise ways in which our environment is deteriorating and our resources are being depleted. It is quite another matter to find ways of controlling this that are manageable by businesses or countries and which the public will accept.

There are, however, some things that limit the problems:

Legislation This is often a blunt instrument, because laws made are not enforced. We have had legislation against litter for very many years, but that does not stop the streets around Kings Cross from being cluttered with paper waste. However, reclamation and pollution control legislation is more successful. Often the penalty is a fine and paying the fine is cheaper than changing the system. Clean-air legislation has been in force for many years and it has worked miracles in cleaning the air of London.

Taxation Effectively, this is saying that we cannot prevent the pollution but we can make you face the cost of removing it. There is a danger that any tax on business for this purpose will be passed on, at least in part, to the consumer. It is argued that high petrol and diesel taxes are designed to make car and lorry users pay the costs of pollution. If this were really so, tax differentials would be quite sharp between leaded and unleaded petrol and between petrol and diesel.

Specific charges If taxation is not feasible, then perhaps the pollution actually caused can be costed and then charged to the business. This sounds fair, but would be costly to administer and may still be passed on to the consumer in many cases.

Bribes Perhaps an unfair comment, but that is what grants, subsidies and tax allowances to find better methods of waste disposal are.

Traffic reduction schemes There are extreme examples, like banning cars from a town centre or complete pedestrianisation. The oldest form is the by-pass, but more inexpensive schemes include park and ride, bus lanes and cycle schemes. Cambridge tried a free cycle scheme for a while and Sheffield, Manchester and Croydon have re-introduced the tram.

Pressure There are many pressure groups whose efforts are directed towards saving the environment. Probably Greenpeace and Friends of the Earth are among the best known. There many local examples of pressure-group influences. Consumers can be very powerful through local action and through TV programmes like *We Can Work it Out* and *Watchdog*. Many of these efforts, however, are focused on righting individual consumer wrongs rather than on protecting the environment.

Conservation One method of conservation is to use wisely, and control the use of, replaceable resources. The best example is probably fishing. Fishing limits help to ensure that fish stocks are maintained. Another form of conservation is to replant. Replanting of trees on a planned basis over time is a long-term strategy, but will only solve the problem when the rate of replanting is greater than the rate of use.

Recycling Recycling is now a major industry. It occurs a lot at an industrial level, but recycling bins for paper, clothing, oil, bottles and cans are now common in every town and local authorities are beginning to collect refuse in ways that enable recycling where it is worth while.

Activity

Work in small groups. Between you, cover the local area. Undertake an audit of ways in which the environment is being abused in your area.

(a) Suggest ways in which this abuse may be removed, minimised or repaired.

(b) How should the cost of protecting the environment be met in these cases?

(c) Discover examples of pressure to protect the environment in your area. How successful is it?

Political constraints

Governments, by their actions, sometimes support and sometimes frustrate the activities of business. Some of the things a government wants to do are political in nature; they are designed to change the fabric of society. After World War II the government decided that many of the essential industries of the country should be in public control. By nationalisation, coal, transport, steel and the utilities were run as single firms controlled by government-created bodies. Subsequently that political decision was gradually reversed by a government believing in private enterprise.

Much that is done in the world is by political agreement or disagreement. One of the greatest influences on UK was, and will be, the creation of co-operative organisations in Europe, which began after World War II and is still developing through the European Union.

During the build up to the millennium, the great 'Jubilee 2000' push was to reduce or remove Third World debt, and continuing major debates are about devolution of power in this country and the exact role of the UK in the **European Union**.

Political decisions play a large part in creating the conditions within which businesses must work. Many are ongoing or predictable and businesses can plan for them or learn to work within them. But some are sudden and unexpected.

Education is an industry in a state of constant change. The pattern of education on offer depends very much on where you live. In some counties there is still selection; in some, secondary schools educate up to 16 and then students go on to either a sixth form college or a further education college. The management role of the staff and governors keeps changing and the educational qualifications towards which students' work change. Surrounding all this there is a pattern of independent schools. Most of the changes described here are the result of political decisions on the structure of our education. Some of these are made at local level and others at national level.

Technology

Technology has always been a great force for change. Every generation sees new inventions that change what we do, what we can buy and how things are made. Technology has changed the pattern of demand and the range and nature of the products that satisfy our needs. Business has been forced to adapt to changing technology in two main ways.

Firstly, the products that firms make now are vastly different from those made just ten years ago. So research must be undertaken to establish how the latest technology can be converted into marketable products.

Secondly, the methods of manufacture have been revolutionised by technology. Computer aided machines – robots, computer aided design and the widespread use of Information Technology have all changed the nature of production and the nature of jobs done by production workers.

Inevitably, just as new technology creates new opportunities, so it leads to business casualties too. Firms that fail to adapt to change can see their markets disappear unless they can develop a unique selling point of employing outdated methods for producing 'traditional products'. Similarly, workforces must adapt to the technological revolution. If firms fail to retrain or redeploy staff whose jobs are replaced by machines then widespread discontent can limit chances of successfully accepting new ideas. The resistance to change is perhaps the major problem that business managers must overcome in order to benefit from the opportunities presented by new technology.

Activity

Find out about changes in your school or college in the last ten years.

(a) Why do you think the changes were made?

(b) What effect have they had on:
   ◆ the local community?
   ◆ businesses in the community?
   ◆ students entering and leaving?

(c) Are there any changes planned for the immediate future?

(d) What do you think are the objectives of those changes?

Activity

Discuss the ways in which technology has changed life:

- ◆ at school or college;
- ◆ in your community;
- ◆ in individual organisations and businesses in your community;
- ◆ in the things you can buy locally;
- ◆ in the way one person known to you does his/her job;

- ◆ in any other way you think is obvious or important in your community;
- ◆ in your personal life as compared with someone your age 10 years ago.

You may find that your relations, the library and old photographs can be of help to you.

Over-to-you

Test revision questions

(60 marks, 1 hour)

1 State two situations in which the state intervenes in each of the following:
   (a) the transport industry;
   (b) the employment of workers;
   (c) the protection of the environment. (6)
2 For each of the examples you chose explain why the state intervenes. (12)
3 Why should a firm develop an attitude of public responsibility? (4)
4 Explain to an individual what personal action could be taken in each of the following circumstances:
   (a) a packet of salad bought locally contains a slug;
   (b) the telephone company has overcharged for its services. (4)
5 State and argue one objective you would expect to be pursued by:
   (a) your local authority;
   (b) the national government. (8)
6 Explain three reasons why you think part-time work has become more common in this country. (6)
7 What is the amount of the current minimum wage? (2)
8 Look around your school or college:
   (a) State and explain three things that you consider are done to ensure your health and safety at work. (3)
   (b) State and argue for one thing that could be done to make your school or college safer or more healthy. (3)
9 Suppose you are a small shareholder in a large business. Why should the law offer you any protection? (4)
10 Discuss the possible benefits to a business of:
   (a) adopting an ethical policy towards the environment, (4)
   (b) observing carefully all health and safety legislation. (4)

Discover and learn

1 Work in groups. Choose a different business each. Find out how the business is affected by each of the constraints discussed in the Chapters 5 and 6.
   (a) In what ways and for what reasons is the business limited by what you have discovered?
   (b) In what ways and for what reasons is the business supported?
   (c) Explain any similarities and any differences you have discovered.
2 What evidence can you find in your community of action taken by the local authority. Explain what you have discovered and explain why it is happening.
3 What evidence is there in the local community of the effects of membership of the European Union?

4 If there is debate in the local community about an issue relating to the environment in which business operates:

(a) Explain both sides of the issue.

(b) Debate the issue.

(c) Explain what may happen if your conclusions are correct. Keep to issues that will influence the pattern and behaviour of local business.

5 Read the case study below and then tackle the questions that follow.

Case study – McDonald's profits are falling

Profits at McDonald's, the hamburger chain, have fallen for seven of the last eight quarters. Sales in its biggest markets are declining. The global store opening programme has been cut back to 650 from a peak of 2000 in 1996. The share price is near a seven year low. Part of the problem is caused by the failure of the American restaurant market to grow. For the last 18 months, fear of economic downturn and the uncertainty caused by terrorist attacks has meant Americans are not increasing spending on meals in restaurants. The fight is on for market share instead. McDonald's has launched a 'dollar menu' to try to win customers from rivals such as Burger King, but they have retaliated. They could both suffer from a 'senseless' price war.

Consumer tastes are also changing. Increasingly sophisticated and health conscious consumers in Europe are attracted to the new ranges of up market coffee houses that offer superior quality, more choice and faster service at slightly higher prices. Ageing populations in Europe are also having an impact on sales of products that are largely marketed at younger consumers.

In Asia, McDonald's have experienced some opposition to new restaurant openings from groups opposed to the 'Americanisation' of their culture. There have been calls for legal restrictions to be placed on the number of new 'imported' restaurants. In India, religious groups complained about the use of beef flavourings in McDonald's fries and this led to negative press coverage. McDonald's has responded to some of these challenges by introducing a 'Made for You' system of customised cooking for each customer. Also a 'New Tastes Menu' has been introduced with a popular chicken sandwich.

Source: Financial Times, 30 November 2002.

Burger King is engaged in a price war with McDonald's

(25 marks, 25 minutes)

(a) Identify, and explain the impact of, four external influences on McDonald's. (8)

(b) Consider, in detail, what could happen to McDonald's if it took no action to respond to these external constraints. (5)

(c) Evaluate the measures you would advise McDonald's to take in order to respond to any two of the external constraints that you have identified. (12)

6 Read the case study below and then tackle the exercises that follow.

Case study – Brotherton Construction plc

The country is just recovering from a period of very low activity in which credit restrictions have greatly reduced the number of houses that Brotherton has built and this has forced some redundancies. With the lifting of these restrictions and the lowering of the rate of interest, Brotherton is already seeing signs of renewed life in the demand for houses. The company has decided it must employ some new workers, but the management are divided between part-time and full-time employment. They are also divided about the pay to be offered. They agree that an hourly rate will be better, with no guaranteed working week and a rate of £4.00 an hour. They have decided to advertise at the local job centre and by word of mouth and to see what applications they get. John Brotherton says he wants the equivalent of eight full-time men and will want to promote one of the existing men to gang manager in charge of the new recruits. To accommodate the expansion, the firm will need to expand the existing yard or to open a new one in

the area. Most of the Board are in favour of a second yard at the other side of town. The problem will be finding a site with good access for the heavy vehicles they use and capable of tight security.

The company has quite a poor health and safety record. It has been prosecuted three times for not observing basic regulations. The directors have just appointed a new manager responsible for health and safety. He is determined to change the culture of the business on this issue.

(26 marks, 30 minutes)

(a) Explain the constraints that may be placed on the firm with respect to:
  ◆ its intended employment policy, (4)
  ◆ the location and use of a new site. (4)

(b) Examine the role that might be played in these situations by:
  ◆ the local authority, (4)
  ◆ the State (i.e. the Law). (4)

(c) Discuss the likely impact on this business of it adopting an improved attitude to health and safety issues. (10)

Summary

In this chapter and the previous one we have recognised that:

● Business is affected by the environment within which it operates. In Chapter 5 we were concerned with the economic aspects of that environment and in this chapter the focus has been on all the other constraints within which business activity takes place. There has been a strong emphasis on the local community from which you can draw rich examples of the dynamics of business behaviour.

● The different forces for change are:
  Social constraints: The effects people have.
  Legal constraints: The State working through the law.
  Environmental constraints: Our world and its changing nature.
  Ethical constraints: The moral code by which we live.
  Political constraints: The effects of government behaviour.
  Technological: The change we create.

● Although these constraints have been considered separately, they are interactive, with many of the things that organisations do being a response to the perceived total effect of these constraints, rather than a consequence of any one of them.

Key words

Definitions of Key words can be found in the Glossary on page 269.

civil law
conservation
economic growth
environment
ethics
European Union
legislation

occupational patterns
price stability
recycling
social costs
unemployment
watchdog bodies

7 Business finance

On completion of this chapter you should be able to:

➤ understand why business activity requires finance

➤ understand the objectives of those who provide finance and become stakeholders in the organisation

➤ show critical understanding of the different sources of business finance and evaluate their appropriateness in different circumstances

➤ analyse the factors managers will consider before deciding on the most appropriate methods of finance

➤ understand the rights and responsibilities of the providers of finance

➤ be able to consider the provision of finance from the point of view of both the organisation and actual or potential stakeholders

Why business activity requires finance

Finance is required for many business activities. Here is a list of just some of the main circumstances in which businesses will require finance:

◆ Setting up a business will require cash injections from the owner(s) to purchase essential capital equipment and, possibly, premises.

◆ All businesses will have a need to finance their working capital – the day-to-day finance needed to pay bills and expenses and to build up stocks.

◆ When businesses expand, further finance will be needed to increase the capital assets held by the firm – and, often, expansion will involve higher working capital needs.

◆ Expansion can be by taking over other businesses. Finance is then needed to buy out the owners of the other firm.

◆ Special situations will often lead to a need for greater finance. For example, a decline in sales, possibly as a result of economic recession, could lead to cash needs to keep the business stable, or a large customer could fail to pay for goods and finance is quickly needed to pay for essential expenses.

◆ Apart from purchasing fixed assets, finance is often used to pay for research and development into new products or to invest in new marketing strategies, such as opening up overseas markets.

Activities

1 Using the list of reasons why businesses require finance, identify:

(a) two situations that are likely to need long-term finance (more than five years);

(b) two situations that might require only short-term finance.

In each case, explain your answer.

2 Sheila and her friend Alison have decided to run their own mobile hairdressing business using the training they have received at college and the experience they both gained working for three years for a local hairdresser. Investigate, locally, the equipment and working stock they will need. From this, estimate the capital they will need to set up the business and survive the first year.

Some of these situations will need investment in the business for many years – or even permanently. Other cases will need only short-term funding – this is usually defined as being for around one year or less. Some finance requirements of the business are for between one and five years and this is referred to as medium-term finance.

The list, given above, of reasons why businesses need finance is not complete – you could probably add to it yourself. The important point to note about this list is that all of these situations are rather different. In practice, this means that no one source or type of finance is likely to be suitable in all cases. Managers will have to decide which type and source of finance is best in each case. Before we are able to assist in this type of decision making, it is necessary to be aware of all of the many sources of finance available to businesses in an advanced economy.

Where does finance come from?

This section deals initially with sources of finance for limited companies – and then considers sole traders and partnerships. Companies are able to raise finance from a wide range of sources. It is useful to classify these into:
Internal Money raised from the business's own assets or from profits left in the business (ploughed-back profits)
External Money raised from sources outside of the business.

Another classification is also often made, as was seen above, that of short-, medium- and long-term finance; this distinction is made clearer by considering Figure 7.1.

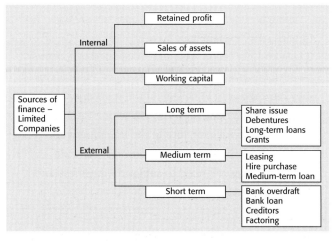

Figure 7.1 Sources of finance for limited companies

Internal sources of finance
Profits retained in the business

If a company is trading profitably, some of these profits will be taken in tax by the government (corporation tax) and some is nearly always paid out to the owners or shareholders (dividends). If any profit remains, this is kept (retained) in the business and becomes a source of finance for future activities. Clearly, a newly formed company or one trading at a loss will not have access to this source of finance. For other companies in the UK, retained profits are a very significant source of funds for expansion. Once invested back into the business, these retained profits will not be paid out to shareholders, so they represent a permanent source of finance.

Sale of assets

Established companies often find that they have assets that are no longer fully employed. These could be sold to raise cash. In addition, some businesses will sell assets that they still intend to use but which they do not need to *own*. In these cases, the assets might be sold to a leasing specialist and leased back by the company. In 1999, Somerfield, the grocery retail company, announced the sale of 50 of its stores to raise finance for investing in other areas of the business.

Reductions in working capital

When businesses increase stock levels or sell goods on credit to customers (debtors) they use a source of finance. When companies reduce these assets – by reducing their working capital – capital is released, which acts as a source of finance for other uses. There are risks with cutting down on working capital, however. As will be seen in Chapter 13, cutting back on current assets by selling stocks or reducing debts owed to the business may reduce the firm's liquidity – its ability to pay short-term debts – to risky levels.

Internal sources of finance – an evaluation

This type of capital has no direct cost to the business, although, if assets are leased back once sold, there will be leasing charges. Internal finance does not increase the liabilities or debts of the business.

However, it is not available for all companies, for example, newly formed ones or unprofitable ones with few 'spare' assets. Solely depending on internal sources of finance for expansion can slow down business growth as the pace of development will be limited by the annual profits or the value of assets to be sold. Thus, rapidly expanding companies are often dependent on external sources for much of their finance.

Activities

1 In each of the following cases, explain briefly why internal sources of finance might be unavailable or inadequate:
   (a) a new business venture between two partners;
   (b) the rapid expansion of a business, which requires expenditure several times greater than current profits;
   (c) the purchase of additional stocks by a retailer just before Christmas.

2 Sheila and Alison have worked out what they need to start their hairdressing business and it is clear that they will need some financial support. Sheila thinks that her parents would help but Alison is anxious to stand on our own feet. She has heard that the Department of Trade and Industry might help them. Contact the Department of Trade and Industry and find out details of the Loan Guarantee Scheme. How could this assist a newly created business?

External sources of finance
Short-term sources
There are three main sources of short-term external finance:
   - bank overdrafts;
   - trade credit;
   - debt factoring.

Bank overdrafts A bank overdraft is the most 'flexible' of all sources of finance. This means that the amount raised can vary from day to day, depending on the particular needs of the business. The bank allows the business to 'overdraw' its account at the bank by writing cheques to a greater value than the balance in the account. This overdrawn amount should always be agreed in advance and always has a limit beyond which the firm should not go. Businesses may need to increase the overdraft for short periods of time if customers do not pay as quickly as expected or if a large delivery of stocks has to be paid for. This form of finance often carries high interest charges. In addition, if a bank becomes concerned about the stability of one of its customers it can 'call in' the overdraft and force the firm to pay it back. This, in extreme cases, can lead to business failure.

Commercial banks are major sources of short-term finance to industry

Trade credit By delaying the payment of bills for goods or services received, a business is, in effect, obtaining finance. Its suppliers, or creditors, are providing goods and services without receiving immediate payment and this is as good as 'lending money'. The downside to these periods of credit is that they are not 'free' – discounts for quick payment and supplier confidence are often lost if the business takes too long to pay its suppliers.

Debt factoring When a business sells goods on credit it creates a debtor. The longer the time allowed to this debtor to pay up, the more finance the business has to find to carry on trading. One option, if it is commercially unwise to insist on cash payments, is to sell these debtor invoices to a debt factor. In this way immediate cash is obtained, but not for the full amount of the debt. This is because the debt-factoring company's profits are made by discounting the debts and not paying their full value. When full payment is received from the original customer, the debt factor makes a profit. Smaller firms who sell goods on hire purchase often sell the debt to credit loan firms, so that the credit agreement is never with the shop but with the specialist provider.

Sources of medium-term finance

There are two main sources of medium-term external finance:

- hire purchase and leasing;
- medium-term bank loan.

Hire purchase and leasing These methods are often used to obtain fixed assets with a medium life span – one to five years. Hire purchase is a form of credit for purchasing an asset over a period of time. This avoids making a large initial cash payment to buy the asset.

Leasing involves a contract with a leasing company to acquire, but not necessarily to purchase, assets over the medium term. A periodic payment is made over the life of the agreement, but the business does not have to purchase the asset at the end. This agreement allows the firm to avoid cash purchase of the asset. The risk of unreliable or outdated equipment is reduced as the leasing company will repair and update as part of the agreement. Neither hire purchase nor leasing is a cheap option, but they do improve the short-term cash flow position of a company compared with outright purchase of an asset for cash.

Medium-term bank loan This will have the same advantages and disadvantages as long-term loans referred to below.

Long-term finance

The two main choices here are **debt** or **equity finance**. Debt finance increases the liabilities of a company. Debt finance can be raised in two main ways:

- long-term loans from banks;
- debentures (also known as loan stock or corporate bonds).

Long-term loans from banks These may be offered at either a variable or a fixed interest rate. Fixed rates provide more certainty, but they can turn out to be expensive if the loan is agreed at a time of high interest rates. Companies borrowing from banks will often have to provide security or collateral for the loan; this means the right to sell an asset, if the company cannot repay the debt, is given to the bank. Businesses with few assets

to act as security may find it difficult to obtain loans – or may be asked to pay higher rates of interest. Alternatively, a small business can apply to the Department of Trade and Industry for the loan to be part of the 'guaranteed loan scheme'. Banks will be more willing to lend if a company has been successful in this application because it gives the bank security of repayment.

Debentures A company wishing to raise funds will issue or sell these to interested investors. The company agrees to pay a fixed rate of interest each year for the life of the debenture, which is often 25 years. The buyers may resell to other investors if they do not wish to wait until maturity before getting their original investment back. Debentures are often secured on a particular asset, which means that the investors have the right, if the company ceases trading, to sell that particular asset to gain repayment. When this is part of the agreement, the debentures are known as mortgage debentures. Debentures can be a very important source of long-term finance – in the British Telecom 1999 accounts the total value of issued loan stock amounted to £3,000 million.

Sale of shares – equity finance All limited companies issue shares when they are first formed. The capital raised will be used to purchase essential assets. Chapter 5 explained the essential differences between private and public limited companies. Both of these organisations are able to sell further shares – up to the limit of their authorised share capital – in order to raise additional *permanent* finance. This capital never has to be repaid unless the company is completely wound up as a result of ceasing to trade.

Private limited companies can sell further shares to existing shareholders. This has the advantage of not changing the control or ownership of the company – as long as all shareholders buy shares in the same proportion to those already owned. Owners of a private limited company can also decide to 'go public' and obtain the necessary authority to sell shares to the wider public. This would obviously have the potential to raise much more capital than from just the existing shareholders. This can be done in two ways:

- Obtain a listing on the Alternative Investment Market (AIM), which is that part of the **Stock Exchange** concerned with smaller companies that want to raise only limited amounts of additional capital. The strict requirements for a full Stock Exchange listing are relaxed.

◆ Apply for a full listing on the Stock Exchange by satisfying the criteria of (a) selling at least £50,000 worth of shares and (b) having a satisfactory trading record to give investors some confidence in the security of their investment. This sale of shares can be undertaken in two main ways:

– Public issue by prospectus: this advertises the company and its share sale to the public and invites them to apply for the new shares. This is expensive as the prospectus has to be prepared and issued. The share issue is often underwritten or guaranteed by a merchant bank, which charges for its services.

– Arranging a placing of shares with institutional investors without the expense of a full public issue.

Once a company has gained plc status it is still possible for it to raise further capital by selling additional shares. This is often done by means of a rights issue of shares. Existing shareholders are given the right to buy additional shares at a discounted price. By not introducing new shareholders, the ownership of the business does not change and, by avoiding expensive merchant bank and advisors' fees, the company raises capital relatively cheaply.

Test Activities

1 Study the three cases below and then tackle the following exercises.

Case study – Dominos goes to market

In 1999 Dominos Pizza Group floated on the alternative investment market by selling £2.5 million worth of shares. Stephen Hemsley, the finance director, stated that the extra capital would be used to open ten more non-franchised stores over the next ten years.

Case study – Peacocks to go public

In November 1999 Peacocks, the discount clothing and houseware retailer, issued its prospectus to the public. The company is going public to raise £42 million (after expenses) to fund further expansion and to repay outstanding debt. The managing director believes that there are great benefits in replacing debt finance with equity or share finance.

Case study – Euro Disney launches new park rights issue

On 10 November 1999, Euro Disney, the operator of Disneyland Paris, announced a rights issue to help finance a second theme park. This will be built in Paris and is due to open in 2002. The rights issue is expected to raise £147 million. The new park will cost three times this amount; the remainder of the finance will be borrowed.

(24 marks, 35 minutes)

(a) Why do you think Domino's Pizza Group decided to join AIM rather than the full Stock Exchange? (4)

(b) Peacocks decided to issue shares by prospectus to the general public. Evaluate this method of selling shares. (4)

(c) What did the managing director of Peacocks mean when he said that there were advantages in selling shares to repay debt? What are the advantages of repaying debts? (6)

(d) Why do you think Euro Disney decided to use a rights issue of shares? (4)

(e) Much of the money for the new park will be borrowed. Why might Euro Disney have decided not to raise all the capital from the sale of shares? (6)

2 Work in pairs. Study the financial pages of a quality newspaper each day for one month. Track the share price of a public limited company of your choice for this period. Make sure your choice is different from the other choices in the class. Plot the share price changes on a graph and read any comments that might relate to these changes in the newspaper.

(a) Try to identify and comment upon at least three reasons for the changes in the share price over this period.

(b) Would these share price changes you have identified make it easier or more difficult for this company to raise finance by the sale of further shares?

(c) Compare your findings with the findings of other pairs in the class. Are there any general conclusions you can draw?

Debt or equity capital – an evaluation Which method of long-term finance should a company choose? There is no easy answer to this question. And, as seen above, some businesses will use both debt and equity finance for very large projects. Debt finance has the following advantages:

- As no shares are sold, the ownership of the company does not change or is not 'diluted' by the issue of additional shares.
- Loans will be repaid eventually, so there is no permanent increase in the liabilities of the business.
- Lenders have no voting rights at the annual general meetings.
- Interest charges are an expense of the business and are paid out before corporation tax is deducted, while dividends on shares have to be paid from profits after tax.
- The gearing of the company increases and this gives shareholders the chance of higher returns in the future. (See the *A2 Business Strategy* book.)

Equity capital has the following advantages:

- It never has to be repaid; it is permanent capital.
- Dividends do not have to paid every year; in contrast, interest on loans must be paid when demanded by the lender.

Other sources of long-term finance

Grants There are many agencies that are prepared, under certain circumstances, to grant funds to businesses. The two major sources in the UK are the central government and the European Union. Usually, grants from these two bodies are given to small businesses or those expanding in developing regions of the country. Grants often come with 'strings attached', such as location and the number of jobs to be created, but if these conditions are met grants do not have to be repaid.

Venture capital Small companies that are not listed on the Stock Exchange – 'unquoted companies' – can gain long-term investment funds from venture capitalists. These are specialist organisations, or sometimes wealthy individuals who are prepared to lend risk capital to, or purchase shares in, small to medium-sized businesses that might find it difficult to raise capital from other sources. This could be because of the new technology they are dealing in, with which other providers of finance are not prepared to get involved. Venture capitalists take great risks and could lose all of their money – but the rewards can be great. The value of certain 'high tech' businesses has grown rapidly and many were financed, at least in part, by venture capitalists.

Factors influencing choice

The decisions taken by managers to obtain finance from a particular source are influenced by many factors: This is shown in Table 7.1.

Time – this will be determined by the use to which the capital will be put	The longer the period over which the financing will be needed, the more likely it will be that longer-term sources of capital will be used
Amount	The greater the amount of capital to be raised, the more likely it will be that either a share issue will be needed or that a combination of equity and debt will be used
Control	If the owners/shareholders do not wish to alter the ownership structure of the business, then either debt finance or a rights issue will be appropriate
Cost	This includes the actual cost of raising the finance, e.g. a public issue of shares by prospectus, and the cost of servicing the finance, e.g. rates of interest; these costs, and others, will have to be assessed before a final decision can be taken
The current financial position of the business, e.g. value of assets available for collateral and the gearing of the business	The greater the proportion of loans to capital employed in the business, the less likely it is that further loans would be advisable
The legal status of the business	Apart from the significance of the distinction between private and public limited companies, the exact form of business ownership will determine the sources of finance available to a firm; it is to these other forms of business ownership that we now turn
Risk	The greater the risk associated with the use of finance, the more likely it is that speculative funding, e.g. venture capital or share capital will have to be found

Table 7.1 Factors influencing choice of finance

Finance for unincorporated businesses

Sole traders and partnerships were referred to in Chapter 5, so only the main distinctions between company finance and unincorporated business finance will be made now.

Unincorporated businesses – sole traders and partnerships – *cannot* raise finance from the sale of shares and are most *unlikely* to be successful in selling debentures as they are likely to be relatively unknown firms. Owners of these businesses will have access to bank overdrafts, loans and credit from suppliers. They may borrow from family and friends, use the savings and profits made by the owners and, if a sole trader

wishes to do this, take on partners to inject further capital.

As was made clear in Chapter 5, any owner or partner in an unincorporated business runs the risk of losing all property owned if the firm fails. Lenders are often reluctant to lend to smaller businesses, which is what sole traders and partnerships tend to be, unless the owners give personal guarantees, supported by their own assets, should the business fail. Grants are available to small and newly formed businesses. One of the most significant sources is the Prince's Trust, which helps the unemployed into the world of enterprise by offering start-up grants for those with sound business plans.

Activities

1 Copy out the following table and complete it by ticking the appropriate boxes alongside each source of finance.

Sources of finance	Long-term finance	Medium-term finance	Short-term finance	Available to unincorporated businesses	Available to private limited companies	Available to public limited companies
Sale of shares to the public						
Sale of debentures						
Leasing						
Debt factoring						
Loans from family						
Take on partners						
Rights issue of shares						
Ten-year bank loan						
Bank overdraft						

2 All banks will lend money. It is their business. To do so they will check out a potential borrower to ensure that they will be repaid and that the business can make the regular interest payments that are required.

Work in groups. Each group should select a bank (different from the others) and research the borrowing potential from that bank.

(a) Find out what the bank manager would need to know before lending money to finance a new business venture.

(b) Find out what the current Bank of England lending rate is. Has this changed over the last three months, and if so, how? Will the change you have identified make it more or less likely that a business will use loan capital for expansion purposes?

Providing finance to a business creates a stakeholder relationship with that business. All stakeholders have certain rights, responsibilities and objectives, but these

will differ between the various sources of finance. This is made clear in Table 7.2, which looks at the three main providers of company finance.

	Rights	Responsibilities	Objectives
Shareholders	Part ownership of the company in proportion to the number of shares owned To attend the AGM and vote, e.g. on election of directors To receive dividend as recommended by the Board To receive a share of the capital if the business is wound up after all debts have been paid	The capital invested cannot be claimed back from the company except when it ceases trading	To received an annual return on investment in shares – the dividend To receive capital growth through an increase in share price Possibly, to influence company policy through pressure at the AGM
Banks	To receive interest payments as laid down in the loan or overdraft agreement To be repaid before shareholders if the company is 'wound up'	To check on business viability before loan or overdraft is agreed; this is both a responsibility to the bank's shareholders and to the business – advice to customers is an important responsibility	To make a profit from the loan. To receive repayment of capital at the end of the loan term To establish a long-term relationship, of mutual benefit, with the business
Creditors	To receive payment as agreed To be paid before shareholders in the event of the business being wound up To attend creditors meetings if the business is put into liquidation	To provide regular statements of amount owing and terms of repayment	To provide credit to encourage the business to purchase stock To establish a relationship built on trust so that credit can be offered with confidence

Table 7.2 Main financial stakeholders

Over-to-you

Test revision questions (60 marks, 1 hour)

1 Outline two reasons why a newly formed business will need finance. (4)

2 Would a pharmaceutical firm's expenditure require short- or long-term finance? Explain your answer briefly. (4)

3 Suggest two ways in which a company might raise finance to pay for the take-over of another business. (2)

4 Explain three factors that would influence the choice of finance in 3. (6)

5 Evaluate briefly the use of a debt factor by a business that is short of cash. (5)

6 With examples, explain the distinction between internal and external finance. (4)

7 Why might a new business find it difficult to raise external finance for its development? (4)

8 Explain what is meant by venture capital. (3)

9 Explain two reasons why the Board of Directors of a public limited company might not wish to raise finance from the sale of additional shares. (6)

10 Outline the advantages to a business of having a bank overdraft rather than taking out a bank loan. (50)

11 Examine why a business might lease new computers rather than buying them outright with borrowed capital. (4)

12 Outline four factors that managers should consider before deciding on the most appropriate source of finance. (8)

13 Evaluate the decision by a business to raise more cash by reducing stock levels by 25%. (5)

Discover and learn

1 Go back to the firm whose fortunes you followed in the case study on page 93. What is its position now? What reasons can you offer for any changes? Do you think it would be more or less likely to find additional funds now if it needed them?

2 Read the case study opposite and tackle the exercises that follow.

Case study – Sharma Taxis

Joe Sharma started his taxi business with just one vehicle. He purchased this vehicle out of his own savings. Initially, he ran his business as a sole trader, but after two years of operation he took on a partner, who had injected further capital into the firm. This had been used to purchase other vehicles and a small garage where maintenance was carried out. The business continued to expand. Joe and his partner decided to convert into a private limited company and shares were sold to business associates, family and employees of the firm. The capital raised from this conversion was used to start a small road haulage department with two vans. As the fleet of vehicles was growing, substantial stocks of spare parts were held to avoid cars and vans being off the road for any longer than was necessary following a breakdown. Regular clients of the firm were offered credit terms of up to two months.

Joe has heard of another taxi business being sold by the owners. It has a fleet of prestige cars and substantial

premises. The Board of the limited company agreed to put a bid in for this business. They agreed that it should be partly financed by floating the company on the alternative investment market with a view to obtaining a full Stock Exchange listing if further expansion was envisaged. The alternative had been to obtain a substantial long-term loan, but the directors were concerned about the chances of an increase in interest rates and preferred the share issue plus the use of some retained profits to buy out the other business. The bid for this firm was successful. The most recent development has been the decision completely to update the computer facilities at the head office. This should lead to efficient scheduling of vehicle use and an update of the accounting and invoicing system. This will allow much speedier sending out of bills to customers.

(24 marks, 25 minutes)

(a) Identify the stages of this business's development where additional finance was required. (4)

(b) At each of the stages you have identified, explain what type of finance was needed. (4)

(c) In your opinion, how could the increase in spare parts and debtors of the business have been financed? (4)

(d) Examine the decision by the directors to float the company on the AIM. (4)

(e) If the company were to expand further, evaluate the case for and against financing this expansion with a long-term loan. (8)

Summary

In this chapter we have recognised that:

● The choice of the most suitable source of finance is a crucial one for all businesses.

● If managers are not aware of all available sources or if they do not consider all of the relevant factors before making the choice, then their business could suffer from inappropriate and costly capital. This finance could prove to be too expensive, too short term or involve serious disadvantages over business ownership and control, which the owners would be most concerned about.

● Inadequate finance can lead to business failure.

● Selecting inappropriate sources of finance can reduce business profits or liquidity or increase the degree of risk to unacceptable levels.

● There are many different types and providers of finance.

● There is a range of factors that managers should take into account before taking the important decision as to which type of financing to use.

Key words

Definitions of Key words can be found in the Glossary on page 269.

Alternative Investment Market (AIM)
bank overdraft
debentures
equity
factoring
grants
hire purchase
leasing
loans
retained profit
Stock Exchange

Part 2

Business decisions and business behaviour

8 The market: definition and structure

On completion of this chapter you should be able to:

➤ define marketing
➤ understand the role and importance of marketing
➤ understand the difference between market orientation and product orientation
➤ understand how marketing fits in with the other activities of a business
➤ understand possible marketing objectives
➤ understand how marketing can lead to the achievement of overall business objectives
➤ define and discuss market segmentation, market growth, and market share

What is marketing?

There are many ways of defining **marketing**. Some of them are more complicated and long-winded than others. P. Kotler (*Marketing Management*, Prentice Hall, 1977) described marketing as 'a human activity directed at satisfying needs and wants through exchange processes'. Here, he is emphasising the importance of exchange, i.e. payment.

Marketing has also been described as a complete system of business activities designed to plan, promote and distribute goods and services to target markets, where they are desired and/or needed. Note the difference between needs and wants/desires. A need is something that is necessary to existence. It fulfils the achievement of physiological needs: the basic requirements for sustaining life, such as food, water, warmth, clothing and shelter. A want is something that a consumer would like to have, but is not necessary for survival, such as ice cream or a trip to an amusement park.

To put it simply, marketing is best described as discovering what the potential consumers want and then supplying it (at a profit).

'At a profit' is in parentheses because profit is usually, but not always, one of the main objectives of a business. In certain state-owned, or charitable, organisations, it may be that the aim is still to find out what the consumers want and then to supply it, but making a profit may not be an essential part of the equation.

The role and importance of marketing

All organisations market themselves. They may not do so intentionally, but simply by producing goods and services and by dealing with customers, they are involved in marketing. If this is the case, then it is better that firms should have a carefully planned marketing strategy rather than a slapdash approach. For a number of years, it was assumed that marketing was only really important for firms dealing in **fast-moving consumer goods** (**FMCGs**), but now it is realised that it is also essential for firms dealing in services and manufacturing. Indeed, organisations such as charities, hospitals, art galleries and even universities are now marketing themselves fairly aggressively.

Marketing is of extreme importance, since it covers many of the functions of management. Design, production, pricing, promotion and distribution are key areas in almost all organisations and they are all under the umbrella or influence of marketing.

Marketing in the UK and Europe has only really grown in importance since the end of the 1950s. The main reason for this rise in the importance of marketing is that, before this time, people did not have the **disposable income** available to demand a large range of products. Since the recovery following World War II, **demand** has grown and many businesses have arisen to satisfy that demand. Also, as incomes have risen, people have satisfied many of their product needs and now demand a far greater number of services than they once did. This accounts for the greater **supply** of restaurants, travel agents and leisure facilities.

The demand for more products and services has led to the emergence of a great number of businesses and brands. In addition, in the UK, there is now more competition from abroad, especially from Europe, following membership of the EU. This increased competition has made marketing all the more important to firms if they wish to survive.

With the improvements in average incomes, fashion has become more important and people's tastes tend to change more frequently. Lifestyles have altered and demands have changed. For example, there is now a whole health and fitness industry, with products ranging from aerobics classes to vitamin tablets. These changes in tastes, fashion and lifestyles are another reason why marketing has become so much more important in recent times.

In the time period we are considering, there have been exceedingly rapid changes in technology. So many products that are now taken for granted were not available 30 years ago, such as mobile telephones, personal computers and CD players. These new and improved products have had to be marketed and now, of course, consumers expect new advances in technology and improvements in products at all times and it is up to the marketers to provide and sell the products. Fear of obsolescence is a much greater worry these days than in times gone by.

To summarise, the role of marketing is immense. It involves all areas of an organisation and successful companies are those that know what their customers really want and then set about supplying it.

Market orientation and product orientation

Marketing focuses on consumer needs and wants and, in modern-day management, it is the consumer who drives product development and production more than the product developer. This is known as a market- or consumer-orientated approach. On the whole, the days of developing a product and then finding a market, a product-orientated approach, are disappearing. However, this still happens to an extent and there are a number of approaches that put the consumer, or market, last:

◆ Product-orientated businesses invent and develop products in the belief that they will then find consumers to purchase them. They believe that they know what the customers want and that if they produce a product of good enough quality, then it will be purchased. This sort of pure research and development is becoming rarer, but there will always be a place for it to some extent. Firms in certain industries, such as pharmaceuticals and electronics, have to operate in this way to survive. The industries are so innovative that to stand still is to risk going out of business.

◆ Production-orientated businesses concentrate their efforts on efficiently producing high-quality, relatively cost-efficient products. The belief is that the products will find a market if the price is relatively low and the product is of a high enough quality. Although production-orientated firms are not as prevalent as other types, they do exist, especially in areas where quality, or safety, are of great importance, such as bottled-water plants or the making of crash helmets.

◆ Sales-orientated businesses tend to produce a product and then concentrate upon different selling techniques and skills, so that they can then clear their supplies. It is argued that some pyramid selling firms work in exactly this fashion.

Activities

1 What is marketing? How do you account for the increase in the importance of marketing in the last 40 years?

2 Attempt to identify five products that have evolved in the last 25 years. Select one of the products and attempt to discover as much as you can about its early marketing.

3 Use your own school or college if you wish and work in groups of four to six. It has become increasingly necessary for all educational establishments to market themselves and what they do. Examine the ways in which your selected school or college markets itself and comment on the success of this. Discuss, in your groups, the strengths and weaknesses of the marketing effort and suggest ways in which the marketing effort could be made more effective.

All of the above approaches take little notice of the consumer and are much more interested in product production and selling techniques.

Market-orientated firms put the consumer/customer first. The business will attempt to produce what the consumers want, rather than try to sell them a product that they do not really want to buy. Market orientation is the most common form of marketing these days and the reasons for it were very well described by Robert Heller, in his book *The Supermarketers*. He said,

It's quite misguided to pursue the technology-push policy – a delusion with much industrial blood on its hands. The myth goes that if you make a better mousetrap the world will beat a path to your door. It has been disproved again and again, never more comprehensively than by the total defeat of competitors who had genuinely stolen technological marches on IBM in mainframe computers ... Despite all such evidence, many allegedly marketing orientated companies still operate on the mousetrap principle: improve the product, they think, and technology push will create the sales.

In fact, success and survival in business depend upon the whole marketing process, which will be covered in this and the next two chapters. Finding out what the consumer wants and then supplying it at a profit requires the following:

- carrying out effective market research and identifying the target groups;
- designing the product;
- assessing the reaction of consumers to both the product and the packaging;
- calculating a suitable price, related to costs of production and what consumers are willing to pay;
- deciding upon a suitable promotional strategy;
- organising the distribution system that will be used to get the product to the market.

Marketing objectives

Objectives are what we attempt, or wish, to achieve. As should always be the case, the **marketing objectives** of a business should relate to the hierarchy of objectives that the enterprise has. The hierarchy of objectives is:

Activities

1 Explain the difference between production-orientated marketing and consumer-orientated marketing.
2 Go to your local shops and identify two products that you think were invented and then marketed and two products you feel were the result of market research and then development and marketing. Explain why you think the individual products were marketed in the way they were.
3 Try to identify products that might be production orientated and sales orientated.

- mission statement;
- long-term objectives;
- short-term objectives;
- departmental objectives;
- set strategy;
- set tactics.

The marketing objectives should come under the heading of departmental objectives and they should reflect the aims of the whole organisation and attempt to aid the achievement of the objectives above them in the hierarchy. The marketing objectives are the outcomes that an organisation is trying to attain through its marketing.

The long- and short-term objectives of the business will have an influence on the marketing objectives. For example, if a firm is attempting to maximise profits, then the emphasis of the marketing strategy will reflect this. In the same way, if a firm is attempting to enter a market and gain a sizeable market share, then its marketing objectives will be different from the previous example.

It is fair to say that whatever the greater aims of an organisation, its marketing objectives will normally be achieved through an appropriate blending of marketing variables. These make up the marketing mix and are discussed fully in Chapter 10. Marketing objectives would normally involve six aspects and we can look at each of these in turn.

Market segmentation

The marketing objectives of a business ought to include an analysis of which market segments the firm wishes to operate in and which market segments they might aim for in the future. It is unusual for a firm to be large enough to attempt to satisfy all of a market, unless the market is a relatively small, usually specialist, one. Because of this, firms usually identify their prime market segments and one of their objectives would be to enter those segments. Thus, a shoe company may decide to aim at the sports shoe and leisure wear segments of the shoe market. They may hope, in time, to move into the work boots segment.

Market share

Once markets, or market segments, have been identified, then firms will normally set objectives relating to the amount of market share that they might hope to gain. Thus, the shoe firm above might set themselves a target of achieving 5% of the sports shoe market and 10% of the leisure shoe market within a period of three years. Obviously, if these market-share objectives are achieved, then new ones emerge. The firm will have to decide whether to attempt to maintain its share, increase the share or move into a new market.

Product development and product range

Firms must set objectives relating to the type, and range of products or services that they wish to develop. This will give them specific areas upon which to focus. In the beginning, our shoe firm might decide to try to develop three different styles of sports shoe and a range of beach shoes. In some ways, the more specific the **product development**, the more the market is being segmented.

Price versus quality analysis

Objectives may be set balancing the quality of the product against the price for which it can be sold. Quality will obviously have an effect upon cost and this, in turn, affects price. Put the other way around, the price that a business thinks it can get for a product may put a restraint on costs and quality. For example, an objective of the shoe firm may be to make the best quality pair of training shoes that can be sold below a price of £30. No-one would pretend that they would be the best shoes on the market, but the point would be that they were the best quality available at that price.

Range of trainers for sale in a typical shoe shop

Sales performance, revenue and profit

Marketing objectives may be set relating to sales (in either volume or revenue terms), revenue gained from specific products or profit gained from particular products.

Distribution strategy

Objectives may be set in terms of how well distributed, or 'placed', the product is going to be. A large pharmaceutical firm may aim to have its products in every chemist shop in the country within a space of two years, or a coffee shop chain may aim to have an outlet in every town with a population over 20,000 in the South East of England.

Segmenting the market

Market segmentation is a vital element of marketing. It is customer orientated and is thus consistent with the concept of marketing. It occurs when the total demand in a market is analysed, so that specific sets of buyers, with distinct characteristics, can be identified.

Once this has been done, then it is possible to design products and services that will apply directly to specific market segments. After this, it is possible to design marketing plans that will then aim the specific products directly at the segments chosen. The act of market segmentation enables organisations to:

- define their markets accurately;
- position various products and brands in the right market area;

- identify gaps in the market that might be successfully filled;
- make more efficient use of marketing resources.

There are three commonly used bases for segmenting markets. The first of these categories is **geographic**. Consumer tastes may vary between different geographical areas and so it may be appropriate to offer different products and to market them in alternative ways in each area. For example, large national breweries offer different brands of beer to different areas of the country, even though they could offer a single brand. They will also promote the products in different ways, because they realise that there are regional differences in attitudes and consumers' tastes.

The second basis for segmentation is **demographic**, i.e. relating to the science of population statistics. This is the most commonly used basis for segmentation and is usually based upon such factors as sex, age, income or ethnic background. For example, manufacturers of washing powders will aim different brands of their products at different ages of consumers. Some brands, such as Bold, will be aimed at the younger end of the market and others, such as Daz, will be aimed at slightly older customers. The promotional strategy for each product is then devised to appeal specifically to the targeted market segments.

The third basis is **psychographic**, which in turn can be split into three main areas: social class, personality characteristics and lifestyles. There are a number of ways of defining social class. One of the most common is to split the population into upper class, upper middle class, lower middle class, upper lower class and lower lower class. These classes are sometimes classified by letters. An individual's social class will have a great influence upon his or her purchasing patterns in many product categories.

In theory, personality characteristics should be very influential. One would expect an aggressive person to have different purchasing patterns from a timid person. The same could be said for impulsive people as opposed to very cautious people. In reality, such personality characteristics are very difficult to identify specifically and to measure accurately. However, many firms especially in their advertising, still do, attempt to appeal to consumers who have particular personality traits. Thus, we see products aimed at outgoing young people who wish to pursue all sorts of relatively dangerous outdoor activities, such as sky-diving or bungee-jumping. Even though it is not possible to measure the market segment accurately, the seller knows that it is there, believes that it is large and is aiming at it. Lifestyle is a very broad term and often overlaps with personality characteristics. Lifestyles tend to relate to activities undertaken, interests and opinions, rather than personality traits.

There are a number of advantages to segmenting the market:

- It enables the division of the market into distinct areas at which the product can be more specifically aimed.
- Small firms, which could not compete in the whole market, are able to concentrate on one or two smaller segments.
- It is possible to design and produce goods and services that are specifically matched to the demand of a more distinct group of consumers.

There are, however, a number of disadvantages. First, there are higher production costs, because it is obviously more expensive to produce a range of products, all aimed at different market segments, than it is to produce a single product aimed at all potential customers. The second disadvantage relates to this point as well. If there is a range of products on offer, then there will be a need for higher levels of stockholding, which will have obvious cost implications. Finally, promotional costs will rise as different strategies are required for different markets and administration costs will also increase as many more products are produced and marketed.

Market growth and market share

The term 'market' is difficult to define. Basically, a market is a group of consumers who have a need to satisfy, money available and the willingness to spend that money. There are two main types of market, consumer markets and industrial markets.

Consumer markets are where the products or services are bought for personal consumption, whereas in industrial markets products or services are for use in manufacture or business, or for resale to other customers.

Market growth is the percentage increase in the size of a whole market. It may be measured in terms of volume, i.e. units sold, or value, i.e. revenue generated. For example, if total sales in a market for sports shoes rose from 24 million pairs at an average price of £32 to 26 million pairs at an average price of £36, then market growth can be measured in the following two ways:

- By volume – the market has risen from 24 million to 26 million, which is an increase of 2 million or 7.69%.
- By value – the revenue has risen from £768 million to £936 million, which is an increase of £168 million or 21.87%.

Market share is the percentage of sales that a single firm has in one market. Again, this might be measured in terms of volume or value. Thus, a firm that sold sports shoes in the above market and had sales of 3.5 million pairs and revenue of £140 million in the second year might measure its market share in the following two ways:

- By volume – the firm sells 3.5 million pairs of shoes in a market of 26 million, which is a market share of 13.46%.
- By value – the firm has sales of £140 million in a market of £936 million, which is a market share of 14.96%.

A market with a high growth rate is obviously one that organisations would wish to be involved in. In the same way, individual firms would wish to have a high market share. This may give a number of advantages, such as a price-setting position in the market and the ability to gain from economies of scale.

There are a number of problems associated with the measurement of market share and market growth. The main one is obvious and can be seen above. It is highly likely that when market growth and/or market share are measured in terms of volume and value, different figures will be obtained, as we have seen in our example. It is thus difficult to make comparisons between firms. For example, there may be a firm in the car industry that specialises in selling high volumes of cars at relatively cheap prices. The firm's market share, if measured in terms of volume, would be high and yet the share measured in terms of value may not necessarily be so large.

Test Activity

Read the case study below and then tackle the exercises that follow.

Case study – The Classic Watch Co.

The Classic Watch company was in trouble. Sales had fallen for each of the last three years. The founder of the company, Harry Brainch, could not understand the reasons behind this crisis. His business had been making the Classic Ladies' wrist watch for the last 20 years and only recently had sales failed to climb every year. The current model had been updated but was still essentially the same design as the original watch. Consumers had been attracted to its simple, robust design and good value. These were very important qualities during the economic crisis that the country had suffered from for much of the last few years. More recently, consumer incomes had started to rise. Old manufacturing industry had been replaced by service sector businesses that offered many supervisory and managerial jobs. Youth unemployment, in particular, had fallen and young consumers had much more money to spend than previously. Both men and women were becoming much more fashion conscious as their consumer tastes changed with higher incomes.

Harry knew his business had to change but he did not know which new styles of watches to introduce. He almost wished a return to the good old days when shoppers were happy to buy a recognised design at a reasonable price.

(20 marks, 30 minutes)

(a) Would you describe the Classic Watch Co. as being product or market orientated? Explain your answer. (4)

(b) Analyse why Harry's original marketing strategy is no longer succeeding in increasing sales. (6)

(c) Suggest, with reasons, how Harry might segment the market for watches in order to increase overall sales. (4)

(d) Evaluate the benefits to The Classic Watch Co. of pursuing a policy of market segmentation. (6)

Over-to-you

Test revision questions (50 marks, 50 minutes)

1 What is meant by the term 'market'. (2)

2 Outline why marketing is important to a business. (5)

3 Explain the difference between product orientation and market orientation. (4)

4 Do you think firms should be market or product oriented? Explain your answer. (5)

5 Why do you think that it is important for Adidas to have marketing objectives? (4)

6 State three possible marketing objectives and suggest situations in which each might be the main marketing target for a business. (6)

7 What is market segmentation? (2)

8 How might a sports shoe manufacturer segment its market? (5)

9 Explain why the sports shoe manufacturer might want to segment its market. (5)

10 Select another product and suggest one way in which the market for it might be segmented. (3)

11 Use a numerical example to illustrate how the total market is growing but an individual firm's market share is falling. (5)

12 Explain why a business might be more interested in market share than market growth. (4)

Discover and learn

1 Take two or three newsagents in your area. How do they compete with each other?

2 Work in a group. Consider the restaurants in your area. In each case:

(a) What segments of the market is each in?

(b) What segments have each avoided?

(c) Explain your findings.

3 Consider the market for any product you choose. Of the outlets in your area, where would you buy that product and why? Do you all agree? If not, why not?

4 Read the case study below and tackle the exercises that follow.

Case study – Tubular Chairs Ltd

Brian Carnes was a strong character and he was determined to set up his own business and not to work for anyone else. In the mid-1970s, he was finishing his marketing degree in Birmingham and he was looking around for a market niche that might suit him. His girlfriend, Jean, was studying furniture design at the Art College and she and Brian used to spend a lot of time going around the local stores looking at various types of furniture. In doing this, Brian began to take an interest in tubular furniture, i.e. furniture made from tubular steel with upholstery attached. In conversation with Jean and people in the stores, he decided that the construction methods were not too complicated and that the mark-up must be reasonable.

On leaving university in July 1974, Brian founded Tubular Chairs in his home town of Stoke-on-Trent. Brian was funded by his father, who invested money from his own wholesale vegetable business, and by the bank, which lent Brian the rest of the necessary capital through a loan that Brian's father guaranteed. In return for his support, Brian's father received a 25% stake in the firm. Jean also moved to Stoke-on-Trent and began to design the furniture that the firm would sell. Having invested

money herself, she also received a 25% share in the firm.

In the early days, the firm grew at a startling, and sometimes alarming, rate. After an initial period of acting as a middleman and simply buying in chairs produced elsewhere and then selling them on, it began to produce and sell Jean's designs.

The marketing policy was all-important in those early days. Jean was designing basic, colourful furniture, which was sturdy, reasonably long lasting and capable of simple and quick production. The furniture was sold at low prices, with a small profit margin, in order to gain high market share. It was sold through large cut-price furniture warehouse chains, which undertook to promote the furniture under their own brand names. The economic climate at the time was difficult, so cheap but reasonably attractive furniture was popular. In no time at all, Brian found that the combination of the firm's market penetration pricing policy and the attention given to below-the-line promotion methods was a great success. By 1980, Tubular Chairs was the market leader in the field and the factory in Stoke was producing large quantities of a wide range of tubular-steel furniture.

Sadly, the good times did not last for the firm. As the 1980s progressed, their type of furniture went out of fashion and sales fell dramatically. The economic boom of the mid-1980s did not mix well with the image of the furniture that the firm was producing. Indeed, the firm was only kept going by its foreign sales, which remained fairly constant throughout the period. Most of these sales were in France and Germany, where the style of furniture remained popular. Brian tried to increase this part of their market and he had some success in selling to Spain and Portugal.

As the 1990s have progressed, the firm has just managed to keep its head above water. In January 1996, in a desperate attempt to change the pattern of things, Brian brought in a firm of management consultants headed by Val Richards, an old university friend. Over a period of three months, Val and her team studied the firm and the markets in which it operated and then produced a report on the situation and recommendations for the future survival of the firm.
A shortened form of the report is given below.

Main points of the report on Tubular Chairs Ltd
Prepared by Val Richards and based upon information relating to the period 1/1/1990 to 31/12/1995.

A. Aim
To identify the current market situation facing Tubular Chairs and to make recommendations for the future.

B. The current situation
The total UK market for tubular design chairs has fallen significantly over the last ten years and the sales of Tubular Chairs Ltd have fallen rapidly in the same period.

Tubular Chairs, once the market leader, has now lost that position to a firm based in Taiwan. The Taiwanese firm has successfully managed to copy the existing range offered by Tubular Chairs and to supply them at a lower price. Consumer research indicates that tastes in furniture have changed markedly in the UK and that people now prefer to spend more on their furniture in the belief that it will last longer and be a saving in the long run. Tubular furniture is now considered to be more

suited to the garden than the sitting room.

The market in the European Union does not yet seem to have gone into decline and, indeed, there has been market growth of 10% between 1990 and 1995. This market, which accounted for 30% of the total sales of Tubular Chairs in 1990, accounted for 40% in 1995.

C. Recommendations
The firm should consider each of the following:
1 A more aggressive pricing policy in order to compete with the Taiwanese competitor, cutting prices and using the economies of scale from the increased output to reduce costs and maintain a profit.
2 Designing a new range of chairs, improving the quality of the materials used in production and aiming at a higher-income segment of the market.
3 Diversification into the production of other types of furniture, such as garden furniture, picnic furniture and camping accessories.
4 Investigating the possibility of expanding its operations in the European Union.
5 Investigating the potential market in the former Communist Bloc countries, such as Poland or Hungary.

In April 1996, a meeting was held between Brian, his father, Jean and Val Richards to discuss the report and to make decisions regarding the future direction of the firm. Brian's father could not see what all the fuss was about and he felt that although times were not good, they were still making a reasonable return on their investment. He suggested that they should leave well alone and carry on as they were. Jean, as one would expect, liked the idea of designing a new range of products and was sure that she could produce something that would appeal and so she was in favour of recommendations 2 and 3 in Val Richards' report. Brian also felt that their products were a little old-fashioned, but he equally felt that there were other markets for them abroad, if they could only get into them. He favoured a combination of recommendations 1, 4 and 5. After much discussion, Brian went away to consider the future of the firm.

(50 marks, 1.25 hours)
(a) Describe how Brian might go about segmenting his market. (5)
(b) Explain the difference between the terms market growth and market share. (4)
(c) Use the following data referring to the UK market, in the context of the case:

Year	Total market sales (1,000s)	Tubular Chairs Ltd sales (1,000s)
1990	200	90
1993	180	85
1995	150	52.5

◆ Calculate the total market sales of Tubular Chairs in the UK and the European Union in 1995. (3)

◆ Calculate the percentage change in the market share of Tubular Chairs, in the UK market, over the period 1990 to 1995. (3)

(d) Using your figures from question (c) and any other relevant data, evaluate the current market position of Tubular Chairs. (6)

(e) Outline Tubular Chairs current pricing policy as revealed in the case, and suggest ways in which it might be 'more aggressive'. (6)

(f) What might be the benefits and the costs associated with diversification into other types of furniture? (6)

(g) Undertake a SWOT analysis of Tubular Chairs. (10)

(h) Evaluate the factors management should consider before entering the names of other European Union countries. (7)

Summary

In this chapter we have recognised that:

● Marketing is of great importance to an organisation.

● The role of marketing is important and it involves all aspects of an organisation's functions.

● Marketing may be aimed at consumers or it may be product, production or sales based.

● Most marketing today is consumer- (market-) orientated.

● It is vital to set marketing objectives and to ensure that they fit in with the overall objectives of the organisation.

● Where necessary, markets should be segmented and the marketers should concentrate upon suitable segments for their products.

● Market growth is desirable for all organisations within a market and the higher a market share that an organisation can achieve, the stronger will its position be.

Key words

Definitions of Key words can be found in the Glossary on page 269.

FMCGs (fast-moving consumer goods)
market growth
market orientation
market segmentation
market share
marketing objectives
product orientation
psychographic
sales orientation

9 Market research

➤ define marketing research and market research and differentiate between the two

➤ distinguish between primary and secondary research

➤ understand some of the different sources of data

➤ understand methods of data collection

➤ understand the importance of sampling

➤ understand sampling methods

➤ discuss research methods and their appropriateness in given circumstances

➤ devise a survey strategy to achieve a given objective

➤ use the data as a base for information gathering appropriate to your project

Marketing research and market research

Market research is the process of discovering relevant primary and secondary information about the demand for a good or service in a specific market.

Marketing research is a much broader and wider-ranging process, which involves the analysis of every single aspect of the marketing sequence. Marketing research involves discovering consumer reaction to many areas of the marketing process. Thus, it might include market research, product development and testing, pricing, promotional aspects, distribution and selling theory and the evaluation of competition.

The terms market research and marketing research are often used to mean the same thing, but this is obviously not the case. In effect, market research is a part of marketing research. However, market research is of great importance and it would be foolish for an organisation to make decisions with no knowledge of the demand factors in their particular market.

Successful market research enables organisations to reduce the risk of making a mistake, when introducing new products. However, there is no guarantee that market research will lead to success. In the two most famous cases of fairly recent years, Clive Sinclair was told that the C5 would be a success and Sony were told that the Walkman would never sell! This just goes to show that market research is not infallible.

The need for market research

◆ *To reduce the risks associated with new product launches.* By investigating potential demand for a new product or service the business should be able to assess with some degree of accuracy the likely chances of a new product achieving satisfactory sales. No research can guarantee success, however. In the 'evaluation of market research' section we consider all of the reasons why market research may give a misleading message about new product success chances.

◆ *To predict future changes.* A travel firm may wish to investigate social and other changes to see how these might affect the demand for holidays in the future. For instance, the growth in the number of single person households may suggest that there could be a rising demand for 'singles'-type holidays.

◆ *To explain patterns in sales of existing products and market trends.* Market research is not just undertaken for new or planned products. It needs to be conducted for existing products too. Cinema attendances in the US fell in 2001. Unless cinema owners are prepared to find out why this happened then they will not be able to take any remedial action to 'stop the rot'.

◆ *To assess the most favoured designs, flavours, styles,*

promotions and packages for a product. Consumer tests of different versions of a product or of the proposed adverts to promote it will enable a business to focus on the aspects of design and performance that consumers rate most highly. These can then be incorporated into the final product.

Marketing research can therefore be used to discover information about:

- market size and consumer tastes and trends,
- the product and its perceived strengths and weaknesses,
- the promotion used and its effectiveness,
- competitors and their claimed unique selling propositions,
- distribution methods most preferred by consumers,
- consumers' preferences for packaging the product.

Primary and secondary research

Primary research is defined as original data gathering from people within your target market. They are called 'first-hand' data as they are being collected by the organisation for the first time for its own needs.

Secondary research is the use and analysis of data that already exist. These data were originally collected by another organisation, often for a different purpose, and are often referred to as 'second-hand' data.

Which one of these research methods should be used first by a business undertaking marketing research for the first time, for example data gathering for a new product launch? Surprisingly, perhaps, it is *secondary* research that should be undertaken first. Why is this? It is because of the benefits that secondary research offers over primary methods.

Assume that a supermarket business in your country was considering expansion abroad. The following data could be obtained from secondary sources, without the manager leaving his desk – which is why it is sometimes called desk research!

- Walmart of the USA has the greatest global market share of any supermarket, with sales in 2000 of US$189 billion.
- Rewe of Germany has more shops than any other supermarket chain – 21,150. This is nearly five times the number of shops that Walmart has. Yet the sales of Rewe, which put it 9th in the world, are

In Germany alone there are 3,500 shops owned by independent Rewe traders plus a further 6,000 branches employing a total workforce of 135,500 employees united under the umbrella of the Rewe trading group.

less than one quarter of Walmart's total. This suggests that the market leader probably has larger shops, on average, than other similar businesses.

- In Thailand, in 2000, there were 102 supermarkets owned by large foreign supermarket groups – in Malaysia there were just 45.
- The Delhaize supermarket group of Belgium earns a greater percentage of its total sales from stores in foreign countries than any of the other leading 20 global supermarket groups.

Essential information about the size of the overall market, whether it is growing or shrinking, the market leader and recent changes in market shares could all be gained from secondary sources. The data referred to above were all obtained from several of the following well-known sources of secondary data:

1 *Government publications.* In most countries sources such as the following from the UK could be referred to:
   - *Social Trends,*
   - *Economic Trends,*
   - *Annual Abstract of Statistics,*
   - *Family Expenditure Survey.*

Therefore, if a furniture manufacturer was undecided whether to produce new designs for teenagers' bedrooms or electric reclining armchairs for the elderly, reference to government publications for the forecasted age distribution of the UK population over the next ten years would be a useful starting point.

2 *Local libraries and local government offices.* If the research data needed were only for a small area – investigating the viability of a new café, for example – then local not national data would be necessary:
- local population census returns with details of total numbers, age and occupation distributions,
- numbers of households in the area,
- the proportions of the local population from different ethnic and cultural groups.

3 *Trade Organisations* produce regular reports on the state of the markets their members operate in. For example:
- Society of Motor Manufacturers and Traders,
- Furniture Retailers Association,
- Engineering Employers Federation.

If a garage owner wanted to start stocking new cars for sale, then details of the type and size of car that is most popular with consumers could be obtained from the first source listed above. Clearly, further research might then be needed to see if, locally, these national data were reflected in consumer demand in the garage's own area.

4 *Market Intelligence Reports.* These are incredibly detailed reports on individual markets and industries produced by specialist market research agencies. They are very expensive but they are usually available at local business libraries. Examples are:
- Mintel reports,
- Keynotes reports,
- Euromonitor.

If the owner of a small hotel planned to expand the business by opening a hotel in the capital city, one of these reports on the hotel and catering market would provide huge amounts of detail on market and consumer trends, eating and holiday 'habits' of consumers, number of tourists and so on.

5 *Newspaper reports and specialist publications:*
- *Marketing journal* – provides weekly advertising spend data and consumer 'recall of adverts' results,
- *The Grocer,*
- *Motor Trader,*
- The *Financial Times* – regular articles on key industries such as IT and detailed country reports – essential for potential exporters.

6 *Internal Company Records.* If the business has been trading for some time a great quantity of secondary data will already be available for further analysis:
- customer sales records,
- guarantee claims,
- daily, weekly and monthly sales trends,
- feedback from customers on product, service, delivery and quality.

It is clear that there is a great range of secondary data available both to existing businesses planning a new market development or a newly formed business. Secondary research should always be the starting point of any market analysis. It will nearly always indicate the focus that subsequent primary research should have. However, on its own, it is rarely sufficient, which is why primary research is also usually undertaken. Before studying the main methods of this type of research, Table 9.1 summarises the advantages and disadvantages of secondary research.

Secondary research gathers background data, but only primary research can provide detailed information from consumers within the firm's target market.

Methods of primary research

Primary – or field – research can itself be divided into *quantitative* and *qualitative* research. The first category refers to finding out the number of consumers who might buy a product and in what *quantities*. This is clearly important information but what is often even more revealing is *why* consumers will or will not buy a particular product. Qualitative research is concerned with discovering the motivational factors behind consumer buying habits. For example, quantitative research might establish the size of the potential market for a new luxury ice-cream. But will consumers buy it for its taste and the quality of its ingredients or because it will be promoted as a 'life-style' branded product that will reflect well on the consumers' image of themselves? Only qualitative research can establish the answer to the last question – and it is important because it will help the business in its pricing and promotional decisions for the new product.

Qualitative research
The main technique of qualitative primary research is interviews with individual consumers or groups of

111

them. These in-depth discussions – often undertaken by psychologists! – will attempt to identify the key factors influencing consumer choice. Different pricing levels and alternative advertisements might be discussed with the

consumers and their reactions will be noted and analysed. These 'focus' groups of consumers are frequently used to assess a new car model. In one such test, all distinguishing name signs on a new car were

Advantages	Disadvantages
Often obtainable very cheaply – apart from the purchase of Market Intelligence Reports.	May not be updated frequently and may therefore be out of date.
Identifies the nature of the market and assists with the planning of primary research.	As it was originally collected for another purpose, it may not be entirely suitable or presented in the most effective way for the business using it.
Obtainable quickly without the need to devise complicated data gathering methods.	Data collection methods and accuracy of these may be unknown.
Allows comparison of data from different sources.	Might not be available for completely new product developments.

Table 9.1 Secondary research

Test Activity

Read the case study below and then tackle the exercises that follow.

Case study

Carlos Sanchez is a chef who specialises in Spanish cuisine. He has just given up his job in a large hotel in the capital city. He has always wanted to work for himself and with his savings he has decided to open his own small restaurant.

Property prices are too high in the capital so he has moved to a small coastal resort about 100 kilometres from the capital. He has many important decisions to make before he starts trading. He is not sure whether Spanish cooking will be popular with the locals and the tourists. He is able to prepare many other types of dishes too. He could open just a restaurant or a take-away too. If he offers take-away meals he could either serve these in plastic containers suitable for microwave heating, which are expensive, or in paper trays, which are cheaper. Carlos has noticed that there are few other restaurants in the area and no take-aways, although one well-known fast food chain has recently closed down. There are no other Spanish-based restaurants. After finding a suitable shop site, Carlos then had to decide whether to decorate it for younger people's tastes with loud pop music or in a more sober style with old-style Spanish music. Carlos began to plan seriously for his new venture – he had not realised that so many decisions would need to be taken before he could start cooking!

(30 marks, 40 minutes)

(a) Would you advise Carlos to do some market research before he opened his new business? Explain the reasons for your answer. (6)

(b) List four areas of marketing research that you would advise Carlos to undertake. (4)

(c) List four sources of secondary research that Carlos could refer to. (4)

(d) How useful would secondary research be for Carlos? Explain your answer. (6)

(e) Carlos believes that primary market research will be necessary:
 ◆ devise a suitable questionnaire,
 ◆ advise him on the most appropriate sampling method to use.

removed and consumers were asked for their reaction to the design, shape and performance of the car. Initial results were very positive – until the consumers were told that it was a Skoda model, a manufacturer with a previously poor reputation. The company knew that consumers would therefore be prepared to purchase the product if they could successfully change the image of the company and its brand name.

Quantitative research techniques

1 *Observation*

Using this approach market researchers observe and record how consumers behave. They can count the number of people or cars that pass a particular location in order to assess the best site for a new business. Researchers can also observe people in shops to see how many look at a new display or take a product from the shelves. A simple stock check can also be used to record sales over a period of time. Results can be distorted, however, if people are aware of being watched and behave differently because of this. Also, observation does not give researchers the opportunity to ask for explanations of behaviour – it only records what actually happens.

2 *Test marketing*

This can take place after a decision has been made to produce a limited quantity of a new product but before a full-scale, national launch is made. It involves promoting and selling the product in a limited geographical area and then recording consumer reactions and sales figures. To be reasonably accurate the region selected must reflect as closely as possible the social and consumer profiles of the rest of the country. In many countries with regional TV stations, one of these regions is chosen as TV advertising can then be focused on just this one area. Test marketing reduces the risks of a new product launch failing completely but the evidence is

not always completely accurate if the total population does not share the same characteristics and preferences as the region selected.

3 *Consumer surveys*

These involve directly asking consumers or potential consumers for their opinions and preferences. They can be used to obtain both qualitative and quantitative research. For example, here are two questions asked in a recent survey of shoppers:

'*How many foreign holidays did you take last year?*'
'*What do you look for in a ideal foreign holiday?*'

The first question is designed to obtain quantitative data which can be presented graphically and analysed statistically. The second question is designed to find out the key qualitative features of a holiday that would influence consumer choice.

There are four important issues for market researchers to be aware of when conducting consumer surveys:

- *Who to ask?* Given that in most cases it is impossible or too expensive to survey all potential members of a target market (called the survey population) it is necessary to select a 'sample' from this population. The more closely this sample reflects the characteristics of the survey population, then the more accurate is the survey likely to be.
- *What to ask?* The construction of an unbiased and unambiguous questionnaire is essential if the survey is to obtain useful results.
- *How to ask?* Should the questionnaire be self completed and returned by post or filled in by an interviewer in a face-to-face session with the respondent? Could a telephone survey be conducted instead?
- *How accurate is it?* Assessing the likely accuracy and validity of the results is a crucial element of market research surveys.

Who to ask? – Sample size and sampling methods

Sample size Generally speaking, the larger the sample, the more confidence can be given to the final results. In surveying consumer reaction to a new advertising campaign for a major brand of chocolate, a sample of ten people is unlikely to be sufficient.

Try to work out why. The first ten people chosen might show a positive reaction to the new advertisement. Yet another ten might show a majority with negative reactions. A sample of ten is too small to be *confident* about the result, as chance variations could easily occur as a result of the limited number of respondents chosen. A sample of 100 or even 1,000 will produce results that will reflect much more accurately the total preferences of the whole survey population. There will be much less risk of pure chance distorting the results. Obviously, a sample of 1,000 is more useful than one of 100, especially if the questions were being focused on particular age or income groups. Once a sample of 100 is broken down into, say, ten different age groups, then there will only be ten respondents from each age band. We have already stated that this is likely to be too few.

What prevents *all* primary research being based on a sample size of 1,000? Cost and time are the two major constraints here – the cost of research increases greatly with the sample size, especially when a specialist firm of market research analysts is used. The results of a survey might be needed quickly to assist managers in making rapid decisions – a sample size of 1,000 will take much longer to organise.

Sampling methods There are several techniques of sampling:

1 *Random sampling*

This method aims to ensure that each member of the survey population has an equal chance of being selected for the sample. It requires an up-to-date 'sampling frame' to be accurate – a sampling frame is a list of people included in the survey population. This is not the same as the total population of the whole country. It would be very rare for a firm to wish to sample from the entire population of a country – from one day old to over a 100 years old! It refers instead to everyone in the target survey population, so, for example, a manufacturer of camping equipment would only be interested in those who go camping. From this survey population a list of names is drawn up and a sample is selected randomly from the list. This can either be done by selecting every nth item in the list (systematic random

sampling) or electronically, by means of computer generated random numbers. The interviewer will then call on the people selected – possibly trying on more than one occasion if they are not at home.

In Business Studies project assignments many students undertake market research and they interview shoppers at the high street bus station at a certain time of day. This is often described as being 'random sampling' – it is not. The sample selected in this way will not be representative because car drivers will not be included and, if conducted during the working day, full-time workers will be underrepresented. A random sample could instead be obtained by using the methods described from a list of all voters, the electoral roll, or even a comprehensive street directory.

2 *Stratified sampling*

This method involves dividing the population into sub-groups and only sampling from those sub-groups that are likely to be interested in the product in question. For example, a new magazine aimed at 12–16 year old girls. It would be pointless and time consuming to select samples from groups other than this particular sub-group. Once the group has been identified, then the sample can be selected by using either random of quota methods.

3 *Quota sampling*

By this method interviewees are selected according to the different proportions that certain consumer groups make of the whole survey population. For instance, if it is already known that, out of all consumers of denim jeans:

male   65%
female   35%

Age
14–20   35%
21–30   35%
31–40   20%
over 41   10%

then the sample selected would conform to the same proportions. Therefore, if there was a sample of 200 people, 130 would be male, 70 female, 70 between 14 and 20 years old, and so on. The interviewer could then either obtain the quotas by questioning the right number of people in the high street or, if a sampling frame was available, the respondents could be selected randomly up to the quota for each group.

4 *Cluster sampling*

When a full sampling frame list is not available or when the product is mainly likely to appeal to specified groups of consumers, for example town or regional newspapers, then cluster sampling will take a sample from just this group – not the whole population. Random methods can then be used to select the sample from this group.

5 *Systematic sampling*

This is where a set numerical formulae is used to choose the sample, for example every tenth or twentieth person is selected. Again, if the population consists of distinct strata, then it is not really a very appropriate method.

6 *Convenience sampling*

In this case, the interviewer selects any convenient place, where large groups of people might congregate, as the location for conducting the interviews. Obviously, this makes the sample quicker and cheaper to conduct, but bias may be introduced by the fact that everyone is from the same location. An example of this might be interviews carried out in large shopping centres or in queues for the cinema.

What to ask – questionnaire design

It is not easy to write an effective questionnaire. The temptation is often to ask too many questions in the hope of gaining every last scrap of information. Yet people may become suspicious or bored with so many questions. Unless it is absolutely essential to know the names and precise ages or income levels of respondents, these questions are best avoided as there will be reluctance to answer them. One way around this is to group income levels together, such as:

'*Please indicate which of the following income levels you are in:*'

$10,000–$20,000

$20,000–$30,000 and so on.

Asking all 'open' questions is not a good idea although questionnaires usually end with one of these. These allow respondents to give their opinion, such as, What do you really think of Jupiter perfume? The

answers to these will be so varied in length and content that the results will be very difficult to put together and to present statistically. A better option might be:

What most attracted you to buying Jupiter perfume?

◆ price ☐ ◆ image ☐
◆ packaging ☐ ◆ widely available ☐
◆ smell ☐

As the design of the questionnaire will greatly influence the accuracy and usefulness of the results it is advisable to undertake an initial pilot survey to test the quality of the questions. Other principles to follow include:

◆ make clear the objectives of the research so that questions can be focused on these;
◆ write clear and unambiguous questions;
◆ try to make sure that the questions follow each other in a logical sequence;
◆ avoid questions that seem to point to one particular answer;
◆ use language that will be readily understood;
◆ include some questions that will allow a classification of results by gender, area lived in, occupation and so on.

How to ask? – self-completed questionnaire or direct interview

Self-completed questionnaires are either sent through the post or filled in by the respondent themselves 'on the spot', for example in a shop. Postal surveys are relatively cheap to send out, a wide geographical area

People are surveyed on how often they use some of the facilities provided by a local council

can be covered and there is no chance of bias from the interviewer creeping in to distort results. However, the response rate to both these and other forms of self-completed questionnaires is nearly always very poor, questions could easily be misunderstood and the sample returned could be biased in favour of those respondents with the most spare time, for example the retired.

Direct interviews are conducted by an interviewer, usually either in the street or in the respondent's home. Skilled interviewers will avoid bias in the way in which they ask questions, and detailed questions can be explained to the interviewee. Follow-up questions can be asked if required. This can be an expensive method but the interviewer will continue their work until the pre-set sample size has been reached – whereas the response to postal questionnaires is always uncertain.

How accurate is it?

Unfortunately, the reliability of primary data can often be called into question. There are three main reasons why primary data may not be as reliable as hoped for.

1 *Sampling bias.* The only really accurate method of primary research is to ask the entire target population – we have already identified the time and cost constraints on this. Results from a sample may be different from those that would have been obtained if the entire target population had been questioned. This is called sampling bias. The less care that is taken in selecting a sample, then the greater the degree of statistical bias that will exist. Therefore, no one can be 100% confident that sample results are really accurate. Statisticians often aim to achieve a '95% confidence level' in their results, which means that

the results can be relied upon in 19 cases out of 20. Generally, the larger the sample, the greater the chance that this 95% confidence level will be met.

2 *Questionnaire bias.* This may occur when questions tend to lead respondents towards one particular answer. Because of this the results are not a completely accurate reflection of how people act or of what they believe.

3 *Other forms of bias.* These might include the respondent not answering in a very truthful way, perhaps because he/she wishes not to admit to spending so much on CDs or clothes!

Market research developments

Increasingly, businesses are turning to electronic means to gather the data their marketing strategies require. Not only can questionnaires be answered over the internet but firms can access the vast quantity of information that electronic data retrieval methods offer them. This is particularly true of retailers such as supermarkets that operate 'loyalty card' schemes. By scanning in the total number and type of goods bought by each consumer, the firms have a complete picture of what each consumer purchases, how often, their age, gender and possibly their income (they would have to provide these details to obtain the loyalty card initially). This allows retailers to target each consumer with advertisements and special offers about just the goods they are most interested in. This form of targeted marketing is cost effective because money is not wasted on promoting, say, dog food to people who do not have a dog.

Primary Research Check List

Who to ask?	Interview or postal questionnaire?
Sampling method?	Open or closed questions?
Sample size?	How to present results?

Test Activity

Read the following questionnaire. It was prepared by Metro Petroleum. The company wanted to research into motorists' petrol buying decisions. They hope that the results will help them to improve their marketing strategies. It was distributed at Metro's petrol stations. Customers were asked to return it, fully completed, during their next visit.

Questionnaire for all petrol customers
Please help us by answering the following questions

1 Name _____

2 Address _____

3 Make and model of car _____

4 Do you buy petrol often?

5 Who buys the petrol, you or your wife? _____

6 How much petrol do you buy? _____

7 Do you always buy petrol at Metro stations? Yes/No

8 Where else do you buy petrol? _____

9 Why do you choose Metro? _____

10 If you drive a company car do you keep the free gifts and special offers for yourself? _____

Thank you for your cooperation – please put the completed questionnaire in the box provided.

(30 marks, 35 minutes)

(a) How effective do you think this questionnaire is? Give reasons for your answer. Include comments on the suitability of each question and the use of a self completed questionnaire. (10)

(b) Assume that you have been asked by Metro to prepare an improved questionnaire.
   ◆ Ask 8–10 questions that you believe will give the type of data that Metro are looking for. (8)
   ◆ Briefly justify why you have asked each question in the form you have. (8)
   ◆ Advise Metro on how the questionnaire should be distributed and collected in. (4)

Over-to-you

Test revision questions

(60 marks, 1 hour)

1 Explain why a sports shoe retailer would find market research useful. (3)

2 Distinguish between primary and secondary market research data. (3)

3 Why is it important to use secondary data, when available, before investing in expensive primary research? (4)

4 Explain two reasons why secondary data might prove to be inaccurate for a firm's specific purposes. (4)

5 State three different ways of collecting primary data. (3)

6 What are the advantages and disadvantages of each of these methods? (6)

7 Explain what a consumer panel is and the circumstances in which one might be used. (5)

8 What is an open question and when might it be useful? (5)

9 Why is it that most questions in a project enquiry should be closed ones? (3)

10 Why is sampling so frequently used in consumer surveys? (2)

11 Evaluate whether a newly formed business should use a small sample of potential customers for a survey. (6)

12 What are the differences between qualitative and quantitative research? (4)

13 Outline two reasons – other than sample size – why primary research could be inaccurate. (4)

14 Explain the difference between a quota sample and a stratified sample. (4)

15 What advantages does primary research have over secondary research? (4)

Discover and learn

1 As a group choose a headline from your local newspaper.

   (a) Agree on questions (not more than three) that you can ask to test the general public's awareness of that issue.

   (b) Each member of the group go and ask ten people those questions.

   (c) Bring back your findings and collate them.

   (d) What do you conclude from your collective findings?

2 (a) Go and research the price of tomatoes in all the shops in which you can find them.

   (b) Decide how you can display the data you have collected in a way that would convey most information to the reader.

   (c) From your research:

- What is the range?
- What is the arithmetic mean?
- What is the median price?
- Is there a modal price?

Which one of these descriptive data would you choose to represent the price of tomatoes? Explain your answer?

3 Suppose you needed to research the market for a new bus service in some part of your area. What secondary data would you seek to use and how would it be of assistance to you?

4 **Case study – Tubular Chairs Ltd**

Using the case study at the end of Chapter 8 (pp. 106), answer the following questions:

(30 marks, 30 minutes)

   (a) Discuss the market research methods that Val Richards and her team might have employed to find the information given in the *Current Situation* section of the report. (15)

   (b) What sampling methods might Val Richards and her team have adopted to gain the consumer research information in the report? (15)

5 Read the case study below and then tackle the exercises that follow.

Case study

A firm is considering opening a sweet and soft drink shop near to your school or college. The owner of the business believes that the success of the shop will depend heavily on the number of students from the school who will buy goods from it regularly. He has asked you to help him research the potential demand from your fellow students for the products to be sold from this shop. He asks to you to collect data concerning current buying habits, amount spent on confectionery items, the number of times students would be likely to visit the shop and so on. He wishes to use the data to attempt to forecast the future sales revenue of the shop.

(a) You decide to conduct a survey of your fellow students. You must decide:

- the questions to ask,
- whether to use a face-to-face interview or a postal questionnaire,
- how many students to include in your sample and how they should be collected,
- how to present the results of your survey.

(b) Undertake this survey. Include just six questions in your questionnaire.

(c) Explain and justify the decisions you make concerning (i) to (iv) above.

(d) When you have completed your findings and presented them in an appropriate way, comment on your results and recommend the action that the business owner should take next.

6 Read the case study below and then tackle the exercises that follow.

Case study – Low market share at Cosmos

The Cosmos Soft Drink Co. Ltd is concerned about its low market share. Despite extensive advertising in newspapers and magazines and colourful displays in most large retailers, sales remained disappointingly low compared with the well-known brands in the market. The image for its drinks that the company was trying to create was a 'sporty' and youthful one. One of the reasons for this was because the directors had found out that the proportion of the population under 18 was expected to increase in the next ten years and the sports participation rates of most age groups were increasing.

The directors were in agreement that the image was the correct one to have and that other factors were to blame for the poor sales performance. They decided to conduct a survey of the general public. This was to be a telephone survey as they believed that quick results were essential to allow them to take the right measures to boost sales. A questionnaire of 30 questions was drawn up asking for details of soft drinks bought and the reasons for purchase decisions, names and addresses of the respondents so that free vouchers could be sent, income levels to identify consumer profiles and many other details that the directors thought might be useful. One hundred people were to be contacted by picking names at random from the telephone directory.

The results of the survey proved to be very disappointing because many calls were not answered, some people refused to answer some of the questions and some of the elderly respondents said that all soft drinks were too sweet and fizzy for them anyway. The directors were no clearer after the survey than before as to what could be done to increase sales of Cosmos soft drinks.

(20 marks, 25 minutes)

(a) What evidence is there in the case that this business has used secondary research methods? (3)

(b) List two sources of such data that Cosmos might have used, if the business was based in your own country. (2)

(c) Analyse four possible reasons why the results of the telephone survey were so disappointing. (8)

(d) Suggest and justify an alternative primary research technique that Cosmos could have used to achieve more useful results. (7)

Summary

In this chapter we have recognised that:

- Market research is not the same as marketing research, it is a sub-set of it.
- Information is relevant data and may be categorised as primary, secondary, quantitative or qualitative.
- Information may be collected by field or desk research.
- Primary information can be collected by observation, experimentation and surveys.
- Questionnaires are usually involved when surveys are being carried out.
- Because it is usually impossible to interview a whole population, or market, some form of sampling usually takes place.
- It is important that the sample is large enough to be significant and that it is representative of the population as a whole.
- Samples may be random or non-random.

Key words

Definitions of Key words can be found in the Glossary on page 269.

observation	quota
probability samples	random samples
qualitative information	sampling
quantitative information	surveys
questionnaires	

10 Market planning

On completion of this chapter you should be able to:

➤ define the marketing mix
➤ understand the requirements of a good product
➤ define and discuss the product life cycle
➤ understand and explain how products can be positioned through the use of portfolio models
➤ understand the influences upon price of different pricing strategies
➤ understand the factors that influence the level of demand
➤ define, calculate and interpret price elasticity of demand
➤ identify and explain different promotional methods
➤ understand and discuss the appropriateness of different promotional strategies
➤ understand different distribution channels and strategies
➤ understand the importance of a strategic approach to marketing
➤ formulate and justify marketing strategies in different situations

The marketing mix

The **marketing mix** is the combination of variables that has to be taken into account when formulating a marketing strategy. Different management theorists will name different variables, but the most common variables are known as the '4 Ps':

◆ product;
◆ price;
◆ promotion;
◆ place.

Some would add packaging as an extra 'P' and others would separate publicity from promotion. However, most still stick with the original variables. In simple words, a marketing mix involves a combination of supplying a product at a price that consumers will pay, making sure that the consumers know that the product exists through promotion and ensuring that the consumers will have easy access to the products through an efficient distribution system.

It is important that the different elements of the mix do not clash and that a firm has a mix that suits its own particular needs. There is no ideal marketing mix, the emphasis upon each element of the mix will vary from firm to firm.

Some firms will emphasise especially the actual product that they are producing. These will tend to be firms who produce high-quality goods that are often technically advanced. Here, they will emphasise quality and will not be so interested in price. If firms make products that are common, have many competitors and are relatively simple, then they will not be so likely to emphasise the product, but will put more emphasis upon price and promotion.

Firms supplying manufacturers with equipment will stress the quality and appropriateness of the product, assuring them that the machinery on offer is the best for the job. In many industries, it is impossible for firms to ignore the marketing mixes of their rivals. Many firms will match the style and content of the marketing mixes of their competitors. A good example of this would be the high-street banks in the UK, such as Lloyds, Barclays, HSBC and the National Westminster Banks.

In the end, all firms are looking to find a 'Unique Selling Point' (USP) somewhere in the marketing mix. This is the point that, in the eyes of the consumers, sets their product apart from its rivals.

The product

A product can be defined as anything that can fulfil a consumer's needs or wants. It may be a good, i.e. tangible, or a service, i.e. intangible. It is sometimes thought to be the most fundamental and important element of the marketing mix, since, if a product does not fulfil the needs or wants of a consumer, then that consumer will not buy the product.

Product development is an important area for any business. In order to be a 'good' product, an item needs to satisfy three major requirements:

◆ The product should be able to fulfil the function for which it is intended. If a product does not do what it is meant to do, then consumers will not buy it. No-one wants a basketball that does not bounce or a chair that collapses when people sit on it. When considering this, the developers of products should be aware of all of the tasks that consumers might expect product to fulfil. People use screwdrivers for a number of tasks, not just inserting and removing screws. Amongst other things, they may use them to open paint tins, mix paint and punch holes in thin wood and metal. They would expect a reasonable screwdriver to be able to perform these functions and so the designers will have to ensure that they do.

◆ The product should be as aesthetically pleasing as can be expected for the price. If possible, products should look good, but this will obviously depend upon the product in question. People do not expect a cheap ruler to look aesthetically pleasing, but they would expect it from a sports car or a pair of earrings. Products that are basic and functional do not normally have to be very visually appealing, but luxury products usually are.

◆ The product needs to be capable of economic production. There is no point in making a product so well that it is functionally perfect and aesthetically wonderful, but so costly to make that the price that would have to be charged to make a profit would not be one that consumers would be willing to pay.

In addition to these three requirements, a firm will also have to consider any legal requirements that might be placed upon their product. Furthermore, in this more enlightened age, firms may also take into account environmental factors that may be encountered by the production process or by the disposal of the product when it has been consumed.

It will be up to the product developers to strike a balance between the above five factors. This balance will normally be decided upon having considered the results of any market research that has been undertaken.

Activities

1 What are the elements of the marketing mix? Use illustrations to show how each different element may be the most important in specific markets.
2 What are the five requirements for a good product?
3 Identify ten different products and, for each one, attempt to rank in order of importance the five requirements for a good product. Explain your reasoning.

The product life cycle

The **product life cycle** looks at the different stages that a normal product will go through in its life, from development to decline and eventual failure. It shows the product's life, over time, measured in terms of sales revenue or, more often, profit. A typical product life cycle is shown in Figure 10.1.

As we can see from the figure, the first stage is that of development, and here we would expect costs and no revenue, since there would be no sales. Thus, the product would be making a loss. The second stage is introduction and the product may be introduced to the whole market or, more likely, it may be tried out on a test market. This is a smaller, normally regional market, which has the same characteristics as the main market. It is thought that, if the product flourishes here, it will do the same in the main market. It must be said that it is normally at this stage that the majority of new products, a figure as high as 75%, fail. If the

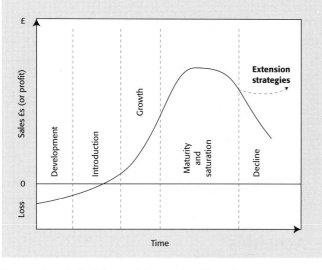

Figure 10.1 Typical shape of the product life cycle

introduction goes well, then the product may move into profit at the end of this stage, but promotional costs are high and so any profit is unlikely to be great.

If the product is successful, it then moves into the growth stage and we will find that sales are increasing, as is market share. It may be that there is marked market growth as well, but this will eventually slow down as the market becomes stable. In this stage, promotional expenditure is still fairly high, but sales are ever increasing and so profits rise. Eventually though, as the market growth slows down, the product enters the maturity and saturation stage, where it has a high market share in a stable market. This makes it a valuable source of funds and profits, since promotional costs are not too high (because the product is well known) and the sales revenue is high and constant. However, for most products, but not all, demand will eventually begin to diminish and the product will move into the decline stage. Sales will fall and profits will do the same. The firm will have to decide whether to cease production and sales of the product or whether to attempt to prolong the life of the product through extension strategies.

Extension strategies are such ploys as:

◆ redesigning the product in order to make it attractive again, such as altering the design of a watch to include an alarm function;

◆ redesigning the packaging in some way, such as making Apple Mac computers coloured;

◆ developing add-on products, such as the male companion doll Ken, which was added to the Barbie range to try to increase sales of Barbie.

The actual shape of the product life cycle will not always, or even often, be like the one that we have just seen. The shape of the curve and the lengths of the stages will vary from product to product. The likely impact that the product life cycle could have on marketing decisions is shown in Table 10.1.

Product portfolio

The **product portfolio** of a firm is sometimes called its product mix. It is the range of products that a firm produces and it is imperative that a firm has a balanced portfolio. Very few firms will be able to survive over time with only one product. As we have seen from the product life cycle, almost all products will eventually go into decline and so firms should have products in all stages of the product life cycle. In this way, the successful products, in the maturity stage, can be used to fund new products that the firm wishes to develop and introduce to the market.

In Figure 10.2 we can see a balanced product portfolio of three goods. However, many firms will have a much larger product mix, consisting of many different products. A good example of this would be ice-cream manufacturers, such as Walls, who produce many different ice-creams and are always adding new products to their range.

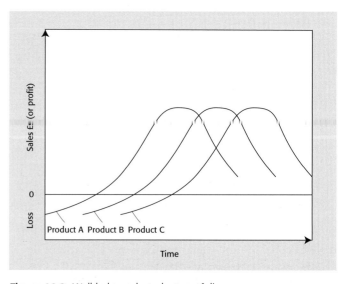

Figure 10.2 Well-balanced product portfolio

Phase of the PLC	Price	Promotion	Place (distribution outlets)	Product
Introduction	May be high compared to competitors (skimming) or low (penetration).	High levels of informative advertising to make consumers aware of the product's arrival on the market.	Restricted outlets – possibly high-class outlets if a skimming strategy is adopted.	Basic model.
Growth	If successful, an initial penetration pricing strategy could now lead to rising prices.	Consumers need to be convinced to make repeat purchases – brand identification will help to establish consumer loyalty.	Growing numbers of outlets in areas indicated by strength of consumer demand.	Planning of product improvements and developments to maintain consumer appeal.
Maturity	Competitors likely to be entering market – there will be a need to keep prices at competitive levels.	Brand imaging continues – growing need to stress the positive differences with competitors' products.	Highest geographical range of outlets as possible – developing new types of outlets where possible.	New models, colours, accessories, etc. as part of extension strategies.
Decline	Lower prices to sell off stock – or if the product has a small 'cult' following, prices could even rise.	Advertising likely to be very limited – may just be used to inform of lower prices.	Eliminate unprofitable outlets for the product.	Prepare to replace with other products – slowly withdraw from certain markets.

Table 10.1 The marketing mix and phases of the product life cycle

Test Activity

Read the case study below and then tackle the exercises that follow.

Case study – Nestlé drops LC1 Go! brand after poor sales

Nestlé has scrapped its probiotic LC1 Go! live yoghurt drink less than three years after it was launched with a £2m TV ad campaign.

The launch of LC1 Go!, a citrus-flavoured low-fat dairy drink was meant to be the company's answer to the fast-growing demand for single-dose bottles of live, friendly bacteria that help the body's digestive system.

A competitor – Yakult – is the biggest seller in a market worth £45m in 2000.

Go! struggled to make an impact and had just 5% market share in 2000, despite its lower price.

Go! was part of a range that included LC1 set yoghurt, which has been withdrawn from the UK for a second time. It was introduced in 1996, then scrapped a year later after disappointing sales. It was relaunched in 1998.

Two years ago, an annual Nestlé report described Go! as an innovation that would strengthen the company's position in Europe.

But poor sales have forced Nestlé to pull the product our of Europe's biggest food markets.

A Nestlé spokesman said the LC1 range was well-received at launch, but added that distribution proved 'difficult to gain and maintain in the face of strong competitive pressure'.

LC1 range: failed to make an impact in market led by Yakult

(20 marks, 25 minutes)

(a) Calculate the value of Go!'s sales in 2000. (2)

(b) Sketch the apparent product life cycle for this product – and justify the 'shape' of your diagram. (4)

(c) Examine the measures that Nestlé could have taken instead of withdrawing this product from the market. (6)

(d) Outline four possible reasons why this product failed to live up to the company's expectations for it. (8)

New product development

As we saw in the product life cycle, new products need a period of development before they are launched onto the market. If a firm is going to have a reasonable and balanced portfolio of products, then it is essential that it develops new products to replace those that become obsolete and to widen the product mix. New products may be completely new or they may be an adaptation of an already existing product. In either case, the process of product development may vary greatly in the time taken to reach the production stage. For some pharmaceutical products, product development may take 15 years or more. However, this is seen to be worth while, because the possible financial rewards are massive. What would be the selling price of a cure for AIDS? In other cases, such as making children's toys, the process may be six to nine months. It is interesting that car firms are attempting to reduce drastically their product development times and some of the Japanese firms are now working on a period of 18 months, as opposed to five years in the 1980s. New product development relies on:

Identifying new product niches This is usually carried out by a mixture of market research and technological prediction. Markets are identified and the consumers are asked what sorts of products they would like to see. In addition, experts in the markets try to foresee what technological breakthroughs might occur

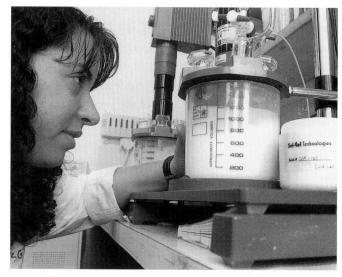

An Israeli company has developed a sunscreen in which the solution is encapsulated in tiny glass bubbles. This invention could give the company a competitive advantage
Source: Popperfoto.

in the market, or might be possible to create. In this way, ideas for new products are generated.

Once the idea of the product has been decided upon, it is necessary to assess whether the product will actually be desirable to the market and whether it will be able to be sold for a profit. Market desirability has normally been indicated in the original market research and so it is usually only necessary to estimate costs and possible revenues in order to predict the profitability factor.

This is often carried out by the building of a prototype.

Developing the product Sometimes, the new products are developed after market research or technological prediction has identified a possible winning product. Occasionally, new products occur as an offshoot of pure research. The most famous example of this is when Teflon, which is used for non-stick frying pans, was discovered as an offshoot of the US space research programme.

When products are developed following research and prediction, the process of development is known as applied research. It is at this stage that the prototype product is developed into the marketable final product. In doing this, it is important that the designers take notice of the requirements for a 'good' product that we considered earlier in this chapter.

Piloting and test marketing the product Once the product has been developed, the firm will normally try it out on a small scale. This will involve producing a relatively small number of the products and then attempting to sell them in a test market, which is representative of the main market that is being targeted. This process should show whether the product can be produced economically and also whether there is a market for it. If the piloting and test marketing of the product is a success, only then will the product be released on the wider market.

Products fail at all stages of the product development process, but if a product reaches the full production stage, there is still no guarantee that it will be a success. There are many reasons why a product may reach the wider market and then fail. Some of them are as follows:

- Competitors release a product that the consumers prefer.
- Changes in technology leave the product dated.
- Tastes change and the product is quickly obsolete.
- The market research was not accurate.
- The costs of production were greater than predicted.
- The product could not fulfil its main functions.
- The pricing estimate was wrong.
- The promotion was not effective and so not successful.
- There were problems of distribution and consumers could not gain access to the product in sufficient quantities.

There are so many possible causes of failure that it is almost miraculous that products succeed at all.

Activities

1 What are the phases involved in the development of a new product?
2 Why do firms produce new products, if so many products fail?

Product positioning

Product positioning places a product in the market in terms of its rivals. It identifies where a product stands in terms of the major characteristics that consumers expect products in that market to have. The first step to take, when positioning a product, is to discover the main qualities that consumers expect from this type of product. This is best shown by an example. Assume that a firm is trying to position a product in the sliced wholemeal bread market. The main expected qualities are discovered by means of market research and it is discovered that they are price and variety of nutrients.

Once the main desired qualities have been identified, then a 'map' can be drawn like the one in Figure 10.3. The existing products in the market are placed on the map and it is then studied in order to decide where the firm's new product should be positioned.

Figure 10.3 Product positioning map

In this case, we can see that there are two main groups of products. There are those that are high in both price and variety of nutrients and those that are low in both qualities. There seems to be little in between.

The firm must now decide where it will place its own product. There are a number of possibilities. First, the firm could aim for a gap in the market. This may be rather risky but, if it pays off, then there may be the chance of substantial profits. A second option is to position the product in with others. In this way, the firm is producing a similar product and hoping for some of the existing market share. This is a less risky option than trying to fill a gap, but the potential profits will usually be much lower.

Firms will sometimes identify more than just two qualities and may position their product against a number of different factors. They may also aim to reposition an existing product by altering it so that it will then occupy a different point on the positioning map. An example of this may be making a product more exclusive and moving it up market or making a product more available and moving it towards the mass market.

Market positioning

In just the same way that a product can hold a certain position in a market, so can a firm. There are a number of different market positions that firms may occupy.

Market leader

This is a firm that is regarded as the main producer in the market. Invariably, the firm will have the largest market share and will normally be a 'price setter', i.e. it will dictate the prices for the market and the market followers will adopt those prices or very similar ones. The market leader will be keen to achieve market growth and may be attempting to drive other firms out of the market. However, in large markets, the small firms often do work that the market leader does not want and the market leader will tolerate them so long as they toe the line.

Market challenger

This is normally the second largest firm in the market, or a new firm that has high aspirations. The aim of the market challenger is to become the market leader. Markets that have a leader and a challenger tend to be very competitive and price wars may well take place as the challenger attempts to gain market share. Supermarkets are a good example and the fight between Tesco and Sainsbury is a constant one.

Market follower

This is a firm in the market that is actually satisfied simply to maintain market share and to follow the market leader. These markets tend to be less competitive in terms of pricing and most competition takes the form of non-price promotion.

Niche marketer

This is a firm that simply concentrates on a specialist, discrete, area of the market, such as a publisher that specialises in publishing only children's books. Niche marketing will be successful if the niche is large enough to be profitable, but too small to be of interest to the larger firms in the market.

Activities

1 Select three different products, identify their main rivals and then attempt to plot a positioning map for each product. Justify your decisions.
2 Select three individual firms, in different industries, and then attempt to position the firms in their separate markets. Explain your positioning.

Price and demand

Price is the amount of money that a consumer is prepared to pay for a good or service. In a wider sense, it is the money value of a good, service, asset or factor input. There are a number of approaches to pricing.

Demand-based pricing

This is where the firm attempts to charge what the market will bear and to gain the highest price that will still clear the amount supplied. In order to undertake demand-based pricing, it is necessary to understand the concepts of the demand curve and price elasticity of demand.

The demand curve is based upon the simple idea that people will buy more at a lower price than they will at a higher one. Although this is not always true, it does apply in the majority of cases. A typical demand curve is shown in Figure 10.4.

As we can see, when the price falls from P to P_1, demand rises from Q to Q_1. Thus, it is obvious that price is one of the most important determinants of demand. Demand will also be influenced by:

- the prices of substitute goods, e.g. buses instead of taxies;

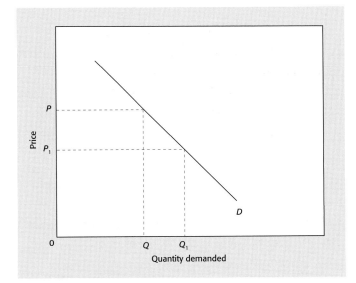

Figure 10.4 A demand curve

- the prices of complementary goods, e.g. eggs and bacon;
- the level of people's incomes;
- the changing tastes of consumers;
- the overall size of the population;
- government policies;
- the distribution of income among the population.

In reality, firms find it very difficult, if not impossible, to draw their demand curves. They actually only have an idea of how demand changes over a very small range of prices. However, if they can understand price elasticity of demand, they can make predictions about what is going to happen to their total sales revenue when they alter their prices.

Price elasticity of demand is a measure of the responsiveness of demand to changes in price. When the price of a product rises, demand will fall, but the question is 'by how much?' If it changes little, then the firm will be happy and total revenue will rise. We say that the price elasticity of demand is inelastic. If it changes a lot, then the firm will be unhappy, since total revenue will actually fall. We say that the price elasticity of demand is elastic. If price and quantity change by the same percentage, then the total revenue will be unchanged and we say that elasticity is unitary (equal to one). The relative levels of price elasticity of demand are shown in Figure 10.5.

The degree of elasticity is normally measured by using the following equation :

Price elasticity of demand (PED)

$$= \frac{\text{Percentage change in quantity demanded}}{\text{Percentage change in price}}$$

The value of PED is normally negative, because a fall in price normally produces a rise in demand. This movement in the opposite direction is called an inverse relationship but it is usual to ignore the negative sign since it is only the extent of change that matters. Table 10.2 shows how different values for PED are classified.

There are a number of factors that will determine the PED of a product:

How necessary the product is The more necessary people consider a product to be, the less they will react to price changes and the more inelastic will be their demand. If a good is considered to be a luxury, then it is likely that the demand for it will be relatively elastic.

How many competitors there are If there are many

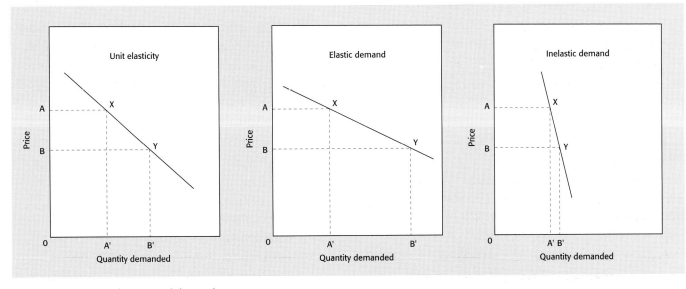

Figure 10.5 Varying elasticities of demand

Value of PED	Classification	Explanation
Zero	Perfectly inelastic demand	The same amount is demanded, no matter what the price. In reality, there is no product that would have this sort of PED.
Between 0 and 1	Inelastic demand	The percentage change in demand is less than the percentage change in price. If a firm faces this sort of demand, it can raise the price, not lose much demand and increase sales revenue. However, this cannot keep happening. As the price continues to rise, demand will become more elastic.
Unitary	Unit elasticity	The percentage change in demand is equal and opposite to the percentage change in price, so any price change will lead to an equal change in demand and the total sales revenue will remain constant. When PED = 1, sales revenue will be maximised.
Between 1 and infinity (∞)	Elastic demand	The percentage change in demand is greater than the percentage change in price. If a firm faces this sort of demand, then it can lower the price, pick up a lot more demand and increase sales revenue.
Infinity (∞)	Perfectly elastic demand	An infinitely large amount is demanded at one price and then demand falls to zero if the price is raised, even by the smallest amount. In reality, there is no product that would have this sort of PED.

Table 10.2 The potential range of elasticity and its effects

competitors, then there are a large number of substitutes for the product and consumers will quickly switch to another brand if the price rises. Thus, the demand for the product will be relatively elastic.

The price of the product If the price of a product is low, people will not really care as much about price increases and so demand will be relatively inelastic. However, as price continues to rise, the demand will start to become more elastic.

In an ideal world, firms will want to produce products that are necessities, with few substitutes. However, this is difficult to do for any length of time, because other firms enter the market, attracted by the inelastic demand and the profits.

Other approaches to pricing
Cost-based pricing

The basic idea is that firms will assess their costs per unit, in some way, and then add an amount on top of the calculated cost. There are a number of different methods of cost-based pricing that may be adopted:

◆ Mark-up pricing is usually carried out by retailers, who take the price that they pay to the producer or wholesaler for the product in question, and then just add a percentage mark up. The size of the mark up usually depends upon a combination of the strength of demand for the product, the number of other suppliers, and the age and standard life of the product. Sometimes it also depends on the tradition of the industry.

	£
Total cost of production	40
50% mark up on cost	20
Selling price	60

◆ Target pricing is where a company decides upon a price that will give a required rate of return at a certain level of output/sales. This is best explained by an example. If a company has costs of £200,000 when making 10,000 units of output and has an expected rate of return of 20%, then it will set its price by working out its total cost and expected return and then dividing the amount by the output.

	£
Total output costs 10,000	200,000
Required return 20%	40,000
Total return	240,000
Price per unit 240/10	24

◆ Full cost (or absorption cost) pricing is where the

company attempts to calculate a unit cost for the product and then adds an agreed profit margin. However, it is not always easy to allocate all of the costs of a firm to a specific product, especially if the firm makes a range of products. It is especially difficult to allocate the fixed costs.

The method differs from cost plus pricing only to the extent that a method of allocating fixed costs among the various products produced has to be found.

◆ Contribution cost (or marginal cost) pricing does not try to allocate the fixed costs to specific products. Instead of this, the firm calculates a unit variable cost for the product in question and then adds an extra amount that is known as a contribution to fixed costs. If enough units are sold, the total contribution will be enough to cover the fixed costs and to return a profit. For example, let us suppose that a firm produces a single product that has direct costs of £2 per unit and that the total fixed costs of the firm are £40,000 per year. The firm sets a contribution of £1 per unit and so sells the product at £3. Every unit sold makes a contribution towards the fixed costs of £1. If the firm sells 40,000 units in the year, then the fixed costs will be covered. Every unit sold over 40,000 will return a profit. Thus, if the firm sells 60,000 units, then the fixed costs will be covered and there will be £20,000 profit realised.

Obviously, it would be good for a firm if it produced a range of products that all made a positive contribution to the fixed costs. Then, each product is 'doing its bit'. As a general rule of thumb, a product that makes a positive contribution to fixed costs should be produced so long as there is spare capacity in the firm, it does not take the place of a product with a higher contribution and there is not another option that has a higher contribution. There are many firms that have excess capacity and hence use contribution cost pricing to attract extra business which will absorb the excess capacity.

Examples are train companies, for which there is substantial excess capacity except in the morning and evening rush hours. Even then, trains tend to run rather empty in one of the two directions. Electricity and telephone companies face the same

sort of situation. For fuller treatment of contribution cost pricing, see Chapter 11.

Competition-based pricing

This is the situation that exists where a firm will base its price upon the price set by its competitors. However, there are a number of different possible scenarios:

◆ Price leadership often exists in markets where there is one dominant firm and other firms simply charge a price based upon that set by the market leader.

◆ Some markets have a number of firms the same size, but prices are still similar in order to avoid a price war. An example of this would be the High Street banks

◆ Destroyer pricing: sometimes, firms will note the price of competitors' products and then deliberately undercut them in order to try to force them out of the market.

◆ Market pricing is where the price charged is based upon a study of the conditions that prevail in a certain market. This is sometimes also called consumer-based pricing, because, when the market is studied, it is in many ways the actions of consumers in that market that are actually being looked at. However, a study of the market is, in fact, more detailed than just looking at the responses of the consumers in the market. A number of different pricing strategies come under the heading of market-orientated pricing:

– Perceived value pricing (customer value pricing) is used in markets where demand is known to be inelastic and a price is placed upon the product that reflects its value, as perceived by the consumers in the market. The more prestigious the brand name, for example Rolex, the higher the perceived value, and so the higher the price that can be set.

– Price discrimination takes place in markets where it is possible to charge different groups of consumers different prices for the same product. An example of this would be airline firms, who charge many different rates for the same journey. Firms can price discriminate if there are different groups of consumers, with different elasticities of demand for the product, and where the firm is able to avoid resale between the groups. This is easier to do with services.

– Pioneer pricing takes place in new markets and there are normally two different approaches that may be taken. The first is penetration pricing, a relatively low price is set and strong promotion takes place in order to achieve a high volume of sales. Firms tend to adopt penetration pricing because they are attempting to gain a large market share. The second approach is market skimming, which usually occurs when a firm does not expect to have a lead in a market for a

Methods	Advantages	Disadvantages
Full cost pricing	The price set will cover all costs of production Easy to calculate for single-product firms where there is no doubt about fixed cost allocation Suitable for firms that are 'price makers' due to market dominance	Not necessarily accurate for firms with several products where there is doubt over the allocation of fixed costs Does not take market/competitive conditions into account Tends to be inflexible, e.g. there might be opportunities to increase price even higher If sales fall, average costs often rise – this could lead to the price being raised using this method
Contribution pricing	All variable costs will be covered by the price – and a contribution made to fixed costs Suitable for firms producing several products – fixed costs do not have to be allocated Flexible – price can be adapted to suit market conditions or to accept special orders	Fixed costs may not be covered If prices vary too much – due to the flexibility advantage – then regular customers might be annoyed
Competitor pricing	Almost essential for firms with little market power – price takers Flexible to market and competitive conditions	The price set may not cover all of the costs of production May have to vary price frequently due to changing market and competitive conditions
Price discrimination	Uses price elasticity knowledge to charge different prices in order to increase total revenue	Administrative costs of having different pricing levels Customers may switch to lower priced market Consumers paying higher prices may object and look for alternatives

Table 10.3 Summary of pricing methods

long time and so attempts to make relatively high short-term profits by charging a high price for as long as the product can hold its strong position. An example of this is pharmaceutical firms, who are given a seven-year monopoly under the Sainsbury Committee rules. They are able to charge high prices in order to recoup their considerable investments in research and to make high profits. It is not uncommon for them to lower their prices in the last year of their legal monopoly in order to hold their market share when other companies enter. A summary and evaluation of pricing methods is shown in Table 10.3.

Test Activity

Read the short case study below and then tackle the exercises that follow.

Case study – The *Daily Times*

The owner of the *Daily Times* newspaper is concerned about falling circulation (sales). He believes that newspaper readers are mainly influenced by price when making their decisions over which papers to buy. He therefore decided to cut the price of his paper from $1.50 to $1.20. In the following week circulation increased by 150,000 copies to 1,650,000. After four weeks, however, sales had fallen back to their original level. The owner was confused about the possible reasons for this and wondered whether he should cut the price again to $1.

(25 marks, 30 minutes)
(a) Calculate the PED in the first week after the price reduction. (4)
(b) Comment on your result in terms of the apparent price elasticity of this product. (2)
(c) Calculate the newspaper's daily revenue just before and just after the price cut. Comment on your results. (5)
(d) Explain two possible reasons why demand fell back to the original level some weeks after the price reduction. (6)
(e) What action would you advise the newspaper's owner take now to increase sales – would a further price cut be advisable? (8)

Test Activity

(12 marks, 15 minutes)
A firm sells three products. The price elasticity of demand is estimated to be:

A –3   **B** –0.5   **C** –1

(a) Explain what these results mean. (6)
(b) Explain what the effect on sales will be for each product if all prices rise by 10%. (6)

Promotional methods and strategies

Firms have a number of communication options, some are controllable and some are outside their control. The non-controllable methods are things such as word-of-mouth communication and independent and objective communication in magazines, such as *Which?* or *What Car?* There are four main methods of controllable promotion used by firms and they would normally employ a combination of those methods in their promotional strategies. The four areas are advertising, sales promotion, personal selling and publicity.

Advertising

Advertising is defined as purchased, non-personal, communication using mass media. These days, it is often called 'above-the-line' promotion. Where the mass media are used, it is expensive and so is only open to larger firms.

There are three main forms of advertising. The first is product advertising, where a firm tries to inform potential customers about the existence of a certain product. Thus, we see product advertisements for Coke or Burger King. The second is institutional advertising, where the firm gives information about its activities or attempts to show itself in a good light. Information about activities may be information regarding changes in opening hours or the starting of a delivery service. Firms may show themselves in a good light by advertising the environmental or charity work that they are involved in. The third form of advertising is primary advertising, where groups of firms, or the government, get together to promote a general category of a good, such as tea or health programmes.

Sales promotion

This covers a whole range of activities that offer incentives to purchase products or features that make the products attractive to the consumer. These activities are often known as 'below-the-line' promotion. They normally come under three headings and are shown in Table 10.4.

Personal selling

This takes place when promotion is carried out on a one-to-one, face-to-face basis. The consumer has the chance to ask questions about the product and the salesperson has the opportunity to gain the trust of the consumer and to tailor each presentation to the specific customer. Personal selling may take place inside retail outlets, where sales people deal with customers, such as in department stores or car showrooms. It may also occur when salespeople go out to sell a product, such as door-to-door salespeople. Examples are Avon Cosmetics, double-glazing or company representatives (reps) who sell to other firms.

A form of selling which is one-to-one and covers an increasing range of goods is through the telephone (tele-sales). Sometimes this is 'cold calling', where the person called is selected at random. More often there is evidence to suggest that the person called might be interested. Minor house developments are often sold in this way.

The big new player on the scene is the Internet, through which anything can be bought. It is expected that the proportion of goods sold in this way will grow rapidly. Effectively it turns the market for most products into a world market.

Salespeople carry out a number of different tasks. They give advice, demonstrate products, take orders, deliver goods, collect payment for the goods, deal with complaints and provide feedback to the firm from customers. There are many advantages to be gained from personal selling, but there is one large drawback of the process: it is expensive! The cost of selection, training and paying a sales force can be very high. However, more and more these days, firms are realising the importance of having quality salespeople, especially in the retail and service-providing companies.

Publicity

This is any promotional information about a firm or its products that is not directly paid for by the firm. Publicity is usually via press releases that the firm issues to the newspapers and magazines in the hope that they will be used. However, it can also occur when celebrities 'plug' a product in a speech or interview. Publicity can be uncontrollable and very damaging, such as during the BSE crisis of the late 1990s and its long-lasting effects on the sales of British beef. Most publicity on consumer programmes, of which there are, on average, two a week, is largely negative as consumers voice their complaints about a firm or a product and the programme follows it up.

Distribution

The physical distribution of products is much more

Methods of below-the-line promotion	Examples
Immediate consumer incentives – techniques that give an immediate benefit to the consumer in return for purchase.	Price reductions on packs; free samples; trial packs; bonus packs (e.g. 50% extra); premiums (e.g. two for the price of one); give aways (e.g. buy the first issue of a magazine and get the second one free); competitions with immediate prizes.
Delayed consumer incentives – techniques that give an eventual benefit to the consumer in return for purchase.	Coupons for future purchases; tokens and trading stamps; mail-in cash refunds; competitions with a specific finish date; charitable offers.
Other sales promotional methods	Point of sale (POS) displays Branding and packaging Exhibitions Sponsorships Credit facilities

Table 10.4 Sales promotion techniques

important than the consumer realises. A firm can have the best products, at the right prices, with excellent promotion, but if the products are not at the selling points when the consumers want them, the firm will soon discover how fickle the buying public can be.

Physical distribution covers the physical movement of products from producers to the eventual selling points. The costs of this are significant and, on average, can account for approximately 20% of the unit costs of a product. This is accounted for by:

♦ the costs of distribution facilities, such as storehouses;

♦ stock holding costs;

♦ transport costs;

♦ communication costs;

♦ costs of unitisation.

Distribution channels are the routes through which products go from the producer to the final consumer. These routes may be simple or complicated. The routes are normally expressed as two types.

Short-channel routes

These are routes where the supplier reaches the consumer either directly or through a retailer. Short-channel routes are shown in Figure 10.6.

Direct supply takes place through mail-order or telephone selling, but the rapidly growing revolution in selling is through the internet. Ecommerce is going to become the norm in the marketing of some goods and

Figure 10.6 Short distribution routes

increasingly common in others (see Tesco story, page 46).

Short-channel supply through retailers is very common and there is often an interesting balance of power between the producer and the retailer. In some cases, the producer is keen to have products sold through the retailer's outlets. An example of this would be a producer of foodstuffs who would be keen to supply to Marks and Spencer. In other cases, retailers, such as garages, are keen to supply a certain product, such as BMW motor cars. The relative power will change with the circumstances of the market. In many cases, producers and retailers work together on such matters as funding, design, promotion and staff training. Obviously, it is in the interests of both parties for products to sell well.

Long-channel routes

These are routes where there is an intermediary (or intermediaries) between the producer and the eventual consumers. Possible long, channel routes are shown in Figure 10.7.

Wholesalers have two main functions, those of 'breaking bulk' and stock holding. Many retailers are too small to buy products in bulk from the suppliers and so wholesalers do it, break the large quantities down into smaller amounts and then add a profit margin, selling smaller quantities to the retailers. The small corner shop is able to buy 24 packs of washing powder from the wholesaler as opposed to the minimum order of 2,400 packs from the supplier. Wholesalers are risk takers, in that the stock could be damaged or, worse still, become obsolete or out of fashion, while they hold it.

Agents are people who have the authority to enter into a contract on behalf of the producer they represent. Agents manage the relationship between the producer

Figure 10.7 Long-channel routes involving intermediaries

and the customer. They do not take legal ownership of the products involved and simply work for a fee or a percentage of the sales value. Agents are especially employed in foreign markets, where a producer may not have contacts or outlets. Agents are common in new car sales and customary in the sale of houses.

The main disadvantage of using long channels of distribution is that all of the intermediaries will add their profit margins and so the price to the final consumer is pushed up all the time. Also, the producer becomes isolated from the market and feedback and communication will be strained.

Activities

1 Which elements of the promotional mix will be most appropriate for the following events (rank the elements in order of importance in each case and explain your reasoning):
   (a) Christmas sales at Next?
   (b) Promoting a local church fete?
   (c) Informing customers of changed opening times at the local corner shop?
   (d) A local garage changing its franchise from Peugeot to Ford?
2 Identify four actual products that each use a different distribution channel. Identify the channel used in each case and explain why this channel is used.

Marketing plans

All firms, even very small ones, should have a marketing plan. No matter how simple, it is essential that marketing is co-ordinated by means of a sensible plan. If this is not the case, then the marketing activity may not be suitable for the market in question and may have elements that conflict. A possible framework for a plan is shown in Figure 10.8. It is useful to look at each step in detail.

Assess the present situation

This may be carried out by looking at the internal situation in the firm and the external market in which the firm is operating. The internal investigation may be carried out by analysing accounts, interviewing employees and assessing the strengths and weaknesses of the firm as part of a SWOT analysis. The external investigation may be carried out by conducting market

research, consulting experts, assessing the opportunities and threats for the firm as the remainder of the SWOT analysis and attempting to forecast where the market will go in the future.

Set marketing objectives

When that the firm has decided where it is now, it needs to ask 'What of the future'? Firms have a number of objectives that they might decide upon, such as:

◆ aiming for a greater market share in their existing markets;
◆ targeting new markets for their existing products;
◆ developing new products for their existing markets;
◆ diversifying into completely new markets;
◆ improving the image of the firm and its products;
◆ increasing profitability;
◆ increasing sales revenue.

The choice of objective(s) will have a great effect upon the marketing plan that needs to be adopted. When deciding upon objectives, the management of the firm will carefully weigh up risk. Some objectives will obviously carry more risks than others.

Devise a marketing plan

Now, the firm is looking at its objectives and asking the question, 'How to get there?' It is important that the

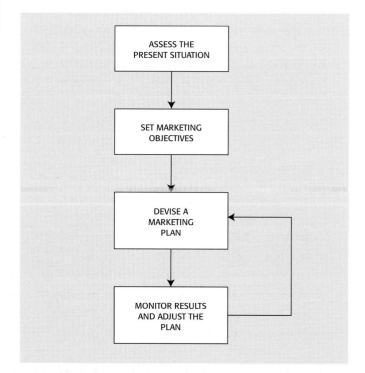

Figure 10.8 Flow diagram of the marketing planning process

plan adopted will achieve the objectives set. It will be a mixture of elements from the marketing mix and it is important that the elements do not clash. Too often, firms may decide to concentrate upon promotion, without considering how they will deal with the extra distribution pressures that may arise. A good example was the problems with McDonalds' 'Two for One' offer. In the same way, they may attempt to lower the price of a product, whilst attempting to raise its perceived consumer value.

Monitor results and adjust the plan

Once the plan has been running for an agreed time, the attainment of the required objectives should be constantly measured to ensure that the plan is operating effectively. If this is not the case, then the plan or the way of working should be adjusted to attempt to achieve the agreed objectives. In too many cases, plans are decided upon, implemented and then left to run with little analysis of their success until it is too late.

Over-to-you

Test revision questions

(60 marks, 1 hour)

1 State and explain the four variables that make up the marketing mix for a soft drink. (8)
2 Explain, with examples, the difference between 'above the line' and 'below the line' promotion. (4)
3 'I believe that the demand for our product is price elastic, therefore we should raise the price to increase sales revenue' Do you agree with this quote from a marketing manager? Explain your answer. (4)
4 Why is packaging so important in the marketing of most consumer products? (3)
5 State three requirements of a 'good product'. (3)
6 Explain two factors that will influence the choice of distribution routes for a consumer product of your choice. (4)
7 Draw, label and explain a product life cycle. (6)
8 Examine the usefulness of the product life cycle concept to a marketing manager. (6)
9 Explain two possible extension strategies that could be adopted for a soft drink. (4)
10 Why is it important for firms to develop new products? (4)
11 Explain how a marketing manager would use the product positioning map on page 125. (4)
12 Why is it important for firms to establish a 'marketing plan'? (5)
13 Outline the steps to be followed in setting a marketing plan. (5)

Discover and learn

1 Visit the furniture shops in your town. What can you learn about the pricing strategy that each has adopted? Explain the reasons for the differences you observe.
2 Work in groups. Select a product advertisement on TV. What is the message the advert conveys? How would you judge a good advert? On the basis of your criteria, is the advert you selected a good one? Justify your answer.

1 **Case study – Tubular Chairs Ltd**

(30 marks, 35 minutes)

Using the information from the case study at the end of Section 7 (p. 106), answer the following questions:

   (a) Outline 3 ways in which these products could be promoted. (6)
   (b) Identify and explain appropriate marketing objectives for Tubular Chairs Ltd. (10)
   (c) Devise a marketing strategy for Tubular Chairs Ltd. (14)

2 Read the case study opposite and then tackle the exercises that follow.

Case study – Dell to continue price cuts as PC sales slow down

'It's only a price war if you are losing money and losing market share'

Dell Computer, the world's number-two computer maker, yesterday promised to continue its price-cutting offensive. This is bad news for other, smaller, computer manufacturers.

The company pledged further cuts in the price of desktop PCs, storage units and computer servers to increase its share of the slowing US PC market.

It said its low stock levels enabled it to pass on price falls in micro chips faster than rivals in the industry; recently, there have been profits warning from Gateway, Apple and Hewlett-Packard.

Dell, which announced its own profits warning this month, has dismayed some analysts by reducing profit margins through discounting.

But Michael Dell, chairman and chief executive, said the move was intended to undercut high-margin rivals,

such as EMC and Sun Microsystems.

'You have not seen the last of our price-cutting,' Mr Dell said yesterday. 'It's only a price war if you are losing money and losing market share. We are gaining market share and increasing revenue.'

Source: Carlos Grande, *Financial Times*, 11 February 2001.

(25 marks, 30 minutes)

(a) What evidence is there in the case that the PED for Dell computers is greater than 1? (3)

(b) Why might the issue of psychological, or perceived value, pricing be important in setting prices for Dell computers? (4)

(c) Analyse the possible reasons for the price cutting strategy used by Dell. (8)

(d) Evaluate the possible long-term impact of this price cutting strategy on both Dell and computer consumers. (10)

Summary

In this chapter we have recognised that:

- Market planning is important.
- Most firms, whether they know it or not, employ a marketing mix.
- Products need to be developed and firms need to have a sensible portfolio of products, which are at varying stages of the product life cycle.
- Positioning of the products of a firm, and the firm itself, in the market is important.
- Firms should adopt a sensible pricing policy that supports their objectives.
- A knowledge of price elasticity of demand is especially helpful.
- Firms should adopt a mixture of promotional methods, within the budget available.
- Distribution needs to be efficient to ensure that products are available to consumers when the consumers require them.
- All firms should have a unique marketing strategy, which reflects the objectives of the firm.

Key words

Definitions of Key words can be found in the Glossary on page 269.

above the line
advertising
below the line
competition-based pricing
cost-based pricing
demand-based pricing
distribution channels
market positioning
marketing mix
personal selling

portfolio models
price elasticity of demand (PED)
pricing
product development
product life cycle
product positioning
promotional strategies
sales promotion

11 Using accounting and financial information

On completion of this chapter you should be able to:

➤ understand why accounting records are kept, which groups use them and why
➤ critically appraise the usefulness of these accounts from the point of the stakeholders
➤ understand and apply the double-entry principle of accounting to simple examples
➤ identify the different costs incurred by business activity and analyse situations in which costs are used by managers
➤ appreciate why overhead costs are sometimes apportioned and the limitations associated with this process
➤ understand the nature and purpose of contribution costing and comment critically on situations in which it might be used

Why keep accounting records?

Most people know that accounts are 'monetary records' of transactions. You probably keep simple records of your own income and expenditures – these would be basic accounts. Why do you do this? Probably because you want to know whether you are spending more than you are earning or to find out if you can afford to book that holiday you promised yourself once the 'AS' levels are over!

All businesses have to keep detailed records of purchases, sales and other transactions. Why is this? The easiest way to answer this question is to ask another one – what would happen if businesses did *not* keep accounting records? Table 11.1 lists some problems that would immediately arise and the groups who would be most affected.

None of these questions could be answered without detailed and up-to-date **accounts** being kept. We can

therefore say that accounts are financial records of business transactions, which are needed to provide essential information to groups both within and outside the organisation.

Internal and external users of accounting information

It is usual to divide the users of accounting information into internal and external users. The managers of a business are termed internal users and they will have access to much more detailed and up-to-date data than other groups. External users include the government, employees and shareholders and other stakeholders of the business. The following list gives details of all users of accounts and the reasons why they need accounting data:

Problem	Groups affected
How much did we buy from our suppliers and have they been paid yet?	Managers and suppliers (creditors)
How much profit did the business make last year?	Managers, shareholders and the tax authorities
Is the business able to repay the loan to the bank?	Managers and the bank
Did we pay wages to the workers last week?	Managers and workers

Table 11.1 Accounts and the interests of stakeholders

Business managers

- to measure the performance of the business;
- to help them take decisions, such as new investments, closing branches and launching new products;
- to control the operation of each department and division of the business;
- to set targets or budgets for the future and compare these with actual performance.

Banks

- to decide whether to lend money to the business;
- to decide whether to allow an increase in overdraft facilities;
- to decide whether to continue an overdraft facility or a loan.

Creditors, e.g. suppliers

- to see if the business is secure and liquid enough to pay off its debts;
- to decide whether the business is a good credit risk;
- to decide whether to press for payment.

Customers

- to decide whether the business is secure;
- to determine whether they will be assured of future supplies of the goods they are purchasing;
- to decide whether there will be security of spare parts and service facilities.

Government and tax authorities

- to calculate how much tax is due from the business;
- to determine whether the business is likely to expand and create more jobs;
- to decide whether the business is in danger of closing down, creating economic problems;
- to confirm that the business is staying within the law in all respects.

Investors, e.g. shareholders in the company

- to assess the value of the business and their investment in it;
- to decide whether the business is becoming more or less profitable;
- to determine what share of the profits investors are receiving;

- to decide whether the business has potential for growth;
- if they are potential investors, to compare these details with other businesses before making a decision to buy shares in a company;
- if they are actual investors, to decide whether to consider selling all or part of their holding.

Workforce

- to decide whether the business is secure enough to pay wages and salaries;
- to determine whether the business is likely to expand or be reduced in size;
- to determine whether jobs are secure;
- to find out whether, if profits are rising, a wage increase can be afforded;
- to find out how the average wage in the business compares with the salaries of directors.

Local community

- to see if the business is profitable and likely to expand;
- to determine whether the business is making losses and whether this could lead to closure;
- to decide whether there is a need to get involved and, if so, how.

Limitations of published accounts

All stakeholders in a business have a use for the published accounts of the business, but how effective are these in giving the stakeholders the information they require? It must be remembered that companies will only release the absolute minimum of accounting information. The directors do not wish sensitive data to fall into the hands of competitors or even pressure groups that could take action against their interests. The rules governing the disclosure of company accounting information are laid out in the Company Acts. Obtaining a copy of the published accounts of a plc will allow you to see what is required by law – and, just as importantly, what is not.

Issues that do not have to be publicised in a company Annual Report and Accounts include:

- details of the sales and profitability of each product or service provided;
- the research and development plans of the business;

- the precise expansion or rationalisation plans of the business;
- the performance of each department or division;
- evidence of the company's impact on the environment;
- future budgets or financial plans.

The data given are all 'past' data concerning the last financial year and this information could be several months old by the time it is published. Stakeholders are often concerned about the accuracy of the published accounts. No company can publish accounts that it knows to be deliberately and illegally misleading – these matters are checked by an independent firm of accountants known as auditors. However, accounting is not necessarily an exact 'science' and there are many areas of compiling accounts where 'judgement' is necessary. These judgements can often lead to a difference of opinion between accountants, e.g. over the precise value of unsold goods or the value of other assets, particularly 'intangible ones' (see Chapter 13). Where companies attempt to put a favourable gloss on their accounts, this is sometimes known as window dressing or creative accounting, because judgements are made that cast the accounts in a more favourable light. For these reasons, published accounts are a useful 'starting point' for stakeholders wishing to investigate the activities of a business, but they are by no means going to provide all of the answers.

Recording business transactions

Every time a business engages in a transaction, e.g. buying materials or selling goods to a customer, the accounting records of the business must include it. In all but the very smallest business, computer programs specially designed for keeping accounts would be used for this task. The job would be undertaken by the business's book-keeper.

How are business transactions actually recorded?

Suppose a single purchase is made by a customer in a shop. Table 11.2 shows the details of the transaction and the records that are kept.

The double-entry principle

Can you imagine the confusion amongst the users of accounts – including 'AS/A' level students! – if every business used different methods and principles in the

Transaction:	Purchase of 1kg of sugar
Effect:	Cash receipts increased by 59p (recorded on till roll)
	Stock of sugar reduced by 1 kg (recorded by computer program)
Documents:	Customer will have a till receipt
	Owner will have sale recorded on till roll
Ledger entries:	(These may be by hand in books of account or on a computer): Sales ledger 59p Cash book 59p
Trial balance:	All sales collated and ledger balances totalled
	All cash receipts totalled and cash book balanced
	All other account balances totalled
	Trial balance checks the accuracy of all entries
Final accounts:	From Trial balance the final accounts for a trading period are produced

Table 11.2 Recording a transaction

recording of transactions and in the compiling of final accounts? It would, for instance, be impossible to make comparisons between business accounts if every accountant had used his or her 'own' methods and techniques. The accounting profession agrees, therefore, to keep to certain very important accounting concepts. Most of them do not concern us until later in the course, but one concept is central to most accounting and you have seen it being used in the example above. This is the principle of **double entry**. It is simple to state since there is a 'dual aspect' to every business transaction and both sides of each transaction should be recorded if the accounts are to balance. The customer who bought the bag of sugar above caused two changes in the business:

- reduction of the shop's stock of sugar;
- increase in the owner's till receipts.

Every transaction has this double effect, as shown in Table 11.3. In both cases there are two sides to the transaction. The double-entry principle requires that both sides should be recorded and, when this is done, the accounts will be accurate and will balance.

Transaction	Dual aspect of the transaction
Sale of goods for cash	Goods have left the business Cash has been received by the business
Purchase of goods by cheque	Goods received by the business Business bank balance reduced

Table 11.3 The dual aspects of transactions

Activity

Identify the dual aspect of each of these transactions writing them out in the same way as in Table 11.3:

- payment of wages in cash;
- purchase of machinery by cheque;
- purchase by a customer of a new car;
- payment by the business of its electricity bill.

Management and financial accounting

There are several different branches of accounting in the UK. Two of the most important types of accountants are financial and management accountants. In general terms, the work of **financial accountants** is to prepare the published accounts of a business. The work of **management accountants** is to prepare detailed and frequent information for internal use by the managers of the business who need financial data to control the firm and take decisions for future success. The work of these two types of accountant is summarised in Table 11.4.

What are the costs of production?

Much of the information collected and used by accountants is concerned with the costs of production. The financial costs incurred in making a product or providing a service can be identified and classified in several ways. The most important categories are:

- direct costs;
- indirect costs.

Direct costs

These costs can be clearly identified with each unit of production and they vary with the level of output. Examples are:

- One of the direct costs of a hamburger in a fast-food restaurant is the cost of the meat.
- One of the direct costs for a garage in servicing a car is the labour cost of the mechanic.
- One of the direct costs in teaching is the salary of the teacher.

The two most common direct costs are labour and materials.

Financial accounting	Management accounting
Collection of data on daily transactions Preparation of the published report and accounts of a business – balance sheet, profit and loss account and cash statement	Preparation of information for managers on any financial aspect of a business, its departments and products
Information is used by external groups	Information is only made available to managers of the business – internal users
Accounts usually prepared once or twice a year	Accounting reports and data prepared as and when required by managers and owners
Accountants are bound by the rules and concepts of the accounting profession. Company Accounts must observe the requirements of the Company Acts	No set rules – accountants will produce information in the form requested
Covers past periods of time	Can cover past time periods, but can also be concerned with the present or on projections into the future

Table 11.4 The work of financial and management accountants

Activity

Identify one direct cost from each of these business activities:
- a carpenter making a wardrobe;
- an insurance company issuing a new motor insurance policy;
- a brewery delivering beer to a hotel;
- a bank agreeing an overdraft.

Why do you think it is important to identify direct costs?

Indirect costs

These costs cannot be identified with a unit of production because they are usually associated with performing a range of tasks or producing a range of products. Indirect costs are often referred to as overheads. Examples are:
- One indirect cost of a farm is the purchase of a tractor.
- One indirect cost of a supermarket is its promotional expenditure.
- One indirect cost of running a garage is the office.
- One indirect cost of running a school is cleaning it.

How do costs relate to the level of output?

It is important for management to understand that not all costs will vary directly in line with production increases or decreases. In the short run, i.e the period in which no changes to capacity can be made, costs may be classified as being:

Fixed costs   These remain fixed regardless of the level of output, e.g. rent of premises.

Variable costs   These vary as output changes, e.g. direct cost of materials.

Semi-variable costs   These include both a fixed and a variable element, e.g. electricity standing charge plus cost per unit used, salesperson's fixed basic wage plus a commission that varies with sales.

Problems in classifying costs

Did you find it easy to classify all of those costs? In practice, it may not be very easy or even worthwhile to classify every cost into the categories explained above.

1 Are labour costs necessarily variable, direct costs? Certainly not, because when labour is unoccupied because of lack of orders, most businesses will continue to employ and pay workers in the short run. Wages then become an overhead cost, which cannot be directly identified to any particular output. Similarly a television presenter may be employed on a fixed-contract salary, which will not be related to the amount of work done. In addition, the salaries of administration, selling and other staff are always considered to be an indirect cost, probably fixed in the short run, because these costs cannot be identified with any one of the firm's products or services.

2 Telephone charges in a busy factory could be directly allocated to each range of products made as long as an accurate and reliable record was kept of the purpose of each call. In practice, this may not be worth while and telephone charges would normally be considered as an indirect overhead expense.

Activity

Identify one indirect cost for each of these businesses:
- a building firm;
- a High Street bank;
- a TV repairer;
- a power station.

Explain why the cost is indirect in each case.

The CEGB's 2,000 MW oil-fired Pembroke power station in South Wales. Oil is the main direct cost and maintenance of the station is an indirect cost.
Source: Electricity Association.

Activity

The management of a small manufacturing firm is attempting to classify the costs of the business to help in future decision making. You have been asked to assist in this exercise. Classify these costs as shown in the following table. Explain why you have classified these costs in the way you have.

Cost	Direct or indirect	Fixed, variable or semi-variable
Rent		
Management salaries		
Electricity		
Piece-rate labour		
Depreciation of equipment		
Hire of company car		
Materials used in production		
Maintenance cost of machinery		

Introduction to costing methods

Managers need to know, as accurately as possible, the cost of each product or service produced by the firm. One reason for this is the need to make a pricing decision. Go back to Chapter 10 and re-read the section on pricing. In fact, buyers of many products will want an estimate or a quotation before they agree to purchase; managers may also need to decide whether production should be stopped, stepped up or switched to new methods or new materials. All of these things would be foolish to think about unless accurate costings were made first. Managers also need to compare actual costs with original targets or budgets and to compare the current period with past time periods. Therefore accurate product cost information is vital and the different approaches to calculating the cost of a product or service will now be considered.

In calculating the cost of a product, both direct labour and direct materials should be easy to identify and allocate or charge to each product. For instance, the materials used in making Product X are allocated directly to the cost of that product. These are not the only costs involved, of course. Overheads, or indirect costs, cannot be allocated directly to particular units of production but must be 'shared' between all of the items produced by a business. There is more than one way of 'sharing' or apportioning these costs and therefore there may be more than one 'answer' to the question: 'How much does a product cost to produce?'

Costing methods: important concepts

Before studying the alternative costing methods, various important concepts need to be understood.

Cost centres   A cost centre is an area of responsibility, such as a department, to which costs can be charged. Examples of cost centres are:
- in a manufacturing business: products, departments, factories, particular processes or stages in the production, such as assembly, for example;
- in a hotel: the restaurant, reception, bar, room letting, and conference section, for example.

Different businesses will use different cost centres, which are appropriate to their own needs.

Profit centres   A profit centre is a section of a business in which both costs and revenues can be identified. Examples of profit centres are:
- each branch of a chain of shops;
- each department of a department store;
- in a multi-product firm, each product line.

Why do businesses use cost and profit centres?   If an organisation is divided into these centres, certain benefits are likely to be gained:
- Managers will have targets to work towards.
- These targets can help to motivate and control a business division.
- The individual performances of divisions and their managers can be assessed and compared.
- Work can be monitored and decisions made about the future.

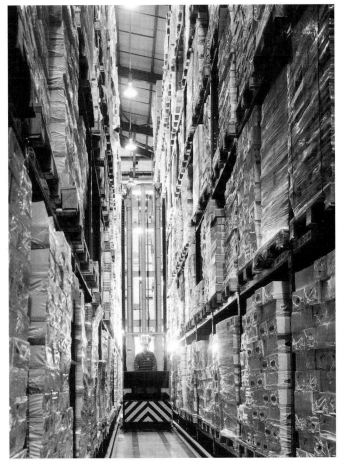

Warehouse at Cambridge University Press – costs of operating this are distribution overheads
Source: Cambridge University Press.

Overheads   They are usually classified into four main groups:

Production overheads   These include factory rent and rates, depreciation of equipment and power.

Selling and distribution overheads   These include warehouse, packing and distribution costs and salaries of sales staff.

Administration overheads   These include office rent and rates, clerical and executive salaries.

Finance overheads   These include the interest on loans.

Unit cost   This is the average cost of producing each unit of output:

Unit cost = Total cost divided by the number of units produced.

A firm produces 20,000 desks at a total cost of £1,000,000. Unit cost is 1,000,000 divided by 20,000 = £50. Clearly, unit cost is an essential step towards pricing the desks.

Test Activity

Case study – Heath Electronics Ltd

The firm produces two product ranges, a pump for central heating systems and an extractor fan. Both products pass through three process cost centres during their manufacture, although different equipment is used for each product.

The direct labour and material costs have been identified and allocated to the two products as follows:

	Pump (£'000)	Fan (£'000)
Machining department:		
Direct materials	100	150
Direct labour	40	10
Assembly department:		
Direct labour	80	40
Testing department:		
Direct labour	30	20
Total direct cost	250	220

The total overheads of the business in 2002 were:

	£'000
Rent and rates	60
Power	20
Administration	80
Depreciation	40
Total overheads	200

(20 marks, 10 minutes)

The management accountant has been asked for the unit cost of both products. In 2002, 50,000 pumps and 40,000 fans were produced. The accountant first uses full costing to arrive at a result for unit cost. He:

◆ identify direct labour costs for each of the pump and the fan, and calculate the total direct labour cost for both products; (4)
◆ express (a) the direct labour cost of the pump and (b) the direct labour cost of the fan as a percentage of the total direct labour cost; (6)
◆ divide the total fixed costs between the pump and the fan in proportion to the use of total direct labour in producing each product; (6)
◆ comment on the method that you have used. (4)

Activity

Identify four possible cost centres within your own school or college. Discuss with the managers or heads of these cost centres the benefits and drawbacks of using this form of organisation. Check with your Bursar/College accountant the accuracy of your answer.

Allocating costs
Full costing technique

Using this method accountants take the total overheads incurred by the organisation and share them on the basis of one simple rule. For example, total overheads could be divided between products and cost centres on the basis of the proportion of total direct labour costs each account for. In the case of Heath Electronics Ltd total direct labour amounts to £220,000. The pump accounts for £150,000 of this total and the fan for £70,000. They will each have to absorb overheads in the same proportions.

The full costing statement now looks like this:

	Pump (£)	Fan (£)
Direct materials	100,000	150,000
Total direct labour	150,000	70,000
% of total direct labour	68.57%	31.43%
Apportioned overheads	136,363	63,637
Total cost	386,363	283,637

Activities

1 Calculate the unit cost of both the pump and the fan using the full costing results.
2 Give reasons why you would or would not be satisfied with these results for decision making, e.g. establishing market prices for the two products.
3 Draw up a new full costing statement, basing your division of the overheads on the basis of total direct costs for each of the products (see Activity p. 131).
4 Recalculate the unit cost for each product on the assumption that the firm actually produces 60,000 pumps and 30,000 fans.

Full costing – an evaluation
◆ Full costing is relatively easy to calculate and understand.
◆ Full costing is particularly relevant for single-product businesses.
◆ All costs are allocated (compare with contribution costing).
◆ Full costing is a good basis for pricing decisions.

But:
◆ There is no attempt to allocate each overhead cost to cost centres on the basis of actual expenditure incurred.
◆ Arbitrary methods can lead to inconsistencies between departments and products.
◆ It is sometimes dangerous to use this cost method for making decisions because the cost figures arrived at can be misleading.
◆ If full costing is used, it is essential to allocate on the same basis over time; otherwise sensible year-on-year comparisons cannot be made.
◆ The average full cost will only be accurate if the actual level of output is equal to that used in the calculation.

Marginal costing or contribution costing approach
This approach to costing solves the problem of the appropriate sharing out of overhead costs in a different way – it does not apportion them at all! Instead, the method concentrates on two very important accounting concepts.
◆ Marginal cost is the cost of producing an extra unit. This extra cost will clearly be a direct cost. For example, if the total cost of producing 100 units is £400,000 and the total cost of producing 101 units is £400,050, the marginal cost is £50.
◆ The contribution of a product is the revenue gained from selling a product less its marginal (direct) costs. This is not the same as profit, which can only be calculated after overheads have also been deducted. For example, if that 101st unit with a marginal cost of £50 is sold for £70, it has made a contribution towards fixed costs of £20. The unit contribution is found as the difference between the sale price (£70) and the marginal cost (£50), i.e. £20.

LUsing accounting and financial information

Case study – Marginal costing/contribution statement for Oxford Printers Ltd

	Novel	Textbook
	£	£
Sales revenue	50,000	100,000
Direct materials	15,000	35,000
Direct labour	20,000	50,000
Other directly apportioned costs	10,000	5,000
Total marginal cost	45,000	90,000
Contribution	5,000	10,000

As can be seen, this statement avoids apportioning overhead costs between these two products. Overheads cannot be ignored altogether, however. They are needed to calculate the profit or loss of the business.

Total contribution for Oxford Printers Ltd = £15,000

If total overheads amounted to £12,000 then:

Profit = Contribution less overheads.

Therefore the business has made a profit of £3,000.

This link between contribution, overheads and profit is a crucial one and you can see the role of contribution costing in pricing decisions if you read Chapter 10.

Test Activity

An electrical assembly firm produces three products. The following data (in £) is available:

Products	X	Y	Z
Unit direct costs:			
Labour	5	7	9
Materials	4	12	10
Selling price	20	30	21

Total overhead costs are £40,000

(10 marks, 10 minutes)

(a) Calculate the unit contribution of each product. (3)

(b) If sales of each product are 1,000, calculate the total contribution of each product. (4)

(c) Calculate the profit or loss made by the firm at the current output level. (3)

Contribution costing and decision making

Contribution costing has very important advantages over full costing when management plans to take important decisions based on cost data.

Should a firm stop making a product?

If a business makes more than one product or provides more than one service, marginal costing shows managers which product or service is making the greatest or least contribution to overheads and profit. If full costing were used instead, a manager could decide to stop producing a good that seemed to be making a loss, even though it might still be making a positive contribution. In cases such as this, ending the production of a good making a positive contribution will reduce the overall profits of the business. The following case study illustrates this point.

Should a business accept a contract or a purchase offer at below full cost?

If a firm has spare capacity or if it is trying to enter a new market segment, marginal costing assists managers in deciding whether to accept an order at below the full cost of the product or service. Hotels often offer very low rates to customers in off-peak seasons, arguing that it is better to earn a contribution from additional guests than to leave rooms empty.

If contracts are accepted or customers gained by using prices below full cost, this can, in certain circumstances, lead to an increase in the total profits of the business. There are dangers in this policy, however:

- Existing customers may learn of the lower prices being offered and demand similar treatment. If all goods or services being sold by a business are sold at just above marginal cost, then this could make earning a profit very unlikely.
- When high prices are a key feature in establishing the exclusivity of a brand, then to offer some customers lower prices could destroy a hard won image.
- Where there is no excess capacity, sales at contribution cost may be losing sales based on the full cost.
- In some circumstances lower priced goods or services may leak into the higher priced market.

In fact many businesses do use contribution-cost selling, but build in ways of ensuring that there is no leak into the higher priced market. For example, railway companies sell Saver and Supersaver tickets, but make the offers exclusive by banning their use for certain days, times or journeys. Gas and electricity companies use time bands for their cheaper priced use of energy. The following case study illustrates this principle of using marginal cost pricing in accepting new business.

Test Activities

1 Read the case study below and then tackle the exercises that follow.

Case study – Onyx Garages

The Managing Director of Onyx Garages Ltd was concerned about the profitability of the business. She had asked for cost details of the three divisions of the business – repairs, petrol sales and spare parts – together with a breakdown of sales revenue. Unaware of the differences between costing approaches, she had asked for overheads to be apportioned on full-cost principles according to labour cost. The data opposite had been provided.

When the Managing Director saw these details, she is quoted as saying: 'If we close down our repair division, then total annual profits will rise – they would have been £15,000 higher last year if we had shut down repairs in 1999.'

Spanner	1998 (£000s)		
	Repairs	Petrol	Parts
Sales revenue (A)	27,000	300,000	68,000
Direct labour cost	15,000	25,000	10,000
Direct materials	5,000	180,000	35,000
Other directly apportioned costs	4,000	10,000	5,000
Apportioned overheads (total £60,000)	18,000	30,000	12,000
Total cost (B)	42,000	245,000	62,000
Profit/(Loss) (A – B)	(15,000)	55,000	6,000

Overall profit made by the business in 1999
= 55,000 + 6000 − 15,000 = £46,000.

(25 marks, 30 minutes)

(a) As a trainee accountant working with this company you have been asked for your opinion on the figures above. Use the marginal costing method and calculate a new costing statement. (10)

(b) Do you agree with the MD that the repairs division should be closed in order to increase overall garage profits? Justify your answer with both quantitative and qualitative reasons. (15)

2 Read the case study below and then answer the questions that follow.

Case study – Bureau Office Supplies Ltd

The Marketing Director of Bureau Office Supplies Ltd was determined to gain a large order for computer desks from a major local authority. There was spare capacity on the production line as a recent contract had been cancelled at short notice. The buyer for the local authority wanted to purchase 1,000 desks at a price of £70 each. Bureau's Marketing Director knew this was a price lower than that offered to most customers. The order was being discussed at a Board meeting and the Production Manager presented the following cost data:

Computer desks full unit cost statement

Direct labour	£25
Direct materials	£30
Apportioned overheads	£30
Full unit cost	£85

The Production Manager was amazed at the willingness of the marketing department to sell the desks for £70 each. 'How can you possibly justify selling these desks at a total loss of £15,000'?', he asked.

Who has the better case? Is the Marketing Director justified in his attempt to capture this order? Is the Production Manager right to be concerned at the apparent loss the order will make?

The appropriate decision depends on answers to the following questions:

◆ Does the order make a contribution to overheads by the price exceeding direct costs?
◆ Is there spare capacity?
◆ Can the order be accepted without further overhead expenditure?
◆ Are other orders likely?
◆ Is there another customer who is prepared to pay a higher price for these goods?
◆ Will the price of the order become known to other customers?

Test Activities

(25 marks, 30 minutes)

1 Use the marginal costing approach to reach your own conclusion on the wisdom of accepting the order discussed in the Bureau Office case study. (10)

2 Prepare a brief report, containing your marginal costing statement, to the Board, together with a recommendation on whether to accept the order or not. Consider both quantitative and qualitative factors in coming to your recommendation. (15)

Contribution costing – a summary

◆ Overhead costs are not allocated to cost centres, so contribution costing avoids inaccuracies and arbitrary allocations.

◆ Decisions about a product or department are made on the basis of contribution to overheads.

◆ Excess capacity is more likely to be effectively used.

But:

◆ By ignoring overhead costs until the final calculation of the businesses profit or loss, contribution costing does not consider that some products and departments may actually incur much higher fixed costs than others.

◆ Emphasises contribution in decision making. It may lead managers to choose to maintain the production of goods just because of a positive contribution.

◆ As in all areas of decision making, qualitative factors may be important too, e.g. the image a product gives the business. In addition, products with a low contribution may be part of a range of goods produced by the firm and to cease producing one would reduce the appeal of the whole range.

Evaluation of the costing approaches
Full costing

Full costing can be useful for single-product firms and as a quick guideline to the costs of products. However, it does have serious flaws for multi-product businesses because the approach does not apportion overheads on a real basis. The final costing figure may, in fact, be inaccurate or misleading. Thus, full costing data could

be used to make comparisons of costs calculated on the same basis over time but it should not be widely used for decision making.

Marginal or contribution costing

Marginal or contribution costing is now the most widely used method for decision making, because it accepts that fixed overhead costs must be paid during a particular time period, regardless of the level of production. This should help management take appropriate decisions when faced with the option, for example, of accepting a new contract or scrapping a product altogether. Marginal costing does have one potential drawback, however. If overheads are set aside for costing purposes, there is a danger that they could be overlooked altogether. This could mean that contribution is confused with profit and pricing decisions for products could ignore the fixed-cost element. Eventually overheads have to be paid for and this important fact must not be forgotten when applying the marginal costing approach.

Break-even analysis

Break-even analysis can be undertaken in two ways:
◆ the graphical method;
◆ the equation method.

The graphical method – the break-even chart   The break-even chart requires a graph with the axes shown in Figure 11.1.

Figure 11.1 The axes for a break-even chart

The chart itself is usually drawn showing three pieces of information:

- fixed costs, which, in the short term, will not vary with the level of output and which must be paid whether the firm produces anything or not;
- total costs, which are the addition of fixed and variable costs; we will assume, initially at least, that variable costs vary in direct proportion to output;
- sales revenue obtained by multiplying selling price by output level.

Figure 11.2 shows a typical break-even chart. Note carefully the following points:

- The fixed-cost line is horizontal.
- The total-cost line begins at the level of fixed costs, the difference between total and fixed costs being accounted for by variable costs.
- Sales revenue starts at the origin; no sales = no revenue (0).
- The variable cost line is drawn to aid your understanding of how the chart is constructed. It is not necessary to the chart and is often omitted.

The point at which the total cost and sales revenue lines cross (E) is the break-even point. At production levels below the break-even point, the business is making a loss; at production levels above the break-even point the business is making a profit.

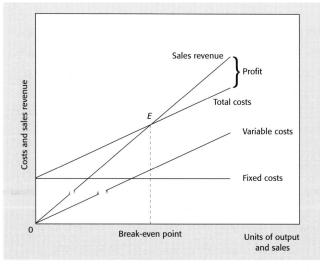

Figure 11.2 A typical break-even chart

Margin of safety The margin of safety is defined as the amount by which sales exceed the break-even point. This is a useful indication of how much sales could fall without the firm falling into loss. For example, if break-even output is 400 units and current production is 600 units, the margin of safety is 200 units.

Test Activity

The following data relates to a single-product business.

Direct labour per unit	£12
Direct materials per unit	£18
Variable overheads per unit	£5
Fixed costs	£200,000
Selling price	£45

Maximum capacity of the factory is 30,000 units.

(15 marks, 15 minutes)

(a) Draw a break-even chart using this data. (10)

(b) Show the break-even point and identify the break-even level of output. (3)

(c) Identify from the graph the profit expected at maximum capacity. (2)

This can be expressed as a percentage of the break-even point, for example:

Production over break-even point = 200 = 33.33%.

If a firm is producing below the point E it is in danger. This is sometimes expressed as a negative margin of safety. Hence if break-even output is 400 and the firm is producing at 350 units it has a margin of safety of −50. The minus sign simply tells us that the production level is below break-even.

The break-even equation A formula can be used to calculate break even:

$$\frac{\text{Fixed Costs}}{\text{Contribution per Unit}}$$

If fixed costs are £200,000 and the contribution per unit of output is £50 then the break-even level of production is

$$\frac{200,000}{50} = 4,000 \text{ units}$$

This is an exact answer and therefore likely to be more accurate than many chart readings. The same method can be used if a manager wants to determine a target profit level and establish the level of output required to achieve it: Suppose the target profit is £25,000. This is treated as if it were an extra fixed cost and the calculation is

$$\frac{200,000 + £25,000}{50} \quad \frac{225,000}{50} = 4,500 \text{ units produced.}$$

Test Activity

Read the case study below and then tackle the exercises that follow.

Case study – Windcheater Roofracks

The sole owner of Windcheater Roofracks needs to expand output as a result of increasing demand from motor accessory shops. Current output capacity has been reached at 5,000 units per year. Each rack is sold to the retailers for £40. Production costs are:

Direct labour	£10
Direct materials	£12
Fixed costs	£54,000

The owner is considering two options for expansion:

Option 1   Extend the existing premises but keep the same method of production. This would increase fixed costs by £27,000 per year, but direct costs would remain unchanged. Capacity would be doubled.

Option 2   Purchase new machinery, which will speed up the production process and cut down on wasted materials. Fixed costs would rise by £6,000 per year, but direct costs would be reduced by £2 per unit. Output capacity would increase by 50%.

(40 marks, 40 minutes)

(a) Drawing the two break-even charts for these options would assist the owner in making this decision, but other issues may have to be considered as well.
  ◆ Construct break-even charts for these two options. Identify the break-even point for each. (12)
  ◆ What is the maximum profit obtainable in each case? (4)
  ◆ If demand next year is expected to be 7,000 units, what would be the margin of safety in both cases? (2)
  ◆ Which option would you advise the owner to choose? Give both numerical and non-numerical reasons for your decision. (10)

(b) The owner of Winchester Roofracks discovers that the fixed costs for option 1 will be 20% greater. Use a break-even chart to determine the new break-even point and then the equation to verify it. (6)

(c) In option 2 the increase in fixed costs is £8,000 and the direct costs fall by £2.50 per unit:
  ◆ explain why the direct costs might fall; (3)
  ◆ determine the new break-even point. (3)

Break-even analysis – further uses

In addition to obtaining break-even points and margins of safety, break-even charts can also be used to demonstrate the impact of different options on the operations of a business. In this way they can assist in the decision-making process. However, they must be used with some caution as indicated in the evaluation section below.

Evaluation of break-even analysis

Benefits of break-even analysis are:
  ◆ Charts are relatively easy to construct and interpret.
  ◆ It provides useful guidelines to management on break-even points, safety margins and profit/loss levels at different rates of output.
  ◆ Comparisons can be made between different options by constructing new charts to show changed circumstances. In the case study above, charts could be amended to show the possible impact on profit and break-even point of a change in the product's selling price.
  ◆ The equation produces a precise break-even result.

The limitations are:
  ◆ the assumption that costs and revenues are expressed in straight lines, which is a major drawback;
  ◆ the problem that not all costs can be reliably or consistently classified as fixed or variable costs;
  ◆ the assumption that everything produced will be sold;
  ◆ the assumption that fixed costs will remain fixed regardless of the level of output.

Activity

Explain why the assumptions that the lines in the break-even chart are straight are not realistic and will limit the usefulness of break-even analysis. Give examples to support your argument.

Over-to-you

Test revision questions

(60 marks, 1 hour)

1 List four potential users of the accounts of a plc such as Tesco. (4)

2 Explain why each of these users would find the accounts useful. (4)

3 Explain what the double-entry principle means. (3)

4 Define what is meant by fixed costs and give three examples for a bakery. (5)

5 Distinguish between direct and indirect costs. (3)

6 Explain how the full cost of a product is calculated. (3)

7 How is the contribution made by a product calculated? (3)

8 The profit made on a product is not the same as the contribution made by it – explain why not. (4)

9 Analyse the advantages and disadvantages of cull costing. (6)

10 Why do managers usually use contribution (or marginal costing) when taking a decision about a special order contract? Support your explanation with simple figures. (8)

11 If a product sells for £15, its variable costs of production are £6 and fixed costs are £18,000, calculate the break-even level of output. (4)

12 Explain two business decisions that could be helped by using break-even analysis. (6)

13 Evaluate the usefulness of break-even analysis in one of the situations described in the answer to 12. (7)

Discover and learn

Obtain a copy of a plc's Report and Published Accounts. You can try either writing to the head office or obtaining one via the company's Internet page. The *Financial Times* operates a company reports service, which enables you to obtain copies from several different companies at the same time.

1 Read both the Chairman's Report and the Chief Executive's Report.
How useful do you think these would be to:
(a) shareholders?
(b) future investors in the company?
(c) the workforce?
(d) competitors?

2 Read the Auditor's report. What is it telling you about the published accounts? Can the readers of the accounts be certain that these accounts are completely accurate and objective?

3 Work in small groups. Consider the setting up of a small business of your choice in your area. Discover or estimate the probable direct and indirect costs of:
(a) setting up the business;
(b) running it in the first year.
You may find that literature available from banks will be very helpful to you in this exercise.

4 Exchange your work with another group and comment upon the data you have been given. Try to be positive in your comments.

5 When your work is returned:
(a) discuss it with the other groups and ensure you know what they mean by their comments;
(b) make the changes they suggest or justify your decision not to make them.

6 Read the case studies and then tackle the exercises that follow.

Case study – Abbey Restaurant

Abbey Restaurant has a good local reputation for first-class meals at first-class prices. It has a loyal customer base, but the manager, Phil, is concerned about the disappointing number of new customers. Total revenue had fallen over the last few months and Phil believed that this was partly due to the closure of the head office of an insurance company. Job losses occurred at all levels of the organisation, especially amongst middle managers. Phil was considering introducing a new menu that would offer less variety and less complicated dishes. He considered that the new items on the menu would be cheaper to produce and he would not have to replace one of the skilled chefs, who had just given in his notice. Phil estimated that the number of customers could increase by 20% per night on average as he had noticed that a recently opened medium-price café–bar was full to bursting virtually every night.

Phil had shown the following financial data to the restaurant's accountant, who started to do some calculations before advising Phil on whether to adopt the new lower-priced menu:

Current situation:	
Sales turnover per month (600 customers @ average of £20)	£12,000
Average variable cost per meal	£7
Overhead costs per month (including salaries of kitchen staff)	£7,000
Proposed new menu:	
Average meal price	£14
Average variable cost per meal	£4
Overheads per month (including salaries of kitchen staff)	£6,000

(30 marks, 30 minutes)

(a) What are the maximum monthly profit figures for the two menu options? (8)

(b) On the basis of your calculations and the financial data provided, would you advise Phil to adopt the new menu? Explain your answer. (12)

(c) What other, non-financial factors should Phil consider before taking the final decision? Explain their significance to Phil's business. (10)

Case study – Cosmic Cases

Cosmic Cases manufacture a range of suitcases. There are four sizes of case, ranging from a small vanity case to a large luggage case with wheels for mobility. The cases are sold mainly through department stores, either as a complete set or, more frequently, as individual items. The latest six-monthly costing statement (see below) had just been prepared, together with the sales figures for the same period. Jill Grealey, the managing director was concerned about the performance of the mid-sized case and wanted to discuss the data with the finance director.

Costing statement for 6 months ending 31/3/2000				
	Vanity case	**Small suitcase**	**Medium suitcase**	**Large suitcase**
Total direct costs	£30,000	£35,000	£12,000	£20,000
Allocated overheads	£15,000	£12,500	£10,000	£10,000
Total costs	£45,000	£47,500	£22,000	£30,000
Total output	5,000	4,000	1,000	1,500

The selling prices to the department stores were:

Vanity case	£15	Small case	£18
Medium case	£20	Large case	£25

(22 marks, 20 minutes)

(a) Calculate the total revenue (price × quantity sold) for each size case. (6)

(b) Calculate the total profit/loss made by each size case. (3)

(c) Calculate the contribution made by each size case. (3)

(d) Jill Grealey wanted to stop production of the mid-sized case. She said to the Finance Director: 'If we stop making this case, then our total profits will rise.' The finance director was convinced that this would be the wrong decision to make. As a management consultant, write a report to the managing director giving your recommendation for the action to be taken with the mid-sized case. You should justify your recommendation with both numerical and non-numerical factors. (10)

Case study – Midtown Imperial Hotel

'We would be mad to accept this special request over £1000 below our normal price and £500 below the cost of providing the conference and audiovisual facilities.'

The hotel manager, Rajesh, was annoyed that Sheila Burns, the Conference Manager of the Imperial Hotel, had even bothered to consult him about the enquiry from the Friends of General Hospital for the use of the conference suite for their annual general meeting involving 100 people. Sheila had been asked for a price to organise the Friends' AGM and had used the normal hotel practice of adding 50% to the total variable cost of the conference, plus the overhead allocation. This had been too much for the charity, so they had requested a reduction and had suggested a lower figure of £2,200. As the AGM was planned for the end of February, a very slack time for all hotels, Sheila had been tempted to take up the offer and had put it to Rajesh for his approval. She knew that many of the Friends were quite influential people with business interests and she believed that this could be to the hotel's long-term advantage.

The costing statement for the conference suite was as follows:

Variable cost per delegate including food, three drinks each and waiting staff	£15
Hotel overhead allocation per conference	£1,000

In addition, the Friends had requested some special audiovisual equipment, which the hotel would have to hire in for the day at a cost of £200

(20 marks, 20 minutes)

(a) Calculate the full cost of the conference for the Friends of the General Hospital. (3)

(b) Calculate the price that the hotel would normally charge for a conference of this size with the equipment requested. (4)

(c) What would the contribution to the hotel's overheads and profit be if the conference suite were let out for £2,200? (3)

(d) Advise the hotel manager on the advisability of accepting this special request for the use of the conference facilities. Include both quantitative and qualitative data in your answer. (10)

Summary

In this chapter we have recognised that:

- There are two types of accounting, financial accounting and management accounting.

- There is a difference in both the nature and purpose of the two types of accounting and these can be explained in terms of the point of view of the stakeholders who are involved and in terms of the uses that are made of accounting data.

- There are various principles of accounting, chief of which is the concept of double entry.

- All businesses have to identify both cost and profit centres and to use costing approaches to allow determination of total costs, unit costs and the contribution that a product might make.

- Contribution costing and full costing may lead to different pricing decisions, which should be understood in the context of pricing decisions considered in Chapter 10.

- Break-even analysis is a forecasting tool for business.

- It can be used in either graphical or formula form.

- There are limitations on the use of break-even analysis.

Key words

Definitions of Key words can be found in the Glossary on page 269.

accounts	indirect costs
break-even analysis	management accounting
contribution costing	marginal costing
direct costs	overheads
double entry	published accounts
financial accounting	semi-variable costs
fixed costs	variable costs
full costing	

12 Cash flow and budgets

On completion of this chapter you should be able to:

➤ recognise the need to control the flow of money into and out of a business

➤ understand the importance of managing cash flow and explain why profit is not the same as cash

➤ construct, interpret and analyse cash-flow budgets

➤ demonstrate understanding of the problems caused by poor cash flow and of ways in which problems can be reduced or removed

➤ show understanding of the nature and importance of budgeting

➤ compare actual and budgeted performance by simple variance analysis and analyse the causes of such variances

Why cash flow is important to business activity

According to the Department of Trade and Industry, more business failures result from lack of cash than for any other reason. This is particularly true for new businesses. Why is cash – and in particular the flow of cash into and out of a business – so important and how can managers try to avoid cash problems developing? Consider these problems resulting from too little cash:

◆ Without sufficient cash flow a business will not be able to pay its many suppliers on time. These creditors may stop supplying goods or impose strict conditions, such as 'cash on delivery'. Discounts will be lost for prompt payment of bills. Other traders may be less prepared to deal with the firm except on a cash basis. In extreme cases, the creditors could take the company (or the business owners if not a company) to court.

◆ Wages and salaries may not be paid on time and this will cause poor motivation, absenteeism, higher labour turnover and industrial unrest.

◆ New capital assets cannot be afforded and this can reduce business efficiency.

◆ Tax bills may not be paid – government has little patience with such cases and, again, could take legal action.

The relationship between profit and cash

'If a business is profitable the firm is certain to have a cash surplus too.' This is one of the most common incorrect beliefs of students of Business Studies. Profit is not the same as cash. A profitable business may run out of cash – called insolvency – whilst a business recording a loss may have a cash surplus. How is this possible? There are several reasons why the profit or loss recorded by a business in one time period will not be the same as its cash balance. Here are two of the most frequently occurring:

◆ A business may be selling more of its output on credit than previously. Therefore, a profit is being made as the goods are being recorded as sold, but the cash payment from customers will be received at some time in the future. This period of credit may leave the firm dangerously short of cash or liquid funds.

◆ Capital expenditure is recorded on the profit and loss account under depreciation as an expense. However, only a proportion of the cost of additional capital spending will be recorded as depreciation each year, yet the total cash payment may occur in the first year.

Activity

Alex Tyrrell is an antique dealer. In June he bought five chairs for £50 cash. He sold them the same day for £30 each. He agreed that half of the money would be paid in cash and the customer would pay the rest in the following month.

(a) Calculate the profit made on the five chairs.

(b) How much cash did Alex gain from the purchase and sale of the chairs in June?

This simple example shows that profit does not equal cash.

Activity

In which of these cases will the cash needs of a business be greater:

(a) ◆ Materials paid for in cash.
   ◆ Wages and materials paid for.
   ◆ Goods produced.
   ◆ Goods sold on credit.
   ◆ Cash received one month later.

(b) ◆ Goods bought for cash today.
   ◆ Goods sold for cash tomorrow.

Explain your answer.

Managing cash flow

Managing the flows of cash into and out of a business is one of the most important tasks of management. In order to do this effectively they will need to assess:

◆ the size and likely timing of cash flows into the business; this will largely depend on how long debtors take to pay their bills;

◆ the size and likely timing of payments out of the business; this will largely depend on the costs of the business and the period of credit offered by suppliers;

◆ whether there are sources of finance to cover periods when cash shortages could arise.

You will notice from the points above that time is of great significance to cash-flow management.

Cash-flow forecasts: the benefits to business

A cash-flow forecast is an attempt by management to plan ahead, to prevent future liquidity problems. Cash-flow forecasts contain estimates of cash receipts and payments over the coming months – these are taken from the budgets of the business. Each month or quarter the anticipated 'cash in hand' or cash deficit (overdraft) is calculated. If an overdraft is predicted, then the firm's bankers must be warned and arrangements made for an appropriate overdraft facility. As a general rule, bank managers are much more prepared to arrange loan facilities for organisations that can demonstrate they have planned their financial needs and shown that they should be able to repay loans. This is particularly the case with new businesses. The preparation of a cash-flow forecast will show the bank manager that the owners of the new business are aware

of the need to manage cash flow carefully. If there is no overdraft arrangement or if it is insufficient, then management will have to take rapid action to overcome a shortage of cash. There will always be periods of the year when large cash surpluses may build up, since most businesses have a seasonal element to their sales. Examples are:

◆ Many businesses expect a boost to sales in the period leading up to Christmas.

◆ A seaside guesthouse will be very much busier in the summer months. In fact it may close in winter.

◆ A florist expects high sales for 'Mother's Day' and for Easter.

◆ Farmers receive most of their income in summer and autumn.

Large cash balances have an opportunity cost in terms of lost interest and plans could be made to use these resources in a more profitable way, e.g. by purchasing short-term investments. Overdrafts have an even greater cost in terms of interest charges.

A typical cash flow forecast is shown in Table 12.1.

Dealing with cash-flow problems

If the cash-flow forecast predicts negative cash flows and negative cash balances, managers have certain options they can consider to tackle this problem:

Reducing or delaying expenditure There may be ways in which the business can cut costs, such as reducing advertising spending or delaying the purchase of capital equipment. Clearly, these decisions would have a beneficial impact on short-term cash flow, but they might have negative effects on business performance in the longer term.

BEL Engineering Ltd						
Cash-flow forecast year (£000s)						
Month	Jan.	Feb.	Mar.	Apr.	May	June
Receipts						
Cash sales	200	220	220	200	200	240
Payments from debtors	120	140	140	220	200	100
Other (e.g. loan received)					50	
Total cash receipts	320	360	360	420	450	340
Payments						
Materials	80	90	90	130	160	190
Labour	50	50	60	60	90	90
Rent	150			150		
Interest		25			25	
Advertising	10	10	10	10	60	10
Electricity	15			15		
Salaries	40	40	40	60	60	60
Purchase of fixed assets		100				280
Total cash payments	345	315	200	425	395	630
Net cash flow	(25)	45	160	(5)	55	(290)
Opening cash balance	25	0	45	205	200	255
Closing cash balance	0	45	205	200	255	(35)

Table 12.1 An example cash-flow forecast

Notes:
- The opening cash balance for each month is the closing cash balance for the previous month.
- Payments from debtors are cash received from debtors for goods previously sold on credit, probably in the previous month for most debtors.
- Net cash flow may be negative and this is indicated in brackets. You can see from the forecast that BEL were expecting a negative net cash flow and negative closing balance in June. What action can the management take to deal with this? The options are looked at after the next task.

Rent or lease equipment rather than buying it outright
This is very common with IT equipment, for example. Such moves reduce short-term cash outflows but will lead to regular, if smaller, payments in the future.

Delay the payment of bills – *extending the credit period*
Suppliers may be unwilling to accept later payment – especially from new businesses with an unknown credit history.

Get cash in more quickly from the sale of goods This could be done in a number of ways:
- Insisting on cash at the time of sale. This could

Test Activity

Read the case study below and then tackle the exercises that follow.

Case study – Tourist Trinkets Ltd
Tourist Trinkets Ltd owns a warehouse supplying souvenir retailers in town.

Forecast sales (£000s) are:

Jan.	Feb.	Mar.	Apr.	May	June
6	8	8	14	16	18

On past experience, 50% of sales will be cash sales. One month's credit is offered for credit sales. Stock is purchased in the month prior to sales. Sufficient stock is purchased to cover the following month's sales. The average mark-up on cost is 100%. Suppliers allow one month's credit on purchases.

Other expenses are:
- labour – £600 per month except May and June when it is expected to be £1,200;
- rent of £1,800 per half year payable in Jan. and July;
- electricity and other charges, £600 per quarter paid in Jan., Apr., July and Oct.;
- advertising of £100 per month except June when it is budgeted to increase to £500;
- interest charges of £1,000 payable in May;
- management salaries of £2,000 per month.

Opening cash balance in January is £1,500.

In January the firm is expecting payment from its debtors of £1,000.

(20 marks, 40 minutes)
(a) Write a note to the manager of Tourist Trinkets Ltd. listing three benefits to the business from preparing a cash-flow forecast. (6)
(b) Prepare a month-by-month cash budget for Tourist Trinkets Ltd for the first six months. Use the same format as that given above. If you are able to use a spreadsheet software package, prepare the cash-flow statement with it. (14)

lead to loss of business as in many industries it is usual to offer customers a period of time to pay for goods purchased.
- Reducing the debtor period. This could also lead customers to taking their custom to other businesses that offer extended credit terms.

- Selling the debts to a specialist institution, such as a debt factor. This option is covered in detail in Chapter 13.
- Using a bank overdraft. This is a flexible source of funds which – up to a predetermined limit – can be varied to meet the changing cash needs of a business. The interest rate tends to be high and it is possible for banks to recall overdrafts at very short notice if they are concerned about the future of a business. This action often leads to failure of the business.
- Obtain a short-term loan, which is less variable than an overdraft and often borrowed at lower interest rates. If there is likely to be a long-term need to increase the cash position of the business – such as during a period of rapid expansion – then a long-term loan would be appropriate.
- An established business could also sell some of its assets – such as buildings – to a leasing company and lease them back. This sale and leaseback option will give an injection of cash into the business, but will lead to continuing cash payments, which have to be allowed for in cash forecasts.

Evaluation of cash budgets

As with any judgement about the future, cash-flow

Activity

Read the case study below and then tackle the exercises that follow.

Case study – setting up in business

Aled Jones was disappointed to hear the news that the Bank of England had announced an unexpected increase in interest rates. He had just submitted his business plan to the bank manager for approval for the business start-up loan and overdraft arrangement he would need to establish his proposed building business. The business was to specialise in building expensive conservatories. Aled had read that the Bank of England had taken the decision to prevent further increases in the inflation – the rate at which prices were rising. Aled's business plan had contained the following cash budget for the first six months of trading:

	March	April	May	June	July	August
Receipts						
Capital injection	5,000	0	0	0	0	0
Start-up loan	15,000	0	0	0	0	0
Cash sales	1,000	3,000	5,000	5,000	16,000	19,000
Payments from debtors	0	12,000	10,000	10,000	12,000	13,000
Total	21,000	15,000	15,000	15,000	28,000	32,000
Payments						
Capital expenditure	10,000	0	0	0	0	0
Labour	2,000	6,000	7,000	7,000	7,000	7,000
Materials	5,000	10,000	8,000	8,000	10,000	12,000
Overheads inc. interest	5,000	7,000	7,000	7,000	9,000	9,000
Total	22,000	23,000	22,000	22,000	26,000	28,000
Net cash flow	(1,000)	(8,000)	(7,000)	(7,000)	2,000	4,000
Opening cash balance	0	(1,000)	(9,000)	(16,000)	(23,000)	(21,000)
Closing cash balance	(1,000)	(9,000)	(16,000)	(23,000)	(21,000)	(17,000)

(a) Explain how the use of a spreadsheet would have assisted Aled in compiling his cash-flow forecast.

(b) Explain *two* ways in which the increase in interest rates could have an impact on the cash-flow forecast.

(c) If inflation did rise, how would this be likely to affect the cash flow of the business?

(d) Discuss the usefulness to Aled of constructing the cash-flow forecast as part of the business plan.

(e) Recommend to Aled three ways to reduce the negative cash flows of his business in the first six months.

forecasts need to be treated with caution. They have several significant advantages, as already noted above, but too much reliance must not be placed upon their accuracy. This would be particularly true for a new business, which was uncertain about future sales levels. Similarly, any business cash forecast could be made inaccurate by changes in the external economic environment, such as movements in interest rates or inflation at a faster rate than anticipated. For this reason, some businesses prepare optimistic and pessimistic cash budgets to reflect these possible changes. This is easy to do on spreadsheet applications and allows businesses to prepare for more than one future scenario.

Budgets and budgetary control: introduction

We all plan for the future to some degree. We plan for the long term – such as career choices – and we plan for the short term – such as how to spend the weekend. This should apply to business organisations too, although the plans of a business are likely to be expressed in financial terms. This process is known as budgeting and a budget is a detailed and financial plan for a future time period. Planning for the future is important for all organisations. If no plans are made, an organisation drifts without real direction and purpose. Managers will not be able to allocate the scarce resources of the business effectively without a plan to work towards. Employees working in an organisation without plans for future action are likely to feel demotivated, as they have no targets to work towards – or to be praised for achieving. If no targets are set, then an organisation cannot review its progress because it has no set objective to achieve.

Setting budgets and establishing plans for future actions would therefore appear to have six main purposes:

Planning Translates the objectives of the firm into intentions for achievement. It gives a sense of purpose to the workforce.

Effective allocation of resources
Allocation to departments

There will be priorities to discuss, since what can be done is always likely to be greater than resources will permit.

Setting targets to be achieved Research shows that most people work better if they have a realisable target at which to aim.

Co-ordination People will have to work effectively together if targets set are to be achieved.
Monitoring Plans cannot be left once in place. There is a need to check regularly that the objective is still within reach. All kinds of conditions may change and businesses cannot afford to assume that everything is fine.
Modifying If there is evidence to suggest that the objective cannot be reached, then either the plan or the way of working towards it must be changed.
Reviewing At the end of the budgetary period, the actual results should be compared with the original budgets.

Key features of budgeting

A budget is not simply a forecast, although much of the data on which it is based will come from forecasts, since we are looking into the future. Budgets are plans that organisations aim to fulfil. A forecast is a prediction of what could occur in the future given certain conditions. Budgets may be established for any part of an organisation as long as the outcome of its operation is quantifiable. Thus, there may be sales budgets, capital expenditure budgets, labour cost budgets and so on.

Co-ordination between departments when establishing budgets is essential. This should avoid departments making conflicting plans, e.g. the marketing department may be planning to increase sales by lowering prices, yet the production department may be planning to reduce output and lower the direct-labour cost budget. These targets will conflict and need to be reconciled.

Setting of budgets should be an exercise in participation. Decisions regarding budgets should be made with the subordinate managers, who will be involved in putting them into effect. Those who are to be held responsible for fulfilling a budget should be involved in setting it. This sense of 'ownership' not only helps to motivate the department concerned to achieve the targets but also leads to the establishment of more realistic targets.

The budget will be used to review the performance

of a department and the managers of that department will be appraised on their effectiveness in reaching targets. Successful and unsuccessful managers can therefore be identified. These stages of involvement in constructing the budget, taking responsibility for its operation and being appraised in terms of success, are the human aspects of the process. They have a very important role to play in the motivation of staff.

How budgets are commonly prepared

Stage 1 The most important organisational objectives for the coming year are established – these will be based on:

- the previous performance;
- external changes likely to affect the organisation;
- forecasts based on research.

Stage 2 The key or limiting factor that is most likely to influence the growth or success of the organisation must be identified. For most businesses this is likely to be sales. Therefore, the sales budget will be the first to be prepared. Care and accuracy are essential at this stage, because an error in the key-factor budget will distort all other budgets as well. For example, if the sales budget proves to be inaccurate, then cash, production, labour budgets etc. will be rendered inaccurate too.

Stage 3 The sales budget is prepared.

Stage 4 The subsidiary budgets are prepared, which will now be based on the plans contained in the sales budget. These will include cash

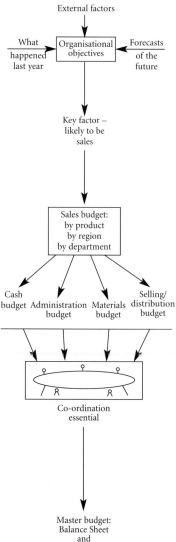

budget, administration budget, materials budget, selling and distribution budget.

Stage 5 These budgets are co-ordinated to ensure consistency. This may be undertaken by a budgetary committee with special responsibility for ensuring that budgets do not conflict with each other.

Stage 6 A master budget is prepared that contains the main details of all other budgets and concludes with a budgeted profit and loss account and balance sheet.

Stage 7 The master budget is then presented to the Board – hopefully for their approval.

Once approved, the budgets will become the operational plans of each department and cost centre within the organisation. However, the overall plan is usually too long a time period to be a stimulating target and will be broken down into short periods like a month or even a week.

Setting budgets – incremental or zero budgeting?

There are several ways in which the budget level can be set. Two of the most widely used are:

Incremental budgeting This uses last year's budget as a basis and an adjustment is made for the coming year. In many businesses that operate in highly competitive markets there may be plans to lower the cost budget for departments each year, but to raise the sales budgets. This puts increased pressure on many staff to achieve higher productivity.

Incremental budgeting does not allow for unforeseen events. Using last year's figure as a basis means that each department does not have to justify its whole budget for the coming year – only the change or 'increment'.

Zero budgeting This requires all departments and budget holders to justify their whole budget each year. This is time consuming, as a fundamental review of the work and importance of each budget-holding section is needed each year. However, it does provide added incentive for managers to defend the work of their own section. Also, changing situations can be reflected in very different budget levels each year.

Budgetary control – variance analysis

At the end of the budgeted period the actual performance of the organisation needs to be compared with the original targets and reasons for differences must be investigated. This process is known as variance analysis. A variance is the difference between budgeted and actual figures. This is an essential part of budgeting for a number of reasons:

- It measures differences from the planned performance of each department.
- It assists in analysing the causes of deviations from budget. For example, if actual profit is below budget, was this due to lower sales revenue or higher costs?
- The reasons for the deviations from the original planned levels can be used to change future budgets in order to make them more accurate. For example, if sales revenue is lower than planned as a result of market resistance to higher prices, then

this knowledge could be used to help prepare future budgets.

The performance of each individual budget holding section may be appraised in an accurate and objective way.

If the variance has had the effect of increasing profit, e.g. sales revenue higher than budgeted for, then it is termed a **favourable variance**. If the variance has had the effect of reducing profit, e.g. direct material costs higher than budgeted for, then it is termed an **unfavourable** or adverse **variance**. These distinctions can be demonstrated by the following self-assessment task. Favourable variances *add* to profit and are shown with a positive sign. Adverse variances reduce profit and are shown with a negative sign.

Activity

With the help of the tables in the case study below tackle the exercises that follow.

Case study – Oasis Cookers Ltd

Oasis Cookers Ltd – (£000s)

	Budget	Actual	Variance
Sales revenue	165,000	150,000	−150,000
less Cost of materials	80,000	70,000	
Labour cost	22,000	23,000	
Gross profit	63,000	57,000	
less Overheads	40,000	43,000	−3,000
Net profit	23,000	14,000	

(a) Calculate the variances missing above and indicate whether they are favourable or unfavourable variances.

(b) Suggest two possible reasons for the variance in:
- sales revenue;
- labour cost.

Department	Budget	Actual	Variance
Selling and distribution	8,000	6,000	
Administration	9,000	8,000	
Production	22,000	27,000	
Personnel	1,000	2,000	

(c) From the Oasis Cookers Ltd. overhead budget and actual results shown above, calculate the variances and indicate whether they are favourable or unfavourable.

Budgets and budgetary control – an evaluation

Setting, agreeing and controlling budgets is time consuming. Budgets can fail to reflect changing circumstances and become inflexible. Budget holders can look upon a budget as a limit up to which they can spend, whether their department needs all of the resources or not. Therefore, is the budgetary process worthwhile?

Try to think of the alternative:

◆ Without a detailed and co-ordinated set of plans for allocating money and resources of the business, who would decide 'who gets what'?

◆ Without a clear sales budget as the cornerstone of the budgetary process, how would departments know how much to produce or to spend on sales promotion or how many people to employ?

◆ Would it be possible to assess how the business had done or how well individual departments had performed without a clear series of targets with which to compare performance?

◆ Without figures to monitor progress during the budgetary period, how would it be possible to know where the business is or to suggest changes that might be made?

◆ Budgets have to be agreed and administered. This gives responsibility and a sense of direction to those delegated to work with them. These human advantages are difficult to ensure without planned money values to work with.

The arguments in favour of some form of budgetary setting and control are clear to many managers.

Over-to-you

Test revision questions

(60 marks, 1 hour)

1 Outline two reasons why existing businesses should prepare cash flow forecasts. (6)

2 Explain why cash flow forecasts are of particular importance for a new business proposal. (4)

3 Examine two factors that could explain why the cash flow forecast for a hairdressing business proves to be inaccurate. (6)

4 Explain how 'sale and leaseback' can improve cash flow. (3)

5 Outline the advantages and disadvantages of two other methods of improving a firm's short-term cash flow. (8)

6 Distinguish between a forecast and a budget. (3)

7 Outline three benefits to a business of introducing a system of budgetary control. (6)

8 Explain the process of setting a firm's budgets for the coming year. (6)

9 What would a sales budget contain? (3)

10 Distinguish between zero and incremental budgeting. (5)

11 What is variance analysis? (3)

12 Outline two ways in which an unfavourable profit variance might arise. (4)

13 Explain why it is important for budget setting to involve participation between managers and those responsible for meeting the budgets. (3)

Discover and learn

1 Refer to the published accounts of a public limited company.

(a) Find out what the retained profits were for the last financial year (retained profits are those reinvested in the business).

(b) Find out the cash balance of the business at the end of the previous financial year and the start of the last one. By how much has the cash balance changed? Is this the same as the retained profit of the business? If not, suggest three possible reasons why the two figures are different.

2 Forecast your own cash income for the next month. Include payments from work, parents, etc. Forecast your monthly cash outgoings under headings such as travel, social, clothes, etc.

(a) Are you forecasted to make a cash surplus or deficit? Record all income and expenditure over this period.

(b) Did you have a cash surplus or deficit?

(c) How different was it from your forecast?

(d) Can you identify why it was different?

3 Find out whether your school or college uses zero or incremental budgeting for departmental expenditure. Try to discover why the choice was made.

4 Read the case studies and then tackle the exercises that follow.

Case study – Gita Fashions Ltd

The bank manager had just been on the telephone to Gita. The bank was not prepared to pay a cheque she had written to her main supplier. 'Did you know that your overdraft has reached its limit of £15,000?' the bank manager had queried. 'We are only prepared to consider continuing with your overdraft arrangement if you come into the office tomorrow with a cash flow forecast for the next three months.'

Gita had never worried too much about finance as this had always been looked after by her partner. He had recently left the business, taking his share of the capital with him. Gita had used her savings to help pay him his share of the business. Now she had no idea how the business had reached such a poor cash position and she certainly could not put any more money in herself.

All that evening she looked over the accounting records of the business, including all recent sales invoices and bills for materials and other expenses. She had managed to arrive at some idea of what the business could expect over the next three months in terms of cash payments and receipts.

Sales were likely to be £12,000 for the next two months (starting in July) and 50% lower than this in the third month. Half of these sales would be for cash. Half would be on one month's credit. She had sold £8,000 on credit in June.

She estimated all overhead expenses to be £6,000 per month. Labour was likely to be £3,000 per month. Materials, paid for one month after delivery, were always one half of monthly sales. They were delivered in the same month in which the goods they were used to make were sold. Opening cash was negative – the overdraft was the opening balance for the three-monthly period.

(25 marks, 25 minutes)

(a) Prepare a three-month cash-flow forecast for Gita's business starting in July. (10)

(b) Would you advise the bank manager to increase the overdraft limit? (3)

(c) What additional information would help you to advise the bank manager? (4)

(d) Explain to Gita how a cash-flow forecast might have helped her business avoid the problem it now faces. (8)

Case study – Karmali Carpets plc

The Managing Director of Karmali Carpets was angry. The profits of the business had fallen for the third year running and he was determined to put all the blame on the Sales Manager, Sarah Fellows. He called her into his office to discuss the latest company results.

'The company's profits have worsened again this year and your department must take the blame – sales revenue was down from what I had expected it to be,' he grumbled. 'Why can't you manage to increase sales each year?'

Sarah expressed real surprise at this complaint. 'What do you mean sales are down? We sold more carpets this year than ever before. I know we had to increase our discounts towards the end of the year, but you are always telling us "if they come through that door, then they go home with a carpet" and we acted on that.'

'But you failed to reach your annual targets that I finalised last month.'

Sarah defended herself by saying 'Those targets were received after most of the year had gone and I never thought they were realistic anyway. I wanted to increase advertising, but you rejected my new campaign because you used the money to buy new computers for the accounts office. How can I be expected to reach your targets, when I don't believe in them myself?'

(20 marks, 20 minutes)

(a) From the text above, which departments in this business would be likely to benefit from a correctly managed system of budgetary control? (4)

(b) Comment critically on the Managing Director's approach to budgeting. (6)

(c) Write a report to the MD outlining the likely advantages to his organisation from a budgetary control system as outlined in this section. Consider the way in which you would advise him to both set and use the budgets. (10)

Summary

In this chapter we have recognised that:

- Business activity needs to be planned and translated into working targets.

- Business activity needs to be controlled in ways that will ensure that actual results are likely to be in accordance with the plan.

- Business activity needs to be reviewed to check whether the actual results were in accordance with the budget. If variances are found these need to be analysed and explanations produced for them.

- Business activity needs to be modified. The effort should be to bring the activity back towards the budgeted outcome. However, in some circumstances the budget may prove to have been unrealistic and it is the budgeted outcome that will need to be changed.

- There are various techniques that are appropriate for carrying out these operations.

Key words

Definitions of Key words can be found in the Glossary on page 269.

budget	incremental budgeting
capital expenditure	unfavourable variance
cash-flow forecasts	variance analysis
favourable variance	zero budgeting

13 The final accounts of a business

On completion of this chapter you should be able to:

➤ understand what the final accounts of a business contain

➤ explain and analyse the significance of the three main final accounts – balance sheet, profit and loss account and cash-flow statement

➤ notes to accounts

➤ limitations

➤ understand the importance of assessing and reducing risk

➤ understand how investments can be appraised using pay back and accounting rate of return methods

➤ understand the nature and significance of working capital

The final accounts of a business

At the end of each accounting period, usually one year, accountants will draw up the final accounts of the business. For companies, these will be included in the Annual Report and Accounts, which are sent to every shareholder. Table 13.1 gives details of the final accounts of limited companies, as these are the accounts you are most likely to come across in your studies

Profit and loss account – what it shows about a business

The profit and loss account records the revenue, costs and profit of a business over a given period of time, usually a year. There are two versions of the profit and loss account:

◆ A detailed profit and loss account can be constructed for internal use because managers will need as much information as possible.

◆ A less detailed summary will appear in the published accounts of companies. The content of this is laid down by the Company Acts and provides a minimum of information. This is because, although the shareholders would use additional information to assess the performance of their investment, the published accounts are also available to competitors and detailed data could give them a real insight into their rivals' strengths and weaknesses.

The version used in this chapter is one based on the published accounts but with additional information where this aids understanding. An example is given in Table 13.2.

The account	What it shows
The profit and loss account	The gross and net profit of the company. Details of how the net profit is split up (or appropriated) between dividends to shareholders and retained profits
The balance sheet	The net worth of the company. This is the difference between the value of what a company owns (assets) and what it owes (liabilities)
Cash-flow statement	Where cash was received from and what it was spent on

Table 13.1 Final accounts of limited companies – what they contain

Profit and loss account for Energen plc for the year ended 29 March 1999 (£m)		
	Sales turnover	3,060
(minus)	Cost of sales	(1,840)
(equals)	Gross profit	1,220
(minus)	Overheads	(580)
(equals)	Operating or net profit	640
(minus)	Interest	(80)
(equals)	Pre-tax profits	560
(minus)	Tax @ 20%	(112)
(equals)	Profit after tax	448
	Appropriation	
(minus)	Dividends to shareholders	200
(equals)	Retained profit	248

Table 13.2 Profit and loss account for Energen Ltd for the year ended 29 March 2003 (£m)

Definitions of terms used

Sales turnover (or sales revenue)

This is the total value of sales made during the trading period; in the example above this is during the financial year ending on 29 March 99. It is most important to understand that, as not all sales are for cash in most businesses, the sales turnover figure is *not* the same as cash received by the business. This point is covered in more detail later. The formula for calculating sales turnover is:

Sales turnover = quantity sold × price.

Therefore, if 120 items are sold at £2 each, the sales turnover is £240.

Cost of sales (or cost of goods sold)

This is the direct cost of purchasing the goods that were sold during the financial year. This figure is unlikely to be the same as the total value of goods purchased by the company during this period as items may have been added to stocks or taken from them. Only the goods used and sold during the year will be recorded in cost of sales. The formula used is:

Cost of sales = Opening stocks plus purchases minus closing stocks

This can be laid out as:

Opening stocks (at the start of the year)	£500
Purchases during the year	£2,500
Total stock	£3,000
Closing stocks (at the end of the year)	(£750)
Cost of goods sold	£2,250

Gross profit (or loss)

This is the difference between sales turnover and cost of sales. This is the final entry in the trading account section of the total profit and loss account.

Activities

1 Calculate gross profit for Cosy Corner Retailers Ltd for the financial year ending 31 March 2001. Show all of your workings.
   1,500 items sold for £5 each; opening stocks were valued at £500; purchases totalled £3,000; closing stocks were £1,000.

2 Cambridge Boxes Ltd sold 3,500 units in the last financial year ending 31 December 2001. The selling price was £4. Opening stocks were 200 boxes. The business purchased 4,000 boxes during the year. All boxes cost the company £2 each.
   Calculate the value of closing stocks and the company's gross profit in 2001.

Overheads

These are costs or expenses of the business that are not directly related to the number of items made or sold. These can include rent and business rates, management salaries and lighting costs.

Operating or net profit

This is the profit made, before tax and interest, but after all costs of sales and overheads have been deducted from sales turnover. This is the final entry in the profit and loss section of the total profit and loss account.

Tax

Limited companies pay corporation tax on their profits before they pay dividends or keep profits within the business.

Dividends

This is the share of the profits paid to shareholders as a return for investing in the company.

Retained profit

This is the profit left after all deductions, including dividends, have been made. This is 'ploughed back' into the company as a source of finance. These last three entries form what is known as the appropriation section of the profit and loss account. This is because it gives details of how net profits have been divided or appropriated.

Activity

Using the layout used above, construct a profit and loss account for Lancashire Traders Ltd from the following data:

Sales turnover – 5,000 items	@ £11.00
Opening stocks	£3,000
Corporation tax rate	20%
Interest paid	£1,000
Purchases	£40,000
Closing stocks	£8,000
Overhead expenses	£12,000
Dividends	£4,000

The balance sheet – what it shows about a business

The balance sheet records the net wealth of a business at one moment in time. In a company this net wealth 'belongs' to the shareholders. Table 13.3 shows an example of a balance sheet for a limited company.

Fixed assets		2,500
Current assets:		
Stocks	120	
Debtors	650	
Cash	20	
	790	
less:		
Current liabilities:		
Trade creditors	450	
Overdraft	30	
	(480)	
Net current assets		310
ASSETS EMPLOYED		2,810
FINANCED BY:		
Long-term liabilities	250	
Share capital	2,000	
Profit and loss reserves	560	
CAPITAL EMPLOYED		2,810

Table 13.3 Balance sheet for Energen Ltd as at 29.3.03 (£m)

Points to note

- Companies have to publish the profit and loss account and the balance sheet for the previous financial year as well in order to allow easy comparison. These have not been included in the above examples for reasons of clarity.
- The titles of both accounts are very important as they identify both the account and the company. Whereas the profit and loss account covers the whole financial year, the balance sheet is a statement of the estimated value of the company at one moment in time – the end of the financial year.

Definitions of terms used

Assets

These include anything of measurable value owned by the business.

Fixed assets

These are items owned by the business that are likely to be kept and used for more than one year. The most common examples are land, buildings, vehicles and machinery. These are all **tangible** assets as they have a physical existence. Businesses can also own **intangible assets** – these cannot be seen but still have value in the business. Examples are:

- patents;
- trademarks;
- copyrights;
- goodwill.

The reputation and prestige of a business that has been operating for some time also gives value to the business over and above the value of its physical assets. This is called the **goodwill** of a business and should normally only feature on a balance sheet just after it has been purchased for more than its assets are worth, or when the business is being prepared for sale. Disputes can arise between accountants about the valuation of intangible assets and there is a current debate regarding the asset value of well-known brand names. There is scope for varying the value of these and other intangibles on the balance sheet in order to give a better picture of the company's position. This is one aspect of 'window dressing' of accounts that can reduce objectivity.

Current assets

Current assets are those that are expected to be converted into cash within one year. The most common examples are stocks, debtors (customers who have bought goods on credit) and cash/bank balance.

Current liabilities

Current liabilities are debts that are likely to have to be repaid within a year. Typical current liabilities include trade creditors (suppliers who have allowed the business credit), bank overdraft and unpaid dividends and tax. Current liabilities are usually referred to as 'creditors – amounts falling due within one year'.

Net current assets

This is the difference between current assets and current liabilities. It is also known as **working capital** and is the finance tied up in the business for the day-to-day operation of the business.

Share capital and reserves

These are collectively called the **'shareholders' funds'**. They represent the capital originally paid into the business when the shareholders bought shares (share capital) or the retained profits of the business (profit and loss reserves) that the shareholders have accepted should be kept in the business. Reserves can also appear on the balance sheet if a company believes that its fixed assets have increased in value (revaluation reserve) or if it sells additional shares for more than their 'nominal' value (share premium reserve).

Capital employed

This is the total of all of the long-term finance of the business. It is the sum of share capital, reserves and long-term liabilities. These funds are used to finance the company's assets and, for this reason, assets employed always equals capital employed.

Activities

1 Copy out this table and indicate in which category the following items would appear on a company balance sheet.

	Share capital	Reserves	Long-term liabilities	Current liabilities	Current assets	Fixed assets
Company car						
Materials in the warehouse						
Four-year bank loan						
Tax owed to government						
Increase in value of company property						
Issued shares						
Cash in the bank						
Money owed to suppliers						

2 Using the layout above, construct a balance sheet for Yorkshire Logistics Ltd from the following data:

Long-term loans	£5m	Vehicles	£10m	Offices	£2m
Equipment	£1m	Stocks	£1m	Cash	£0.2m
Creditors	£2m	Unpaid tax	£1.5m	Debtors	£3m
Share capital	£6m	Reserves	£2.7m		

Assets employed

This is the total of fixed assets plus current assets less current liabilities. This is an important value, which is used in the analysis of accounts.

Long-term liabilities

These are the long-term loans owed by the business. These are due to be paid over a period of time greater than one year and include loans, commercial mortgages and debentures.

Cash-flow statement

Cash-flow statements are not examined in detail at 'AS' level Business Studies. The most important point to remember is that these statements explain to the users of accounts why the profits (or losses) made by a business are not the same as its cash flow. This surprises many students. Surely a profitable business has money in the bank? Clearly it must be true that a loss-making business is short of cash. The answer to both these questions is *not necessarily*.

Capital and revenue expenditure

What is the difference, in accounting terms, between a business purchasing a van and purchasing the fuel to fill the tank? There is expenditure involved in both cases, but one purchase is of an asset that will be kept and used by the business for several years. The petrol will be used up in the process of using the van in the day-to-day activities of the business. The purchase of the van is called **capital expenditure**; the purchase of the petrol is an example of **revenue expenditure**.

Any item bought by a business and retained for more than one year, i.e. the purchase of fixed assets, is capital expenditure. Any expenditure on assets that are used up within one year, such as stocks for resale or printer cartridges, is revenue expenditure.

How do accountants record these two types of spending in the accounts?

Case study – M and G Taxis Ltd. Cash flow statement

M and G Taxis Ltd made a net profit of £200,000 last year. The two major shareholders, Mike and Gina Campbell, were therefore surprised to find that, at the end of the year, their business had a bank overdraft. Their accountant explained to them that out of net profit they had bought new taxis costing £50,000. In addition, the business had repaid a bank loan and several major customers had delayed paying their accounts. There had therefore been an increase in the debtors of the business; services had been supplied profitably to customers but not yet paid for. The accountant showed them the following simplified version of a cash-flow statement:

M and G Taxis Ltd cash-flow statement for the year ending 31 December 2001

Net profit	£200,000
less Increase in debtors	(£60,000)
less Purchase of new fixed assets (taxis)	(£50,000)
less Repayment of loan	(£100,000)
Net change in cash	(£10,000)

As the business had only started the year with a cash balance of £2,000, the statement above helps to explain the current bank overdraft of £8,000.

Activity

Copy out this table and complete it by writing either revenue or capital in column 2 and a brief explanation of your decision:

Expenditure	Capital or revenue spending	Reason
Purchase of computers for use in administration		
Salaries of the administration staff		
Stock bought for resale		
Maintenance costs of the building		
Extension to the existing offices		

Revenue expenditure is easy to deal with. All revenue expenditure is on assets and expenses that give short-term benefit to the business – within one year. They will all be recorded in full on each year's profit and loss account and will therefore reduce that year's profits – with the exception of the unsold stocks, which will be entered under 'closing stocks'.

Capital expenditure is more complicated. Consider this situation. A removal business purchases two new trucks, which are expected to last for ten years. This is obviously capital expenditure on fixed assets. If the cost of these trucks was recorded as an expense immediately and recorded on the profit and loss account, there would be two serious disadvantages for the business:

◆ The trucks would not appear as fixed assets on the balance sheet because they had been recorded as an annual expense. This would lower the value of the business below its true worth – after all, the trucks will have value many years from now.

◆ This year's profits will be low as a result of the entire cost of the trucks being recorded straight away – and profits in later years will be higher because they do not bear any of the charge of this purchase.

How then, is capital expenditure recorded on the accounts? By a process called depreciation.

Depreciation of assets

Nearly all fixed assets will depreciate or decline in value over time. It seems reasonable, therefore, to only record the cost of each year's depreciation as a cost on each year's profit and loss account. This will overcome both of the problems referred to above:

◆ The assets will retain some value on the balance sheet each year until fully depreciated or sold off.

◆ The profits will be reduced by the amount of that year's depreciation and will not under- or over-record the performance of the business.

Depreciation may be defined as the decline in the estimated value of a fixed asset over time. Assets decline in value for two main reasons:

◆ normal wear and tear through usage;

◆ technological change, making either the asset or the product it is used to make obsolete.

Used computers and facsimile machines collected throughout Japan – depreciation rates on technological equipment are often very high
Source: Popperfoto.

Planning and decision making

Whilst accounting must provide the data with which to look backwards, learn from experience and modify behaviour in order to ensure that objectives are achieved, it must also enable managers to look into the future and plan. We are interested in two of the ways in which a firm may do is before making an investment which might prove unwise or unprofitable. The data for this are always present knowledge and the experience to predict, but even the best predictions are guesswork. Examples of potential investment decisions could include:

◆ a decision by a clothes manufacturer whether to extend the range of clothing offered for sale;

◆ a decision by a butcher shop whether to open a branch on a large newly built housing estate;

◆ a decision by a bus company whether to run a bus route linking local villages with the nearby town;

◆ a decision by a supermarket whether to open a café for its customers.

At the heart of all these decisions is a risk. The management in each case will want to know whether the costs will be greater than the benefits. Accounting can provide for them the financial data upon which the decision will be made and the techniques to enable the analysis to be completed. But accounting data are never sufficient, on their own, to make the decision. We return to that consideration after looking at two of the techniques for assessing an investment. The benefit of an investment does not necessarily lie in increased income, but the benefits can come from savings made or from reduced costs.

Investment appraisal – what information is necessary?

In judging the profitability or desirability of an investment project the following information will be useful:

- the cost of the investment, including, in the case of equipment and machinery, installation cost;
- the estimated life expectancy – over how many years can returns be expected from the investment;
- the expected net returns or net cash flows from the project. These are the expected returns from the investment, less the annual running costs of it.

The two methods we consider here are:

the payback period,
average rate of return (also known as the accounting rate of return).

Payback method

The payback period is the length of time it takes for the net cash inflows to pay back the original investment. If a project costs £2m and is expected to pay back £500,000 per year, the payback period will be four years. This can then be compared with the payback on alternative investments. A payback example is shown in Table 13.4.

Year	Annual net cash flows	Cumulative cash flows
	£	£
0	(500,000)	(500,000)
1	300,000	(200,000)
2	150,000	(50,000)
3	150,000	100,000
4	100,000	200,000

Table 13.4 Cash flows of a second investment

It is normal to refer to 'Year 0' as the time period in which the investment is made. The cash flow at this time is therefore negative – shown by a bracketed amount. What is the payback period in the example above? It occurs in the third year, but when during this year? If we assume that the cash flows are received evenly throughout the year (this may not be the case, of course) then payback will be at the end of the 4th month of the 3rd year.

How do we know this? At the end of year 2:
£50,000 is needed to pay back the remainder of the initial investment.
£150,000 is expected during year 3.
£50,000 is a third of £150,000
One third of a year is the end of month 4!
You might find it easier to use the following formula to find out which month in a particular year payback occurs:

month of payback is

$$= \frac{\text{additional cash inflow needed}}{\text{annual cash flow}} \times 12$$

$$= \frac{£50,000}{150,000} \times 12$$

$$= \text{4th month}$$

Why is the payback of a project considered to be important?

Managers can compare the payback period of a particular project with other alternative projects in order to put them in rank order. Alternatively, the payback period could be compared with a 'cut-off' time period that the business may have laid down, e.g. they will not accept any project proposal which pays back after five years. There are several reasons why payback period is considered important:

- a business may have borrowed the finance for the investment and a long payback period will increase interest payments;
- even if the finance was obtained internally, the capital has an opportunity cost of other purposes for which it could be used. The speedier the payback, the quicker the capital is made available for other projects;
- the longer into the future before a project pays back the capital invested in it, the more uncertain the whole investment becomes. The changes in the external environment which could occur to make a project unprofitable are likely to be much greater over ten years than over two;

◆ some managers are 'risk averse' – they want to reduce risk to a minimum so a quick payback reduces uncertainties for these managers;

◆ cash flows received in the future have less real value than cash flows today, as a result of inflation. The quicker money is returned to an investing company the higher will be its real value:

> an increasing number of investments rely on modern technology and an asset which pays back over a long time or even a medium period, may be obsolete before it has paid back.

The payback method has the following advantages and disadvantages.

Advantages:

1 It is quick and easy to calculate.
2 The results are easily understood by managers.
3 The emphasis on speed of return of cash flows gives the benefits of concentrating on the more accurate short-term, forecasts of the project's profitability.
4 The result can be used to eliminate or 'screen out' projects which give returns too far into the future.
5 It is particularly useful for businesses where liquidity is of greater significance than overall profitability.

Disadvantages:

1 It does not measure the overall profitability of a project – indeed it ignores all of the cash flows after the payback period. It might be possible for an investment to give a really rapid return of capital but then to offer no other cash inflows.
2 This concentration on the short term may lead businesses to reject very profitable investments just because they take some time to repay the capital.
3 It does not consider the timing of the cash flows during the payback period.

Evaluation

The payback method is often used as a quick check on the viability of a project or as a means of comparing projects – but it is rarely used in isolation from the other investment appraisal methods. It is of greatest value in times of high inflation and when the investment has a high technological element.

Accounting rate of return

It measures the overall profitability of an investment as a percentage of the initial investment something that payback does not do. If it is possible to demonstrate that Project A returns, on average, 8% per year while Project B returns 12% per year, then the decision between the alternative investments will be an easier one to make.

Table 13.5 shows the expected cash flows from a business investment into a fleet of new fuel-efficient vehicles. The inflows for years 1–3 are the annual cost savings made. In year 4, the expected return from selling the vehicles is included.

Year	Net cash flow
0	(£5m)
1	£2m
2	£2m
3	£2m
4	£3m

Table 13.5 Expected cash flows

Calculation of ARR – the four steps involved:

1 Add up all of the positive cash flows.
2 Subtract the cost of the investment.
3 Divide by the life span of the investment in years £4M/4 = 1.
4 Calculate what % this figure is of the initial capital cost by this formula:

$$\frac{\text{average annual profit}}{\text{initial capital cost}} \times 100$$

Example of ARR – new vehicle fleet:

Add up all positive cash flows = £9m
Subtract cost of investment = £9m – £5m = £4m
Divide by life span = £4m/4 = £1m
Calculate the % return = $\frac{£1m}{£5m} \times 100$
= 20%

The result indicates to the business that, on average, over the life span of the investment, it can expect an annual return of 20% on its investment. This could be compared with:

◆ the ARR on other projects,

◆ the minimum expected return set by the business – the so-called criterion rate.

In the example above, if the business refused to accept any project with less than a return of 15% the new vehicle fleet would satisfy this criterion. But if the criterion rate was 25% the investment would be rejected.

The advantages and disadvantages of the average rate of return:

Advantages:

1 It uses all of the cash flows – unlike the payback method.
2 It focuses on profitability which is the central objective of many business decisions.
3 The result is easily understood and easy to compare with other projects which may be competing for the limited investment funds available.
4 The result can be quickly assessed against the pre-determined criterion rate of the business.

Disadvantages:

1 It ignores the timing of the cash flows. This could result in two projects having similar ARR results but one could pay back much quicker than the other.
2 As all cash inflows are included, the later cash flows which are less likely to be accurate are incorporated into the calculation.
3 The time value of money is ignored. Time value of money is an important part of many decisions of this kind but we do not consider it until the A2 part of the course. If, however, you are doing a project which is about investment appraisal you might like to read about the concept called discounted cash flow in the text for the second part of the advanced level course. This is a widely used measure for appraising projects but it is best considered together with payback results. The two results then allow consideration of both profits and cash flow timings.

Forecasting cash flows in an uncertain environment

Investment appraisal methods require cash flow forecasts. With long-term investments this can mean forecasting many years ahead and the chance of external factors upsetting forecasts become considerable. The original investment into the Channel Tunnel involved assessing returns 20 years after it was due to open – and

---

Activity

A manufacturing business is planning an investment programme to overcome a problem of demand exceeding capacity. It is considering two alternative projects involving new machinery. The initial outlays and future cash outflows are given below:

Year	Project X (£)	Project Y (£)
0	(50,000)	(80,000)
1	25,000	45,000
2	20,000	35,000
3	20,000	17,000
4	15,000	15,000
5	10,000	–

Project Y machinery is forecast to have a life expectancy of just four years.

(a) Calculate the payback for both projects.
(b) Explain which project should be selected if payback was the only criterion used – and why.
(c) Calculate ARR for both projects.
(d) The business has a cut-off or criterion rate of 11% for all new projects. Would either project be acceptable under this restriction?
(e) Taking both the results of payback and ARR together, which project would you advise the business to invest in, and why?
(f) What additional information would help you advise the business on the more suitable project?

---

the opening date was many years after the project began. The scope for external changes affecting the revenue forecasts – based on market research – was very great. For instance, the state of the French and UK economies influences the amount of freight and tourist traffic. Technical problems with the tunnel operations could hit revenues – as with a fire in 1997 which could not have been foreseen at the appraisal stage. The level of air fares – which have fallen dramatically since the tunnel opened – will also impact on demand levels.

These uncertainties cannot be removed but the existence of them must be constantly borne in mind by managers when considering the results of investment appraisal. The decision makers also need to be informed of the market research techniques used and the degree of confidence that can be put in the results. Manufacturers' data concerning the performance of an asset, such as machinery or a vehicle, may need to be

The Channel tunnel shuttle train emerges from the tunnel. Revenue and cost forecasts proved to be very unreliable due to unforeseen events
Source: Popperfoto Reuters.

verified so that claims of output or efficiency can be confirmed. Therefore, several factors could make the forecast of future cash flows unreliable:

♦ the quality of the information available;
♦ the degree of care with which the information is collected;
♦ the basis of estimates of the possible market, prices and cash inflows;
♦ the nature of the product or service being provided;
♦ the stability of the external environment;
♦ the activities of competitors.

Qualitative factors – investment decisions are not just about profit.

Investment appraisal techniques provide numerical data which are important in making decisions. However, no manager can afford to ignore other factors which cannot be so easily expressed in a numerate form and may have a crucial bearing on the decision. These are referred to as qualitative factors and may include:

(a) The impact on the environment and the local community. The growing concern about environmental issues is forcing businesses to consider carefully plans for developments in sensitive areas. The bad publicity stemming from the announcement of certain investment plans may dissuade managers from going ahead with the project due to the long-run impact on image and sales. An example is the dispute over rail routes to the Channel Tunnel.

(b) Closely related to this is the risk that certain projects may not receive planning permission and this would preclude continuing with the scheme. It is the duty of local planning offices to weigh up the costs and benefits of a planned undertaking and to act in the best interests of the community. Members of that community will often have a direct role through a public enquiry or may set up a pressure group to make their views known and persuade a particular outcome.

(c) The ways in which the workforce may react, particularly where any investment may lead to redundancies, to redeployment or to extensive re-training. The savings of a change may be considerable but expenses may arise from unexpected factors, such as strikes, absenteeism, lateness and other indicators of unrest and unease among the workforce.

(d) The aims and objectives of the business which must be a key consideration. The decision to close bank branches and replace them with Internet and telephone banking services involves considerable capital expenditure – as well as the potential for long-term savings. Managers may, however, be reluctant to pursue these investment policies if there is concern that the aim of giving excellent and personal customer service is being threatened. Similarly, the decision to replace large numbers of workers with labour-saving machinery may be reversed if the negative impact on industrial relations appears to be too great. An investment opportunity may prove viable on the basis of financial data but managers will think long and hard about entering a field where there is no history of success for the firm and no assurance of marketing successfully. Firms have often refused to move into new market areas because they are not familiar with them and there are spectacular examples of eventual success of a venture which initially firms rejected. Many very successful pop groups and authors can tell tales of initial rejection.

(e) Different managers are prepared to accept different degrees of risk. No amount of positive quantitative data will convince some managers, perhaps because of previous experiences, to accept a project which involves a considerable chance of failure.

Understanding of the 'other factors' involves in an investment decision is to be aware of the whole picture. Examiners expect to see this kind of awareness and expect you to be clear that investment decisions are never made on the basis of the financial data alone but by assessing all the evidence and coming to a balanced judgment.

Working capital – meaning and significance

Working capital is often described as the 'life blood' of a business. It is the finance needed for everyday expenses, such as the payment of wages and buying of stock. Without sufficient working capital a business will be illiquid. This position can be measured and analysed by using the two liquidity ratios referred to above; the results of these will be low when illiquidity is a problem.

The simple calculation of working capital is: current assets less current liabilities. You will remember from the section on the balance sheet that current assets are stocks, debtors and cash in the bank and the tills. Virtually no business could survive without these three assets, although some business owners refuse to sell any products on credit so there will be no debtors. This is very rare for businesses beyond a certain size. Where does the capital come from to purchase and hold these current assets? Most businesses will obtain some of this finance in the form of current liabilities – overdrafts and creditors are the main forms. However, it would be unwise to obtain all of the funds needed from these sources. For one thing, the liquidity ratios would be at very low levels. Another point against this approach is that it will leave no working capital for buying additional stocks or extending further credit to customers when required.

How much working capital is needed?

Sufficient working capital is essential to prevent a business from becoming illiquid and unable to pay its debts. Too high a level of working capital is a disadvantage; the opportunity cost of too much capital tied up in stocks, debtors and idle cash is the return that money could earn elsewhere in the business – invested in fixed assets perhaps. The working capital requirement for any business will depend upon the 'length' of this 'working capital cycle'. Figure 13.1 shows the simple cycle in a business that makes things, but neither seeks nor offers credit. Credit to purchasers given by the business will lengthen the time before a sale is turned into cash. Credit received by the business will lengthen the time before stock bought has to be paid for. To give more credit than is received is to increase the need for working capital. To receive more credit than is given is to reduce the need for working capital.

Managing working capital

There are business dangers from both *too much* working capital and *too little*. Working capital therefore needs to be managed. It is managed by concentrating on the four main components of the cycle:

◆ debtors;
◆ creditors;
◆ stock;
◆ cash.

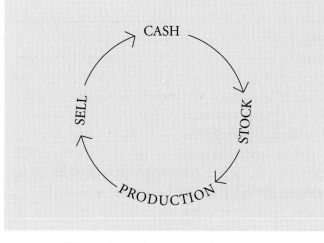

Figure 13.1 The simple working capital cycle

Debtors
People who business money.

Debtors can be managed in many different ways, as follows:

- Not extending credit to customers – or extending it for shorter time periods. Will they still buy from this business? Will a major aspect of this business's marketing mix have been removed? There are dangers in this approach. Many customers now expect credit and will go elsewhere if it is not offered.
- Selling invoiced sales to specialist financial institutions acting as debt factors. These businesses will 'buy' debts or invoiced sales from other concerns having an immediate need for cash. This will involve a cost, however, as the factors will not pay 100% of the value. The factoring businesses must make a profit for themselves.
- By being careful to discover whether new customers are creditworthy. This can be done by requiring references – from traders or from the bank is common – or by using the services of a credit enquiry agency.
- By offering a discount to clients who pay promptly.

Credit

Credit can be managed in two main ways, as follows:

- Increasing the range of goods and services bought on credit. If a business has a good credit rating this may be easy, but in other circumstances it is difficult. The danger is that an unpaid creditor may refuse to supply.

- Extend the period of time taken to pay. The larger a business is, the easier it is to extend the credit taken. This is often a great burden for small businesses that trade with larger ones.

Stock

Stock can be managed in the following ways:

- keeping smaller stock balances;
- using computer systems to record sales and therefore stock levels, and ordering as required;
- efficient stock control, stock use and stock handling so as to reduce losses through damage wastage and shrinkage;
- just-in-time stock ordering. There are dangers here if demand has not been forecast correctly, if there is a sudden change in demand, if suppliers are unreliable or if there are delivery difficulties.

Cash

Cash can be managed by:

- use of cash-flow forecasts, which have already been considered;
- wise use or investment of excess cash;
- hold low cash reserves and plan for overdraft facilities made with the bank if the need for more cash arises.

A permanent increase in working capital

When businesses expand, they generally need higher stock levels and will sell a higher value of products on credit. This increase in working capital is likely to be permanent and so long-term or permanent sources of finance will be needed, such as long-term loans or even share capital.

Activity

List the following businesses in order of their likely working capital requirements (highest working capital first):

- shipbuilder,
- fresh fish shop,
- further education college,
- second-hand car dealer,
- newsagent.

Activity

Read the case study below and then tackle the exercises that follow.

Case Study – Directphone Ltd

Directphone Ltd operates a direct insurance service to motorists. As part of a recent expansion programme, the finance director calculated that stocks of stationery, such as insurance certificates, would have to rise by 10% from £10,000. More motorists would be encouraged to use the company by being offered extended credit terms. This would increase debtors to an estimated £50,000 from the existing £40,000. Cash reserves to pay out for accidents would rise to £35,000 from £30,000. The only current liability was creditors (garages that had not yet been paid for accident work). This amounted to £40,000 and the director hoped to be allowed to increase this to £50,000.

(a) Calculate the proposed increase in the working capital requirements of the business resulting from the expansion.

(b) Discuss how the finance director might finance this increase in working capital.

Over-to-you

Test revision questions

(60 marks, 1 hour)

1 What does a profit and loss account indicate about the performance of a business? (4)
2 Explain the difference between gross and net profit. (3)
3 What does the appropriation section of a profit and loss account contain? (3)
4 With examples, explain the difference between current and fixed assets. (4)
5 What does capital employed mean? (3)
6 How is net current assets (also known as working capital) calculated? (3)
7 Differentiate between long-term and current liabilities, with examples. (4)
8 Give two examples of capital expenditure for a manufacturing business – justify your selection. (4)
9 If a project, costing £3m, has annual net cash flows of £1.2m, calculate the payback period. (4)
10 Evaluate the payback method of investment appraisal. (4)
11 In the example in 9, the project lasts for six years. Calculate the ARR. (4)
12 Evaluate the ARR method of investment appraisal. (4)
13 Why are there always uncertainties in calculating future cash flows from an investment project? (4)
14 Explain the importance of working capital to any business. (4)
15 A building firm is very short of working capital. The owner is planning either to demand cash payment from customers before he starts work on a project or to delay paying suppliers by one more month. Evaluate these two methods of working capital management. (8)

Discover and learn

1 Consider an improvement to facilities for your school/college common room which would cost at least £5,000:
   (a) Explain why it would be a valuable addition and what the benefits would be.
   (b) Analyse all the quantifiable costs and revenues or savings.
   (c) On the basis of this data conduct a pay back and accounting rate of return analysis.
   (d) Consider all the 'other factors' which should be considered and on the basis of all the evidence, make and justify your decision.
2 Using a car magazine or a car price guide, find out the following information about a particular model of car, for example a 1.6 Ford Focus:

(a) new price;

(b) retail value after one year;

(c) retail value after two years.

Calculate the percentage decline in the value from new both one year and after two years.

A car hire firm has ten Ford Focus cars. It keeps them for two years on average. Comment on the fact that it uses straight-line depreciation for all of its fixed assets.

3 Read the case study below and then tackle the exercises that follow.

Case study – Highfield Leisure Ltd

The following accounts refer to Highfield Leisure Ltd, which operates several amusement arcades in seaside resorts in the UK and hires out machines to pubs and clubs.

Profit and loss account for the year ending 31 March 2003

(2002 figures in parentheses. All figures in £m)

Sales turnover	320	(330)
less Cost of sales	120	(100)
Gross profit	200	(230)
Overhead expenses	150	(145)
Net profit	50	(85)
Interest	10	(5)
Pre-tax profits	40	(80)
Tax @ 50%	20	(40)
Profit after tax	20	(40)
Dividends	15	(15)
Retained profit	5	(25)

Balance sheet as at 31 March 2003

(2002 figures in parentheses. All figures in £m)

Fixed assets		80	(75)
Current assets:			
Stock	10		(15)
Debtors	25		(20)
Cash	0.5		(2)
	35.5		(37)
less:			
Current liabilities	30		(25)
Net current assets		5.5	(12)
ASSETS EMPLOYED		85.5	(87)
Financed by:			
Long-term liabilities	40		(46.5)
Share capital			
(£1 ordinary shares)	30		(30)
Reserves	15.5		(10.5)
CAPITAL EMPLOYED		85.5	(87)

(a) Define working capital and state the present working capital of the company in the year 2000.

(b) Stock is found to be overvalued by 20% for 2000.

Recalculate working capital.

(c) Using the data in any way you consider appropriate, what comments would you make about the success of this business from the point of view of:

◆ a trade creditor?

◆ a potential investor?

Summary

In this chapter we have recognised that:

- The final accounts of a business are its statement to stakeholders and to the world at large of the present position of the business.

- An important part of understanding final accounts is the language and concepts that are involved.

- A number of different values including ratios are used to assess companies on the basis of their accounts.

- The ratios and other calculations are an aid to decision making and not answers in themselves.

- Action that could be taken to solve problems is not always wise and there are factors, other than the numbers themselves, that are often more important.

Key words

Definitions of Key words can be found in the Glossary on page 269.

assets employed
balance sheet
capital employed
capital expenditure
cash-flow statement
current assets
debtors
dividends
final accounts
fixed assets
goodwill
gross profit
gross profit margin

intangible assets
investment appraisal
net current assets
net profit
operating profit
overheads
profit and loss account
retained profit
revenue expenditure
sales turnover
stock
tangible assets
working capital

14 Planning the workforce

➤ show the need for organisational objectives to be met

➤ understand the importance of workforce planning

➤ consider the importance of recruitment, induction and training to an organisation

➤ understand the roles of induction and the different types of training

➤ explain why some organisations have a high labour turnover

➤ discuss workforce planning needs in given circumstances

➤ explain the nature of a contract of employment and the things it covers

➤ explain why workers may be dismissed and procedures to protect them

➤ explain work situations in which the law intervenes

The need to achieve business objectives

One of the most important ingredients of any successful organisation are the people who work for it. The extent to which the organisation's objectives are achieved will depend, to a great extent, on the effectiveness and efficiency of its employees. It is important, therefore, that managers ensure employees understand and are in sympathy with the aims of the organisation. This may not always be the case.

Consider the situation of Bill, who has been working for the same firm for the past 25 years:

◆ He has not been promoted.

◆ He is quite happy with the wages he earns.

◆ He is quite content to remain in his job until he retires.

How might Bill's objectives differ from those of the organisation?

The organisation intends to operate in the most efficient way so that it can produce the desired output at the lowest unit cost and make a profit. We could say that the objective of the firm is a reasonable return on capital employed. Bill's objective is to continue to earn a reasonable wage without causing himself any stress. Obviously there is a real problem here for a manager. How can the two different sets of objectives be brought together?

Activity

Talk to four people you know who have different types of jobs. Ask them:

(a) Why they go to work?

(b) What they see as their objectives?

(c) Consider whether or not these objectives would be appropriate to the organisation they work for.

(d) If you were their manager, or the owner of the firm, would you be happy with them?

People at work

People come to work for all kinds of reasons, ranging from the need to earn money to the need to be with other people. Managers must use their skills to provide a match between the aims of employees in coming to work and the aims of the organisation, which may range from making a profit to providing an effective and efficient service. There is a further difficulty. We live in an era of change. Businesses are dynamic and are changing because of a number of factors. Technology is changing and this may necessitate people having to adapt to new techniques or machinery, or indeed having to retrain to do a job that is completely different from the one they used to do. People are often not happy with this kind of change, and indeed may fear it. Bill, who is

A new industrial estate, with many small businesses. Each of these firms needs to plan its future workforce needs

happy simply coasting along doing the same job day after day, may be frightened by the prospect of new challenges. Therefore, managers have to be skilled in their approach if they are to avoid tension in the workplace.

Workforce planning

Good planning can help an organisation run smoothly. Lack of planning often leads to disaster. The right kind of labour is rarely easy to obtain and without an appropriate well-balanced labour force it will be very difficult to achieve the objectives of the organisation. The mix of labour needed must first be determined and then a statregy designed which will either obtain those who are needed through recruitment or by training existing staff. The workforce plan involves looking at the present workforce and the future requirements, as well as at the means by which these future requirements can be met. The organisation needs to look at all the different types of workers it requires. These will include managers, technical experts, clerical workers, skilled manual workers and semi-skilled workers or unskilled workers. Obviously the number and pattern of employees will depend on the type and size of the organisation. However, all of these people have a crucial part to play. Planning is important all the time but some

Activity

Read the case study below and then tackle the exercises that follow.

Case study – R Wilkins Ltd

R Wilkins is a small firm, which has been operating in the same town for the last 50 years. Many of the workers have been with the organisation for a long time and there has been a tradition for the sons and daughters of workers to come into the firm when they leave school. The company produces crafted wood products for a fairly small market. There has never been any real pressure exerted on the workers and there was always a casual feel to the production process. Old Mr Wilkins is about to retire and his son, who has been to Business School, is about to take over. He would like to become involved in exporting. He would also like to invest a large amount of money in new technology, such as computer-controlled lathes. However, none of the current workers have any experience of this type of technology.

(a) Outline the problems that you think Wilkins will have if he introduces this new strategy.

(b) How would you suggest he might try to introduce it with the minimum of disruption to the workforce?

(c) Explain how the objectives of the workforce and the organisation are different in this case.

factors make **workforce planning** particularly crucial. Among them are:

- People leave at all times and for a variety of reasons.
- The firm should be ready to replace them.
- This may be a time to employ different skills.
- It may be an opportunity for internal rather than external appointment.
- It may be a time to initiate or respond to change.
- Reasons for the departure need to be known and analysed.
- Technology constantly requires a revision of the workforce.
- Redundancy, retraining and/or new employment must be planned.

Redundancy and retraining need to be carefully planned as they always have the potential to cause major problems within the organisation. For example, if people feel that there is a chance of redundancy, it will cause uncertainty and unrest, may lead to industrial disputes and certainly will lead to a reduction in efficiency. Such situations often persuade workers to leave who are among those the firm would wish to retain. However, the most common aspect of workforce planning lies in the successful recruitment of new employees.

Recruitment

It is important that organisations obtain the best workforce available if they are to meet their objectives and compete successfully. As far as possible, the employees need to be chosen so that they meet exactly the needs of the organisation in order to reduce the risk of conflict between their personal objectives and the objectives of the organisation. Many organisations will

Test Activity

Read the case study below and then tackle the exercises that follow.

Case study – Workforce planning at Cameron Sweets Ltd.

By accepting the resignation of three key production line workers, Roman Kauls knew that he would be lucky to meet the staff needs of Cameron Sweets over the next six months. The three workers had been attracted away from the firm by the offer of higher wages and better conditions in a local bakery. As HR manager, Roman had been planning the workforce numbers for the future. He had collected data from both the marketing department on estimated sales figures and the production department for details of the new machines being installed next month. Price reductions by Cameron's leading competitor was making accurate forecasting difficult – taking last year's results and adding on 5%, the standard practice in this business, would no longer be accurate enough.

The new machinery was fully automated and there would be no more manual packing at the end of the line. The machine would need reprogramming for each new type of sweet and the operations manager had also expressed concern about maintaining such complicated machinery. To add to Roman's problems, two of the women in the materials preparation department had announced that that they would be applying for maternity leave over the next three months. With all of these issues occurring, Roman's plans were thrown into further confusion by a leaked report from the government that suggested a plan to introduce a law making 48 hour, or longer, working weeks illegal.

(30 marks, 40 minutes)

(a) Define the term 'workforce planning'. (3)

(b) Explain the possible consequences to firms, such as Cameron Sweets, of not having a workforce plan. (7)

(c) Outline five factors from the case that will influence either the number of workers or the skill levels of workers needed by the business over the next year. (10)

(d) To what extent will it be possible accurately to predict the workforce needs of Cameron Sweets over the next 12 months? (10)

be involved in recruitment fairly frequently, as they need to replace workers who die, retire, are dismissed or who move to another job. In addition to this they may need to recruit for expansion.

Work is increasingly technological with greater capital intensity and changing requirements of workers. Craft skills are less significant and the ability to use computerised equipment and work as a team is becoming more important. Organisations have to recruit for these reasons so that they will not be left behind by change.

Test Activity

Read the case study below and then tackle the exercises that follow.

Case study – Brendon Plastics plc

Brendon Plastics is a medium-sized firm in its industry employing 350 workers. In its community it is a large employer with a relatively high labour turnover. In one month the need to recruit new employees arose from:

- two who had retired at 65;
- one who had died;
- two who had been dismissed;
- three who had found other employment;
- the creation of a new section requiring ten staff at different levels;
- the division of two jobs, the work of which had grown.

Two of the staff in the new section will have management responsibilities and will need both qualifications and experience in plastic moulding techniques. Both the jobs that need dividing are in administration and will require experience and computing skills. All the other jobs are on the shop floor and require neither experience nor qualifications.

(15 marks, 20 minutes)

(a) Outline the processes that you think might be necessary for successful recruitment. (6)

(b) Discuss ways in which the appointment of:
- shop-floor workers;
- management workers;
- administrative staff;

may need different processes. (9)

Processes employed by firms and channels through which they will work differ from one organisation to another, but all will begin by reflecting on the consequences of a person leaving and the opportunities this offers. The organisation will wish to find the employee best suited to its needs. This is a process that requires great care because, once you have engaged someone, dissimal can be difficult.

Once the organisation has decided on the vacancy, it needs to complete a **job analysis**. This involves gathering together all the facts relating to the job. It may be necessary for managers to observe the job being done (provided it is not a new job!), or to ask the person who currently does the job what is involved. This is quite important, as very often managers may not fully realise what the job entails.

Once this information has been gathered, the next step in the process is to draw up a **job specification**. This will include items such as the basic job details, a summary and purpose of the job, who the employee will be responsible to, the conditions of employment such as salary, holidays etc., any training that will be required. It is important that the job specification is accurate, as this will determine what the prospective employee understands the job to be.

The **job advertisement** can then be drawn up and this must be clear so that prospective candidates are not misled. Job advertisements are normally placed in newspapers, trade journals, employment agencies, careers offices, etc. In certain cases where levels of expertise are required, they may be placed in universities or further education colleges. The cost of recruitment must not be unnecessarily high, but for many jobs, the widest possible pool of prospective employees must be reached. However, there are many jobs where applicants can be found from the contacts of existing employees or by placing a card in the window.

As soon as **applications** are received, then the organisation will select the ones from people they might want to interview. It is unlikely that all applicants will be interviewed, because usually there will be many more applications than can be coped with. In addition, some of the applicants may not be suitable or qualified for the job. To interview them would be a waste of time both for the organisation and the applicant. This process of selecting a small number from which the choice can be made is called short-listing. For many jobs references

Activity

Work in groups of four. Each individual select a job. Any job will do. It could be one you do yourself or one that is done by a member of your family. If you were appointing to that job:

- What would you expect the employee to be able to do?
- What qualifications or experience do you think would be needed?
- What qualities would you look for in a potential employee?
- Draw up an advertisement based on the answers to these questions.
- Discuss your advertisement with the others and amend if you think it is necessary.
- Decide where you would advertise and why.

Activity

Employers are required to show no bias of any kind in the recruitment of employees. Discuss the four advertisements you prepared in your group. Do you think there are any unfair things in the advertisements? If so, comment upon them and change them so that they are fair and will attract the kind of people who are needed.

What do you think are the strengths and weaknesses of the advert?

will be asked for so that prospective employers can have some support for, and confirmation of, the qualities and suitability of the applicant. This approach is most likely where qualifications and experience are demanded or where there is a need to protect the organisation from bogus applicants.

Applicants can then be called for **interview**. At interview they will be asked a number of questions to determine their suitability for the job in terms of their qualifications and experience. However, suitability of the person from the point of view of personality and ability to fit in with others with whom they will be working is also important. The type of job that is being interviewed for will clearly determine the format of the interview. What applicants sometimes forget is that an interview is a two-way opportunity. It is as important for the applicant to be satisfied that this is the right job and in the right organisation as it is for the potential employer to be satisfied. Taking a job because it is offered is one of

the commonest reasons for dissatisfaction at work, for absenteeism and for rapid decisions to leave.

After the interviews have taken place, the decision will be made. Those who have been involved in the interview will discuss the various applicants as individuals, as well as how well they have answered the questions put to them. It is important that everyone on the interview panel is in general agreement as to the successful applicant(s). Some organisations provide unsuccessful applicants with feedback on the reasons why they were not appointed. This can be a very useful exercise for candidates.

Activity

Consider the following job advertisement. Do you think it is a good one? Is there anything missing? Is it legal?

JOHN BROWN LTD

Required, young man as an office employee.

No previous experience is required.

Grade C at least in GCSE English and Maths.

A neat and tidy appearance is essential.

Contact 0234 56789. Ask for Mr Smith.

Induction

The costs of recruitment are very high. No business wants to recruit more often than is necessary, so a big effort must be made to ensure that recruits stay. The first stage of this is called induction. You will remember what it was like starting at a new school with few friends. You wanted to settle as soon as possible, but there were many things you did not know. In working situations this feeling can be much worse unless the firm sets out to ensure that you fit into the culture of the organisation, know where things are, the work group of which you will be a part and what job you will have to do. All of this is undertaken in most firms through a specially provided induction programme, which sometimes lasts up to a week. It is not training for the job; it is training to be in the job, designed to make you feel part of the firm and confident that you know what to do and where to go. Time and money spent in this process may well pay dividends later as employees will settle quickly and will operate as efficiently as possible. Done well, it will reduce the expense of having to go through the recruitment process all over again and may more than pay for itself in that way.

Features of an induction programme are likely to be:

- familiarisation with the workplace and its amenities;
- introduction to important personnel;
- introduction to work mates;
- awareness of the culture, workings and objectives of the business;
- awareness of times and working practices;
- awareness of health, safety and fire drills and precautions;
- requirements when absent, ill or late.

Training

Training is an ongoing process and does not simply apply to the new entrant to the organisation. Because of continuous change in technology and processes, it is important that all staff, from shop floor to management, are trained in an ongoing fashion. Some will require training because they are being asked to do different things, being deliberately multi-skilled or being groomed for promotion. Training is expensive, but failure to train or poor training is even more expensive since it can lead to, or make worse, a number of potential problems. Among these are:

- poor quality;
- increased wastage;
- poor motivation and morale;
- absenteeism and increased labour turnover;
- lost sales and customers;
- damage and accidents.

On-the-job training

Management needs to establish who needs to be trained within the organisation, in other words, to identify the gaps. Training is only necessary because there is a gap between what a firm wants from an employee and what the employee is currently able to do. Even someone who is highly skilled may not be able to use that skill in precisely the way the employer wants. For example, someone highly skilled in computing may not be familiar with the hardware and software the firm is using or with the procedures the firm has adopted. For someone in this position training may be minimal and may be quick, but it is still essential.

Once gaps are identified and analysed, programmes can be constructed to deal with these gaps. These programmes may evolve within the company and it may be necessary to train someone to be a supervisor. Very often, people who have been good at their job are promoted to supervise others. For example, students employed to work at the checkout in a superstore are first trained by an employee who is already skilled in the job. This usually takes place outside normal hours.

However, it may be that some trainers need basic training so that they can get the best from other people. Very often the way that trainers communicate with trainees is as crucial as the task that is being learnt.

This kind of training is an example of what is known as on-the-job training and is essential where jobs must be done in a particular way and involve interpersonal skills.

1 You will certainly have seen teachers in training in your school or college and you may even have been taught by one of them. If you have, you will have noted that they are often supervised to ensure both the effectiveness of their progress and the quality of your learning,

2 You may have been to the hairdressers when a new employee is being trained. The employee can only learn by cutting hair, but this does pose a risk for the customer whose hair is being cut. The first customers are often volunteers or people who are being charged less.

On-the-job trainees are often less efficient than an experienced worker, take longer, waste more materials or make mistakes, which have to be put right. This is a natural part of the learning process.

Off-the-job training

The training of many personnel will take place off the job, particularly in the early stages. Those who have to work machines are often first taught in the training school or on reserved machines that are not used for production. Teachers spend a long time in academic and training college courses before they undertake their first teaching practice. Most organisations, nowadays, are anxious that their senior personnel, people they see with potential for promotion and managers undergo regular development programmes. These may be carried out at universities or further education colleges. It may be that there will be a formal qualification at the end.

One problem for organisations may be that they will train their personnel (often paying for the training), only to discover that those people will move to another organisation simply because they are now better trained. However, this is a risk that organisations are prepared to take. It is vital that people with responsibility are well trained and well motivated if they are to use their skills to help the organisation to meet its objectives.

Any training programme must be monitored and apparent results recorded. A debriefing for both the trainees and the trainers enables evaluation. There is always room for improvement and there are always changes in circumstances that must be taken into account. Valuable lessons can be learnt for the future. It is wise to involve employees in the training process, not only afterwards, but also in allowing them to help decide what training they need. This gives a real sense of ownership to the process and is likely to result in a better outcome. Managers need to be aware that they may not have all the answers as far as training needs are concerned.

Labour turnover

Labour turnover is the number of people who leave an organisation in a given period of time. A rough guide can be given by expressing the number who leave as a percentage of those employed:

Employees	540
Number who left in the year	124
Labour turnover for the year	$124/540 \times 100 = 23\%$

But this not very helpful. There are many reasons why people leave organisations. Some of them are not really part of a labour turnover problem and have to be accepted. These include:

◆ those who retire at 60/65, who die or are too ill to continue;

◆ those who leave because the family is moving;

◆ those the firm has dismissed;

◆ those who were only employed short term, e.g. students.

All of these must be excluded from any analysis, although there may be something to learn from reasons why people had to be dismissed. Unexpected labour turnover is expensive and the reasons for it must be found. Only when the reasons are identified can a solution be sought.

1 If many people are leaving within a short time of being employed the reasons are likely to lie in the suitability of recruitment, in the quality of induction or in the initial training activity.

2 If the leavers are concentrated among male employees or among female employees, then the conditions of employment or of working together may be an issue.

3 If there is a high concentration within one or two departments, then the cause is likely to lie in conditions of work or in leadership style.

4 If many of the workers leaving are moving to a competitor or to a given local firm using similar skills, the answer is likely to lie in wages, in conditions of employment or in working practices.

Whatever the reason, if people are not happy in the work they are doing, they are certainly not being as efficient as they could be, and the objectives of the organisation will not be met. In addition, if people are leaving, the firm is having to recruit and train new people, and this is also very expensive. It is also important for the organisation to consider its reputation. It is certain to be the case that many employees who are moving on are not enhancing the reputation of the organisation they have left.

Activity

In small groups, discuss why you think there could be a turnover of labour within an organisation. Try to discuss a firm known to you. Perhaps you can get information from:

(a) the firm in which you work or which you yourself have left;

(b) the firm in which you are doing the Project;

(c) a friend or relative who has changed jobs.

Dismissal

There may be occasions when an employee has to be dismissed for one reason or another. It could be that the employee is unable to do the job to the standard that the organisation requires. On the other hand, it may be that the employee has broken one of the crucial conditions of employment. However, before dismissal can happen, the organisation must be seen to have done all that it can to help the employee reach the required standard or stay within conditions of employment. There should be support and, if necessary, training for

DENIM BLUES Levi's has slashed 13,000 jobs in the past two years and closed 24 US factories and four European plants

Levi's can lay claim to being the world's biggest clothing brand but it has failed to spot what has been happening among its core 15 to 24-year-old market.

Outwitted by the vagaries of fashion, Levi's has seen its share of the key US market plunge to 17 per cent compared with 31 per cent a decade ago. It has suffered similar declines in Europe.

Throughout these troubled times rivals have been busy. VF Corporation, makers of the Wrangler and Lee brands, has increased its share of the denim market from 18 to 25 per cent share, while Gap has gone from 3 to 5 per cent.

Levi's global sales fell in 1998 to $6bn from $6.9bn the year before with worse expected for 1999. Its debts have soared to $1.8bn. It has incurred $1.3bn of restructuring costs since 1997 as it has scrambled to cut costs, shutting American and European factories and laying off workers.

Last week it had to renegotiate its borrowings with a consortium led by Bank of America with the new credit facilities secured against the company's assets, including its world famous Levi Strauss trade mark. If Levi's fails to repay $200m a year over the next two years the banks can take control of the brand name.

Source: Damian Reece, *Sunday Telegraph*, 13 February 2000

the person concerned. It is important from the organisation's point of view that it does not leave itself open to allegations of **unfair dismissal**.

Sometimes employees become involved in gross misconduct, which may be stealing or some other serious offence. If this happens, the organisation can dismiss with immediate effect, without pay or notice. However, if an employee is late regularly, then the organisation must give warnings and follow the agreed disciplinary procedure before dismissal can take place. This usually involves verbal warnings followed by written warnings, before dismissal is thought to be 'fair'.

If someone is off work, because of illness, for a long period of time and it is unlikely that they will return for some time to come, then, after consulting medical experts, it may be that the employee can be dismissed or continue to be employed on lower wages in accordance with the contract of employment. The employee needs to be given full notice and full pay during the period of notice.

Whether or not a dismissal is unfair is a matter of fact to be decided by a tribunal. It is the right of every employee to claim unfair dismissal. To show that a dismissal is fair employers need to be able to show that one of the following is true and, except in the case of gross misconduct, the agreed procedures have been followed:

- inability to do the job in a situation where necessary and sufficient training has been given;
- a continuous negative attitude at work, which has affected the employees or the work of others adversely;
- continuous disregard of required health and safety procedures;
- deliberate destruction of an employer's property;
- continued harassment of other employees.

There are certain situations in which dismissal has been considered unfair or in breach of employment law. These include:

- pregnancy;
- a discriminatory reason, e.g. race, colour or religion;
- being a member of a union;
- a non-relevant criminal record; if the employer has previously been unaware of a criminal record, it is not a reason for dismissal unless it is central to the

job, e.g. a cashier convicted of stealing from the till or a schoolteacher convicted of child abuse. A firm cannot be required to reinstate someone who has been unfairly dismissed, but failure to do so or to employ in another capacity is likely to be reflected in the damages awarded to an employee whose case has been successful.

Redundancy

One of the most difficult situations for an organisation is when it is required to make someone redundant. If the problems of Levi Strauss (see above) are not solved they could easily result in redundancy. This can happen if a job that someone has been doing is no longer required and there is no possibility of that person being re-employed somewhere else in the organisation. Redundancy may also happen if, due to budget cuts, the firm needs to reduce its workforce. If redundancies are to take place, then set guidelines are normally followed to ensure that the correct person or people are made redundant. Often the principle is 'last in, first out'. People who feel that they have been unfairly treated can go to an Industrial Tribunal, which will consider their case and make a ruling. People who are made redundant are given redundancy payments, which will have been worked out with unions in advance and which are related to the employee's wages and the length of time employed by the firm. Many firms faced with having to lose some members of the workforce will often try to do so by natural wastage, i.e. by not replacing all or some of those who leave. Where this does not work or is insufficient, they will often pursue a policy of voluntary redundancy. However, an invitation to leave is often a high-risk strategy because those who are easily employable elsewhere are often the ones a firm needs to keep.

The law at work

There are a number of laws that are in place to protect both the employee and the employer. These laws cover issues such as employment rights and **health and safety** issues. It would be impossible for every employee to know the law inside out, but unions will protect their members and if workers think they have a problem concerning law at work, then they should contact their union

representative. The issue of **employment law** is a huge area, so we will mention briefly the more important points.

When someone starts to work for an organisation, they enter into a **contract**. This is a legally binding agreement between the employer and the employee and is designed to protect the rights of both. It is not necessary, in all cases, to issue an actual contract, but it is necessary that the employee has particulars of its main points and knowledge of where full details can be found. The main features of such a contract are shown in Table 14.1.

Name of firm	Guzzlers Restaurant
Job title	Kitchen porter
Responsible to	Chef
Start work	1 Jan. 2001
Hours	15 hours per week
Pay	Hourly, 10% above minimum wage
Holidays	14 days per annum, rising to 21 days after three years
Notice	One week either side
Pension scheme	None
Trade union membership	None in business but membership recognised
Discipline	See staff handbook; copy supplied

Table 14.1 Features of a contract of employment

A contract does not have to be exchanged immediately, but, as soon as you commence work, its terms and conditions apply. That is why the date of starting work is so important. All kinds of entitlements and responsibilities begin at that time.

Employees should expect standards of safety to be good. All businesses must have a code of practice for health and safety and must conform to that code. This applies to a wide range of organisations, including schools and churches. Among the things that must be provided for at work are:

- establishing and continuously maintaining a safe and healthy work environment;
- ensuring conditions of work are safe and healthy, e.g. the temperature is reasonable or clothing to compensate is provided;
- ensuring that the space in which workers must

work is sufficient for the nature of the task and the kinds of movement that are necessary;

♦ ensuring sufficient provisions for health, e.g. toilets and wash facilities;

♦ ensuring that the equipment used is safe and that the actions necessary on the part of employees to keep it safe are undertaken;

♦ ensuring that employees wear clothing appropriate to the product and the processes – standards of clothing and hygiene are particularly high where food or food-related products are being produced;

♦ ensuring habits of safety through training and the promotion of good safety habits;

♦ warning where hazardous areas, activities or substances are. Training to make work effective and safe in these circumstances; action to ensure unauthorised personnel do not intrude.

The law intervenes to protect the weaker party in many different situations. You will find comments about the support given by the law in all the contexts in which this is important. Nowadays, it is directives from the EU, as much as law passed in the UK, that determines how employees are protected in the work situation.

Details of the names of Acts of Parliament or of directives may be of interest, but they are not required; neither are any features of legal procedure.

Over-to-you

Read the case study below and tackle the exercises that follow.

Case study – Brankscoombe Copy Services

Branskcoombe Copy Services is expanding its business to include the servicing of office equipment. For this it will require four engineers, one office assistant and two maintenance staff. All will be expected to have driving skills and a clean licence. The engineers will be expected to have some experience in the servicing of office equipment. The engineers will have to work closely with the sales staff since they will also be expected to advise potential customers as to the most suitable equipment for their needs and to install that equipment. All staff will be expected to push for the purchase of Branskcoombe brands of software, paper and other accessories.

(a) Devise a job description for the engineers and from it a suitable advert.

(b) Explain where you would place this advert and why.

(c) The firm has no induction programme at the moment. Advise the management on a suitable induction programme for the new personnel.

(d) What training needs would you expect the firm to provide and what method(s) of training would you consider best?

Test revision questions

(60 marks, 1 hour)

1 List four objectives that an individual working for an organisation might have. (4)

2 What is meant by a 'workforce plan'? (4)

3 Explain four factors that will influence the number of staff needed by a manufacturing business in 12 months time. (8)

4 Outline four problems to a firm as a result of a high labour turnover. (8)

5 State a formula for calculating labour turnover. (3)

6 What limitations does this measure of labour turnover have? (3)

7 Evaluate whether a business should commit a large budget to staff training. (8)

8 Explain three reasons why it might be necessary for a worker to be dismissed from an organisation. (6)

9 Evaluate whether laws relating to employment protection are helpful to businesses. (6)

10 What is meant by voluntary redundancy and why might employers try to encourage this? (4)

11 Should a business strictly observe all health and safety laws? Explain your answer. (6)

Discover and learn

1 Work in groups. Using your part-time work experience analyse what kind of induction programme some local firms run for new employees. Compare your findings with others in your group and comment on those things that appear to be good practice.

2 Consider the student induction programme for your own school or college.

(a) Did it meet your needs?

(b) How can it be improved? Explain your answer.

3 The following data refer to the Asian Airlines:

	2000	2001	2002
Staff employed	200	200	220
Staff leaving	30	40	55
No. of staff absent (average)	15	20	30
Productivity index 2000 = 100	100	95	90

(a) Calculate labour turnover and absenteeism rates for all years.

(b) Explain possible reasons for the trends in the data.

4 Refer to the Levi case study on page 185.

(24 marks, 35 minutes)

(a) Why did Levi get its 'workforce planning' so wrong? (8)

(b) Outline two likely effects on the workforce that remain of these redundancies. (8)

(c) Analyse four factors that will influence Levi's workforce plans over the next few years. (8)

Summary

In this chapter we have recognised that:

- Individual employees will also have objectives, which may be different from those of the organisation.
- It is important for the organisation to have a plan that will consider their employment needs.
- In order to run efficiently, an organisation must be very careful in selecting its workforce.
- It also needs to induct carefully and train the workforce so that it gets the best from the men and women who work for it.
- There are employment laws that affect both the employer and the employee, both of whom have rights that need to be considered.
- Employees are the most important resource that any organisation can have.
- It does not matter how technologically advanced the machinery is or how educated the senior managers are, if the workforce are not motivated and do not have objectives that closely match those of the organisation, then efficiency will be lost.

Key words

Definitions of Key words can be found in the Glossary on page 269.

contract of employment
employment law
health and safety
induction
labour turnover
off-the-job training
on-the-job training

organisational objectives
recruitment
redundancy
training
unfair dismissal
workforce planning

15 Motivation and leadership

On completion of this chapter you should be able to:

➤ understand and explain the importance of motivation to business success
➤ demonstrate how motivation can reduce conflict and increase co-operation
➤ show understanding of the theories of selected writers
➤ explain and apply those theories to business situations

What is motivation – and why does it matter?

In business, motivation is the desire to see a job done quickly and well. Motivation results from the individual's requirement to achieve objectives and to satisfy needs. The best-motivated workers will help an organisation achieve its objectives as cost effectively as possible. Motivated workers will also be trying to reach their own personal goals. Employers need to be aware of what these are because the greatest motivation will develop if workers feel that, through working towards the objectives of the organisation, they are achieving their own.

Unmotivated staff will be reluctant to perform effectively and quickly and will offer nothing other than the absolute minimum of what is expected. It was seen above how important improved motivation could be to the level of productivity and thus the competitiveness of the business. Highly motivated staff will be keen to stay with the firm, reducing the costs of labour turnover. They will be more likely to offer useful suggestions and to contribute in ways other than their contractual obligations. They will often actively seek promotion and responsibility. All of these benefits have an impact on business efficiency, levels of customer service and unit costs. A summary can be found in Figure 15.1.

Some indicators of poor staff motivation are shown in Table 15.1.

Figure 15.1 Gains resulting from motivated staff

Absenteeism	Deliberate absence for which there is not a satisfactory explanation; often follows a pattern
Lateness	Often becomes habitual
Poor performance	Poor quality work; low levels of work or greater waste of materials
Accidents	Poorly motivated workers are often more careless, concentrate less on their work or distract others, and this increases accidents
Labour turnover	People leave for reasons that are not positive; even if they do not get other jobs they spend time in trying to do so
Grievances	There are more of them within the workforce and there might be more union disputes
Poor response rate	Workers do not respond very well to orders or leadership and any response is often slow

Table 15.1 Some indicators of poor staff motivation

Activity

Work in small groups. Discuss the reasons why you think people go to work. Why may these be different depending on the kind of organisation they work for?

Discuss the different motivations to work that might exist for:

(a) a kitchen porter;

(b) someone who works on a production line;

(c) a potter who hand throws her products;

(d) the owner of a computer servicing business.

Conflicting views

In any situation people may well come into conflict with one another. This can be a very good thing if they are prepared to discuss their views with other people. If people are prepared to listen to one another, very often better solutions can be produced. It was for this reason that Mary Parker Follett (*Dynamic Administration: Collected Papers*, Pitman, 1941) argued that conflict was not only inevitable it was desirable.

It is often the case that in organisations people do come into conflict. This may be because the objectives of an individual may be different from those of the organisation. It can be very useful for workers to talk to others in the organisation in order to minimise conflict. However, conflict can be a good thing and may be used constructively to solve problems. Listening to the views of those who operate the machines can sometimes solve production problems. Organisations can save large amounts of money in this way. Therefore, it is important for the leadership style to lend itself to this approach.

It has to be said that if people are happy at work there is much less chance of unhelpful conflict arising. Managers and leaders must have their finger on the pulse of the organisation so that potential difficulties can be spotted and, hopefully, sorted out before major problems arise.

Motivation in theory: how can workers be motivated to work well?

There are many theories of motivation but in this chapter we will concentrate on four of the best-known theorists. Students are advised to read about others too and should feel free to use the thinking of other theorists in situations they come across during their studies.

F.W. Taylor (1856–1917) and scientific management

Taylor made the first serious attempt to analyse worker motivation in order to advise management on the best ways to increase worker performance or productivity. The techniques he used – of establishing an idea or an hypothesis, studying and recording performance at work, altering working methods and re-recording performance – are still used in modern industry. This approach has become known as 'scientific management' due to the detailed recording and analysis of results that it involved.

His main aim was to reduce the level of inefficiency that existed in the US manufacturing industry. Any productivity gains could then, he argued, be shared between business owners and workers. The scope for efficiency gains in early twentieth century manufacturing plants was huge. The vast mass of workers were untrained and non-specialised. They were poorly led by supervisors and managers with little or no formal training in dealing with people. There was usually no formal selection or appraisal system of staff and many were recruited on a daily or weekly basis with no security of employment.

How to improve productivity – Taylor's scientific approach

1 Select workers to perform a task.

2 Observe them performing the task and note the key elements of it.

3 Record the time taken to do each part of the task.

4 Identify the quickest method recorded.

5 Train all workers in this quickest method and do not allow them to make any changes in it.

6 Supervise workers to ensure that this 'best way' is being carried out and to time them to check that the set time is not being exceeded.

7 Pay workers on the basis of results – based on the theory of economic man.

The theory of 'economic man' was widely held, and Taylor himself supported this notion. The view was that man was driven or motivated by money alone and the only factor that could stimulate further effort was the chance of earning extra money. This formed the basis of Taylor's main motivational suggestion – wage levels based on output. He always maintained that workers should be paid a 'fair day's pay for a fair day's work' and that the amount should be directly linked to output through a system known as 'piece rate'. This means paying workers a certain amount for each unit produced. To encourage high output a low rate per unit can be set for the first units produced and then higher rates become payable if output targets are exceeded.

Results of Taylor's work

The results of his research revolutionised the way work was organised in many industries. The emphasis on increasing efficiency and productivity was greeted by industrial leaders as a route towards greater profits. Workers' leaders were more suspicious as they believed that it would lead to more work but no more pay or benefits. They did not necessarily believe Taylor's view that the fruits of higher efficiency would be shared between workers and business owners.

The Taylor approach was widely taken up by the manufacturers of the early twentieth century who were introducing the first forms of mass production and flow line techniques. Workers specialising in one task, strict

management control over work methods and payment by output levels were important features of successful production line techniques. These principles were the driving forces behind all mass production until the 'Japanese style' of working and people management became more widespread from the 1960s onwards. Even before this, other research had been undertaken on people's behaviour at work and doubt was being cast on the simplistic nature of many of Taylor's assumptions about worker motivation. The views of these other researchers is considered next, after an evaluation of Taylor's scientific management approach has been made (see Table 15.2, page 192).

Elton Mayo (1880–1949) and the human relations theories

Elton Mayo is best known for his 'Hawthorne Effect' conclusions. These were based on a series of experiments he and his team conducted over a five-year period at the Hawthorne factory of Western Electric Co. in Chicago. His work was initially based on the assumption that working conditions – lighting, heating, rest periods and so on – had a significant effect on workers' productivity. Experiments were undertaken to

Ford factory in the 1930s – early mass production manufacturers adopted Taylor's approach
Source: Courtesy of Ford Motor Company.

Taylor's approach	Relevance to modern industry
Economic man	Some managers still believe that money is the only way to motivate staff. However, the more general view is that workers have a wide range of needs, not just money, that can be met, in part at least, from work.
Select the right people for each job	Before Taylor there had been few attempts to identify the principles of staff selection. The importance he gave to this is still reflected in the significance given to careful staff selection in nearly all businesses.
Observe and record the performance of staff	This was widely adopted and became known as 'time and motion study'. Regarded with suspicion by workers as a way of making them work harder, it is still employed as a technique but often with the co-operation and involvement of staff.
Establish the best method of doing a job – method study	Again, this is still accepted as being important as efficiency depends on the best ways of working being adopted. However, the Taylor approach of management giving instructions to workers with no discussion or feedback is considered to be undesirable. Worker participation in devising best work practices is now encouraged – see 'kaizen' below.
Piece work payment systems	This is not now a widely used payment system. Quality may be sacrificed in the search for quantity – workers will vary output according to their financial needs at different times of year and it discourages them from accepting changes at work in case they lose some pay. In most of modern industry, especially service industries, it has become very difficult to identify the output of individual workers.

Table 15.2 Evaluating how relevant Taylor's views and methods are today

establish the optimum working conditions and, as in all good scientific practice, the output of a control group was also recorded and this group experienced no changes in working conditions at all. The results surprised all observers – as lighting and other conditions were changed, both improved and worsened, so productivity rose in all groups *including* the control group. This forced Mayo to accept that:

◆ working conditions in themselves were not that important in determining productivity levels;
◆ other motivational factors needed to be investigated further before conclusions could be drawn.

Subsequent experiments were carried out with a group of assembly line workers. Changes to rest periods, payment systems, assembly bench layout and canteen food were made at twelve week intervals. Crucially, before every major change, the researchers discussed the

new changes with the work group. At the end of the experiments the working conditions and hours of work were returned to how they had been before the start of the trial. Output rose far above the original level. Clearly, other motivational factors were operating to increase productivity completely separate from the conditions of work.

The Hawthorne Effect – the conclusions of Mayo's work

Mayo drew the following conclusions from his work:

◆ changes in working conditions and financial rewards have little or no effect on productivity;
◆ when management consult with workers and take an interest in their work then motivation is improved;
◆ working in teams and developing a team spirit can improve productivity;

- when some control over their own working lives is given to workers, such as deciding when to take breaks, there is a positive motivational effect;
- groups can establish their own targets or norms and these can be greatly influenced by the informal leaders of the group.

Maslow (1908–1970) and the hierarchy of human needs

Abraham Maslow's research was not based solely on people in the work environment and his findings have significance for students of psychology and sociology too. He was concerned with trying to identify and classify the main needs that humans have. The importance of his work to business managers is this. Our needs determine our actions – we will always try to satisfy them and we will be motivated to do so. If work can be organised so that we can satisfy some or all of our needs at work then we will become more productive and satisfied.

Maslow summarised these human needs in the following hierarchy (see Figure 15.2 and Table 15.3).

This hierarchy was interpreted by Maslow as follows:
- individuals' needs start on the lowest level;
- once one level of need has been satisfied, humans will strive to achieve the next level;
- self-actualisation or self-fulfilment is not reached by many people but everyone is capable of reaching their potential;
- once a need has been satisfied it will no longer motivate individuals to action – thus when material needs have been satisfied the offer of more money will not increase productivity;

- reversion is possible – it is possible for satisfaction of one level to be withdrawn, for example a loss of job security, and for individuals to move down to the next level.

Limitations of Maslow's approach

Criticisms of Maslow's hierarchy include:
- not everyone has the same needs as is assumed by the hierarchy;
- in practice it can be very difficult to identify the degree to which each need has been met and which level a worker is 'on';
- money is necessary to satisfy physical needs yet it might also play a role in satisfying the other levels of needs, such as status and esteem;
- self-actualisation is never permanently achieved – as some observers of the hierarchy have suggested.

Figure 15.2 Maslow's hierarchy of needs

Level of need	Business conditions which could allow for the needs to be met
Self-actualisation – fulfilment of potential	Offer challenging work that stretches the individual – this will give a sense of achievement. Opportunities to develop and apply new skills will increase potential.
Esteem needs	Offer recognition for work done well. Status, advancement and responsibility will gain the respect of others.
Social needs	Working in teams or groups and ensuring good communication to make workers feel involved
Safety needs	Offering a contract of employment with some job security. A structured organisation that gives clear lines of authority to reduce uncertainty. Ensuring health and safety conditions are met.
Physical needs	Income from employment – high enough to meet essential needs.

Table 15.3 Significance of the hierarchy of needs to business

Jobs must continually offer challenges and opportunities for fulfilment otherwise regression will occur.

Test Activity

(15 marks, 20 minutes)
Examine the similarities and differences you consider exist between the research findings of Mayo and those of Maslow. (15)

Herzberg (1923–2000) and the 'Two factor theory'

Despite basing his research on just 200 professionally qualified workers, Herzberg's conclusions and famous two factor theory have had the greatest impact on motivational practices since Taylor's work almost 60 years earlier. His research was based around questionnaires and interviews with employees with the intention of discovering:

◆ those factors that led to them having very good feelings about their jobs and
◆ those factors that led to them having very negative feelings about their jobs.

His conclusions were that:

Job satisfaction resulted from five main factors – achievement, recognition for achievement, the work itself, responsibility and advancement. He called these factors the 'motivators'. He considered the last three to be the most significant.

Job dissatisfaction resulted from five different factors – company policy and administration, supervision, salary, relationships with others and working conditions. He termed these 'hygiene factors'. These were the factors that surround the job itself (extrinsic factors) rather than the work itself (intrinsic factors). Herzberg considered that the hygiene factors had to be addressed by management to prevent dissatisfaction, but even if they were in place they would not, by themselves, create a well-motivated workforce.

The consequences of Herzberg's two factor theory for business

1 Pay and working conditions can be improved and these will help to remove dissatisfaction about work; but they will not, on their own, provide conditions for motivation to exist. Herzberg argued that it was possible to encourage someone to do a job by paying them – he called this movement. However, movement does not mean that someone wants to do the job – that would require motivation. Motivation to do the job, and to do it well, would only exist if the motivators were in place. Herzberg *did not* claim that pay did not matter, but that it **moves** people to do a job not **motivate** them to do it.

2 The motivators need to be in place for workers to be prepared to work willingly and always to give of their best. Herzberg suggested that they could be provided by adopting the principles of 'job enrichment'. There are three main features of job enrichment and if these were adopted then the motivators would be available for all workers to benefit from:

◆ **Complete units of work**. Typical mass production methods leave workers to assemble one small part of the finished product. This is not rewarding, can be boring and repetitive and prevents the worker from appreciating the importance of what they are doing as part of the overall production system. Herzberg argued that complete and identifiable units of work should be assigned to workers, and that this might involve teams of workers rather than individuals on their own. These complete units of work could be whole sub-assemblies of manufactured goods, such as a complete engine assembly in a car plant. In service industries it could mean that a small team of multi-skilled people, such as waiters, chefs and technicians for IT/video equipment, provide all of the conference facilities in a hotel for a business conference rather than many people doing just one small and relatively unimportant task before moving on to another part of the hotel. 'If you want people motivated to do a good job, give them a good job to do,' as Herzberg put it.

◆ **Feedback on performance**. This type of communication could give recognition for work well done and could provide incentives to achieve even more.

◆ **A range of tasks**. To give challenge and to stretch the individual, a range of tasks should be given some of which may be, at least initially, beyond the workers' current experience. This, in quite a large measure, ties in with the 'self-actualisation' level in Maslow's hierarchy.

3 A business could offer higher pay, improved working conditions and less heavy-handed supervision of work. These would all help to remove dissatisfaction but they would all be quickly taken for granted. If work is not interesting, rewarding or challenging then workers will not be satisfied or will not be motivated to offer their full potential whatever the pay level offered to them.

Evaluation of Mayo's research

Since Mayo's findings were published there has been a trend towards giving workers more of a role in business decision making – this is called participation. Personnel departments, which hardly existed in the early years of the twentieth century, were established to try to put the 'Hawthorne effect' into practice. The idea of involving workers, taking an interest in their welfare and finding out their individual goals has opened up new fields of research for industrial psychologists and this area of study is now regarded as an important component of university business courses.

This development of the 'people' side of business has taken industry away from the engineer focused and purely money motivated views of Taylor. This trend was sustained by the work of two other famous researchers.

Evaluation of Herzberg's work

Although other researchers who have used Herzberg's methods have failed to arrive at quite such clear-cut conclusions, there is little doubt that the results he drew from his work have had a significant impact on business practices. Team working is now much more widespread with whole units of work being delegated to these groups. Workers tend to be made much more responsible for the quality of their own work rather than being closely supervised by a quality-controlling inspectorate. Most firms are continually looking for ways to improve effective communication and group meetings allowing two-way communication are often favoured. It would be wrong to conclude that this is all Herzberg's doing, but there is little doubt that his work

Test Activity

Read the short case study below and then tackle the exercises that follow.

Case study – Three workers discuss the work they do in their different businesses

Maria was a self-employed market researcher. She earned a reasonable salary but it was not the same every month as it depended on how much work she had been able to gain. 'I really like my work as it is very interesting and I am very much appreciated by the firms I work for. I do not work with a regular team of people but that does not bother me. I earn enough for my needs and I would not take a higher-paid job in a large firm as I do not like being told what to do by supervisors.' Asif's experience was different. He worked in a shop. He enjoyed the group of friends he worked with and really felt part of the team. He thought the money was good

too. However, he considered that his work was not appreciated and was not challenging enough. 'I would look for another job which gave me more responsibility and recognition but for the present I do not want to give up the friends I have made. The interesting jobs, like displaying stock and deciding on which new items should be sold, are all done by the managers.' Imran spoke up too, 'You are both very lucky. My present job is only temporary and although the pay is reasonable I have been told that my contract could end at any time. I am very keen to find a more permanent position.'

(15 marks, 20 minutes)

(a) Assess which level of Maslow's hierarchy each of these workers seems to be on at present. Explain your answer. (6)

(b) Discuss Asif's current level of motivation and how it could be increased by referring to Herzberg's 'hygiene factors' and 'motivators'. (9)

and the publicity given to the research conclusions led to a hastening of the trends that may have occurred much more slowly without his intervention (see Table 15.4).

Hygiene factors	Motivating factors
Wages	Things about the job
Conditions of work	Efforts made are recognised
Culture of the organisation	Responsibility
Relationship with bosses	Opportunity to develop
Treatment at work	Opportunity for promotion
Feelings about work and own efforts	Success
Controls and limitations	Self realisation at work
	Status

Table 15.4 Herzberg's two-factor theory

Motivational theories – how useful are they?

They provide us with a starting point and a framework for analysing and discussing the main motivational issues. The research undertaken has been criticised for its lack of rigour and follow-up work, yet the basic ideas that have been covered in this chapter are still talked about and evaluated many years after the initial findings were published. In examination terms, it is important not to spend too long describing research methods. It is more important to identify the most appropriate theory to the question set and to explain the relevance of it to business decision makers. It is the application of the motivational theorists' ideas – and the potential difficulties in applying them to certain situations – that are most likely to concern your examiners.

Douglas McGregor

McGregor was a social scientist, and from his experience he developed what has become known as the **Theory X** and **Theory Y** approach. What McGregor said has often been misquoted. His theories are not about motivation but about attitudes.

McGregor saw the attitudes of managers to workers as lying on a line between two extremes. His Theory X in many ways demonstrates one extreme, the traditional approach to management, which involves high levels of discipline, control, obedience and conformity. In other words, the managers tell the employees exactly what to do and when and where to do it. McGregor's Theory Y demonstrates the opposite extreme. In this he argues that managers assume that people enjoy mental effort and will actually be self-disciplined if they are committed to the objectives of the organisation.

The inference is that managers who adopt a Theory Y attitude to workers will explain and share the objectives of the organisation. Theory Y implies that people will respond to rewards, although, interestingly, McGregor says that these do not necessarily have to be monetary rewards.

McGregor also says that the majority of people have the ability to demonstrate initiative, which is not the gift of a few but of many. Managers need to be able to create situations within the work setting where subordinates can demonstrate their initiative. This would be for the general good of the organisation, as well as for the individual.

However, this view may represent a challenge to managers, who may feel threatened by a situation where they have less control and where others may be coming up with good ideas. Table 15.5 shows these two extreme attitudes.

What managers assume	
Theory X	**Theory Y**
Workers are lazy	Workers are keen
Workers need to be pushed	Will work on their own
Workers need control	Workers can be self-directing
Workers need threats and punishment	Workers respond to rewards and recognition
Workers avoid responsibility	Workers seek responsibility
Workers have no ambition or initiative	Workers are ambitious and seek to show initiative

Table 15.5 Theory X and Theory Y

In practice most managers are somewhere between those two extremes. Those close to Theory X manage in an autocratic way, whilst those closer to Theory Y are much more flexible and democratic in their approach.

It is unwise to assume that the autocratic approach is always wrong. There are people who like to be directed and controlled and there are situations in which there is little value in the democratic approach:

1 In every group of people there is likely to be at least one who prefers to be controlled and directed, likes

being told what to do and when to do it. This person will often fail to achieve if deprived of the firm direction needed. Most teachers will identify at least one student like that in every group.

2 Some situations require immediate action and the unquestioning obedience of the workforce. This is true, e.g. in military situations, in the police force or the fire service.

The work of these theorists should not be seen as purely theoretical. They have much to offer managers as they seek to understand and motivate their workers. It is clear that managers need to be close to those they control if the findings of the theorists are to be applied. In today's ever-changing and often difficult organisational setting, innovative and creative management is necessary. No longer will people tolerate simply being told what to do; nor can it be assumed that they will be motivated only by money.

We need to talk

All of us spend a lot of time communicating with other people. We can do this in all kinds of ways:

- by speaking to them face to face;
- by using the telephone;
- by sending faxes or emails;
- by sending letters, memos and various other pieces of paper;
- by using our body language;
- by indirect means like notice boards and other people;
- by ignoring people; this often conveys a very strong message.

It is essential that we communicate with other people, in both our business and private lives, but what is even more important is that the **communication** is effective and can be understood. How often have we got ourselves into difficult situations, simply because our message has been misunderstood or misinterpreted? This can cause real problems of frustration or even anger and a breakdown in a relationship.

Within an organisation, the process of communication is absolutely vital if the organisation is to achieve its objectives. Poor communication can cause mistrust and suspicion amongst the employees and this can lead, at best, to a reduction in motivation and production. At worst, it leads to very poor industrial relations. It has been said that a manager in an organisation can spend as much as 80% of his working day communicating with others. It has also been suggested that 80% of all industrial problems arise or are made very much worse through poor communication. There are some very common factors that result in communication being poor:

- The words used can cause problems. This is most common when one person is using technical

Activity

Read the case study below and then tackle the task that follows.

Case study – Benson and Co.

Benson and Co. is a small clothing firm, which makes clothing principally for a major high-street store. The contract to supply the store is very valuable to the firm as it offers a ready market for the products and a good return. However, the store is very demanding in terms of delivery times and of the quality of the goods. Indeed, it sends its own quality-control expert to take random samples in the firm. Bensons' have been told that if they cannot meet delivery deadlines, the contract will not be renewed. The nature of the work is that the employees, mostly female, are each involved in one process only. They tend to operate on a very solitary basis and have little time together, except at the limited tea-break time. The employees are paid using the piece-rate system.

The management of Bensons' is concerned that production is not as good as it might be; the quality controller has noticed an increasing number of problems and morale seems to be low amongst the workers. There also seems to be an increasing rate of absenteeism. Jobs could be in danger.

You have been called into Benson and Co. as a management consultant to advise on the situation. Bearing in mind what we have been considering about motivation, write a short report giving your opinion and advice on the way forward.

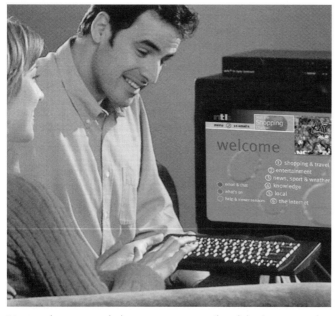

More and more people have access to email and the internet and the communication doors they open
Source: ntl.

language that the other person does not understand. Examples are passing on accounting information or talking about computers.

◆ The tone of a message will often cause problems. It is not what you say but how you say it that conveys the message.

◆ Timing can be crucial. If someone gets a message too late, after someone else, when they are not concentrating or in poor circumstances, it can be ignored, forgotten or misunderstood.

◆ People's feelings and emotions can influence how a message is received. If we do not like someone or do not trust them we are likely to disbelieve what we are told. If we trust or like them, we may believe something that should not be accepted. Sometimes status gets in the way. When a boss gives a message, it is often believed and acted upon. When a subordinate gives one, it is commonly ignored.

The strengths and weaknesses of communication methods are listed in Table 15.6. To get communication right we have to pay careful attention to:

◆ ourselves as senders and our awareness of the person to whom the message is being sent; if the receiver cannot understand or interpret the message, the communication is a waste of time;

◆ the nature of the message; there is no point in sending urgent messages through a slow medium,

Activities

1 Try a game of Chinese whispers in the class as a whole. Start a slightly complex message at the front and pass it towards the back by word of mouth. Relay the final message to the rest of the class.

2 Figure 15.3 shows different kinds of communication net. Try them out and discuss your conclusions.

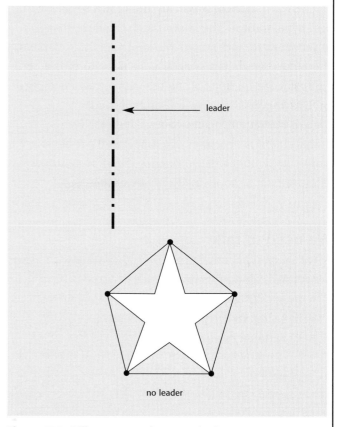

Figure 15.3 Different types of communication net

3 Choose any problem known to you from the news, local activity or what happens in your school or college. Discuss the extent to which better communication would have helped.

4 A lesson can be delivered in any one of the following ways:

(a) all talk with you listening and making notes;

(b) by using dictation;

(c) by using a case study;

(d) by using visual aids;

(e) by using a marker board or overhead projector;

(f) by brainstorm or discussion;

(g) by question and answer.

Discuss circumstances in which each of these methods might be either a good way or a bad way.

e.g. second-class post, or confidential information in a way that allows open access;

◆ the response we hope to get; abrupt unfeeling messages will not work where we need co-operation or want to make a sale;

◆ timing; sending out bills to arrive on Christmas Eve is not likely to be received kindly;

◆ the nature of the medium; some are not suitable for all messages; some are too costly, some are too slow, some are inappropriate for the receiver;

◆ the purpose of the communication; the objective is always to change someone's behaviour so that you get the response you seek; in some cases it is to encourage a purchase, in others to get into higher education or to get a job.

Method	Strengths	Weaknesses
Oral	Direct	Need to listen carefully
	Can be varied	Affected by noise
	Easy to understand	Passive
	Easy access	No permanent accurate record
	Can be questioned	Can be distorted
	Quick	Quickly forgotten
Written	Recorded	Often difficult to read
	More structured	No body language
	Easy to distribute	Feedback slower
	Cannot be varied	No immediate response
	Message identical	May be misinterpreted
		Costly and time consuming
Visual	More interactive	Needs close attention
	Demands attention	Sometimes too fast
	Often easier to remember	Not always clear
	Creates greater interest	Interpretations vary
Technological	Great speed	Cannot always be received
	Interactive	Relies on receiver
	Creates interest	Is expensive in hardware
	Encourages response	Not universal
	Ignores boundaries	Can be intercepted
	Good image	Diminishes personal contact

Table 15.6 Strengths and weaknesses of communication methods

Motivating people in practice

Firms have objectives and they relate to the outcomes of business activity. To achieve these outcomes they will have to motivate the workforce. The theorists give us some idea of what might motivate people and clearly effective communication is an essential feature. What methods are commonly employed?

Wages and salaries

Almost all surveys produce a strong indication that people think they are motivated by money, and up to a point we all are. Some are more money conscious than others; hence the way that people are paid tends to be the starting point. Among the most common methods are:

Time-based wages Employees are paid by the hour and the total wage they earn is determined by the total time worked. Workers may also be paid overtime rates. This could be one and a half times or twice the normal hourly rate. Overtime is voluntary, but can be a very good way of earning extra money for special times of the year, such as holidays or Christmas. No worker can be required to work overtime. At certain anti-social times, such as night working, working week-ends and bank holidays, the basic rate is likely to be increased. Time-based wages put the emphasis on quality and on taking your time over a job.

Output-based wages Employees are paid according to the output they achieve. For example, someone may be involved in a job where they pack socks into boxes. The number of boxes packed will determine how much they earn. Often, in this situation, people decide how much they want to earn during a week and work accordingly. They may have packed enough boxes in three days to earn what they regard as a sufficient wage. They will take two days off work. In most cases, managers are happy with the arrangement, because they know that, if they insisted on workers attending for five days, they would simply slow down and not actually pack any more boxes. This type of payment is often for boring, repetitive jobs and puts the emphasis on the quantity of work done rather than on the quality.

Activity

John is in a job where he is paid by the hour. He earns £4.75 an hour. This week he has worked for 37 hours and has done 5 hours overtime at time and a half.

Calculate his gross pay for the week.

Salary   Employees are paid an annual amount of money, which is then divided into monthly payments. It is usually the case that staff, rather than manual workers, are paid in this way. In many salaried positions, it is not possible to earn overtime, any extra work done outside normal working hours is regarded as part of the job. This is true in the case of teachers and most managers. It puts the emphasis on getting the job done. It is particularly suitable when the job cannot be limited by either time or output and tends to convey status to the receiver as compared with wage earning. However, many salaries are lower than the annual amounts earned by some wage earners.

Commission   This is when a percentage of a sale price is given to the employee as an incentive to sell more goods. Sales people may well be paid by a basic salary plus commission. In some cases, the basic salary is quite low and so encourages the person to sell as much as possible. It is up to the individual what the final amount earned will be. The more they sell, the more they earn. In other cases, people can be paid on a commission-only basis. Commission is often earned in professional occupations like that of the auctioneer, the estate agent and the art dealer. Estate agents and auctioneers may get commission payments from both the buyer and the seller.

Profit sharing   This is meant to ensure that the workers strive to meet the objectives of the firm because they will share in the resultant profits. Such shares in profit are often described as bonuses and paid out at worker-friendly times of the year like Christmas and holidays.

Share options   These make the worker a shareholder in the business and thus give a permanent stake in the success of the business. They often have only a short-term effect because the workers sell their shares.

Productivity agreements   Often negotiated with unions. Extra payments are made when the productivity of the workforce improves to a targeted extent. Improvements in efficiency of this kind benefit all stakeholders.

Test Activity

Read the case study below and then tackle the exercises that follow.

Case study – Business expansion needs workforce support

Ursula and Jin-Ho had established their retail store selling mobile phones six years earlier. They were now ready to embark on an ambitious expansion programme. This involved opening three new stores a year. They had sufficient capital but they were worried about the staffing needs for these extra stores. How should they attract and keep the best staff? Ursula wanted to make the new store managers fully responsible for the performance of each branch and to reward them with a 'share option' scheme that would give them the chance to buy company shares at preferential rates. In addition, she wanted a profit-sharing scheme for all employees. This would involve sharing 20% of annual profits amongst all the staff in proportion to their annual salaries. Jin-Ho was not keen on either proposal. He suggested a commission-based pay scheme for the shop staff and a performance-related pay bonus system for the managers. The bonus would be paid if the managers reached the annual sales targets that would be set, taking the area and size of each shop into account. He was unhappy about taking profits out of the business. 'As it is still a young company with ambitious growth plans we need to reward our existing shareholders, including ourselves, and put as much back into the firm as possible', he had said.

Whichever system they adopted they both agreed that it would have to encourage all staff to contribute fully to the future success of the business.

(30 marks, 40 minutes)

(a) Explain the differences between the payment systems mentioned in this case study. (9)

(b) Examine the advantages of each of these two proposed payment schemes. (9)

(c) Using all of the information available to you and your knowledge of payment schemes, recommend and justify suitable pay systems for shop workers and managers. (12)

Non-financial motivation

In many instances, we can use non-monetary methods of motivation. As Herzberg indicated, people are motivated by things other than pay. In jobs that do not motivate of themselves, absenteeism and lateness become common once pay has reached an acceptable level. Among the approaches most commonly used are:

Goal setting   Employees and supervisors can sit down together and negotiate achievable goals. Where this is done in a supportive climate, it can motivate people. It is important, however, that the goals have been understood and agreed by the workers. Obviously the goals that are set need to be realistic as far as the workers are concerned and yet, at the same time, they need to benefit the organisation. Honest communication is essential at the meeting where the goals are set so that there is no confusion. It is easy sometimes for people to agree to things and yet, when they consider more carefully, they realise that they have bitten off more than they can chew. This will benefit no one.

Employee participation   There are various methods of involving the employees in the running of the business. It should be noted, however, that there is a difference between employee involvement, which may only involve single workers, and employee participation, which is a principle whereby employees are seen to be an important and fundamental part of the process of management within the organisation. This process may well involve workers being on the boards of companies. When workers are involved in the decision-making processes, and effectively in the running of the company, it is expected that they will support fully the company philosophy and strategy. Employee participation can take a number of forms:

◆ Financial involvement where the employees actually have a capital stake in the organisation. This may be through profit sharing or share option schemes.
◆ Job involvement, when employees can contribute to the way their own jobs are organised. Because they have a say in working conditions and practices, there should be fewer complaints. Also it would be expected that job satisfaction can be improved.
◆ Managerial involvement, when employees sit on joint decision-making committees. The most likely committee is the Health and Safety committee.

Employees feel that management is prepared to listen to them in terms of possible improvement to processes or indeed simply on more day-to-day issues. It is important in this situation that suggestions are acted upon, otherwise the basis of trust is lost. If effective employee participation is to take place, then the culture of the organisation must allow it and indeed foster it. The management style must be open and democratic and levels of trust must be high. Smaller organisations tend to lend themselves more easily to participation because discussions probably already take place as a matter of course. Larger organisations have difficulties, such as those associated with ineffective communication systems, as discussed above. It is important that comments made are passed on to senior management, even if the comments seem critical. There is a temptation for middle managers to ignore the critical comments in order to save embarrassment. However, when this happens, trust will be lost and participation will not be a success.

Job rotation   Jobs are rotated on a regular basis so that the workers can be involved with a range of operations and not simply be doing the same repetitive task day after day. This also enables workers to see how their particular function fits into the general scheme of things and how, without their contribution, the product could not be completed. A side effect of this scheme is that there can be a greater flexibility in the workforce. However, job rotation does not really work when it is just movement from one similar boring job to another. It does tend to work when it is based on multi-skilling and a genuine difference in the job being undertaken.

Job enlargement   Tasks are broadened or deepened so that employees become involved in a greater range of tasks. The result is a greater awareness of the overall process, as well as greater job satisfaction.

Job enrichment   Employees often become involved in decision making and have much greater responsibility. The process often involves a slackening of outside supervision.

Quality circles   These are groups of employees who meet together on a regular basis to discuss issues such as the quality and level of output and safety. The groups try to devise ways of solving problems and implementing solutions. This approach has the benefit of involving the workers directly in the process of problem-solving and strategic management within their area. Undoubtedly motivation is increased as a result. There is also a greater sense of pride and achievement. There is an opportunity for the organisation to use expertise in the workforce and also the chance to see whether or not workers have potential for supervisory or management positions.

Flexible timings   This allows personnel to decide the hours they will work. It is suitable for workers with children who must be taken to school or in situations where transport is difficult and or unreliable like 'rush hours'. Generally there is a core time when workers must be in work, but choice around it. It is normal to have a limit both to the number of excess and missed hours that may be built up.

Perks and status symbols   These are most common among management and include such things as a company car, a well-furnished office, a fancy title or a parking space.

Appraisal   It may seem strange to include this as a motivator, and yet, used properly, that is exactly what it should be. Too often it is assumed that this is a method that an organisation uses to check up on employees. It has been regarded negatively and in many ways that is unfair. An effective appraisal system will be a two-way communication process where employees can discuss with their superiors their achievements over the previous period. They can then discuss ways to improve their performance. This may be an ideal way for management to discover fundamental difficulties, perhaps, in the shop floor processes. If the processes can be improved, this will be of advantage to both management and workers. Where such appraisals are genuinely two-way, it also provides valuable information on the communication and leadership skills of supervisors.

Does leadership style matter?

Every organisation needs effective leadership if it is to succeed. There are natural leaders. We come across them whether it is as captain of the sports team or simply the person who always seems to take the lead in a discussion group. It is important that those who manage organisations have leadership ability, whether natural or learned, that will enable them to take people with them. The leader may have very sound and well thought out objectives, but if those who are to be led will not follow, then the objectives will never be achieved.

There are formal leaders within organisations who are appointed to have a managerial roles. Organisations must realise the potential of the informal

Activity

Work in small groups. Discuss the qualities you think a good leader should have. Is anyone in your group a good leader? Give reasons. Is a leader born or can leadership be learned?

leader. He or she is the person people naturally look up to and who may not have, as yet, a formal leadership responsibility. Managers should be aware of possible leaders and give them some sort of responsibility. This could be by inviting them to sit on a consultation committee within the organisation, or possibly even by having them as a worker representative on the board. The natural talents of these people need to be harnessed for the good of the organisation. In simple terms, it is better to have people with informal leadership skills working for rather than against the organisation's goals.

Leaders lead in different ways according to their natural traits and according to the situation. The main leadership styles are (see also Table 15.7):

Authoritarian   This type of leader has control, avoids discussion, issues instructions, often without explanation, and is unwilling to listen to subordinates. This style can cause major problems in an organisation where people have experience in what they are doing. Workers will feel unvalued and resentment will quickly build. However, where workers are inexperienced, this style of leadership may be effective, at least in the short term. It is of course, appropriate where the luxury of discussion may not be available, e.g. in a war situation. Such a leader has much in common with the Theory X attitude to management.

Democratic   This type of leader will encourage discussion, will involve others in decision making, will consult and generally will try to help the employees to grow in terms of performance and self-worth. This type of manager needs to be prepared to be flexible in terms of views held and must, of course, be willing to delegate responsibility. Complex problems can often be approached using this management style. There is opportunity to use the talent and experience of others. However, workers need to feel comfortable with this approach and need to feel that their views are genuinely considered. There is no point in a manager paying lip service to this approach and then proceeding with plans that have already been decided upon. Here you will recognise a Theory Y attitude.

Laissez-faire   It has been said that this type of manager is not really a manager at all. He/she will be involved only in crisis management, reacting to situations and not managing them. He/she will simply leave things alone until they go wrong. There is no sense of strategic management. In today's organisational climate, it is doubtful if this management style would succeed. Nevertheless there are situations in which the

Style	Main features	Drawbacks	Possible applications
Autocratic	Leader takes all decisions. Gives little information to staff. Supervises workers closely. Only one-way communication. Workers are only given limited information about the business.	Demotivates staff who want to contribute and accept responsibility. Decisions do not benefit from staff input.	Defence forces and police where quick decisions are needed and the scope for 'discussion' must be limited. In times of crisis when decisive action might be needed to limit damage to the business or danger to others.
Democratic	Participation is encouraged. Two-way communication is used which allows feedback from staff. Workers are given information about the business to allow full staff involvement.	Consultation with staff can be time consuming. On occasions, quick decision making will be required. Should staff be involved in all aspects of the business? Some issues might be too sensitive, e.g. job losses; or too secret, e.g. development of new products.	It is most likely to be useful in businesses that expect workers to contribute fully to the production and decision-making processes, thereby satisfying their higher-order needs. An experienced and flexible workforce will be likely to benefit most from this style. In situations that demand a new way of thinking or a new solution then staff input can be very valuable.
Paternalistic	Managers do what they think is best for the workers. Some consultation might take place but the final decisions are taken by the managers – there is no true participation in decision making. Managers want workers to be happy in their jobs.	Some workers will be dissatisfied with the apparent attempts to consult, while not having any real power or influence.	Used by managers who have a genuine concern for workers' interests but feel that 'managers know best' in the end. When workers are young or inexperienced this might be an appropriate style to employ.
Laissez-faire	Managers delegate virtually all authority and decision-making powers. Very broad criteria or limits might be established for the staff to work within.	Workers may not appreciate the lack of structure and direction in their work. This could lead to a loss of security. The lack of feedback – as managers will not be closely monitoring progress – may be demotivating.	When managers are too busy (or too lazy!) to intervene. May be appropriate in research institutions where experts are more likely to arrive at solutions when not constrained by narrow rules or management controls.

Table 15.7 Summary of management styles

Activity

Work in small groups

(a) Consider the part-time jobs that people have. Discuss the type of management style that you think exists in the organisation you work for. Give reasons for your decisions.

(b) Outline the management style of those who teach you. How appropriate do you consider that style is:
- for them;
- for you;
- for the task they have to undertake?

style works. In such circumstances it is known as management by exception and involves refusing to interfere in a situation or a process unless something goes wrong.

Paternalistic   This type of manager will ask for opinions, but will then persuade employees to accept his/her point of view. In a sense this is playing at democracy, but being autocratic. Again, it will not be successful with experienced staff, who will soon become frustrated and disenchanted, but it is common in small firms where the boss is seen more as the 'father' of the whole team than as a boss.

The style of leadership that is adopted will depend very much on:
- the organisation and its culture;
- the subordinates (what kind of temperament do they have? are they experienced?);
- the managers themselves;
- the task that is to be performed;
- the conditions and circumstances of the task.

The most successful managers are those who can adapt their style to suit different situations, although it is true

Activity

Which form of leadership/management style would be most appropriate in the following circumstances? You should give reasons for your answers:
- the army;
- a small computer software company that employs 12 people;
- a large engineering company where there has been a history of industrial unrest.

to say that people tend to display one of the styles. It may not be easy for someone who is naturally democratic to become autocratic, or the other way round. Managers can be sent on training courses to improve their management skills and to make use of theory, but it still remains true that the best managers have a feel for the job.

Theories of leadership

Trait (or qualities) theory

This theory suggests that leaders are born rather than made. People are born with certain characteristics and come from a certain background that would make them leaders.

Style theory

This suggests that leaders use a different style, as indicated in the last section. This could be authoritarian, democratic, laissez-faire or paternalistic. Researchers have looked at how different styles affect performance. The findings showed that, while people tend to experience more job satisfaction when working under a democratic leader, the level of productivity is only very slightly higher.

Contingency

Fiedler is the best-known theorist here. He suggested that the style of leadership depended upon the task being done, how much power the leader had and the relationship the leader had with the workers.

Best-fit approach

Managers need to assess the situation and then adapt their leadership style to fit it.

Management by objectives

The suggestion is that managers and subordinates closely discuss the objectives that are desired and how the subordinates can contribute to the achievement of these. There are obvious benefits of this kind of approach:
- Motivation is improved. As discussed above, there is greater motivation for employees when they are involved in the process of deciding on objectives and how best they can be achieved.
- Managers are forced to plan and develop

objectives. They are also forced into a process of discussion and consultation.

- ◆ The structure of the organisation will be improved as managers can see more clearly where the weaknesses and strengths lie.
- ◆ Benchmarking is provided and this helps managers to control the situation better.
- ◆ Workers are working towards realistic targets.

There are also problems with this approach:

- ◆ The approach is very time-consuming because it involves so much discussion.
- ◆ Frustration can arise when objectives cannot be met because of external factors.
- ◆ Some organisations do not lend themselves to this approach. Perhaps there has traditionally been a very strong authoritarian approach to management.
- ◆ New skills need to be developed to cope.

Over-to-you

Test revision questions
(100 marks, 1 hour, 40 minutes)

1 Explain what is meant by 'labour productivity'. (3)
2 Show how an increase in labour productivity can reduce unit costs of production, by using a numerical example. (4)
3 Outline three factors that can lead to an increase in labour productivity. (6)
4 State three features of Taylor's research that might be relevant to modern manufacturing industries. (3)
5 Outline the main findings of Mayo's Hawthorne research. (4)
6 Examine the significance of one feature of the Hawthorne effect to management interested in increasing worker productivity. (3)
7 Explain why studying human needs is believed to be an important part of motivation theory. (4)
8 Give an example of how it is possible for an individual to revert to a lower level of Maslow's hierarchy of human needs. (2)
9 Consider two different levels of Maslow's hierarchy and explain how these needs could be satisfied at work. (6)
10 Consider two possible limitations of the ideas contained on Maslow's hierarchy for a manager keen to improve workplace motivation. (4)
11 Differentiate clearly between Herzberg's motivators and hygiene factors. (6)
12 Why did Herzberg consider it important to differentiate between 'movement' and 'motivation'? (3)
13 Outline the three key features of job enrichment. (6)
14 Why might it be difficult to implement job enrichment into a place of work? (3)
15 Outline the differences between McGregor's 'Theory X and Theory Y' approach to managers' assumptions about workers. (3)

Discover and learn
1 Investigate a local organisation and determine what style of management is used. Justify your conclusions.
2 Visit a local supermarket. From your observations, do you consider the workforce is, in general, well motivated. Support your conclusions.
3 Undertake your own research into motivational factors. Construct a simple questionnaire using Herzberg's two best-known questions concerning job satisfaction and job dissatisfaction. Ask these questions of as many working people as you can – a minimum of ten would be useful. Give each of the respondents the list of factors that Herzberg considered to be both hygiene factors and motivators and see if your research supports his findings. Write a report about your findings which are either likely to agree with the original research, or not. If not, try identify and explain the factors that *do* give job satisfaction to your respondents.

   You could ask teachers and support staff at school, parents, friends, neighbours or your workmates if you have a part-time job.

4 Read the case study below and then tackle the exercises that follow.

Case study – Why women are happier in their work than men

The world of work is a better experience for women than it is for men, according to a survey. Asked to rate their job satisfaction on a scale of one to seven, they scored an average of 5.56 while males scored 5.22. Experts appear divided over the reasons why women appear to get more out of their work than men. Many women

Many women find companionship and job satisfaction working in retail.

work part time and have job-sharing schemes which, the survey found, increased job satisfaction as they could pursue other interests too.

In addition, older workers get the greatest satisfaction from their jobs while university graduates are the most dissatisfied of all, according to the survey of 30,000 employees. Employees generally enjoyed their first years at work but then job satisfaction falls between the ages of 30 and 40. But employees over 60 gained the greatest satisfaction from their work. Professor Andrew Oswald of Warwick University, who conducted the survey, said, 'the young are just happy to have a job. As they grow older they realise that ambitions and needs may not be so easily fulfilled.' It seems that we all start off thinking we will reach the top in our careers but most of us are forced to adjust. 'The older we get the

more settled and content with our role at work we get', he added.

Graduates are often frustrated by the lack of challenging work on offer. They are often forced to take low-skilled jobs for which they are over-qualified in order to pay off debts. The survey also revealed that long hours at work did not turn people off their jobs.

Employees of small businesses and non-profit-making organisations, such as charities, were happier at work than those working for big companies. David Hands, of the Federation of Small Businesses, said, 'There is a greater camaraderie (friendship) in small firms than in big companies.' Workers feel less involved and less secure in bigger firms. He added, 'It is more relaxed in small firms and people enjoy it more. Many also get more responsibility which adds to their satisfaction.'

Source: Adapted from *Daily Mail*, November 2000.

(35 marks, 45 minutes)

(a) Identify three factors that seem to influence job satisfaction and explain them in terms of Maslow's hierarchy of needs. (6)

(b) Explain in terms of the features of job enrichment why it might be easier for small firms to motivate staff than big businesses. (9)

(c) Discuss the extent to which it might be possible for large firms to use Herzberg's motivators to improve the level of worker motivation. (10)

5 Read the case study below and tackle the exercises that follow.

Case study – Plast-flower Ltd

Plast-flower Ltd is a medium-sized firm employing 58 workers. George Wilkenson was the founder of the firm and is its current manager. He is very autocratic in his approach to running the firm. People tend not to question his decisions, but it is obvious that productivity is low. There is also resentment among the workers because they are not being consulted about anything. They believe that there is much they could contribute that would improve productivity.

George is considering retirement and selling the firm to the highest bidder. Existing managers are very keen to buy, thinking they know how to make a success of the firm.

   (a) Advise them on how they might motivate the workforce.
   (b) Consider ways in which resentment can be reduced.
   (c) The unrest has created a number of hostile informal groups. How should the new managers react to these?

6 Read the case study below and then tackle the exercises that follow.

Case study – Leadership styles at McNuggets

As one of the largest take-away food restaurant chains in Asia, McNuggets had established a reputation for cheap meals of consistent quality with rapid customer service. Research surveys had established that the public appreciated that, no matter which town or country they were in, they could always depend on buying exactly the same range of dishes, at similar prices with the same quality standards. This reputation was built on a very detailed training programme for staff – failure to pass the test at the end of the course or failure to observe the methods and work practices taught would lead to demotion or dismissal. Every single activity of the workers was laid down in company regulations. Here is a list of just some of them:

◆ All customers to be greeted with the same welcome.
◆ Chicken nuggets to be cooked for exactly two minutes in oil at 100 degrees C.
◆ A portion of French fries to contain 150 grams, to be salted with 10 grams of salt and to be kept for no more than five minutes before sale – they would then have to be disposed of.
◆ Staff to be trained to specialise in undertaking two tasks within the restaurant.

The managers at McNuggets prided themselves on the fact that they had 'thought of everything' and that workers did not have to use any initiative – all problems had been foreseen and there was a set procedure to deal with all of them.

Workers were well looked after. The pay rate per hour was reasonable, there were free uniforms and staff meals, bonus systems were paid to staff who, in the managers' view, had given the best customer service each month. Regular meetings were held at which information about branch performance was discussed with the staff. They were encouraged to air their views but they were told that they could not, under any circumstances, change the method of working laid down by McNuggets Head Office. Despite what the managers considered to be good working conditions, the staff turnover was very high and absences were a problem.

(30 marks, 40 minutes)
   (a) Which style of leadership/management seems to be used at McNuggets? Justify your answer. (4)
   (b) Using your knowledge of motivational theorists, how would you account for the apparent low levels of motivation at McNuggets restaurants? (8)
   (c) Discuss how the management style could be adapted in an attempt to improve motivation of staff within these restaurants. (8)
   (d) To what extent is the style of management used at McNuggets appropriate for a business such as this? (10)

Summary

In this chapter we have recognised that:

- Workers need to be motivated if the organisation is to achieve its objectives.

- There are different approaches to motivation, but it is important to note that money is not the only motivator. Indeed there are situations when money will not motivate at all.

- There is a very wide range of non-monetary ways of motivating. Experience shows that these often satisfy the higher needs and hence are successful.

- Although many ways have been tried, motivating workers engaged in dull or repetitive jobs is not easy. The modern approach is increasingly towards quality circles and team working.

- There are many styles of leadership that can be used within an organisation and, in many ways, these are best used by adapting them to the situation.

- Many people have leadership potential and some of the time they may not be in positions of authority. It is important that the organisation makes use of them in both formal and informal situations.

- Leadership style will impact upon the performance of individuals and, ultimately, it is the performance of individuals that will reach the organisation's objectives.

Key words

Definitions of Key words can be found in the Glossary on page 269.

authoritarian	McGregor
communication	motivation
democratic	movement
Herzberg's two-factor theory	paternalistic
	quality circles
hygiene factors	salaries
job enrichment	scientific management
laissez-faire	Taylor
Maslow's hierarchy of human needs	Theory X and Theory Y
	wages
Mayo	

16 Management and organisation

What is organisation?

All structures need organisation to make them work efficiently. This section explains how organisations are built and how they enable a business to perform more effectively. No two organisations are really the same. Each has its own history and culture. In many ways this is dictated by the traditions of the business and the objectives and attitudes of its owners and managers. Most businesses started off small with one owner completely involved in the workings of the business. The owner will have developed a view of the world, and a way of working through which the culture of the business was developed. That, in turn, will have changed with time. Out of this culture objectives and strategies for achieving them will have arisen and, to make achievement possible, a structure will have been built and modified as needed. Whatever the cultural framework, the success of the business depends on the skill with which it is managed.

What do managers do?

It is not easy to precisely define the role of management. It is easier to recognise a business that is poorly managed than it is to pinpoint the specific features of good management in a successful business. Badly managed businesses will be poorly organised, will often have poor staff motivation and resources will be wasted or inefficiently used. In addition, the business is unlikely to have long-term plans or objectives and will, as a consequence, lack direction and purpose. By identifying these common problems of failing businesses perhaps the following definition of management – or effective management – can now be offered:

> Managers are responsible for setting objectives, organising resources and motivating staff so that the organisation's aims are met. Managers 'get things done' – not by doing all jobs themselves but by working with and through other people.

Managers do not all use the same style of leadership and different managers will approach problems and decisions in very different ways, but the key features of management are common to all. These are best explained by reference to some of the best-known management writers, such as Fayol and Drucker. By combining the main ideas of these two writers we can arrive at the following list of management tasks or operations.

The role of management

1 Setting objectives and planning. All good managers think ahead. Senior management will establish overall strategic objectives and these will be translated into tactical objectives for the less-senior managerial staff. The planning needed to put these objectives into effect is also important. A new production or marketing objective will require the planning and preparation of sufficient resources.

2 Organising resources to meet the objectives. This is not just about giving instructions. People throughout the business need to be recruited carefully and encouraged to take some authority and to accept some accountability via delegation. Senior managers will ensure that the structure of the business allows for a clear division of tasks and that each section or department is organised to allow them to work towards the common objectives.

3 Communicating with and motivating staff. The importance of this has already been investigated – a management failure to encourage staff to become actively involved in and concerned about the business's performance will often lead to poor business results. The significance of developing staff

---

Test Activity

Read the case study below and then tackle the exercises that follow.

Case study – Allstyles department store

Rebecca Allahiq's working day was busy and varied. She had recently been appointed as General Manager of the Allstyles department store. This was a large shop in the city centre. It had ten departments selling a wide range of products from men's and ladies' clothes to carpets, furniture and electrical goods. A film crew from the local TV company had asked if they could film a typical working day for a programme they were making about different people's working lives. Rebecca agreed and the ten minute programme used six different clips of film with Rebecca involved in the following activities:

1 Meeting with all departmental managers to explain the store's pricing and promotional strategy for the next 'End of season sale'. At this meeting she expected all managers to inform staff of the price reductions allowed and the way in which goods should be presented in the sale so that consumers would have a clear message about the promotion.

2 Attending a planning meeting with senior executives from Head Office to agree the sales targets for the store for the next 12 months. Rebecca explained that the opening of a competitor's store very close to hers was a factor that should be taken into account.

3 Presenting three shop workers with 'Reach for the stars' badges for outstanding sales records over the last month. She had her picture taken with them for publication in the store's internal newspaper.

4 Reviewing the poor performance of the electrical products division with the manager. Poor staff absence figures had contributed to this problem and Rebecca suggested that the manager should attend additional training sessions on staff motivation and monitoring of staff performance.

5 Meeting with builders, architects and planners to discuss progress on the new store extension. Rebecca was concerned that they were not working closely enough and the project could fall behind schedule.

6 Settling a dispute between two departmental managers over which department should be able to stock a new electronic exercise bicycle – sports or electrical goods? It was agreed that it could not appear in both because of lack of space, so sports would stock it for six months next to gym equipment. Sales would be monitored closely and if it did not do well then relocation might be possible.

(20 marks, 25 minutes)

(a) Identify all of the different management roles that Rebecca fulfilled during this busy day. (6)

(b) Outline the personal qualities that you think Rebecca needed to carry out all of these roles successfully. (6)

(c) Examine the problems that this store might encounter if Rebecca was not an effective manager. (8)

so that they are encouraged to employ all of their abilities at work is now widely recognised.

4 Co-ordinating activities. As the average size of business units increases – especially true for multi-nationals – so the need to ensure consistency and co-ordination between different parts of each firm increases. The goals of each branch, division, region and even all staff must be welded together to achieve a common sense of purpose. At a practical level, this can mean avoiding the situation where two divisions of the same company both spend money on researching into the same new product, resulting in wasteful repetition of effort.

5 Measuring and controlling performance against targets. Management by Objectives establishes targets for all groups, divisions and individuals. It is management's responsibility to appraise performance against targets and to take action if under-performance occurs. As Herzberg pointed out, it is just as important to provide positive feedback when things keep going right!

Delegation: the art of management

If a business is small it will be owned and operated by one person, who will do each of the required tasks with varying degrees of skill. Some things will be very well done, whilst others will be poorly done, for none of us can do all things well. As a business grows, there is the opportunity to employ and with employment the chance to share work. The best way is to let the new person do the things you are not good at as far as this is possible. From this sharing of work some specialisation will develop and the whole job will be done with greater effect. This is the simple notion, but how effective it is will depend on the extent to which the owner/manager has learnt to delegate. The owner is still the owner with the responsibilities of the business; these cannot be passed on. Authority to do things can be delegated. For many owners and managers **delegation** is both the most necessary and the hardest thing to do.

There are three aspects of delegation:

Authority   The delegate must have the authority to undertake the tasks selected. This will come in part from ability to do the job, in part from the external trappings of the job such as an office, a title and perhaps a uniform, but largely because the superior passes it on.

Authority must be clear and certain, e.g. the power to spend money and the limit on how much, the power to hire and fire. It is the passing on of authority that many superiors find most difficult.

Responsibility   The delegate will be responsible to an immediate superior. What the responsibilities are and to whom the delegate must be responsible are usually indicated in a job description. The superior will expect correct, effective and efficient use of the powers given and that the resources are used for the purposes for which they were intended.

Accountability   The boss is still accountable both in law and in fact. He/she has chosen this method of working, has recruited and trained the delegate and has made the decision that the delegate is capable of exercising the powers given efficiently. The accountability remains firmly at the top.

Principles of good delegation

Poor delegation simply leads to poor results and often to chaos since nobody knows what is happening. Among the principles of good delegation are:

◆ The nature of the task(s) should be clear to both sides and to those who will work with the delegate.
◆ The manager must ensure, perhaps by training, that the delegate is capable and will undertake the task in ways that support the objectives of the business.
◆ Results expected and the timing of them should be clear and realistic. Many delegations are spoiled by expectations that are unrealistic.
◆ The delegate must have sufficient and known authority. This is partly personal, but authority must be supported by the system.
◆ Those who need to know must be informed.
◆ Limitations of authority should be clear.
◆ The manager's ultimate accountability should be clear.
◆ Reporting requirements should be clear.
◆ Sources of advice and access to them should be spelt out.

The potential limits of delegation

Delegation is not a universal solution to all problems of a business. There are limits to it and these are:

◆ The costs in time, money, resources and possibly poor outcome. Small firms can afford to delegate very little and autocratically led ones will be reluctant to do it. The benefits must be thought to exceed the costs.

♦ The need for uniformity. Different people do things in different ways and want to show their initiative and individuality. Some firms want 'organisation people' who will always work in prescribed and predictable ways. This often prevents growth and results in lost opportunities.

♦ The size of the organisation or task. Small firms delegate little and tasks that are either too small or too large often remain undelegated.

♦ The expectations of the customer. Heads of schools often find it difficult to delegate because parents expect to see them and not someone junior. Vicars often find it difficult to delegate to lay persons because people will not want to see anyone other than the vicar.

♦ The attitudes and philosophy of the management.

♦ The quality of the recruits or of the personnel training.

♦ In some cases there needs to be a high degree of control and this hampers the style and effectiveness of the delegate.

♦ The need for confidentiality.

Co-ordination

The more that work is devolved, the more it has to be co-ordinated and the greater pressure there is for working together and for good communication. However many players there are, the organisation has to work as a team to ensure the achievement of overall objectives. Among the things that often make co-ordination difficult are:

Conflicting departmental objectives   A common example involves marketing and production. Marketing may push for a high level of sales and/or for short delivery dates. The production department may not be able to produce what has been promised in the time given or may have to produce at a level of output, which increases unit costs of production. On the other hand, production may want to produce at the lowest cost per unit and this may produce an output that is either too great or too small for marketing's needs. Every department works out an annual draft budget and the total of these is almost always in excess of the amount available. Here, departments have to prioritise

Advantages of delegation	Disadvantages of delegation
Releases managers to undertake a more strategic role.	If the task is not made clear, if training is not provided and if sufficient authority is not transferred then delegation will be unsuccessful.
Shows trust in subordinates and this motivates staff to do well.	
Develops and trains staff for more senior positions and is one way of assisting people to achieve their potential (self-actualisation).	Managers may delegate boring jobs that they do not want to do – this will not prove to be motivating.

Table 16.1 Delegation – advantages and disadvantages

expenditure needs and to compromise with each other in order to ensure that overall business objectives are met.

Matters of common policy   Activity within large firms when it is totally centralised is very rarely effective, but some things do have to be matters of agreed common policy. Where this is not the case, problems often arise. Where it is the case, some degree of freedom is lost by each of the line departments. Common policy is most often about issues like recruitment, promotion, training and finance.

Formal and informal organisation

A formal organisation tightly controls the things that happen within it. Activities are grouped into departments, both roles and role interaction are well defined and everybody knows exactly what they are doing and who they work with. You would expect all marketing to take place within the marketing department and that there will be little cross activity.

♦ Effective specialisation and division of labour should ensure that people are experts at what they do and that mistakes are rare.

♦ There are established procedures, which ensure that most problems are expected and dealt with in a set way.

♦ Communication methods are well tried and tested and work effectively.

Benefits	Costs
Workers have more than one focal point	Not always possible to observe
Improves the morale of the group	Difficult to monitor and control
These advantages may be capable of good use by the business	May develop objectives hostile to the objectives of the business
Communication can be easier through the identified leader who, once on side, can bring the group along	The group may be resistant to change, particularly where change will break the group up or threaten objectives;
	Very often groups form precisely because members want to resist a particular change
Once on side, the group can be a powerful force ensuring that business objectives are met	

Table 16.2 Potential costs and benefits of informal groups

Activities

1 Explain the difference between formal and informal groups.
2 Discuss the informal groups that exist within your school or college. In the case of each one (a) is it on balance supportive, or (b) does it make life more difficult.
3 In what ways might any one of these groups be enabled to support the objectives of the school/college?

Of course, the real world is not like that; people are variable and sometimes absent, technology breaks down and new, unknown, problems occur all the time. No organisation can be perfect; no organisation can behave with perfect predictability and efficiency.

Informal organisation defines very broad roles and allows the participants to work out what is to be done, when and by whom. Interaction is never predictable because it depends on the people involved and the circumstances. All organisations must have elements of this because informal relationships such as work groups, interest groups and friendship groups are bound to develop in any business as it grows. Informal groupings can be used very effectively to the advantage of a business. However, they can also cause major problems in that they may pursue objectives that are in conflict with those of the organisation. Table 16.2 shows the potential costs and benefits of informal groups.

All organisations need structure

Organisational structure is the internal, formal framework of a business that shows the way in which management is linked together and how authority is transmitted. A typical business structure is one that is based on departmental lines, and these departments are divided according to function or the type of work carried out. Structures can be illustrated by means of an organisation chart. Traditional structures, showing functional structure, is shown in Figures 16.1 and 16.2.

Figure 16.1 Chart for Small Firm Ltd

These charts displays a number of important points about the internal organisation of this business. It shows:

◆ who has overall responsibility for decision making;
◆ the formal relationships between different people and departments – individual workers can identify their position in the business and who is their immediate 'line' manager;
◆ the way in which accountability and authority may be passed down the organisation – this is called the chain of command;
◆ the number of subordinates reporting to each more senior manager – this is called the span of control;
◆ formal channels of communication both vertical and horizontal – this will aid the investigation of communication problems if messages are not being received in time by the correct people;
◆ the identity of the supervisor or manager to whom each worker is answerable and should report to is made clear.

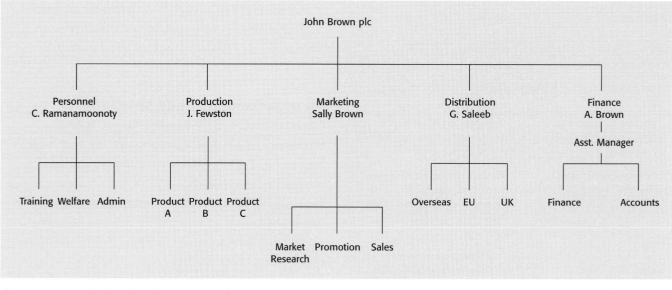

Figure 16.2 Organisation chart for Large Firm plc

Different types of organisational structure

There are several structural systems that a business might adopt – we will analyse the two most common ones.

1 *The hierarchical (or bureaucratic) structure.*
This is one where there are different layers of the organisation with fewer and fewer people on each higher level – Figures 16.1 and 16.2 demonstrated this. In general terms it is often presented as a pyramid (see Figure 16.3).
Advantages:
Many businesses are still organised in this way as decision-making power starts at the top but may be passed down to lower levels. The vertical divisions do not have to be based on functional departments – they could be based on region or country or product category, for example consumer goods and industrial goods. The rungs on the career ladder of a keen and ambitious employee are illustrated by the different levels of hierarchy. The role of each individual will be clear and well defined. There is a clearly identifiable chain of command. This traditional hierarchy is most frequently used by organisations based on a 'role culture', where the importance of the role determines the position in the hierarchy.
Disadvantages:
Such a structure tends to suggest that one-way (top downwards) communication is the norm – this is rarely the most efficient form. There are few horizontal links between the departments or the separate divisions, and this can lead to lack of co-ordination between them. Managers are often accused of tunnel vision because they are not encouraged to look at problems in any way other than through the eyes of their own department. This type of structure is very inflexible and often leads to change resistance. This is because all managers tend to be defending both their own position in the hierarchy and the importance of their own department.

2 *The matrix structure.*
This approach to organising businesses aims to eliminate many of the problems associated with the hierarchical structure. This type of structure cuts across the departmental lines of a hierarchical chart and creates project teams made up of people from all departments or divisions. The basic idea is shown in Figure 16.4.

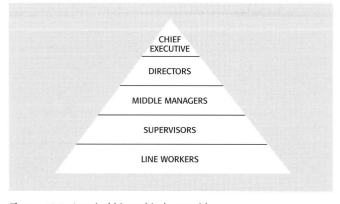

Figure 16.3 A typical hierarchical pyramid

	Finance Dept	Production Dept	Marketing Dept	Human Resources	Research & Development
Project Team 1					
Project Team 2					
Project Team 3					

Figure 16.4 A matrix organisational structure

This method of organising a business is task or project focused. Instead of highlighting the role or status of individuals it gathers together a team of specialists with the objective of completing a task or a project successfully. Emphasis is placed on an individual's ability to contribute to the team rather than their position in the hierarchy.

Advantages:

It allows total communication between all members of the team, cutting across traditional boundaries between departments in a hierarchy where only senior managers are designed to link with and talk to each other. There is less chance of people focusing on just what is good for their department. This is replaced with a feeling of what is good for the project and the business as a whole. The cross over of ideas between people with specialist knowledge in different areas tends to create more successful solutions. As new project teams can be created quickly, this system is well designed to respond to changing markets or technological conditions.

Disadvantages:

There is less direct control from the 'top' as the teams may be empowered to undertake and complete a project. This passing down of authority to more junior staff could be difficult for some managers to come to terms with. The benefit of faster reaction to new situations is, therefore, at the expense of reduced bureaucratic control, and this trend may be resisted by some senior managers. Team members may have, in effect, two leaders if the business retains levels of hierarchy for departments but allows cross-departmental teams to be created. This could cause a conflict of interests.

Test Activity

Read the case study below and then tackle the exercises on page 216.

Case study – Thames Valley Cars Ltd

Jim Mah founded the Thames Valley car hire business six years ago. He started out as a sole trader with just three vehicles. His business now employs 33 people and it has a fleet of 2,000 vehicles. Jim is chief executive. He has four fellow directors. They are in charge of finance, vehicle repairs, marketing and administration. The latter role includes dealing with all staffing matters. The finance director has three accounting assistants. The director in charge of vehicle repairs has two supervisors who report to him – one for the day and one for the night shift. They each have six mechanics working under them. The marketing department contains four people – one sales manager and three junior sales assistants. Administration has six office staff who take all the bookings and responsible to an office supervisor who is under the direct control of the director.

This type of structure has served the business well but Jim is concerned about the impact of further expansion on the organisation. In particular he is planning two developments for the future – one would involve renting trucks to other businesses and the other would be setting up a new office in another country.

(20 marks, 25 minutes)

(a) Sketch the current organisational structure of Thames Valley Cars Ltd. Include all staff on your chart. (6)

(b) Do you think the current structure is appropriate for the business? Give reasons for your answer. (6)

(c) Discuss how Jim might resolve the problem of devising a suitable structure for the two new developments he is planning. (8)

Key principles of organisational structure

Levels of hierarchy   Each level in the hierarchy represents a grade or rank of staff. Lower ranks are subordinate to superiors of a higher rank.

The greater the number of levels the greater the number of different grades or ranks in the organisation. A tall organisational structure has a large number of levels of hierarchy and this creates three main problems:

- communication though the organisation can become slow with messages becoming distorted or 'filtered' in some way;
- spans of control are likely to be narrow – see below;
- there is likely to be a greater sense of remoteness, amongst those on lower levels, from the decision-making power at the top.

Chain of command   This is the route through which authority is passed down an organisation – from the Chief Executive and the Board of Directors. Whereas, typically, orders are passed down the hierarchy, information, for example about sales or output levels, is sent upwards.

Span of control   This refers to the number of subordinates reporting directly to a manager. Spans of control can be either wide – with a manager directly responsible for many subordinates – or narrow – a manager has direct responsibility for a few subordinates. This difference would be illustrated on an organisation chart as shown in Figure 16.4.

Delegation   This is a very important principle which can have far-reaching effects on both the organisational structure and the motivation levels of subordinate employees. Delegation means the passing down of authority to perform tasks and take decisions from higher to lower levels in the organisation. As Herzberg and other researchers pointed out, this process can be very beneficial to motivation. Generally, the wider the span of control, the greater the degree of delegation that

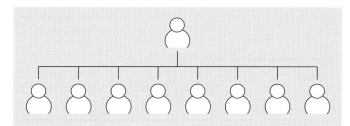

Figure 16.4a Span of control of 8 (wide) – this is likely to encourage delegation

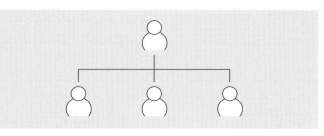

Figure 16.4b Span of control of 3 (narrow) – this is likely to lead to close control of subordinates

is undertaken. Imagine a manager with a span of control of 15 subordinates. It might be impossible to closely control the work of each of these every day – the manager would be allowed no time for more important 'strategic' matters. Thus, the manager will delegate authority to his staff and he will trust them to perform well. Clearly, they are accountable to the manager for good performance; but he or she retains ultimate responsibility for the work done in the department whether it was delegated to others or not.

Centralisation and decentralisation   These two principles are linked to delegation. Centralisation means keeping all of the important decision-making powers with head office or the centre of the organisation. There will be minimum delegation to managers in other areas, departments or divisions of the business. Decentralisation is the opposite and means passing decision-making authority to managers in other areas, departments or divisions in the business, allowing decisions to be taken away from head office. This must involve delegation. A centralised organisation would insist on all sections of the business following the same procedures and gives the business a feeling of uniformity and consistency. Head office will be able to exert considerable control over all operations. Decentralised organisations will allow staff to be empowered and this demonstrates trust in them. Decisions will be taken 'closer to the action' in terms of junior managers being more aware of local factors or closer to the consumers themselves.

Advantages of centralisation	Advantages of decentralisation
A fixed set of rules and procedures in all areas of the firm should lead to rapid decision making – there is little scope for discussion.	Allows more local decisions to be made which reflect different conditions – the managers who take the decisions will have local knowledge and are likely to have closer contact with consumers.
The business has consistent policies throughout the organisation. This prevents any conflicts between the divisions and avoids confusion in the minds of consumers.	Develops more junior managers and prepares them for more challenging roles.
Senior managers take decisions in the interest of the whole business – not just one division of it.	Allows delegation and empowerment and these will have positive effects on motivation.
Central buying should allow for greater economies of scale.	Decision making in response to changes, for example in local market conditions, should be quicker and more flexible as head office will not have to be involved every time.
Senior managers at central office will be experienced decision makers.	

Table 16.3 Centralisation: advantages and disadvantages

Test Activity

Read the case study below and then tackle the exercises that follow.

Case study – Majestic Cinemas plc

Majestic Cinemas owns one of the largest chains of cinemas in Asia. It operates in more than ten countries. The current organisational structure is shown below:

The new Chief Executive, Paul Lee, is concerned that this structure does not give the business sufficient flexibility. The former head of the corporation was very autocratic in approach and had centralised nearly all major decision making. There was minimum delegation as he had not believed the staff could be trusted, even with day-to-day decisions. All procedures were clearly laid down from head office, including the opening times of each cinema, the types of films to be shown, the range of drinks and snacks to be sold and so on. He had been reported as saying that, 'Our customers know where they are with Majestic – they do not want to see us change the way we do things. In any case, by buying our films centrally we can keep costs down.'

Paul did not believe in this approach. He had been educated abroad and had travelled extensively. He recognised the differences in tastes, culture and population trends that existed across the region. He considered that decentralisation was essential in many areas of the business. He wanted to develop and train younger staff to manage cinemas and to

> stamp their own style and personality on them. The ageing middle management would, he felt, oppose all of these moves. He wondered if they were really necessary – after all, the cinema managers could send him daily attendance figures over the internet each day and he could use video conferencing to contact them at any time. Paul realised that he had a job on his hands to change the culture of the organisation – but measures had to be taken to cut costs and to remain competitive.

(26 marks, 35 minutes)

(a) What is the span of control of the film purchase director? (2)

(b) How many levels of hierarchy are there in the cinema buildings department? (2)

(c) Outline three drawbacks of a centralised structure in this business. (6)

(d) Explain how Paul might decentralise the decision making in this business. (6)

(e) Discuss the consequences to the business and to the cinema managers of decentralising decision-making authority to them. (10)

McDonald's, familiar in many towns, throughout the world, has grown into the world's largest food service organisation

Roles What an employee is expected to do within the business. It would have been outlined in the job description and often will change with time as an employee undertakes new tasks and responsibilities. When roles are not clearly defined, it leads to inefficiency. Sometimes an employee may have more than one role and this can lead to **role conflict** and to problems for the firm.

1 Jean Brewer is both Head Teacher of a school and a junior member of the French Department. John Duckham is head of French. Jean has to be careful not to allow her overall authority affect her departmental relationship with John and he has to develop a working relationship with her as a junior member of his department. A common problem in a school but often a difficult one.

2 John Francis is Head of a small local limited company and Jennifer Platt is a secretary in his firm. However,

outside business Jennifer is Mayor of the town and leader of the Council, whilst John is a newly elected council member.

Specification Similar to role. Relates to the details of a job and its relationship to other jobs. It is the basis of recruitment, of delegation and of authority. Appraisals are often undertaken with reference to the job specification.

Problems with line and staff relationships

The line in a business involves people at differing levels but in the same activity, e.g. Production or Marketing. There are some things in which they are involved which may need skills or expertise from outside. People who come in to provide these are called staff personnel. Examples of this happening include:

- ◆ The firm will have made decisions that given activities ought to be conducted in accordance with agreed and centralised policy, for example: recruitment and training.

- ◆ Some activities are highly specialised and need experts who may not be found in the line concerned. Some of these may work for the firm as a whole and need to visit branches from time to time, for example: computer specialists, auditors from finance.

- ◆ From time to time the organisation will consult experts about broad issues that affect every department of the firm. These may relate to efficiency and need a work study expert, or to rationalisation and involve questions of redundancy.

The main problems with this approach are often ones of attitude and uncertainty about control. The Head of the department and the managing team do not like what they often consider interference in their domain. This is particularly difficult when the staff member advising about computers or auditing the books is a junior member of another line and is advising or even instructing much more senior members of the firm. Specialist skills often tend to cut across seniority and status. Often, line personnel do not see the benefits of specialist support or consultants in their midst, but they do see the cost in money and the disruption of work of their department. It often creates uncertainty and even

fear when the issues are rationalisation or work study. Departmental managers have been known to be unhappy when books are being audited or when the personnel department is making decisions about how a job should be advertised or even who should be recruited. They naturally want to have the last word in these situations.

Smaller firms have to contract out a number of services that they would like to do in house but do not have the facilities or staff for. They would simply not be cost-effective. This could apply to computer services or to market research.

Activity

Case Study – Hoy and Sons

Hoy and Sons have asked you to help with some problems. Currently they employ 20 people and their main product is garden ornaments. They sell these to one retailer, who has six branches. They are unhappy with reliance on a single customer. This gives them two immediate problems:

◆ They need to investigate the market and find ways of penetrating it.
◆ They think they should use technology to cope with stock levels, ordering, invoicing and billing.

They have asked you to decide which specialist they should employ. They can't afford both. Write a short report advising them. You may wish to suggest that neither should be employed, but you must justify your advice. You will need to investigate the costs of employing either staff or agencies and consider the benefits in each case.

Activity

Explain what is meant by a line and staff structure. How does this work in your own school or college? How are the academic line and the pastoral line interlinked? Are there any problems in this?

Discuss the organisational structure of your school or college and comment on its strengths and weaknesses.

Over-to-you

Test revision questions
(60 marks, 1 hour)
1 Why do organisations need a formal structure? (3)
2 Give three benefits of a typical hierarchical structure. (3)
3 Explain two drawbacks of a typical hierarchical structure. (4)
4 Explain the benefits and weaknesses of a matrix structure. (6)
5 What is meant by a 'long chain of command'? (3)

6 What is meant by a 'wide span of control'? (3)

7 Explain why some businesses have a centralised structure. (3)

8 Explain how the organisational structure of a business might change as it expands. (3)

9 State two factors other than the size of business that could influence the organisational structure. (2)

10 Discuss the importance of delegation to a business. (6)

11 Explain why delegation might involve a conflict between trust and control. (4)

12 Distinguish between accountability, responsibility and authority. (6)

13 Outline two problems associated with a 'long chain of command'. (4)

14 Explain the link between the width of span of control and the degree of delegation exercised in a business. (4)

15 Would you advise a multi-national furniture retailer to adopt a centralised management structure? Explain your answer. (6)

Discover and learn

1 (a) Draw an organisation chart for your school or college. Identify the levels of hierarchy – you may need to ask the Principal about these! Attempt to correctly identify the span of control of each section head or head of department.

   (b) Would you describe this organisational structure as being hierarchical or matrix based? If the former, is there any aspect of the school or college which is based on a matrix system?

   (c) Evaluate this organisational structure in terms of:

   ◆ speed and accuracy of communication,

   ◆ the average span of control,

   ◆ the degree of delegation used – ask heads of department about this but check that the Principal is aware of your research.

   (d) Suggest and draw a new organisational structure and explain the benefits that you believe it could have over the existing one.

2 Read the case study below and then tackle the exercises that follow.

Case study – Hotels group set for major management shake up

It is reported today that the Empire Hotel group is to undergo a radical management overhaul. The group has been criticised in the financial press for poor performances in recent years. The blame is put at the door of senior management who have been slow to respond to changing consumer needs for hotel accommodation and the growth of the business conference industry. Rising consumer incomes have made consumers much more demanding about the services they expect. The standard in many Empire hotels leaves a lot to be desired. In addition, they tend to have very old-fashioned conference facilities and need new IT and video equipment to keep up to industry standards. Some staff are reported to be leaving for other hotel chains which offer much more responsibility to hotel and departmental managers. Excell Hotels, for example, give their hotel managers much longer training than Empire but also give them much more freedom when they have qualified. One Excell manager was quoted as saying, 'We are given so much authority early on in our careers and we report directly to senior management which gives such immediate feedback.' It is reported that complaints from top managers or requests for new resources from hotels take three weeks before being considered in the Empire organisation because of the number of middle managers who are asked to give their views. Excell Hotels also have an excellent reputation for local food dishes and decorations that reflect local culture and traditions. At last, Empire seem to be responding to this criticism. They have appointed several new design and catering experts to advise their own departments – yet the changes being proposed are causing some friction amongst the existing established line managers.

(18 marks, 20 minutes)

(a) Outline the problems that Empire Hotels seem to be experiencing due to a long chain of command. (6)

(b) Why might existing senior managers be unwilling to delegate? (4)

(c) Discuss the impact on the performance of this business of adopting a much more widespread policy of delegation. (8)

3 Read the case study below and answer the questions that follow.

Case study – Ahmed Ltd

Ahmed is a small private company. It employs 15 workers and is managed by Ahmed himself. The company produces computer software and has been very successful and profitable. A similar company in a nearby town is on the market and Ahmed is considering the possibility of buying it. It employs 30 people and has also been profitable. The reason for the sale is that the owner is moving to Australia to take control of a large sheep farm that has been left to her. Ahmed sees this as an opportunity to expand his capability, to widen his market and increase his profits. He is unsure of possible pitfalls associated with growth and does not know whether it is worth the hassle.

(a) What are the organisational problems of bringing two similar companies together? How can these be overcome with least hassle and pain?

(b) How might Ahmed's role change and what difficulties might he face in these changes?

(c) What structure, in broad terms, would you suggest Ahmed should consider, given that he will continue to operate from both branches.

Summary

In this chapter we have recognised that:

- Organisation is vital.

- Those who work within a business have to be used in conjunction with other resources to meet the aims and objectives of the business.

- People need to be organised in such a way that they know what their function is and how it fits into the rest of the organisation and that they are highly motivated to perform it well.

- Organisation charts are often used to show the internal structure visually and compactly.

- They give a good indication of chain of command, span of control and division of labour.

- Some hierarchies are tall and these tend to be large businesses. This gives rise to difficulties and such difficulties are often overcome by flattening the organisation chart or by using alternative approaches to structure, where they will work.

- Most large businesses are, in fact, a complex of different approaches.

- There is an increasing occurrence of matrix approaches, which enable workers to be multi-skilled and to work in teams.

- All approaches have their strengths and weaknesses. The real need of every organisation is to find and maintain the best fit.

Key words

Definitions of Key words can be found in the Glossary on page 269.

authority	objectives
centralisation	organisation
chain of command	organisation charts
delegation	role conflict
hierarchy	roles
matrix aproach	span of control

17 Organising production efficiently

Production

Production is the measured quantity of output that a firm produces in a given period of time. Thus, if we look at the daily and weekly figures for the output of cane chairs at The World of Cane Ltd, a furniture producing firm (Table 17.1), we can see that it has two methods for measuring production, daily and weekly. Thus, we can see that the firm's production for the Friday of Week 1 was 107 chairs and that the weekly production for Week 3 was 528 chairs. Production, often called output is expressed in terms of units of the commodity being produced.

Production is the process of combining resources, such as land, labour, capital and management, in order to produce commodities – goods and/or services. The four resources mentioned above, land, labour, capital and management, are known as the factors of production.

Land is not simply land itself, but also includes all resources grown on or found under the ground. It also includes all the resources found in the sea! Labour is the human factor and capital is described as any man-made aid to production, ranging from machinery to a simple shovel. Management is the combining factor and is there to ensure that production takes place efficiently and smoothly. Whether goods or services are being produced, it is necessary to combine the factors of production. Thus, someone producing cane chairs, as in our example, will have to combine a production unit (factory), machinery, raw materials and labour in order to manufacture the chairs. There will also be a need for people who provide support services, such as accountants and human resource workers. In the same way, someone providing a service, such as a hairdresser, will need to combine a working unit (salon), equipment and labour, as well as support services.

	Week 1	Week 2	Week 3	Week 4
Monday	110	115	112	108
Tuesday	106	112	109	107
Wednesday	98	95	101	99
Thursday	104	98	102	105
Friday	107	103	104	105
Weekly total	521	523	528	524

Table 17.1 Measuring output

Production can be broken into three separate types:

◆ Primary production is the production or extraction of 'natural' materials. It is mainly in three areas, farming, fishing and mining.

◆ Secondary production is the production of manufactured, tangible, goods. It also includes the construction of buildings. The goods or buildings would be made using raw materials from the primary sector.

◆ Tertiary production is the production of intangible services. Services may be aimed at normal consumers or at businesses. These are known as direct services and commercial services respectively. Direct services are things such as taxi rides and manicures. Commercial services might be the provision and upkeep of potted plants for the offices or office cleaning services. Some services may be both direct and commercial, such as banking, insurance and legal services.

When producing, firms have to ask themselves a number of questions and make a number of decisions. The most common questions are:

◆ What product to produce? This will depend upon whether the firm is one that invents its own products and then convinces consumers that they want them or one that researches the market and produces what consumers want. This is the difference between product- and market-orientated production. In addition, obviously, the firm will have to consider the profitability of producing certain products. At the end of the day, no private company can produce in the long run without making a profit, not even Amazon.com!

◆ How to produce the product? The actual production method to be used will depend upon a number of factors, not least the type of product involved, and we will look at different production methods later in this section.

◆ Where to produce the product? The siting of the productive unit can be crucial to a firm. It will be influenced by many factors, such as proximity to the market, proximity to raw materials and suppliers, the cost of land, availability of labour and suitable infrastructure, social factors and government influence. It may also be influenced by personal factors. This is more likely with small firms, which are often set up in an area because

Primary production – dairy cattle after they have been milked

Mercedes Benz plant is expected to produce 30,000 A class compact cars a year
Source: Popperfoto.

Tertiary production – hotel supplying accommodation and conference facilities

the owner lives there and has no desire to move.

◆ How big should the firm be? The scale of the productive unit will be influenced by a number of factors and these will be considered later in the section.

◆ How should production and quality be controlled? Quality is hugely important in all industries and the control of production is necessary in order to ensure that commodities are produced efficiently and to the correct standard.

◆ How should the product be distributed? Production is pointless unless the products are distributed efficiently to the customers. Different distribution channels have been explained in Chapter 11. It is true that one of the major problems of the modern world is still effective distribution. In parts of the world people are starving and yet we have lakes and mountains of food and an agricultural policy that, through milk quotas and 'set-aside' policies, deliberately restricts the production of food.

Productivity, production and efficiency

Productivity is not the same as production and the two should not be confused. Production is the measured quantity of output that a firm produces in a given period of time. Productivity can be defined as a measure of the ratio of output to any of the firm's inputs – usually labour and capital. If a firm becomes more productive, then it has become more efficient, since productivity is an efficiency measure. The most common measures of productivity are:

Labour productivity =

$$\frac{\text{Total output in a given time period}}{\text{Quantity of labour employed}} = \frac{\text{Output}}{\text{per worker}}$$

Capital productivity =

$$\frac{\text{Total output in a given time period}}{\text{Quantity or value of capital employed}} = \frac{\text{Output per}}{\text{capital input}}$$

Nearly all firms are trying at all times to increase productivity – even if total production is not increasing. Business can do this by employing fewer but more technologically advanced machines.

Improvements in prductivity usually lead to a

reduction in the unit costs of production. If the cost of labour and capital inputs does not change then any increase in output per worker or output per machine will lead to a fall in unit costs. in competitive markets this could give firms a crucial advantage.

Productivity can be increased in several ways:-

1 *Better, quicker, more reliable machinery.* Machines and equipment are being updated and replaced with great frequency in many businesses. These improvements should allow the operators to increase output in any time period. For example, the phone assembly worker may have been provided with a more modern soldering tool. The telephonist might have been equipped with a more modern switchboard allowing more than one call to be held in a queue.

2 *Better training of workers.* If workers are encouraged to learn the latest techniques of working and improve their skill levels then this should speed up their work processes.

3 *Improved motivation levels.* Most workers can be encouraged to work harder and more effectively – to avoid time wasting or to suggest better ways of working. Evidence suggests that when workers want to do a job and see the point in doing it well then productivity levels often increase.

4 *More effective management.* Workers may be prevented from working more productively by inept or inefficient managers. Parts and components may fail to arrive on time, there may be insufficient staff appointed to operate key machines or they might just be poor 'people' managers.

In all of these ways, and often by using a combination of them, output per worker per time period can be increased. What benefits does such an improvement in productivity offer to the business? The main advantage

Type of work	Productivity per worker per hour 2000	Productivity per worker per hour 2001
Mobile phone assembly	25	30
Telephonist (number of calls handled)	10	11

Table 17.2 Examples of labour productivity

is the reduction in unit or average cost. Consider these figures for the mobile phone assembly factory:

Labour wage cost per hour on assembly line: £10
Output per hour per worker 2000: 25 units
Output per hour per worker 2001: 30 units
Average assembly cost per phone:

$$2000 = \frac{£10}{25} = 40 \text{ pence per phone}$$

Average assembly cost per phone:

$$2001 = \frac{£10}{30} = 33.3 \text{ pence per phone}$$

This reduction in cost might not sound much, but if the same increase in productivity was repeated throughout the factory then a substantial saving on the cost of each phone could be made. This will improve the firm's competitive advantage and, possibly, its profitability.

Remember – an increase in productivity, other things being unchanged, will reduce unit costs.

Three additional points about productivity:

1 *Productivity is not the same as total production.* Productivity is a relative concept – it compares the quantity produced with the quantity of input (for example labour). Production is an absolute measure. Therefore, if a factory employed 10% more workers, production might rise by 10% too, BUT the level of productivity remains the same.

2 *Increasing productivity is really only effective if quality is maintained.* To take the telephonist example above, if more calls per hour are being answered but at the expense of careful customer service then the success of the business could be damaged.

3 *Productivity is difficult to measure for many service tasks.* How, for example, could the productivity of a fireman or lifeguard in a swimming pool be assessed when for most of the time they are not putting out fires or saving lives!

4 *Capital productivity can also be measured.* This is calculated by dividing total output by units of capital employed.

Traditional production methods

There are a number of production methods that are available to a firm when it is considering 'How to produce the product?' The choice of production method will depend upon a number of factors, including:

The nature of the product   Some products can only be produced in a certain way because of the type of products that they are. For example, bridges need to be produced by job production, since it would hardly be sensible to have a flow production line for bridges. Personal services like hairdressing are obviously job production.

The total demand for the product   This will determine the quantity of the product required in each time period and this, in turn, will have an effect upon the choice of production method. Mass production clearly depends upon the existence of a large market.

The factors of production available   This will affect the choice of method, as will the current state of technology.

The level of quality and precision required   This will also be a factor.

The size of the firm and its funding   This will be a factor because, when firms are small, they often cannot

Test Activity

(12 marks, 15 minutes)
Copy out this table and fill in the blanks. Each assembly worker earns £200 per week.

Year	Total output	Number of assembly workers	Productivity per worker per week	Unit labour cost
2001	500	10	–	–
2002	700	11	–	–

afford the more automated methods of production, even if they would be more efficient. There are three main production methods:

- ◆ job production;
- ◆ batch production;
- ◆ mass or flow production including mass customisation;
- ◆ cell production.

We will consider these in detail.

Production methods

There are several different ways in which goods and services can be produced. They are usually classified into:

- ◆ job production,
- ◆ batch production,
- ◆ mass or flow production (including mass customisation),
- ◆ cell production.

Job production

This is normally used for the production of single, one-off, products. These products are frequently large and are often unique. Thus, good examples of job production would be the Channel Tunnel in the UK or the new Yangtze dam in China. However, products do not have to be large to be produced by job production. Individual wedding cakes and made-to-measure suits are also examples of job production. In order to be considered job production, each individual product has to be completed before the next product is started. Thus, at any one time, there is only one product being made.

New, small, firms often use job production, before they get the chance to expand. Job production enables specialised products to be produced and tends to be motivating for workers, because they produce the whole product and can take pride in it. However, this sort of production tends to be expensive, often takes a long time to complete, and is usually labour intensive. The labour force also needs to be highly skilled and this is not always easy to achieve. Aston Martin is an example of a very expensive car that is individually produced for the needs of each customer. Each engine is hand built and carries a plate with the engineers name on it.

Test Activity

Read the case study below and then tackle the exercises that follow.

Case study – Westlife Jeans Ltd.

The Operations Manager at Westlife Jeans Ltd. is concerned about the declining rate of productivity in the factory. He has collected the following data from factory records:

	2000	2001	2002
Total output of jeans (units)	50,000	55,000	60,000
Staff employed	20	24	30
Machines used	10	12	15

Each worker is paid £3,000 per year and this has not changed for three years. New staff have been employed and put into the production department with little training. The additional machines were purchased second-hand and some of them have proven to be unreliable. The operations manager has been told to increase productivity within six months as it is believed that the major competitor to Westlife Jeans has 20% lower unit labour costs. Although the marketing department admit that the higher quality of Westlife's jeans allows higher prices to be charged the lack of cost competitiveness is cutting into profits.

(30 marks, 35 minutes)

(a) For each year:
- ◆ calculate labour productivity and
- ◆ capital productivity in the Westlife factory. (6)

(b) Analyse the likely reasons for the trends in productivity that your results indicate. (12)

(c) By calculating unit labour costs for each year, explain why declining productivity could be a major problem for this company. (6)

(d) Suggest and evaluate two methods that the operations manager could use to improve productivity over the next six months. (6)

Batch production

Batch production involves the production of products in separate batches, where the products in the batch go through the whole production process together. The production process involves a number of distinct stages and the defining feature of batch production is that every unit in the batch must go through an individual production stage before the batch as a whole moves on to the next stage.

The most quoted example of this form of production is a baker making batches of rolls. First, the dough is mixed and kneaded. Then, after being left for a time, the dough is separated into individual amounts, the right size for rolls. After this, the rolls are baked together and then they are left to cool. When they have cooled, they are put on display in the shop and another batch can be prepared. Each roll has gone through the process with the other rolls in the batch and all the rolls have undergone each stage of the batch before going on to the next stage.

Baker removing rolls from oven. He will now begin preparing the next batch
Source: Sainsbury.

Batch production allows firms to use division of labour in their production process and it enables some gain from economies of scale (see page 231). It is usually employed in industries where demand is for batches of the product – such as different school uniforms. It also allows each individual batch to be specifically matched to the demand and the design and composition of batches can be easily altered. However, there are drawbacks. Batch production tends to have high levels of work-in-progress stocks at each stage of

the production process and the work may well be boring and demotivating for the workers.

Batch production should not be confused with flow production. Some firms produce 'batches' of products using a flow production system, for example a soft drinks firm may bottle a batch of 20,000 cans of orange drink before resetting the line and producing a 'batch' of another drink. This is not, however, batch production. The individual items are free to move through the process without having to wait for others, so it must be flow.

Flow production

The process of flow production is used where individual products move from stage to stage of the production process as soon as they are ready, without having to wait for any other products. Flow production systems are capable of producing large quantities of output in a relatively short time and so it suits industries where the demand for the product in question is high and consistent. It also suits the production of a standardised item that only requires minimal alterations. An example would be a Pepsi Cola production plant like the one in Ho Chi Minh City, Vietnam. Here, the product is standardised in that it is a can of soft drink of a standard size. The system is flow production because the cans move through the various stages independently. However, the firm can make changes to the contents of the cans and the labelling on them without having to alter the flow production system. They are capable of producing Pepsi, Sprite, and Schweppes Soda Water on the same production line.

It is essential that the flow production process be very carefully planned, so that there are no disruptions in the system. In a perfect system, the production process would be broken down so that all of the stages were of equal duration and producing equal output levels.

Flow production has a number of advantages over other types of production. Labour costs tend to be relatively low, because much of the process is mechanised and there is little physical handling of the products. The constant output rate should make the planning of inputs relatively simple and this can lead to the minimisation of input stocks through the use of just-in-time (JIT) stock control (see Chapter 18). Quality tends to be consistent and high and it is easy to check the quality of products at various points throughout the process. The main disadvantage is the high initial set-up cost. By definition, capital-intensive, high-technology, production lines are going to cost a great deal of money. In addition, the work involved tends to be boring, demotivating and repetitive.

Test Activity

Read the case study below and then tackle the exercises that follow.

Case study – Sunburst Bakeries

Sunburst Bakeries is a supplier of all kinds of bread and cakes to leading supermarkets. It has a huge factory that makes the entire range of products – no finished items are bought in from other bakers. Production facilities are split into three main areas. Different production methods are used in these three areas. The demand patterns for three of the best-known Sunburst products are very different. Standard loaves are bought by supermarkets every day, all year round. There is some variation in demand through the seasons – but very little. Large family sized cakes are mainly bought at weekends – whereas doughnuts are most often bought mid week for children's lunch boxes. Finally, the business is famous for its hand-made wedding cakes, each one to a different design. There have been rumours in the factory that one section of the factory that uses batch production might be converted into flow line production.

(15 marks, 15 minutes)

(a) For each of the products referred to above, suggest and justify an appropriate production method. (8)

(b) Explain the possible effects on Sunburst's stock levels and profitability if it replaced all batch production with flow line production. (7)

Recent innovations in production methods

The search for production methods that could combine the advantages of job production – flexibility and worker satisfaction – with the gains from flow production – low unit costs – have led to some important recent developments. These have been greatly aided by tremendous advances in technology such as computer aided design (CAD) and computer aided manufacturing (CAM). These have allowed much quicker developments of new products, designs that feature many common components and robotic

machinery that can be switched to making a range of parts – not just one. In addition, developments in the organisation of the production flow line have reduced the alienating effects of typical mass production. The emphasis on repetitive, boring tasks has been a major factor in poor worker motivation.

Mass customisation

This process combines the latest technology with multi-skilled labour forces to use production lines to make a range of varied products. This allows the business to move away from the mass marketing approach with high output of identical products. Instead, focused or differentiated marketing can be used which allows for higher added value – an essential objective of all operations managers. So, Dell computers can make a customised computer to suit your specific needs in a matter of hours. By changing just a few of the key components – but keeping the rest the same, low unit costs and maintained with greater product choice.

Cell production

Cell production, fully known as cellular production, is a form of flow production, but the flow production system is separated into a number of self-contained mini-production units, known as cells. The idea is supposed to have started in the USSR and its aim is to create motivation and 'friendly' competition.

Each individual cell will have a team leader and then, below that, a single level of hierarchy made up of workers trained in a number of tasks – multi-skilled staff. The performance of each individual cell is measured in a number of ways against preset targets. These targets will include such things as output levels, quality, lead times and cash targets. Cells are responsible for the quality of their own complete units of work (see Figure 17.1).

The cell system has led to significant improvements in worker commitment and motivation and this, in turn, has led to significant increases in productivity. Success depends upon a well-trained, multi-skilled work force. One of the most noted success stories for cell production is Lucas Industries, which introduced the system to its automotive electrical plants. Within two years, productivity had risen by 25%, the reject level had fallen by 20%, and there had been an 80% reduction in work-in-progress stocks.

Figure 17.1 How cell production might be organised in an assembly plant

Activity

Read the case study below and then tackle the exercises that follow.

Case study – In search of quality in quantity

The spread of mass customisation techniques across industries is starting to spell an end to the old production line. Mass production, based on standardised parts and processes, was introduced by Henry Ford in his car plants early in the 20th century. It greatly cut the costs of making each unit but the main drawback was that all goods coming off a single production line were identical. In *mass customisation* the line can be varied to make different products in small batches.

Caterpillar, the US supplier of construction and power equipment, says that virtually all of the 11,000 engines it makes each year are different. The variation comes from changes to 10–20 per cent of the 1,000 parts that go into each product. Software for the engine controls can also be varied. Cessna makes a wide range of general aviation aircraft from single engine piston to business jets on several different production lines. Of the 17 different models produced last year, Cessna produced and delivered over 1,200 planes to customers. By producing a variety of models, Cessna was able to market its products to a much wider range of customers.

Mass customisation needs:

- advanced and flexible capital equipment, for example there are now car paint robots that can paint vehicles in 'one-off' colours in between lines of cars in standard colours;

Cessna 172 Skyhawk is the best-selling aircraft of all time
Source: Cessna Aircraft Company.

◆ skilled and well-trained workers to operate this
machinery and to be able to adapt it to make
different products;
◆ product designs that contain as many standardised
parts as possible in different versions;
◆ reliable suppliers able to supply slight variations in
standard parts or components.

The consultancy Strategic Horizons says examples of
mass customisation have increased greatly in the last
few years. 'Some time this century mass customisation
will be the main form of manufacturing.'

Source: Adapted from *Financial Times*, 30 May 2001.

(20 marks, 25 minutes)

(a) Explain the difference between traditional flow (or mass) production and mass customisation methods of production.
  (5)

(b) Examine the benefits of mass customisation to *either* a computer manufacturer *or* a dress making business. (6)

(c) List three of the factors that are necessary for mass customisation to be successful. For each one, explain why you
  consider it to be important. (9)

	Job	Batch	Flow	Mass customisation
Main feature	Single One off items	Each item in a batch of identical products passes through each stage of production together.	Large-scale production of identical products.	Flow production with many common components and processes but some differences too. These allow different products to be made.
Essential requirements	Highly skilled workforce	Labour and machines must be able to switch to making batches of other designs.	Specialised, expensive but efficient capital equipment. High, steady demand for identical products.	Many common components and flexible equipment and skilled labour.
Main advantages	Able to undertake specialist projects or jobs, often with high value added.	Some benefits from economies of scale. Faster and lower unit costs than job production.	Low unit costs as a result of economies of scale and high productivity.	Low unit costs with ability to produce a range of different goods, almost 'to order'.
Main drawbacks	High production costs. Time consuming.	High levels of stocks in the form of unfinished goods at each stage of the production process.	Inflexible – often very difficult if not impossible to switch to producing a substantially different product.	May require expensive redesign of products to achieve compatibility of components and processes.

Table 17.3 Summary of main production methods

The scale of operations

There is no perfect size for a business and, in the UK, there are thousands and thousands of firms of all sizes. Most firms begin in a small way, quite simply because it requires less capital investment. In order to discuss the size of businesses, we need to look at the different ways that are used to measure business size. These are:

Turnover   This method values the total sales of the firm over a period of time, usually one year. The 1985 Companies Act used this method to differentiate between firms and stated that firms with a turnover of less than £1.4 million were small, those between £1.4 million and £5.75 million were medium-sized and those over £5.75 million were large.

Number of employees   This is another popular method and simply uses the number of employees directly employed by the firm to act as an indicator of size and a means of comparison. The 1985 Companies Act used this method, as well as turnover, and said that those firms that employed fewer than 50 workers were small, those that employed between 50 and 250 were medium-sized and those with over 250 employees were large. Obviously, this can be misleading, because some industries, by definition, are capital intensive and so may be very big in terms of turnover and yet small in terms of the number of people employed.

Profit   This is sometimes used, but it is not ideal. First, there may be large fluctuations from year to year and, second, small firms may make very large profits and extremely large firms may make losses.

Capital employed   This is also sometimes used and simply measures the total funds raised in the firm via equity (shareholding) and borrowing.

Stock market value   This may be used for firms that are quoted on the Stock Exchange, but it will tend to be rather variable from year to year as the share price fluctuates.

The actual size of a firm will be influenced by a number of factors and these should be considered:

The finance available   As has already been stated, most firms start small because funds are limited. In the same way, the majority stay small simply because they cannot achieve sufficient investment for growth.

The market in which the firm is working   Some markets do not have demand in sufficient quantity to support large firms. Additionally, some markets do not suit large-scale production and so will not have large-scale production units (i.e. firms). An example of this would be producers of specialist rock-climbing equipment or the makers of stamp albums. Some firms that provide services will also be small, if the demand is limited, e.g. tattoo parlours.

The objectives of the owners and management of the firm   The objectives, and the level of ambition, of both the owners and managers of a firm must have an impact on the size and potential growth of the organisation. Many people are happy to reach a certain size, often rather small, and lack the ambition to attempt to grow. Often they see the necessary risks as being too great and they are satisfied with what they have already achieved. If growth is to be attained, then much hard work, stress and risk will have to be endured and this may well not be attractive to the owners and management.

Many firms will grow over time and they do so for a number of reasons. They may grow in order to ensure survival, reduce risk and increase market share. They may also be chasing increased profits. Sometimes, firms grow simply because of the ambition and lust for power of their owners. One of the main reasons for growth is to gain cost advantages and thus to increase profitability; this will be dealt with next.

As organisation grows ⟹ unit cost reduces.

Economies of scale

As has just been said, one of the major advantages gained by increasing the scale of an organisation is the cost economies that simply stem from being larger. These are known as economies of scale and they are defined as 'any fall in unit costs that arises from an increase in the scale of the organisation'.

Economies of scale may be split into two types, internal and external. Internal economies are the unit cost reductions that arise directly from the growth of the firm itself. They have been classified into the following groups:

Commercial economies   One of these is purchasing economies, where firms are able to buy in bulk and so gain cost advantages through discounts for large orders. A good example is the ability of large retailers to buy much more cheaply than small shops. Many small shops do their best to compete in this respect by joining buying groups like Spar. Distribution economies, where large firms can take care of their own distribution and thus reduce costs, would also be included under this heading. Marketing economies also fit in here. Marketing costs do not rise at the same rate as output and so unit costs fall. For example, the costs of advertising to sell 50,000 units will not be significantly increased if the firm expands to produce 80,000 units. Many fixed costs will not increase with size and so overheads can be spread over more units and unit costs will fall. This would apply to such things as administration costs and research and development costs.

Managerial economies As businesses grow, they are able to departmentalise their management functions and there is a gain from the use of specialist employees in areas such as accounts, sales, marketing and human resource management.

Technical economies As businesses expand, they are able to use capital, technology and techniques that are not available to smaller firms and there is often a unit-cost advantage to be gained. In small firms, the owners and managers often have to be able to turn their hands to a range of activities and cannot gain from specialisation. Computerisation does not become cost-effective until the business is at least medium-sized.

Financial economies Because larger organisations are considered to be a safer investment, institutions that lend money tend to be more prepared to advance loans to them and will accept lower interest rates for doing so. This will be reflected in lower unit costs.

Risk-bearing economies As firms grow, they often expand into areas that were not involved in their original activities. This is to say that they diversify. If they expand into activities that relate to their supplies of raw materials, or into the selling of their products, they will lower their costs by dealing with their own supplies and selling. This can be a significant saving. It also provides greater security if either the source of supply or the market is guaranteed.

External economies are the unit-cost advantages gained by any firm in an industry as the industry grows. External economies can be particularly large if the firms in a specific industry are mostly concentrated in one geographical area, such as the steel industry in Sheffield. Different causes of external economies of scale are:

Concentration economies As we have said, if an industry concentrates in one area, then there are a number of advantages that can accrue. These may include:

- the emergence of a skilled local labour force;
- the development of a local tradition for the

industry and specialist courses run in local educational establishments;

- suppliers and those involved with the industry moving nearer and thus reducing transport costs and improving the pool of knowledgeable advice;
- support from the local authorities, keen to see the industry stay in the area.

In such situations even the smaller firms in the industry are also able to benefit.

Information economies As industries grow, they often set up information services that are of help to all of the firms in the industry. The tourist industry is a good example.

Diseconomies of scale

It is often argued that there is also a downside to growth and that there will be factors that will force unit costs upwards as organisations expand. These factors are known as diseconomies of scale and, whilst they are not as powerful as economies of scale, they must be taken into consideration. There are two main types:

Human diseconomies As organisations grow, workers tend to lose a sense of belonging and feel less important. This can be very counter-productive and lead to a loss of morale and motivation, which in turn leads to inefficiency and higher unit costs.

Information diseconomies As organisations grow, the number of levels of hierarchy increases and there is a tendency for information channels to become unwieldy.

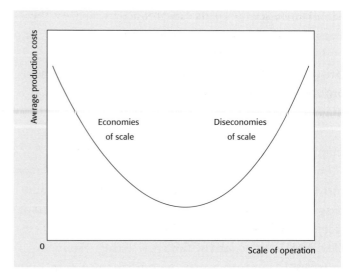

Figure 17.2 The impact of economies and diseconomies of scale on average costs

When this happens, information is often blocked or distorted and decision-making suffers. In addition, decisions take longer to make and so the firm becomes less efficient.

Capacity utilisation

Capacity is the amount of output that a firm can produce, whilst minimising its unit costs. It is, in effect, the ideal output for a productive unit, if the unit is working efficiently. Obviously, a firm will wish to use its productive unit up to capacity, since this is usually the cost-effective level of output.

Capacity utilisation is a measure of the extent to which the maximum capacity of a productive unit is being employed. It can be measured by a simple equation:

$$\text{Capacity utilisation} = \frac{\text{Actual output}}{\text{Capacity}} \times 100$$

If a firm can achieve a high level of capacity utilisation, then it will be able to spread its fixed costs over a high level of output and so will reduce the unit cost of output. This can best be shown by an example:

Plant capacity	100,000 units per year
Actual production	60,000 units
Capacity utilisation	$60,000/100,000 \times 100 = 60\%$

If the firm has fixed costs of £240,000, then the unit fixed cost is £240,000/60,000, i.e. £4 per unit. If output is increased to 80,000 units per year, then the capacity utilisation becomes 80% and the unit fixed cost falls to £3 per unit.

As can be seen, if firms can produce to capacity, then there is a definite cost advantage to be gained. However, firms can only maximise output if the demand for the product exists, if the resources are available and if they are able to use their productive resources at their most efficient level.

There are also potential drawbacks to operating at full capacity for a considerable period of time:

- Staff may feel under pressure due to the work load and this could raise stress levels. Operations managers cannot afford to make any production scheduling mistakes as there is no slack time to make up for lost output.
- Regular customers who wish to increase their orders will have to be turned away or kept waiting for long periods. This could encourage them to use other suppliers with the danger that they might be lost as long-term clients.
- Machinery will be working flat out and there may be insufficient time for maintenance and preventative repairs. This lack of servicing may store up trouble in the form of increased unreliability in the future.

For these reasons many firms attempt to maintain a very high level of capacity utilisation but to keep some spare capacity for the unforeseen eventualities that can always occur in business.

Some production methods depend upon intensive usage of capital and others rely on high levels of labour. If a production system employs a high level of capital relative to the other factors of production, then it is said to be capital intensive. An example of this would be any large car production plant, e.g. the Ford works in Dagenham. Obviously, the set-up costs of a capital-intensive plant are usually high, so the investment can only be justified if the demand for the product being produced is high and relatively stable. Also, since capital intensity implies flow production, the product needs to be a standardised one, so that it can be produced on a production line, with minimal variations.

Some production systems do not lend themselves to the use of large amounts of capital and actually employ a high level of labour relative to the other factors of production. This type of system would be called labour intensive. Small firms are often labour intensive, as are production systems that require high levels of expertise, such as the making of top-quality cricket balls. The majority of service industries, such as insurance companies or estate agents, tend to be labour intensive.

The needs of the market may well strongly influence the level of production, particularly if that market is inclined to seasonal variation. In such circumstances normal working becomes difficult and there is a need to provide for working under or above long-term capacity levels. Often, for Christmas, firms have to do this. Means have to be found of increasing the volume of goods on the market. Typical methods of dealing with this almost always either increase unit costs or reduce profits per unit and include:

- working a shift pattern with up to three shifts a day;
- extending the working day in other ways. Shops will stay open for much longer days leading up to Christmas;

- the post office employs additional postmen at the same time and hotels increase their staff in high season. Most vacation employment for students is based on needs like this;
- working overtime which is normally at a higher rate of pay. The EU working time directive prevents such overtime being compulsory in many instances. Some industries have contingency plans for dealing with emergency situations of this kind which they can bring into operation quickly. The hospital and fire services are examples.

Dealing with the other side of the problem is not so easy. Those firms who have part-time staff may be able to react flexibly and relatively quickly to the need to reduce production levels but many do not and this leads to stockpiling and its inherent costs. This used to be a major feature of the motor industry. Many firms react to this situation by finding ways of getting rid of stock through sales and offers, some can move flexibly from the production of one line to another. In extreme situations the situation will lead to redundancies and closure of branches. The closure of a significant number of Barclay Bank branches because they no longer need the capacity of so many branches is an example. One way of coping is to stay deliberately very slim in the knowledge that it is easier to increase capacity temporarily than it is to reduce it.

Resource management, wastage and the environment

Resources are relatively scarce and have a cost. They must be used rather than wasted. For those resources which are non-renewable to be wasted – coal, oil, minerals – is a permanent loss to the economy. The greatest of these losses is in the failure to make best use of labour. One and a half million people being unemployed means the loss of 1.5 million working days every day. This is in addition to the loss of spending power, dignity and respect which being unemployed entails. Pollution also wastes because it damages and destroys and because it is often costly to remove.

Firms have become much more conscious of these issues and are demonstrating significantly more corporate responsibility about them. This is more likely to be because being 'green' is increasingly good for image and for profits.

Environmental audits

Environmental audits have become a relatively common undertaking for larger firms these days. This is where the firm carries out a review of its effect on the environment in which it operates. The review may be carried out by outside experts or undertaken internally and then verified by independent consultants. The environmental audit would normally look at such things as waste management, material usage, energy usage, efficiency of transport, compliance with legislation and impact on the surrounding countryside. Certain areas of the environmental audit can be positively beneficial for the firm. Improvements in waste management, material usage, energy usage and transport efficiency can be cost saving for a firm. However, meeting legislative requirements and ensuring that the surrounding countryside is preserved can impose costs on a firm that although necessary, are significant.

The legal aspects of production

Firms face a number of legal restrictions and requirements upon their production processes and methods. Some of them will relate to measures to minimise any pollution that may be caused in the production process, but the main laws attempt to protect the workers involved in the process and relate to health and safety.

The Health and Safety at Work Act (1974) places a legal obligation upon employers to safeguard the health, safety and welfare of their workers, whilst they are at work. The Act includes the provision and maintenance of safety equipment and clothing, the maintenance of reasonable temperatures in the workplace, the provision of breaks from work and protection against dangerous substances. Employers have to protect their employees' health and safety 'as far as it is reasonably practicable'. The more potentially dangerous the production process, the more care employers will be expected to take.

All employers have to prepare a written statement of the policy that they have adopted for the health and safety of their employees. It is up to them to ensure that the employees know what the firm's policy is. However, the law also places responsibilities upon the employees, who are obliged to act in a way that takes reasonable care of their own, and other people's, safety. The employees are obliged to obey the health and safety rules that have been set down by the organisation. If employers, or employees, fail to comply with the set rules, then legal action can be taken against them. The Health and Safety Executive is a government department that attempts to ensure that the Act is carried out in companies throughout the country. Their inspectors have the right to enter businesses and check that they are complying with the Act.

Over-to-you

Test revision questions

(60 marks, 1 hour)

1 What is meant by the term 'added value'? (4)
2 How is added value related to the production process? (4)
3 Explain why the term production includes services. (3)
4 Think about your journey to school or college each day. What public services do you use? Explain your list. (4)
5 Write down the equation for measuring each of:

   (a) labour productivity; (2)   (c) capital utilisation. (2)

   (b) capital productivity; (2)

6 Select a method of production and say why it would be the best for each of the following:

   (a) consultation with a solicitor; (5)   (c) baking hot cross buns. (5)

   (b) manufacturing pins; (5)

7 Explain what a diseconomy of scale is and give an example. (4)
8 What is the meaning of the term 'spreading fixed costs' and what is its effect? (4)
9 Explain why waste management is important. (4)
10 What factors would you include in an environmental audit? (4)
11 Explain the advantages and disadvantages to a business of operating at full capacity. (8)

Discover and learn

1 Work in groups. Choose one firm each. Discover its methods of production. Discuss the appropriateness of those methods and comment on the findings of the whole group.
2 Work in groups. Cover as much of your area as you can. Observe ways in which the environment is being damaged and suggest realistic business solutions to the problems.
3 Are there any actual or potential examples of the advantages of concentration economies in your area? If you find them, explain why the industry selected is concentrated in your area.
4 Read the case study below and tackle the exercises that follow.

Case study – Hard Hats Ltd

Jamie Pither started up Hard Hats Ltd in 1980. It is located on the north coast of Wales, on the edge of a small village, five miles from Rhyl. Jamie rented a unit, on a recently built industrial estate, which he has since been able to purchase outright with the help of a mortgage from the bank.

In the early days, the firm only produced safety helmets for construction workers. By necessity, it was a small operation. Jamie dealt with all of the management functions and he employed two workers, one to operate the machine that produced the shells that formed the basis of the safety helmets and the other to attach the straps and cushioning parts and to pack the finished products. All parts, other than the shells, were produced elsewhere and then bought-in.

Since then, Hard Hats has grown, although it is still not a large concern. From 1985 onwards, Jamie had realised the need for diversification and had identified other areas where he could perhaps sell products that were easily capable of being produced in his existing premises. Over the period, he began to produce safety helmets for cyclists, mountain-bike enthusiasts, skate boarders, roller skaters and, most recently, in-line skaters. Indeed, it seemed that whatever the latest craze, there was a potential market for Jamie's products.

By the end of 1997, employment in the firm had expanded to 11 people, in addition to Jamie. There are now two machines for producing the various shells, each with its own highly skilled and trained operator, eight people who work as assemblers and packers, and a works manager, Howard Pedley, who is responsible for the ordering of all materials and supplies, stock control and the general running of the production floor. Jamie continues to deal with all other management functions, which are mostly marketing and accounting.

Production is organised partly on a batch-production basis and partly on an assembly-line basis. When an order is received, then a batch of the necessary style of safety shells is produced on one of the machines. The machines are computer programmable and so change-overs are relatively quick. The machines are quite reliable but, when they do break down, the firm from which they were bought repairs them. The supplier guarantees that an engineer will be on site within two hours, but production is obviously stopped on that machine whilst it is being repaired. The same firm is responsible for the regular maintenance of the machines. The machines are three years old and Jamie is considering changing them. On average, one of them breaks down once a month and production is lost for four hours. Production from each machine averages 120 units per hour and the firm usually works one shift of eight hours each day. However, if there is a rush on, then workers are often asked to work up to two hours of overtime per weekday or an extra four hour shift on a Saturday. Lately, it is often necessary to have to work a total of at least four hours overtime per week. Indeed, the workers now expect this and are unhappy on the odd

occasion that it does not occur. The firm guarantees delivery of orders within ten days of an order being placed. Although the average time for fulfilling an order is nine days, there are a growing number of occasions when the firm is unable to meet its stated delivery time and this is causing problems with customers.

As a batch is being produced, the shells are deposited onto one of the two, small, conveyor belts. It is then the job of one of the workers to stick the relevant brand-name onto the shell, of another to attach the chin straps to the helmet, of a third to put in the cushioning materials and of a fourth to pack the helmets and label the boxes. Workers are moved from one position to another on the same line or to the other line, but there is no doubt that it is tedious work and motivation and morale are not high amongst these workers. On average, one worker is away from work for one day per fortnight. When this happens, production is, obviously, slowed down a great deal. Normally, the workers can keep up with the output of the machines, but, when they are short-handed, they can only

Hard hats are an essential piece of safety equipment on all building sites.

assemble and pack an average of 200 units per hour. When the machines are being reprogrammed for a new batch, the assembly workers are expected to prepare the materials necessary to assemble and pack the batch. This is supervised by Howard Pedley.

Because of the nature of the product, quality control is obviously of great importance. The firm has earned the right to use the kitemark logo of the British Standards Institute and there is no doubt that this is an enormous help to sales. It is rare for a consumer to buy a product of this type if it is not carrying the BSI mark. Quality control is considered to be the job of everyone involved in the production process and all of the workers have the right to hold up production if they think that there is something wrong. They receive a weekly bonus as long as the average reject rate from customers stays below one in one thousand, which it invariably does. The workers take this role very seriously and it acts as a boost to morale.

Lately, the quality of some of the bought-in chinstraps has given some cause for concern. Jamie has just changed to a new supplier, based in Taiwan and the quality of some batches has been rather variable. In order to guard against stock-outs, because of the distance that deliveries have to cover, a large buffer stock is being carried and this is also a concern, since it is tying up capital. However, the prices charged by the Taiwanese firm are considerably lower than European Union (EU) suppliers and this enables Jamie to have lower prices than his competitors with the same profit margins.

Howard Pedley works to a fairly traditional system when he is dealing with the stock control at the firm. He works on a maximum and minimum stock-level basis and, knowing the usual delivery times, he reorders stocks and ensures that these never go below the minimum stock level. Jamie is worried that far too much money is tied up in stocks and he is keen to reduce stock levels. Howard feels that any change might jeopardise output. None of the suppliers is that reliable and there have been occasions where deliveries have taken twice as long as normal to arrive. Current stock-control figures for bought-in components, and some production information, are shown in Table 17.3.

Jamie Pither has noticed an increasing demand from abroad, mostly France and Italy. He feels that this is a very good sign, since he has not attempted to promote his products in these countries. He has now researched the potential markets and has found that all of the activities that he supplies for are popular in France and Italy and that cycling, especially, is much more popular there than it is in the UK. Competition is keen, but Jamie's prices are very competitive. He is keen to expand his market, but he is aware that it would involve a marked increase in weekly production levels. He has estimated that, if things went as planned, he might have to double output over a period of eighteen months.

	Logo transfers	Chin straps	Cushioning materials	Boxes and labels
September 1997	10,000	120,500	12,000	22,000
October 1997	12,000	132,000	15,500	20,500
November 1997	10,000	121,500	14,000	19,000
December 1997	10,500	94,000	18,000	21,000
January 1998	11,000	126,500	22,000	21,500
February 1998	10,500	122,000	25,000	20,500

Average daily production is 1,800 units. Average weekly production is 10,000 units. The usual delivery times, following an order, are as follows:

Logo transfers	3 days
Chin straps	4 weeks
Cushioning materials	1 week
Boxes and labels	2 days

(40 marks, 1 hour)
(a) ◆ Evaluate the production method used at Hard Hats. (10)
   ◆ Discuss any improvements that you feel might be made to the production method. Explain your reasoning. (10)
(b) Identify and explain any economies of scale that Jamie Pither might expect to gain as his firm expands. (10)
(c) How would you classify Hard Hats in terms of size? Explain your reasoning. (4)
(d) Explain any disadvantages associated with production that might arise from the fact that Hard Hats Ltd is a relatively small firm. (6)

Summary

In this chapter we have recognised that:

- There are three types of production: primary, secondary and tertiary.

- Firms should try to produce as efficiently as possible, in order to minimise unit costs and to avoid wastage of resources.

- Traditional production methods – job, batch and flow – have been improved in many cases by recent innovations, such as cell and lean production.

- Firms of all sizes exist in the economy.

- Large firms benefit from economies of scale, although diseconomies may also exist.

- It is sensible for firms to utilise as much of their capacity as possible.

- Some firms are capital intensive and others are labour intensive.

- Firms have an obligation to avoid waste, to manage their resources effectively and to protect the environment.

- Firms should strive to protect their workers in the workplace.

Key words

Definitions of Key words can be found in the Glossary on page 269.

batch production	flow production
capacity utilisation	job production
capital intensity	just-in-time (JIT)
cell production	production
diseconomies of scale	Kaizen
economies of scale	labour intensity
environmental audit	resource management

18 Controlling operations

On completion of this chapter you should be able to:

- ➤ define quality
- ➤ understand the importance of quality to both suppliers and consumers
- ➤ identify methods of attempting to ensure quality
- ➤ understand the difference between inspected and built-in quality control
- ➤ understand the implications for motivation and training of built-in quality control
- ➤ describe and understand different approaches to attaining quality, including total quality management, benchmarking, Kaizen and continuous improvement, quality assurance and quality circles
- ➤ identify the different types of stocks
- ➤ understand the purpose and costs of holding stocks
- ➤ appreciate the opportunity costs of holding stocks
- ➤ construct and interpret stock control charts
- ➤ define just-in-time (JIT) stock control
- ➤ understand the implications for the firm and its suppliers of JIT
- ➤ understand the requirements of successful approaches to JIT

What do we mean by quality

Quality is not easy term to define. However, consumers judge quality every time they make a purchase. Quality does not necessarily mean 'the best that can possibly be produced', because high costs would then make the product unsaleable. A high-quality product is one that best fulfils the particular needs of consumers at a price that they are willing to pay.

The minimum standard demanded by consumers is that the product should 'work' – that it is fit for the purpose intended. A washing machine that does not operate or a clothes line that breaks will be of no value to consumers whatever the price. Beyond this minimum quality level, consumers will expect more if they pay a higher price. Quality can also be assessed in terms of the original specifications for the product. When designing a product or introducing a new service a firm will specify certain quality standards, such as exact size, weight, performance standards, reliability, customer service times and so on. Failure to meet these standards will allow the firm to recognise that it is failing its own quality tests. When a customer is really

important then these product specifications will be laid down after discussions between the customer and the producer.

The *advantages* of producing quality products and services are:

- ◆ easier to create customer loyalty;
- ◆ saves on the costs associated with customer complaints, for example compensation, replacing defective products and loss of consumer goodwill;
- ◆ longer life cycles;
- ◆ less advertising may be necessary as the brand will establish a quality image through the performance of the products;
- ◆ a higher price – a price premium – could be charged for such goods and services. Quality can therefore be profitable.

Quality control techniques

There are three stages to effective quality control:

1 *Prevention.* This is the most effective way of improving quality. If the design of the product

239

follows the requirements of the customer and allows for accurate production then the other two stages will be less significant. Quality should be 'designed into' a product.

2 *Inspection.* Traditionally this has been the most important stage – but it has high costs and these could be reduced by 'zero-defect' manufacturing that is the aim of total quality management.

3 *Correction and improvement.* This is not just about correcting faulty products but is also concerned with correcting the process that caused the fault in the first place. This will improve quality in the future.

Inspecting for quality

Traditionally, quality has been checked by inspecting products at the end of the production process. Some checking might take place at different stages of the process but the emphasis was on the quality of the finished article. Quality inspection is expensive – qualified engineers have to be used – and such checks can involve damaging the product, for example dropping computers to see if they still work! As a result, a sampling process must be used and this cannot guarantee that every product is of the appropriate quality.

When quality checks are used during the production process then statistical techniques are used to record and respond to results. A typical quality control chart is

shown in Figure 18.1 for the recording of weights of loaves of bread.

If the recorded weight falls outside of the warning limits then action needs to be taken to improve the accuracy of the production process.

Weaknesses of inspecting for quality

The key point about *inspected quality* is that it involves a group of quality control inspectors who check the work of workers. There are several problems related to this approach to quality:

1 It is looking for problems and is therefore negative in its culture. It can cause resentment amongst workers as the inspector believes that he has been 'successful' when he finds faults. In addition the workers are likely to look upon the inspectors as management employees who are there just to check on output and to find problems with the work. Workers may consider it satisfying to get a faulty product passed by this team of inspectors. This level of mistrust cannot be good for working relationships and the overall levels of morale in the firm.

2 The job of inspection can be tedious, so inspectors become demotivated and may not carry out their tasks efficiently.

3 If checking only takes place at specific points in the production process then faulty products may pass through several production stages before being picked

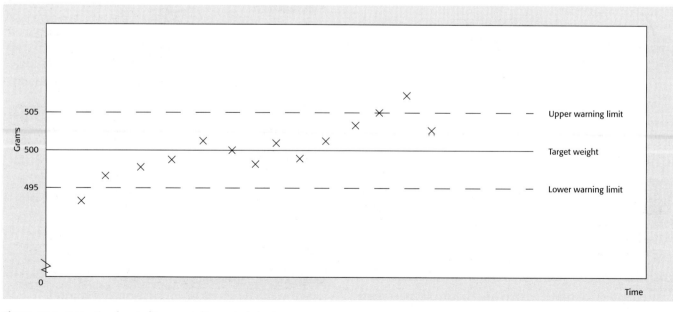

Figure 18.1 Inspecting for quality – a quality control chart

up. This could lead to a lot of time being spent finding the source of the fault between the quality checkpoints.

4 The main drawback is that it takes away from the workers the responsibility for quality. As the inspectors have full authority for checking products, the workers will not see quality as their responsibility and will not feel that it is part of their task to ensure that it is maintained. Ultimately, this lack of responsibility is demotivating and will result in lower-quality output.

Inspecting for quality therefore has many weaknesses. It is hardly surprising that there has been a move away from this approach in recent years.

Quality assurance

Quality control is about checking to ensure that products and services come up to an agreed standard. Quality assurance is setting and agreeing those standards throughout the organisation and making sure

Case study – Quality assurance has been a key component in the success of McDonald's restaurants

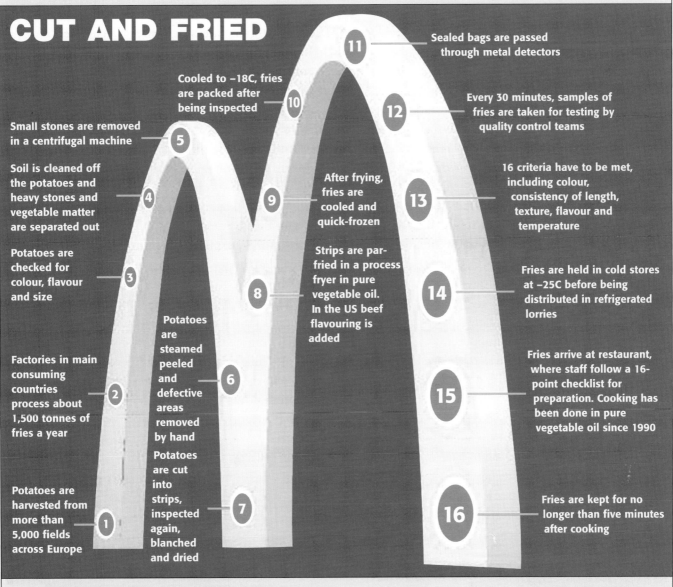

CUT AND FRIED

11 Sealed bags are passed through metal detectors

10 Cooled to –18C, fries are packed after being inspected

12 Every 30 minutes, samples of fries are taken for testing by quality control teams

5 Small stones are removed in a centrifugal machine

4 Soil is cleaned off the potatoes and heavy stones and vegetable matter are separated out

9 After frying, fries are cooled and quick-frozen

13 16 criteria have to be met, including colour, consistency of length, texture, flavour and temperature

3 Potatoes are checked for colour, flavour and size

8 Strips are par-fried in a process fryer in pure vegetable oil. In the US beef flavouring is added

14 Fries are held in cold stores at –25C before being distributed in refrigerated lorries

2 Factories in main consuming countries process about 1,500 tonnes of fries a year

6 Potatoes are steamed peeled and defective areas removed by hand

15 Fries arrive at restaurant, where staff follow a 16-point checklist for preparation. Cooking has been done in pure vegetable oil since 1990

1 Potatoes are harvested from more than 5,000 fields across Europe

7 Potatoes are cut into strips, inspected again, blanched and dried

16 Fries are kept for no longer than five minutes after cooking

Quality assurance standards for McDonald's French fries
Source: The Times, 25 May 2001.

that they are complied with so that customer satisfaction is achieved. The quality assurance department will need to consider all areas of the firm such as:

- *Product design* – will the product meet the expectations of consumers?
- *Quality of inputs* – quality must not be let down by bought-in components.
- *Production quality* – this can be assured by total quality management (TQM) (see extension work).
- *Delivery systems* – customers need goods and services delivered at times convenient to them.
- *Customer service including after sales service* – continued customer satisfaction will depend on the quality of contact with consumers after purchase.

Many quality assurance departments aim to receive recognition for the quality control framework they have in place. This is done by qualifying for an internationally recognised qualification such as ISO 9000. Inspectors will assess the firm's quality standards and the systems they have in place to monitor their achievement of these standards. If the inspectors are satisfied, the firm will gain an ISO 9000 certificate. This can then be used in the business's own promotional material and it is likely to attract customers. Many government contracts are only awarded to firms that have gained this certificate. The competitive edge that such an award can offer to firms could be significant.

To obtain the ISO 9000 certificate the firm has to demonstrate that it has:

- staff training and appraisal methods,
- methods for checking on suppliers,
- quality standards in all areas of the business,
- procedures for dealing with defective products and quality failures,
- after-sales service

The benefits for a firm of being forced to establish a quality assurance framework and to have this externally monitored are clear. There are, however, drawbacks such as costs of preparing for inspection and bureaucratic form filling to gain the certificate.

Modern approaches to achieving quality
Total quality management (TQM)
This is not a technique; it is a philosophy of quality

being everyone's responsibility. The aim is to make all workers at all levels accept that the quality of the work they perform is important. In addition, they should be empowered with the responsibility of checking this quality level before passing their work on to the next production stage. This approach fits in well with the Herzberg principles of job enrichment. TQM should almost eliminate the need for a separate quality control department with inspectors divorced from the production line itself. TQM uses the concept of the 'internal customer'. The internal customer is the next department in the production process. If the work from the previous process is below standard then it will be rejected – just as a customer would reject it. Each department is therefore aiming to satisfy the next department (the internal customer) by passing on the best-quality products. Every department is obliged to meet the standards expected by its customer(s). These departmental relationships are sometimes known as quality chains. All businesses can therefore be described as a series of supplier and customer relationships.

TQM aims to cut the costs of faulty or defective products by encouraging all staff to 'get it right first time'. This is in contrast to traditional inspected quality methods that considered quality control as being a cost centre of the business. Under TQM, if quality is improved and guaranteed then reject costs should fall and the demand for the products rises over time.

However, TQM will only work effectively if everyone in the firm is committed to the idea. It cannot just be introduced into one section of a business of defective products coming from other sections will not be reduced. The philosophy requires a commitment from senior management to allow the workforce authority and empowerment, as TQM will not operate well in a rigid and authoritarian structure.

Benchmarking
The full title for benchmarking is 'best practice benchmarking'. It involves management identifying the best firms in the industry and then comparing the performance standards – including quality – of these businesses with those of their own business. This comparison will identify areas of the business that need to improve to meet the standards of quality and productivity of the best firms.

Stages in the benchmarking process:

1 *Identify the aspects of the business to be benchmarked.* This could be decided by interviewing customers and finding out what they consider to be most important. For example, research may reveal that the most important factors are reliability of the product, speed of delivery and after-sales service. These are the areas that the firm would first benchmark.

2 *Measure performance in these areas,* for example reliability records, delivery records and the number of customer complaints.

3 *Identify the firms in the industry that are considered to be the best.* This process might be assessed by management consultants or by benchmarking schemes operated by government or industry organisations.

4 *Use comparative data from the best firms to establish the main weaknesses in the business.* These data might be obtained from firms by mutual agreement, from published accounts, specialist industry publications and contact with customers/suppliers.

5 *Set standards for improvement.* These might be the standards set by the best firms or they could be set even higher to create a competitive advantage.

6 *Change processes to achieve the standards set.* This may require nothing more than a different way of performing one task, but more substantial changes may be necessary.

7 *Re-measurement.* The changes to the process need to be checked to see if the new, higher standards are being reached.

Benchmarking is not a 'one-off' exercise and to be effective it should become a continuous process to achieve long-term improvements in productivity and quality.

Benchmarking – an evaluation
Benefits include:

Case study – Benchmarking is key to efficiency

Lord Simon is former Chief Executive of British Petroleum. He introduced benchmarking at BP.

'Knowing the opposition and where it is making better profits is one of the most crucial bits of information you can get in business,' says Simon. 'In BP we faced the fact that American companies always achieved a higher return on capital than UK equivalents. Why should this be? We set ourselves a target to equal or exceed Exxon, at that time the best performer, within five years. It was a great way of focusing the mind.'

Simon, who achieved his target in 1997, now promotes the benefits of benchmarking to all firms, especially to small and medium enterprises. 'They need clear data on where competitors are extracting greater profit margins, whether in production, marketing or distribution. Such data can change, enabling better decisions about how to allocate resources.'

Benchmarking also offers a powerful tool for improving the focus and motivation of everybody in the company.

'When managers talk to staff about the need for change it can seem like just another demand,' says Simon. 'But if staff look at a benchmark and see the competition is doing better, they say, if they can do that, so can we.'

Closing the Gap, a DTI (Department of Trade and Industry) report, has thrown up startling variations in performance.

The top 25% of companies achieve profit margins five times greater than those in the bottom quartile. They achieve 98% supplier accuracy and delivery reliability against 60% accuracy and 85% reliability for bottom quartile companies. Spending on training is 10 times greater and staff absenteeism rates up to 75% lower than in the bottom quartile.

These findings do not vary greatly by sector, suggesting that high-achieving companies perform well across a variety of different industries.

Source: Sunday Times, 5 September 2001.

- Benchmarking is a faster and cheaper way of solving problems than firms attempting to solve production or quality problems without external comparisons.
- The areas of greatest significance for customers are identified and action can be directed to improving these.
- It is a process that can assist the firm to increase international competitiveness.
- Comparisons between firms in different industries, for example customer service departments in a retailer compared with a bank, can encourage a useful cross over of ideas.
- If the workforce is involved in the comparison exercise then their participation can lead to better ideas for improvement and increased motivation.

Limitations include:

- The process depends on obtaining relevant and up-to-date information from other firms in the industry. If this is difficult to obtain then the benchmarking exercise will be limited.
- Merely copying the ideas and practices of other firms may discourage initiative and original ideas.
- The costs of the comparison exercise may not be recovered by the improvements obtained from benchmarking.

Kaizen and continuous improvement

Kaizen highlights the difference between western and eastern approaches to problem solving that existed up to a few years ago. Now, the majority of large firms adopt the eastern approach. Traditionally, the western approach involved keeping production up to a certain mark, and then looking for one-off improvements in the form of inventions or alterations to the production process. The eastern approach, the Kaizen approach, has been to strive for 100% perfection by continuously attempting to improve the efficiency of the production process, even if it is only by a barely discernible amount.

This can be shown by means of a diagram; see Figure 18.2. The eastern producers are aware that 100% perfection is not possible to achieve, but they believe that to strive for it must lead to improvement. They also benefit by adjusting their production process in a gradual manner, avoiding much of the unrest and uncertainty that tends to be attached to the managing of

more major change. It is for these reasons that many firms in Europe and the USA have taken up the idea of a Kaizen programme.

In a Kaizen programme, the main target is the elimination of waste of all types. Waste is defined as any activity that adds cost, but not value, to a product. There are three main problem areas identified for production that need to be dealt with and these are:

Muda This is the Japanese word for waste. This is considered to be the most important area and different forms of *muda* are specified. The two most commonly used are 'idling *muda*', which is the time wasted when an employee is idle and waiting for work to arrive, and 'motional *muda*', which is the time wasted through unnecessary movement by an employee during that employee's part of the production process.

Mura This is the inconsistent or non-regular use of a machine or worker.

Muri This is the imposition of excessive demands upon machines or workers.

Kaizen programmes attempt to use the mental abilities of all of the workers and also to improve their manual skills. Workers are expected to assess their roles in the production process and to make suggestions in order to attempt to improve their part of the process. Any idea that cuts half a second or more from the process will be considered and, if possible, implemented.

The process of Kaizen has a knock-on effect and improvements in one part of the production system will require improvements further down the line, if

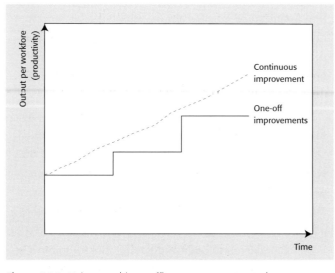

Figure 18.2 Kaizen and 'one-off' responses contrasted

bottlenecks are not to occur. For example, if a worker on a production line that assembles cars finds a way to save 5 seconds from the time it takes to weld the roof panels to the support struts, then the workers who are responsible for the next process must also find a way to save 5 seconds or there will be a build up of work-in-progress stocks. In this case, there would be no increase in production levels. This example highlights the need for all workers to be involved in a Kaizen programme, if a firm is to benefit fully from the process.

Quality circles

Quality circles are another Japanese initiative that has gained considerable significance over the last few years. Quality circles are small groups of workers, usually between five and ten, who meet voluntarily in order to discuss methods of improving productivity and quality in their work areas. Usually, an appointed 'facilitator' leads the group. The main aims of the group are to involve workers in problem solving, thus giving them motivation, and to use the expertise of those who are nearest to the production process, the production workers themselves.

Quality circles are not a means of quality control. They are actually a means of quality and productivity improvements and, as such, are often employed as an integral part of a Kaizen programme.

The importance of education and training

It should have been noted that all of the approaches mentioned above, TQM, benchmarking, Kaizen programmes, quality assurance and quality circles, require input and expertise from the workforce. If this is the case, then the approaches will only be successful if the employees are educated and have been trained to understand their role in the firm and the aims of the firm.

Because of this, there has been an emphasis upon the importance of education and training in industry over the last ten years and this will not die down. Management are beginning to realise the real benefits that can accrue from a talented and skilled, even multi-skilled, workforce. Worker participation requires workers who are able to cope with their empowerment and who are able to contribute fully to the chosen quality attainment system.

Controlling stocks

Firms have a number of different types of stocks that they need to order and control. There are two main types of stocks, product stocks and production process and administrative stocks. The first type, product stocks, are certainly the most important. Product stocks may be split into three distinct categories:

- ◆ stocks of raw materials and bought-in components;
- ◆ work-in-progress stocks;
- ◆ stocks of finished goods.

Stocks of raw materials and bought-in components

These are kept in order to make sure that there are no hold-ups in production caused by late delivery of stocks or by the delivery of faulty stocks. Although the recent trend is to minimise, if not eliminate, these stocks (see the section on Just-in-time [JIT] Stock control), firms do not always do so. JIT involves relatively small, frequent, orders of stocks and it may be that there are large savings to be made by bulk-buying stocks, which will more than outweigh the gains from JIT.

Work-in-progress stocks

These are the stocks of semi-finished products that build up, or are purposely kept, at various stages of the production process. Sometimes, work-in-progress stocks will build up because there is a bottleneck in the production system. At other times, firms will stockpile work-in-progress stocks at certain points on the production system where shortages are known to occur.

Whatever the reason for the existence of these stocks, they signify a production system that is not working efficiently and that should be investigated, analysed and altered. This would be a perfectly appropriate situation for the setting up of a Kaizen programme.

Stocks of finished goods

These are kept to make sure that customers can be supplied, even if there are hold-ups in production or surges in demand. Firms are quite rightly worried that if customers fail to find the product they are seeking, then they will move onto another product that is available and never return to the original choice. There is no doubt that this does happen, but in certain markets this is not the case and firms do try to minimise stocks of finished products. For example, car firms now produce to order and gone are the days when there would be huge numbers of finished cars sitting in parking lots waiting for a customer. In most car firms, it is the order that instigates production and, if orders are not received, then production will not take place.

Production process stocks are maintenance equipment and spare parts that it is necessary to hold in order to keep the production process running. Administration stocks are items that are necessary to run the administration of the firm, such as stationery items and spares for office equipment. These types of stocks are normally much less important than production process stocks, although they can be quite significant in some service industries, such as insurance or banking.

The benefits and costs of holding stocks are summarised in Table 18.1.

Benefits	Costs
They enable the production process to continue when unexpected events occur	Stocks tie up working capital and they have an enormous opportunity cost
Finished goods stocks keep customers happy when they are looking for a product	The actual costs of storing and handling stocks are high
Large-scale buying of input stocks often gains cost advantages through purchasing economies of scale	There is always the danger that stocks may deteriorate, become obsolete, or go out of fashion
Large-scale buying of input stocks reduces the frequency of stock-handling requirements that apply to JIT stock control	Theft of stock is a problem in some businesses

Table 18.1 Benefits and costs of holding stocks

Stock control charts

In situations where firms do hold stocks, then they often use charts to show what their present stock situation is and also to trigger reordering. These charts are frequently computer-generated these days. They are nonetheless useful and should be considered. The traditional chart shows maximum and minimum stock levels, reorder levels, at which point new stock must be ordered, and delivery times. By definition, the charts show a perfect situation and they are based upon three main assumptions:

◆ all stocks are delivered on time, in the correct quantity;
◆ there are no faulty stocks;
◆ stock is used up at a constant rate (see Figure 18.3).

After the initial order, stock is used up at a constant rate and when it falls to the reorder level, a new order for stock is placed, equal to the difference between the maximum and minimum stock levels. The delivery should arrive as the stock level reaches the minimum level and should then take the stock level back to maximum.

Usage is very unlikely to be constant, waste will occur and delivery on time cannot be guaranteed. Also, there is no guarantee that the reordering will take place at exactly the right moment, although computer ordering

Figure 18.3 A typical stock control chart

Activities

1 Distinguish between the different types of stocks a firm may hold. Use examples to illustrate your answer.

2 A firm keeps a stock of brass brackets, which it uses at the rate of 500 a week. No more than four weeks supply of stock is required, but stock must not fall below 1.5 weeks supply. If the initial order is for 1,000 brackets and the delivery time is one week, draw a stockholding chart that shows the minimum and maximum stock levels, the re-order level and the delivery time.

3 If the firm doubles its usage of the brass brackets, redraw the stockholding chart to show the new situation.

has helped here. However, these types of stock control diagrams can still be very useful, so long as the possible inaccuracies are borne in mind and not ignored.

Test Activity

Refer to the stock control chart below.

Stock control diagram for Saiko Trading Ltd

(20 marks, 20 minutes)
(a) What factors may have determined the size of the maximum stock level? (4)
(b) What size of order was received at the end of January? (2)
(c) In weeks, what was the lead time between ordering goods in March and receiving them? (2)
(d) Suggest why stocks fell to zero in April. (4)
(e) Discuss the problems Saiko Trading Ltd might experience from the pattern of stock usage shown by the chart. (8)

Just-in-time (JIT) stock control

Starting in Japan this approach to stock control is now influencing stockholding decisions in businesses all over the world. JIT requires that no buffer stocks are held, components arrive just as they are needed on the production line and finished goods are delivered to customers as soon as they are completed.

The principle is easy to understand but much less easy to put into successful practice. For JIT principles to be successfully introduced there are certain very important requirements that a business must ensure are met:

1 *Relationships with suppliers have to be excellent as they must always be prepared to supply the components as and when required with a very short lead time.* This often means that a firm will only have one, or at most

two, suppliers for each component so that a relationship of mutual benefit can be built up.

2 *Production staff must be multi-skilled and prepared to change jobs at short notice.* There is no point in a worker continuing to produce the same item all the time if this leads to stocks building up. Each worker must be able to switch to making different items at very short notice so that no excess supplies of any one product are made. For example, if a worker in a clothing factory usually makes men's denim jeans but demand is falling then the worker should be able to switch to making other garments that are still in demand.

3 *Equipment and machinery must be flexible.* Old-fashioned manufacturing equipment tended to be designed to produce one range of very similar products. It might have taken days to adapt it to making other types of products. This equipment would be most unsuitable for JIT-based systems. The machinery would have to produce large batches of one type of component before being converted to making another item. Stocks of each item produced would be needed to cope with demand while it was producing other goods. Modern, computer-controlled equipment is much more flexible and adaptable – often able to be changed with no more than a different software program. In this way very small batches of each item can be produced which keeps stock levels to an absolute minimum. However, such equipment is expensive and, as a result, JIT may not be so appropriate for small or underfinanced firms.

4 *Accurate demand forecasts will make JIT a much more successful policy.* If it is very difficult for a firm to predict likely future sales levels then keeping zero stocks of materials, parts and finished goods could be a very risky strategy. Demand forecasts can be converted into production schedules that allow calculation of the precise number of components of each type needed over a certain time period.

5 *The latest IT equipment will allow JIT to be more successful.* Accurate data-based records of sales, sales trends, re-order levels and so on will allow very low or zero stocks to be held. Similarly, if contact with suppliers can be set up with the latest electronic data exchanges then automatic and immediate ordering can take place, when it is recorded that more components will shortly be required.

6 *Excellent employee–employer relationships are essential for JIT to operate smoothly.* Any industrial relations problem could lead to a break in supplies and the entire production system could grind to a halt. It is no coincidence that many of the businesses that have adopted JIT in Japan and in Europe have a 'no-strike' deal with the major trades unions.

7 *Quality must be everyone's priority.* As there are no spare stocks to fall back on it is essential that each component and product must be right first time. Any poor-quality goods that cannot be used will mean that a customer will not receive goods on time.

Advantages	Disadvantages
Reduces capital invested in stocks and reduces the opportunity cost of stockholding.	Any failure to receive supplies of materials or components in time caused by for example a strike at the supplier's factory, transport problems or IT failure, will lead to expensive production delays.
Costs of storage and stockholding are reduced.	
Space released from holding of stocks can be used for a more productive purpose.	Delivery costs will increase as frequent small deliveries are an essential feature of JIT.
Much less chance of stock becoming outdated or obsolescent. Less stock held also reduces the risk of damage or wastage.	Order administration costs may rise because so many small orders need to be processed.
The greater flexibility that the system demands leads to quicker response times to changes in consumer demand or tastes.	There could a reduction in the bulk discounts offered by suppliers because each order is likely to be very small.
The multi-skilled and adaptable staff required for JIT to work may gain from improved motivation.	The reputation of the business depends significantly on outside factors such as the reliability of supplying firms.

Table 18.2 The advantages and disadvantages of JIT stock control

Over-to-you

Case study – Hard Hats Ltd

Using the information from the case study, which can be found at the end of Chapter 17, tackle the following exercises:

(a) ◆ The maximum stock level for cushioning materials is 25,000 sets and the minimum is 10,000 sets. Weekly usage for the four weeks from the 1 February is 10,000 sets. Stating any assumptions that you have made, draw a stock-holding chart for the four weeks to show the maximum and minimum stock levels and the reorder levels. Indicate clearly the points where new orders need to be made.

   ◆ Evaluate the current stockholding policy for all of the materials held at Hard Hats Ltd.

(b) Hard Hats Ltd is continuing to expand and Jamie Pither has decided that a change in the location of the firm would be of benefit. Evaluate factors that Jamie should take into account when he is deciding upon the new location.

(c) Develop a strategy that Jamie Pither might adopt in order to improve the motivation of the production workers.

(d) Write a report considering the firm's approach to quality and make recommendations for a strategy that might be employed to improve quality control in the firm.

Read the case studies below on conflicting experience with just-in-time and then tackle the exercises that follow.

Case study – Nissan cuts stock to almost zero

Nissan's car factories now operate on an average of just 1.6 day's worth of component and raw material stocks. This is one of the lowest in the entire motor industry. Computer links with suppliers, which are often located in the same area as the Nissan factories, allow special coded messages to be sent from the Nissan production line. These contain details of the models and colours of cars being assembled. The supplier, for example of car carpets, then knows that it must supply particular colours of carpets directly to the factory. In fact, some suppliers will make up to 120 deliveries in a day. The parts are taken straight to the assembly line – they do not pass through a traditional warehouse first. Nissan production control directors claim that this method brings huge savings in stock holding and internal stock handling as well as great space-saving advantages.

Final assembly area – Nissan Sunderland, UK   *Source*: Nissan.

HOW NISSAN LEADS THE CAR INDUSTRY IN 42 MINUTES

9am: Microchip on body of car sends electronic order to the supplier via computer

9.10am: Carpet cut and trimmed to specification

9.25am: Batch loaded on to lorry to be delivered to Nissan

9.30am: Driver unloads and takes carpets to assembly line

9.42am: Carpet fitted into car. Other components are supplied and fitted in a similar fashion

Case study – Toyota production is halted

A fire at a major supplier of parts to Toyota's Japanese factories has brought all car production to a stop. Toyota's JIT production system relies on suppliers delivering only the necessary volume of vehicle parts to the assembly line at precisely the point in the manufacturing process at which they are required. The problem is that when things go wrong at just one supplier – Aisin Seiki's fire for example – the lack of stock of parts can lead to serious problems. Toyota always relies on one supplier for all major parts because it believes that this brings huge economies of scale. These suppliers not only have to agree to be 100% reliable – excluding events such as fires or earthquakes – but also accept that they must design parts for Toyota's cars themselves. This special relationship with suppliers have helped Toyota reduce its costs by $820m in each of the past three years.

(20 marks, 25 minutes)

(a) Examine the benefits to both Nissan and Toyota of:
  ◆ the JIT system of stock control that both use; and
  ◆ the reliance on just one supplier for each major component. (12)

(b) Using evidence drawn from the articles and from your own knowledge, examine the potential drawbacks to the adoption of the JIT concept for manufacturing businesses. (8)

Summary

In this chapter we have recognised that:

- The concepts of quality, quality control, stocks and stockholding are important.
- Quality as an objective and work must be to specification, neither above it nor below it.
- Firms must supply quality products if they wish to succeed.
- There are many possible ways of attempting to ensure quality, but more recent systems make quality the responsibility of every single member of a firm.
- Inspected quality control is a waste of resources and is also demotivating for the shop-floor workers.
- There are various types of stocks, but holding stocks has high monetary and opportunity costs.
- Stocks can be controlled by means of stock control charts, but the lower the stock levels, the better, in most cases.
- JIT is a method of attempting to do this.

Key words

Definitions of Key words can be found in the Glossary on page 269.

benchmarking
just-in-time
quality
quality assurance

stock control
total quality management
   (TQM)

19 Revising effectively

Introduction

In modular courses such as OCR Business Studies, examinations can come quickly and frequently. The AS unit examinations are assessed at above GCSE standard but below full A level standard. If you prepare well for these units and gain some encouraging results then you will be well positioned to take the subject further, to A level and, possibly, consider it as one of your options for degree study at University. You will need to get off to a good start – especially if your school of college enters you for one of the January units in year 12. This chapter plans to help you make that good start. It covers essential information about the three AS units, what examiners are really looking for and how to prepare for the pre-issued case studies. We start by looking at the specific examination requirements in Table 19.1.

Unit 1 – 2871 Businesses, Their Objectives and Environment

This is a written paper based on a short pre-issued case study. The case may be taken from a recent newspaper article or other source and will focus on a real business situation. There will be five compulsory questions.

Unit 2 – 2872 Business Decisions

This is a written paper based on unseen data. Four compulsory 'data-response' questions have to be completed in 45 minutes.

Unit 3 – 2873 Business Behaviour

A pre-issued case, longer than Unit 1, will be the basis for four compulsory questions. The case will include quantitative data, such as business accounts.

Unit	Name of Unit	Format	Duration	Total paper marks	AS level weighting	A level weighting
2871	Businesses, their Objectives and Environment	Pre-issued case	1 hour	45	30%	15%
2872	Business Decisions	Data response	45 minutes	45	30%	15%
2873	Business Behaviour	Pre-issued case	1 hour 15 mins	60	40%	20%

Table 19.1 The AS Units

(See end of chapter for sample papers plus selected examples of mark schemes.)

What the examiners are looking for – the examination skills

Examiners are told to identify and reward the following skills (see also Table 19.2).

1 **Knowledge**   Clearly, you would not expect to do well in a Business Studies examination if you did not show relevant subject knowledge. This knowledge and understanding can be demonstrated in a number of ways: by the use of accurate definitions of business terms, by stating appropriate ratios or formulae or by detailing appropriate material from the Business Studies specification. This knowledge is, hopefully, gained throughout the AS course and needs to be revised thoroughly before each Unit examination. Accurate knowledge of the work that you have covered is **essential** to succeed but, surprisingly perhaps, it is not **sufficient** to do well. This is because the AS examinations only allow 30% of their total marks for demonstrating knowledge – the remainder of the marks are for the other skills.

Look at Question 1 of the Unit 1 specimen paper. This is worth two marks. It requires nothing more than an understanding of the data – this is called level 1. Therefore, these two marks will be awarded for this skill and nothing else.

TIP 1: If the question says 'State' or 'List' or 'Define' then the examiners are not expecting a long answer with much discussion and debate. In fact, you will be wasting your time. Just give the essential information requested – enough to demonstrate good knowledge and understanding.

TIP 2: Remember that all the knowledge in the world, the most perfect and detailed knowledge base, will never earn you more than around four marks from a 16-mark question. Once sufficient knowledge has been demonstrated, it is time to move on to the other skills! A few points well argued and supported by relevant evidence is the best approach.

2 **Application**   This means applying the knowledge and understanding that you have to the problems and issues contained in the data (Unit 2) and case studies (Units 1 and 3). This requirement is so easily missed by candidates – yet once the skill has been grasped it

is a very effective way of boosting total marks. Twenty-six per cent of AS marks are for putting the answer into the context of the business situation presented to you.

Here is a good example of **no** application. In a case study about a business making heavy tractors and earth-moving equipment, one question asked candidates to explain suitable methods of market research that this business could use. There were many answers that ignored the **context** and referred to asking consumers on the high street! The best answers contained references to research done from building firms and the construction industry.

Now look at Question 1 in Unit 2 specimen paper and the mark scheme. Level 2 marks are awarded for such application.

TIP: **All** questions require application to the case study or data response material apart from the pure knowledge based questions such as 'List' and 'State'. You could therefore lose over one quarter of the total marks if this is ignored.

3 **Analysis**   This means using the ideas, techniques and theories of Business Studies to help explain your answer. This could be done in any number of ways – it pays to note carefully what the question is asking. Here are some examples:

'Analyse the likely effect on profits of an increase in price for this product'.

In answer to this question you would certainly gain analysis marks if you explained, accurately, how price elasticity of demand would influence the revenue earned by this business following a price change. This is a business technique that you are using to help explain the answer.

'At what level of output will this firm break even?'

Clearly, you are being asked to use the business technique of break even analysis. By using this correctly, you will be demonstrating skills of analysis.

'Explain why quality circles might help to increase productivity in this business'.

Analysis would be demonstrated in this case by referring to the work of one or more motivational theorists. By applying their work and conclusions to the likely impact of quality circles you would be showing a full explanation of how theories of the subject can be used to help underpin and support your answer. This would be clear analysis.

Now look at Question 3 in Unit 2 specimen paper and the mark scheme. See how business ideas are being suggested as possible answers to this question in order to earn analysis marks. Level 3 marks are awarded to candidates who show this analysis.

TIP: Look out carefully for the 'analysis' prompt words such as 'Analyse', 'Explain', 'How might', 'Calculate', as these will require the use of business theories, techniques or ratios.

4 **Evaluation** This means showing judgement. It might involve weighing up arguments behind a business decision and coming to a reasoned conclusion or recommendation. It might mean considering the advantages and disadvantages of an issue and showing judgement in considering them. Other questions might ask for a distinction to be drawn between fact and opinion. It carries 20% of total AS marks but will be much more important than this for some of the questions on each Unit examination. The key prompt terms will be: 'Evaluate', 'To what extent', 'Discuss', 'Recommend', 'Justify'.

Now look at Question 4 Unit 2 specimen paper and the mark scheme. See how the top marks – level Four – are only awarded if **both** advantages and disadvantages are considered and weighed up.

TIP: Do not waste time evaluating your answer unless requested to do so. If asked for a recommendation, make sure that you give one, but to be worth any marks it must be supported by evidence and reasoned argument drawn from the case study material.

Skill	What examiners look for	AS weighting %
Knowledge and understanding	Accurate and relevant subject content	30
Application	References to the case study or data that are relevant to the question	26.5
Analysis	Use of relevant Business Studies ideas and theories to help answer the question	23.5
Evaluation	Reasoned argument and judgement supported by evidence	20

Table 19.2 The skills – a summary

Levels of response

You will have noticed by now that examiners are asked to mark according to 'levels of response'. Some questions have four levels, others three and so on – depending on the skills being sought in the answer. Examiners assess 'from the top down', seeking the extent to which an answer gives them what they really want from the question. Only the best candidates are likely to offer that response so each answer is tested successively against each lower level until the level is found that corresponds with the skills shown by the student. If a level is not found, then no marks can be awarded!

As we have seen, the fact that there are four possible levels does not mean that there will always be four, or that the mark 'band' for each will necessarily be equal. It is sufficient to demonstrate a particular level *once* in an answer and this will then define the minimum mark for the whole answer.

At AS more emphasis is put on levels 1 and 2 – knowledge and application and less emphasis on analysis (level 3) and evaluation (level 4). This means that good understanding of subject matter and application of it to the case can gain you a good mark overall. You should, of course, show the higher skills when the trigger or key term in the question shows that those higher skills are demanded.

Dealing with pre-issued case studies

Both Units 1 and 3 are based on pre-issued material. The purpose of this pre-issue is to give some real focus to your revision and to allow more time in the examination room for writing rather than reading. Once the case study has been released by the Board teachers, students may use it in whatever ways are considered appropriate.

What follows is one way of using the case. This approach does not have to be used. It is based on these assumptions.

◆ Two copies of the case will be needed – i.e. a photocopy will be needed.

◆ The teacher will need some time to study the case before it is issued or worked with.

◆ Two weeks before the examination is enough and three weeks ample.

◆ The examination is not competitive. Co-operation

between students in the run up to the examination is to everybody's advantage and nobody's loss.

The plan – as instructions to students:

- Work in small groups of 4–6.
- Read through the first copy of the case. Check on your understanding of it as a piece of English. Check your understanding of each technical word or phrase.
- Divide the case into approximately equal units or sections – allocate one unit per group. Include all data and tables as part of a unit.
- Follow the activity below.

Using the second copy of the case

Analysing the case in the way described above will have left you with a mass of knowledge about the case. It is now time to focus on the business itself and the issues or problems that the business faces. These will be the sources of most of the questions. The following structure should help you.

What are the key characteristics of the business?

- Large or small?
- Service or manufacturing?
- Limited or unlimited liability?
- PLC or Ltd?
- Capital or labour intensive?
- Main internal strengths and weaknesses?

How is the business managed?

- What are the aims and objectives? Are they clearly stated?
- Leadership style?
- What is the culture of the business?
- Do the staff appear motivated?
- How are the staff motivated?
- Is the focus on shareholders or stakeholders?

Activity for pre-issued case material

1 Read the whole case.

2 Read your part and ensure that you understand it. Discuss this with members of your group.

3 Now concentrate on your section alone.

   (a) Highlight all words and phrases in your part that have business-studies meanings.

   (b) Check your list with members of your group and agree.

4 With reference to each of the identified things you should be able to:

- define it;
- give examples;
- explain it;
- use it in context;
- understand uses;
- understand limitations.

5 Bring your completed work back to class. Present it and photocopy it for all students. You should now have a complete portfolio of words and phrases.

6 Read through your portfolio alone and with your group. Highlight anything you do not understand and bring questions back to the next lesson.

7 With reference to your identified words and phrases, trace links backwards or forwards with repetitions of the same idea or with associated ones.

8 Check any association that the ideas may have with the diagrams or tables in the case.

9 Identify the main issues and themes and allocate one/ two as required fairly among members of each group.

10 Revise your area(s) of the syllabus and create notes for the rest of the class. *Do not try to identify any questions. Trying to create model answers is a dangerous waste of time. Do look at past questions of AS-level standard that are on your topic and make sure you can answer them* or come back with questions you need to ask and debate in class.

11 Try some questions that require different levels of response.

What are the key external influences on the business?

- How competitive is the market it trades in?
- What is the likely income elasticity of the product?
- Is there excess capacity in the industry?
- Is it sensitive to any particular macro-economic changes?
- Does the firm face any particular social or ethical issues?

What are the key characteristics of the managers?

- How experienced are they?
- Do they seem to have common aims for the business?
- Do they seem prepared to delegate?
- Do they react quickly to external events or are they swept along by them?
- Any others – relevant to each particular case

Revision strategies and preparing for the examinations

Step 1 – getting organized

- Ask your teacher for a copy of the specification – use the guidance notes as a checklist when you are revising. Tick off each topic as you revise and understand it.
- Ask your teacher for a full copy of the mark schemes for the specimen papers – and obtain as many past papers with mark schemes as possible. These are invaluable for seeing how marks are awarded for the different skills that we have already identified.
- Put your notes in order with a clear set of 'dividers' so that each topic is easy to refer to. Use the same subject and topic headings as in the specification for your dividers.
- Plan your revision time carefully. A revision timetable is an excellent idea as it allows you to allocate a certain amount of time to each important topic area. Be as detailed as possible in your timetable, for example: 'Thursday – Revise Business Accounts' is not detailed enough. Better to lay out your timetable like this: 'Thursday: 9.00a.m. to 9.30a.m. revise costs and costing methods'.

Step 2 – revision techniques

Everybody has their own favoured methods of revision. This section is not aiming to make you change your methods if you are happy with them and if they work! However, you may like to consider these approaches, especially if you are not satisfied with how you currently prepare for examinations:

1 Short revision sessions but many of them! Psychological studies have shown that our learning abilities decline sharply after around 30 minutes of intensive study. Arrange your timetable so that in each day you have several 30 minute sessions with breaks in between – not just one *session* of several hours.

2 Use active revision techniques. Reading obviously has a place in revision – but it is a passive form of revision. Active methods have been shown to be more effective. These include:
- re-writing notes in a different style;
- making new notes, e.g. from this textbook;
- making spider diagrams or mind maps with key words and terms (see Figure 19.1);
- testing yourself with simple written tests that you can mark yourself, for example, lists of definitions;
- writing answers to past questions or the specimen papers – try to do these in the correct time allocation;
- revising with others and testing each other;
- making easy to refer to revision cards containing a few key facts, figures or diagrams. An example is shown in Table 19.3.

Step 3 – during the examination

Virtually all candidates manage to lose marks by the way they tackle the examination and by the way they write their paper. Some lose many marks – enough to take them down a grade or two. The main reasons are set out below. The interesting thing is that they are common mistakes, which all teachers warn about.

These comments are based on significant mark reductions in actual scripts. To demonstrate them, 50 scripts were chosen at random across a wide mark range. In 80% of these scripts at least on C grade was lost. What follows concentrates on the mistakes and hence is essentially a list of ***Don't's***.

1 **Ignoring the case or data altogether**   The importance of applying the answer to the case or the

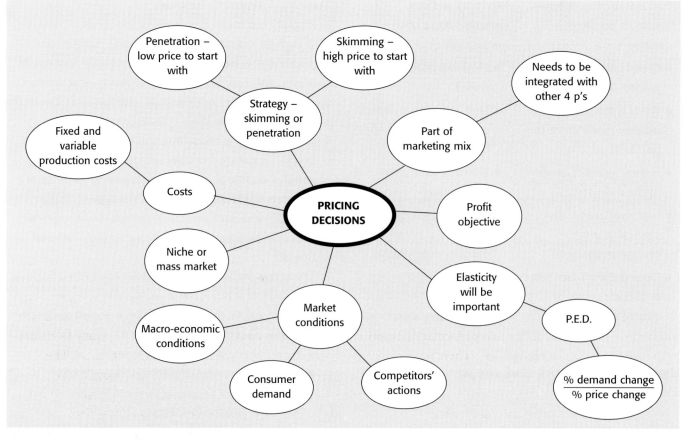

Figure 19.1 A sample mind map to help revision

Specification area: Operations Management

Economies of scale
Definition: The benefits gained by firms as they increase the scale of operation that lead to reductions in unit costs.

Causes
(a) Purchasing – bulk buying discounts.
(b) Financial – lower interest rates; public issue of shares.
(c) Marketing – fixed cost of advertising campaign spread over higher output.
(d) Technical – advanced, efficient equipment can be afforded.
(e) Managerial – Specialists employed in each area.

Table 19.3 A sample revision card

data in the question has already been explained. Many marks in our sample were missed, often by candidates who clearly knew a lot about Business Studies, because they failed to refer to the case in their answer.

2 **Poor timing**   A last question not attempted or with a skeleton for an answer and evidence of haste in one or two of the last questions are all very common. The paper times and mark allocations are shown on Page 251. After re-reading the case study and reading the data in Unit 2 you have, approximately one minute for each mark awarded. This is not very much time, but it is enough if you use it well and do not go over time on any one question.
You may have time at the end of the examination which you can profitably use to improve an answer. To make this possible *leave a good long gap between answers* so that any additional points that can be made are made as part of the answer and not elsewhere on the paper.

3 **Failing to read the question carefully**   This is a real problem with all examinations but, potentially, an even greater problem with pre-issued case studies. There is a real danger, proven from our sample of 50 scripts, that candidates answer the question they thought would appear on the paper and not the actual question. You must avoid this, question

'spotting' is not an ideal way to prepare for pre-issued cases anyway, but when it leads candidates into writing a pre-prepared answer to a question that did not actually appear it is positively dangerous! So:

- check that you understand what the key or prompt word is asking you;
- read the whole question at least twice to ensure you understand its full implications;
- re-read the question as you write your answer to check that you are being consistently relevant.

4 **Not showing your working** Examiners **always** expect working to be shown for any answer involving calculations. In this way, marks can still be awarded for your attempt at an answer, even if you did not arrive at the correct result. Sixteen out of our sample of 50 candidates failed to show working and, as eight of them arrived at an incorrect result, they were awarded no marks at all for that particular question!

5 **Failure to use subject language** There were many instances where time was wasted or marks lost because answers were too long and vague. The candidates had not taken advantage of the opportunity to make their answers clearer and shorter by using the language and terminology of the subject.

6 **Too much knowledge – not enough analysis and evaluation** The different examination skills have already been explained but there are many students who still believe that AS examinations are just about demonstrating lots of knowledge. Some answers can be very long but they contain nothing but subject material with no attempt to:

- be selective,
- be critical,
- be analytical in using their knowledge,
- be judgemental.

Knowledge and understanding alone will gain a maximum of 30%, which is why your revision programme should not just focus on reading notes. It must be more active than this and should include studying – and doing past papers – and looking very carefully at examiners marks schemes to judge how marks are being awarded for the four skills that we discussed above.

Final points

The jump from GCSE to AS level is a big one and has to be made in just a few short months. The additional time that you now have to revise each AS subject – compared with perhaps ten GCSEs – can be used wisely to ensure that you are prepared for the challenge ahead. The absolute importance of application, analysis and evaluation skills has been made clear. If you are able to demonstrate consistently that you are aware of these skills and can demonstrate them relevantly then you will lift your answer above the majority of candidates answers that fail to do this. Examiners are not emotional people when they mark – but the sight of a candidate's answer that shows good subject knowledge combined with an excellent awareness of the case will always lead to an appropriately generous response – and when the points made are also analysed and evaluated then a Grade A becomes a distinct possibility!

OXFORD CAMBRIDGE AND RSA EXAMINATIONS
Advanced Subsidiary GCE

SAMPLE PAGE

BUSINESS STUDIES

Businesses, Their Objectives and Environment

2871

Unit 1 – 1 hour

Case study

CRUISING FOR TROUBLE

War has broken out in the cruise industry – and to the victor will go leadership of one of the fastest growing parts of the holiday market.

Battle commenced in late 2001, when Carousel, undisputed market leader, launched a bid to fight the merger provisionally agreed between its smaller rivals R & R and Caribbean Cruises.

Carousel would certainly prefer the merger not to go ahead. RCC, as the merged company would be known, would leapfrog Carousel to become the biggest operator, measured by number of berths. That is not a slot Carousel will give up lightly. R & R's shareholders are shortly due to vote on the merger. The onus is on Carousel to come up with a tempting offer to R & R's shareholders if it wants to prevent the merger. If enough money is offered, R & R's shareholders could vote against the proposed merger and then vote to allow Carousel to take them over.   5   10

Carousel can take credit for creating the market in its current form. Its strategy of targeting ordinary Americans has fuelled the spectacular industry growth in the US and Europeans are now taking to the seas with similar enthusiasm. Over the past decade, Carousel has increased its passenger capacity by an average of 11 per cent a year and now carries more than 2.6 million passengers a year.   15

R & R and Caribbean Cruises have both been significant beneficiaries of the growth in the market (see fig.1). At least until 11 September 2001 that is. Like the rest of the travel industry, cruising suffered a big drop in demand in the wake of the New York attack. R & R alone immediately lost around 20,000 bookings. There are now signs of recovery, although only because of big price cuts. All three companies are confident that the drop in demand is just a temporary blip in the otherwise smooth progress of the cruising market. They had better be right: R & R and Caribbean Cruises between them have 14 ships with a total of 30,000 berths on order. Carousel is also expected to take delivery of a further 14 offering more than 34,000 berths.   20

Only 12 per cent of Americans and less than 2 per cent of Europeans have been on a cruise; however, in a recent survey more than half said they would like to. It was these growth prospects, rather than thoughts of cutting costs or shedding jobs, that prompted R & R and Caribbean Cruises to get together.   25

When the deal was announced, the two companies pointed to the great geographic fit. As its name suggests, Caribbean Cruises' strength is cruises to the tropical islands while R & R operates in the Mediterranean cruising market. Caribbean Cruises is relatively stronger in the US and R & R in Europe. The newly merged company would certainly be a force to reckon with.   30

A shipping industry insider said yesterday:

> A merger is not the same as a take-over, and there are different implications for R & R and its stakeholders with each option. If Carousel want to make a take-over bid, the board of R & R will want a clear unconditional offer on the table very soon in order to consider the merger and the take-over simultaneously. R & R's board can then make a recommendation to their shareholders. Whether Carousel makes a serious offer or not, the industry is in for a long spell of stormy weather.   35   40

Answer **all** questions:

1 State the nature of the market growth in UK passengers as shown in Fig. 1.   (2)

2 The holiday industry is in the tertiary sector of the economy. Giving an example of each, identify
   the other two sectors of business activity.   (4)

3 Analyse Carousel's likely objectives in its proposed take-over of R & R.   (9)

4 Discuss the main influences on the operation of R & R.   (14)

5 Evaluate how the stakeholders in R & R may be affected by the proposed take-over by Carousel. (14)

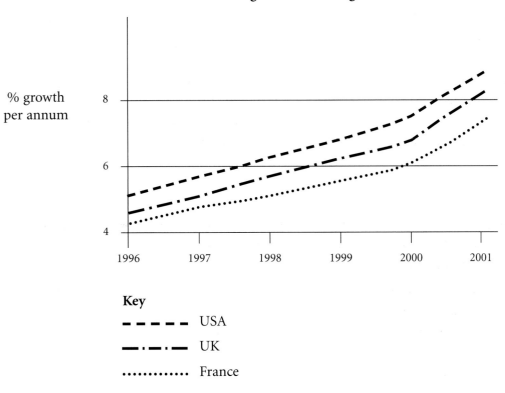

Cruising Market Passenger Numbers

Fig. 1

OXFORD CAMBRIDGE AND RSA EXAMINATIONS
Advanced Subsidiary GCE

BUSINESS STUDIES

2872

Business Decisions

Unit 2 – 45 minutes

Thorntons plc manufactures, distributes and retails a range of high quality chocolate and toffee confectionery. Despite slow growth in the confectionery market overall, the business continues to increase sales. It is the market leader in the premium end of the boxed chocolate market. Among the population Thorntons has both high positive customer awareness and a large degree of brand loyalty. The company has identified four market segments, each of which has different customer needs:

- Gifts
- Personal treat
- Family share
- Children

The marketing mix must reflect these different needs in a complementary and coordinated manner in order to maximise sales. However, over ambitious sales forecasts last Easter led to an excess of Easter eggs at the end of the selling period. These subsequently had to be sold at a discount. Sales are highly seasonal, see Table 1.

Table 1: Seasonal sales patterns

Significant date	Percentage of full years sales	Time period
Christmas	35%	7 weeks
Valentines day	5%	2 weeks
Mothers day	7%	2 weeks
Easter	15%	4 weeks
Fathers day	3%	2 weeks

Thorntons has 410 of its own stores and 127 franchises. The business aims to increase the proportion of franchises. The following information relates to a potential franchise opportunity.

Table 2: Financial information relating to a potential Thorntons' franchise

SET UP COSTS

Initial fee	£10,000
Shop fitting costs	£25,000
Opening stock and other start up costs	£10,000

EXPECTED NET CASH FLOWS

Year	Net cash flow
1	£10,000
2	£15,000
3	£20,000
4	£20,000
5	£20,000

Thorntons manufactures on two sites and uses batch production methods. It handles its distribution using its own fleet of vehicles. Orders are placed over the phone and then processed, picked up, despatched and delivered within 48 hours. The company recruits seasonal staff to work in its warehouse:

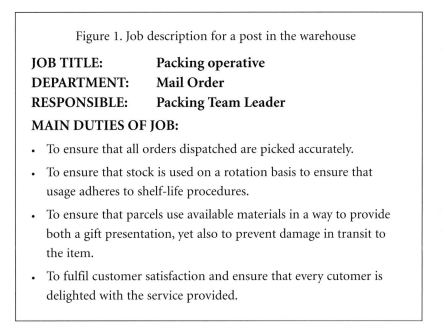

Figure 1. Job description for a post in the warehouse

JOB TITLE: **Packing operative**
DEPARTMENT: **Mail Order**
RESPONSIBLE: **Packing Team Leader**
MAIN DUTIES OF JOB:

- To ensure that all orders dispatched are picked accurately.

- To ensure that stock is used on a rotation basis to ensure that usage adheres to shelf-life procedures.

- To ensure that parcels use available materials in a way to provide both a gift presentation, yet also to prevent damage in transit to the item.

- To fulfil customer satisfaction and ensure that every cutomer is delighted with the service provided.

(Adapted from Thorntons plc Annual report 2000 and www.thorntons.co.uk)

1 (a) Outline **two** methods that Thorntons might use to research the nature of its market. (4)
   (b) Evaluate the ways in which Thornton could maintain a high positive awareness of their brand among the population. (12)

2 A potential franchisee is considering taking a Thorntons franchise for a five year period. Using the data in Table 2, calculate:
   - The payback period
   - The accounting rate of return (ARR). (8)

3 Analyse the advantages and disadvantages to Thorntons of using batch production. (7)

4 Evaluate Thorntons' policy of recruiting waterhouse staff on a seasonal basis. (12)

Selected Examples of Mark Schemes 2872 Unit 2

1 (a) Outline two methods that Thorntons might use to research the nature of its market. (4)

Field research methods – questionnaires, surveys, interviews, observations, focus groups, consumer panels etc.

Desk research methods – sales figures, orders/number of hits on the website, demographic data, government statistics, trade/industry journals etc.

Possible explanation/application: Some indication of the nature or influence of the business or its market in relation to the chosen method or consideration of issues re validity and bias. As a large company Thorntons may use a specialist market research agency to carry out research.

| Level 2 | Method(s) explained/applied to the business | (4–3) |
| Level 1 | One or two Method(s) stated | (2–1) |

2 Analyse the advantages and disadvantages to Thorntons of using batch production (7)

Advantages

Nature of the goods sold by Thorntons is such that there are many different versions within one item for sale such as a box of chocolates. Therefore would need different batches of different products made e.g. chocolates with different fillings. Allows for seasonal variation in products e.g. Easter eggs, chocolate Christmas decorations etc. Can respond to changes in demand.
Allows some specialisation of the workforce and use of specialist machinery – lowering costs.

Disadvantages

Storage costs while all the other flavours in the box of chocolates are made – particularly as these are foodstuffs which are perishable. Also potential wastage as goods are moved around the factory. Downtime while the machinery is cleaned and reset/changed over. Specialisation may mean jobs are boring – motivational issues.

Level 3	Analysis demonstrated by considering the implications for the business	(7–6)
Level 2	Understanding of concepts involved demonstrated in context	(5–4)
Level 1	Appropriate concepts and issues identified	(3–1)

4 Evaluate Thornton's policy of recruiting warehouse staff on a seasonal basis (12)

Benefits

Sales are seasonal so only pay for people when they are really needed. Low level jobs that do not require high levels of training. Need only pay low levels of wages for these types of jobs. People move on before they have a chance to get bored of the job. May fit in with lifestyles of some of these workers e.g. students. These types of workers may keep returning to the job.

Limitations

Cost of recruitment process, cost of training up new staff, lack of experience, lack of continuity, more errors, quality control may be more difficult. May be difficult to recruit people if the surrounding area is affluent or the economy is doing well.

Level 4	Evaluation of the relative importance of the advantages and disadvantages of the policy.	(8–7)
Level 3	Analysis demonstrated by considering the implications for the business.	(6–5)
Level 2	Understnding of concepts involved demonstrated in context.	(4–3)
Level 1	Appropriate concepts and issues identified.	(2–1)

OXFORD CAMBRIDGE AND RSA EXAMINATIONS
Advanced Subsidiary GCE

SAMPLE PAGE

BUSINESS STUDIES

Business Behaviour

2873

Unit 3 – 1 hour 15 minutes

Case study

EDUCATION IS FUN LTD (EIFL)

Adam and Danielle Vernon established EIFL in January 1991. Adam had been made redundant by a major multinational and this affected his outlook. When he set up EIFL he wanted to build an atmosphere of trust and involve all his fellow workers as colleagues in the business. At the same time, he wanted to have managerial and financial control. Adam and Danielle are proud of their achievements in EIFL. They have never taken a dividend and always ploughed back all the available profit. 5

EIFL sells educational toys and equipment for children aged up to five years. There are at present two groups of consumer. The first consists of children who spend the day with a parent, child minder or nanny. The second consists of children at nursery or school, which can be state or independent. There are many different types of nursery or school, with various age-ranges, often depending on the area. The customers who make purchasing decisions are parents, heads of nurseries or schools, and purchasing managers in local education authorities. The distribution of sales revenue between type of customer is shown in Table 1. 10

EIFL manufactures about half its sales volume in its factory near Basingstoke. Three other firms make the rest for EIFL. This way Adam feels that they can keep a check on their own performance by setting external benchmarks and that spreading the production reduces risk. Danielle, on the other hand, feels that EIFL loses economies of scale. Both Adam and Danielle are concerned about the decline in quality of their in-house production. Rejects are rising as are returns from customers. They have lost an account with a small local education authority. 'The trouble is we are all so busy at the moment, neither Adam nor I have enough time to monitor things properly,' Danielle said to herself. 15 20

EIFL has always sold largely through mail order. Personal customers order by answering advertisements placed in newspapers, family magazines and the like. The cost of these advertisements has been kept down by regular volume placements for a year at a time. This has been effective in the past, although Adam and Danielle are now beginning to question this. EIFL has achieved sales to schools through a catalogue. This is produced and sent each year in May, when headteachers know their school numbers and financial budget for the following academic year (September to August), and therefore can place orders for delivery in summer or early September. 25 30

Adam and Danielle are considering plans for marketing for the next three years and are asking themselves a number of questions. What are the right distribution channels? Mail costs are high and the service could be unreliable. Should they set up their own delivery service? Danielle is interested in investigating e-commerce and the possibility of sales through this medium: which of their existing customers would use it and were there any new customers which this would attract? Should they consider approaching some of the major retail outlets to find out if they would stock their products? What effects would introducing an intermediary have? There seemed to be a move towards parents placing their children in nursery schools rather than keeping them at home. What were the implications? 35 40

No plans for development could be made without taking into account the financial position. The most recent balance sheet and profit and loss account are shown in Table 2 and Table 3 respectively. These tables continue the trends that had become apparent in recent years. Danielle's concerns included sales revenue, profits and profitability, stocks, debtors, the overdraft and the interest burden. The overdraft was secured along with the mortgage on the premises, of which EIFL owned the freehold. The premises were probably worth double their book value at current property market prices. However, the interest burden was rising. At the last meeting with the bank manager, he had told Danielle that the bank's 45 regional office had just asked him to investigate EIFL's credit position. Alarmed by this Danielle had decided to budget more carefully and had drawn up Table 4.

50

All these financial concerns were distracting the Vernons from issues concerning the organisational structure. No organisation chart existed for EIFL and, if there were one, it would look very flat. Despite Adam's desire to involve the workforce, many of them felt alienated. There are thirty-six employees as shown in Table 5.

55

Right from the start, EIFL practised job enrichment by default: all the non-office staff were expected to know how to do each other's job without any job demarcation. As this had been a time of high unemployment locally and nationally, this had been accepted. Now that the company had grown, the workforce was unhappy with the general state of affairs. Jenny, who had been with the company since the start, moaned to several of her colleagues during the coffee break one day, 'The trouble is that Adam and Danielle practise the opposite of what they preach. The problem we have is that they are each the production, marketing, human resources and accounting departments all rolled into one. They delegate nothing and communicate nothing, not even to each other at times. They rush about from job to job, leaving tasks half-complete. Sometimes they give different jobs to the same person within 10 minutes of each other. It's a classic case of the right hand not knowing what the left hand is doing.'

60

65

The general dissatisfaction was such that the entire workforce met out of hours privately to discuss the situation. Particular points of concern were the absence of written contracts, no proper structure to the business, no training or promotion schemes and the general lack of involvement and consultation. There was a firm determination to tell Adam and Danielle of their concerns. On hearing of these concerns, the Vernons were shocked that the workforce felt this way and began to consider how to respond.

70

75

Table 1 Sales Revenue by Customer

	Forecast 2003	Actual 2002	Actual 2001	Actual 2000
Individuals	33%	38%	51%	63%
Independent nurseries and schools	42%	39%	29%	25%
State nurseries and schools	25%	23%	20%	12%
	100%	100%	100%	100%

Table 2 Balance Sheet of EIFL
at 31 December 2002

	£	£	£
Fixed Assets			
Premises		750,000	
Plant & equipment		500,000	
Current Assets			
Stock	599,000		
Debtors	562,500		
Cash	18,100	1,179,600	
			2,429,600
Current Liabilities			
Creditors	375,000		
Overdraft	560,000		
Tax due	47,200		
			(982,200)
			1,447,400
Share Capital	75,000		
Revenue Reserves	897,400		
Revaluation Reserve	100,000		
Mortgage	375,000		1,447,400

Table 3 Profit and Loss Account
Profit and loss Account for EIFL for the year ending 31 December 2002

	£	
Sales		2,463,000
Opening Stock	425,000	
Purchases	1,039,000	
	1,464,000	
Closing Stock	(599,000)	
Cost of Sales		(865,000)
Gross Profit		1,598,000
Total Expenses		(1,480,000)
Net Profit		118,000
Tax	47,200	
Net Profit after Tax	70,800	

Table 4 Cash Flow Statement: January–March Actual, April–May Forecast

Year 2003 to date

PAYMENTS	Jan	Feb	Mar	Apr	May
Purchases	87,000	92,000	98,000	85,000	96,000
Production expenses	22,000	33,000	42,000	42,000	41,000
Wages and salaries	59,000	62,000	72,000	72,600	77,500
Office expenses	4,500	4,500	4,500	4,500	4,500
Utilities and business rates etc	2,200	2,101	1,896	1,963	2,003
Interest on mortgage	3,125	3,125	3,125	3,125	3,125
Overdraft interest	4,667	4,578	4,699	4,979	5,068
Marketing and distribution costs	5,000	5,200	5,412	6,523	6,637
TOTAL PAYMENTS	187,492	206,504	231,632	220,690	235,833
TOTAL RECEIPTS	180,000	192,000	198,000	210,000	225,000
NET CASH FLOW FOR MONTH	(7,492)	(14,504)	(33,632)	(10,690)	(10,833)
OPENING BALANCE	(541,900)	(549,392)	(563,896)	(597,528)	(608,218)
CUMULATIVE NET CASH FLOW	(549,392)	(563,896)	(597,528)	(608,218)	(619,051)

Table 5 Workforce

	Full time	Part time	Total
Production	10	7	17
Packing	4	6	10
Warehouse	3	3	6
Office	1	2	3
TOTAL	18	18	36

Answer **all** the questions.

1 (a) Refer to the balance sheet in Table 2 and cash flows in Table 4. Forecasts for June 2003 are as follows.

Purchases	£81,000
Production expenses	£42,500
Overdraft expenses	£ 5,159

The tax liability is due to be paid in June 2003.

All other relevant figures are the same as in May 2003.

Calculate the overdraft required at the end of June 2003. (6)

(b) Discuss how setting budgets can help the Vernons to manage EIFL efficiently. (10)

2 Advise the Vernons how to meet the concerns of the workforce. (16)

3 'EIFL manufactures about half its sales volume in its factory near Basingstoke. Three other firms make the rest for EIFL.' (Lines 15-16) Evaluate Adam's and Danielle's differing views on this, making clear whose argument you support. (16)

4 Assess the main factors that Adam and Danielle should consider before deciding whether to sell EIFL's products via the internet. (10)

Glossary

above the line Using the media to advertise or promote goods and services for sale.

absenteeism Absence from work which is not acceptably explained.

accountability The fact that workers with responsibilities must be accountable to a supervisor or manager.

accounts The financial records of a business. Accounts should be kept for all activities which have a money value.

acid-test ratio Relates liquid assets (cash and debtors) to current liabilities as a tighter test of the liquidity of a business.

advertising Informing or persuading potential buyers about a product or service. Normally involves one or more of the media. Designed to increase sales.

AIM The Alternative Investment Market through which companies can gain access to further capital. The market is designed to give support to smaller companies.

appraisal Any method of evaluating the performance of an employee, often against set targets with new targets set for the coming period. Appraisal is often two way.

articles of association This document sets out the internal rules of a limited company, e.g. types of shares and powers of directors.

assets employed The assets used in a business. Usually found by adding working capital + fixed assets + intangible assets.

audit A check on the accuracy of the accounting process, the truth and fairness of the accounting statements and the probity with which the cash flows into and out of the business have been undertaken and accounted for.

authoritarian leadership A style of leadership/management that keeps all decision making at the centre of the organisation. Lower levels of the hierarchy are given little delegated authority and communication is usually just one way.

authority The requirement and the status to get something done. Authority is passed down the line and the delegated is accountable to the delegator for ensuring that it is done.

average rate of return A method of investment appraisal which measures viability in terms of the average return per year (see also pay back period).

balance sheet The view of the value of a business at a point in time. This is usually the end of the trading year. It provides a 'true and fair' view of the position of the business at that time. Can be presented in a variety of forms.

bank overdraft The negotiated right to take more money from a bank account that is in it. An upper limit to the right is always stated.

batch production Simultaneous production or completion of a process, of several units at the same time. Example the cooking of loaves of bread.

below the line Promotion of a product through such methods as 'two for the price of one', demonstrations and displays, special offers.

benchmarking Seeking to identify best practice in any aspect of production and in any organisation and then adopt it in the production process.

book value The value placed on an asset in the accounts of a business. Usually based on original cost less provision made for depreciation.

break-even point The point at which total costs are equal to total revenue. Can be found graphically or by use of a formula. It is a form of forecasting on which production decisions may be made.

Budget (a) A planned allocation of resources (usually money) to a particular purpose, e.g. production costs or a planned target for receipts, e.g. sales revenue.
(b) The (usually) annual plan which the Chancellor of

Glossary

the Exchequer puts before parliament outlining the intended approach for the raising and using of money in the coming year. These plans are embodied in the annual Finance Act and in other appropriate legislation.

business cycle   The changing pattern of business activity over a period of time (see diagram of page 77).

capacity   The capability of a firm to produce.

capacity utilisation   A measure of the efficiency with which capacity is being used. The more fully facilities are being used the less waste and inefficiency there should be.

capital   (a) One of the factors of production, the wealth that makes business possible.

(b) The amount of money used within a business.

capital borrowed   That part of the capital obtained from loans.

capital employed   The capital which a business uses against which the profit can be measured to provide the primary measure of profitability. Consists of capital borrowed plus capital owned or the net assets of the business.

capital expenditure   Money which is spent out to increase the assets of a business. This is in contrast to revenue expenditure, see below.

capital intensity   The extent to which capital is used in preference to other factors of production. For example the Docklands Light Railway is fully automated and has no drivers. It is highly capital intensive.

capital owned   That part of the capital which belongs to the owner(s) or to shareholders.

cash flow   The movement of cash into and out of the business. The business needs a positive cashflow to survive, i.e. inflows greater than outflows.

cash flow forecast   A cash budget which plans or forecasts the likely flow of cash into and out of a business in a given period of time.

cell production   The workforce is divided into a number of self-contained units (cells). Each cell produces the whole of the product or at least several stages of it.

centralisation   The tendency to keep control within a central office or among the management team. It is common to centralise financial matters and often buying decisions.

chain of command   The levels of hierarchy within an organisation. Command passes down the levels from the top to the bottom. The chain is the linked levels in a line from top to bottom.

civil law   The law which regulates relationships between two or more people and provides a means of settling non-criminal disputes.

cluster sample   Relatively intense sampling of the same small area, e.g. sampling a single constituency in a general election.

communication   Any process, by any method, which is designed to influence the behaviour of someone, or the actual processes by which this is done.

competition   The situation where there is more than one firm in the market for the same goods or for close substitutes.

competition-based pricing   Setting a price for a product or service by taking into account prices charged by competitors.

conservation   The act of saving resources or areas and of using them wisely. An example is the careful maintenance of stocks of fish by limiting catches.

consumer marketing   Attempting to sell to consumers rather than to businesses.

consumers   Those who use a product or service. They are not always the buyers, e.g. baby clothes.

contract   A legally binding agreement between two parties. Contracts need not be in writing but it is normal to have some evidence of their existence, e.g. a receipt for a purchase. Some contracts have to be written, e.g. one to buy a house or business.

Contract of Employment   A legally binding agreement to provide work (employer) and to undertake that work (employee). An employee must be given particulars of the contract but does not always have to be given an actual, formally written contract.

contribution costing   Costing which ignores fixed costs and bases decisions only on the difference between the sale price of a unit and its variable cost. This difference is called the contribution.

co-operatives   Organisations run by a group of people each of whom has a financial interest in its success and a say in how it is managed.

corporation tax   The tax levied on the profits of companies.

cost-based pricing   Determining price by adding a mark-up to the unit cost. There is a traditional mark-up associated with many industries.

creditors   Those who are still to be paid for goods or services. It is usual to distinguish between trade creditors, e.g. for raw materials, and expense creditors, e.g. for advertising. Creditors help to finance business by providing time to pay.

criminal law   The law which establishes which acts are punishable and the means, through the criminal courts, of bringing wrong doers to justice.

current assets   Those assets of a business which constantly change their nature in the flow of daily business activity. The main elements of current assets are stock, debtors and cash.

current ratio   The most familiar of the ratios which measure liquidity. It relates total current assets to current liabilities. A tighter ratio best suited to firms with high stock values, is the acid test ratio (see above).

debentures   Loan certificates. Usually long-term loans at a fixed rate of interest, sometimes secured against a specified asset in which case they are mortgage debentures.

debtor days ratio   Calculates the number of days taken to collect debts. Helps to measure the extent to which debts are really a liquid asset. A business would normally look for a ratio below 30 days. However it is frequently much longer.

debtors   Those who owe a firm money. Some businesses try to avoid debtors (cash and carry) and most will wish to see some evidence of credit worthiness before granting credit.

decentralise   The tendency to spread control and to delegate authority, e.g. from head office to the branches of a business.

decision accounting   That part of the accounting process, sometimes called management accounting, which prepares accounting data and analyses it, in order to enable decisions to be made. It also monitors processes to ensure progress towards objectives is maintained.

delegation   The passing down the line of authority to do something. The responsibility remains with the delegator.

demand   (a) The desire for a good or service backed by the ability and willingness to pay for it.
(b) The amount of a commodity actually purchased per unit of time at a given price.

demand-based pricing   Often called 'what the traffic will bear' it is based upon the amount the consumer will pay.

democratic leadership   A leadership style that allows the majority opinion of staff to influence decisions. It involves a great deal of participation from the workforce but can be time consuming.

depreciation   The way accountants assess the fall in value of an asset as a result of use and passage of time. Shown as an accumulated amount in the balance sheet and as an annual provision in the profit and loss account.

development   Often used in conjunction with research. Taking something which has been invented or discovered a stage further with a view to production.

direct costs   Costs which are attributable to a particular product, process or service.

direct taxes   Taxes levied directly on income, e.g. income tax and corporation tax.

directives   Decisions made by the EU which national parliaments must bring into their own law. An example is the Directive on working hours.

diseconomies of scale   Factors in a production situation resulting from the increasing scale of operations which increase unit costs of production, e.g. having to work overtime or holidays.

dismissal   The act of terminating a contract of employment. It is a formal procedure in most cases and, if not carried out in accordance with procedure, may be unfair.

Glossary

disposable income   What is left of net income after all necessary payments have been made. The income earner has a choice as to how disposable income will be spent. For many people disposable income is very small.

distribution channels   The route taken from producer to consumer. The shortest is direct selling and the commonest through an agent, dealer or wholesaler to the retailer and then the customer.

dividend   Part of the disposable profit of a company is paid out to shareholders. This is worked out on a per share basis and is a dividend on each share. Preference shares receive a fixed dividend. Ordinary shares carry no entitlement to receive a dividend but actual dividend is unlimited.

double entry   Reflects the fact that every transaction has two sides and that both should be recorded, e.g. if I buy a kilo of sugar, the cash of the retailer is increased by its price and the stock of sugar reduced by one kilo.

economies of scale   Factors which lead to a falling unit cost as output rises. The major factor here is usually the spread of fixed costs over an increasing number of units as output rises. But there are also economies which arise from specialisation, from greater capacity utilisation or from bulk buying.

efficiency ratios   Those ratios which focus on the measurement of efficiency, e.g. how well fixed assets are utilised can be shown by relating gross profit or net profit to fixed assets.

employment law   All legislation which regulates contracts of employment, conditions of work and ways in which employees can be dismissed.

empowerment   Transferring authority to act to workers. A form of delegation but it is less specific, offering choice to the worker in many situations.

environment   All aspects of the surroundings, conditions and circumstances within which business operates.

environmental audit   Methods intended to assess a company's corporate responsibility by costing the contributions it might make to environmental damage against the benefits which accrue from exercise of corporate responsibility towards the environment.

equilibrium point   The point when the market is in balance, i.e. the amount demanded is equal to the amount supplied.

equity   Share capital but often used to refer to the whole of the shareholders' funds in a company.

ethics   A set of moral principles by reference to which we would expect our own lives and the practices of business to be conducted. There is no universal agreement about what these principles should be.

European Union   The union of countries in Europe who have agreed to act collectively rather than nationally. The number of countries in the Union has grown considerably since the Treaty of Rome in 1957. The Union is set to grow even bigger.

exchange rate   The rate at which one currency is traded for another.

excise duties   Taxes on commodities, e.g. cars, beers, cigarettes.

export duties   Taxes which would be levied on selling goods to other countries by the home countries.

factoring   The process of selling an outstanding debt to a debt collecting business. Often undertaken when a business needs to avoid cash flow problems. Most businesses factor high purchase debts at the time the HP agreement is made.

factors of production   The inputs upon which production of goods and services is dependent. These are land (natural resources), capital, all forms of work (labour) and managerial skill (enterprise). There is an increasing tendency for capital to be more and labour less significant in the combinations which producers create.

favourable variance   A difference between budgeted and actual results which is to the benefit of the business, e.g. sales greater than budgeted would be regarded as a favourable variance as would costs less than forecasted.

final accounts   Those documents and reports which collectively sum up the activities and position of a business at the end of a trading period. Minimum requirements in this respect are laid down for public limited companies by the Companies Acts.

finance   Support for business which enables activity, usually money but it is sometimes time.

financial accounting   That aspect of accounting which records all the day-to-day transactions of the business, audits, records and completes the periodic financial statements.

fixed assets   Those assets whose purpose and nature do not change over time. They are recorded at historical cost (what was paid for them) and revalued as required, in various ways. Premises, vehicles and machinery are examples.

fixed costs   Those costs which, in the short run, do not vary with output.

flow production   In its major form it is mass production. Producing by completing the stages on an assembly line. Flow production may not produce the whole article.

formal groups   Groups which have been deliberately created, e.g. the classes in a school or the Health and Safety Committee at work. They exist only to complete their function and their objectives are determined from outside the group. Membership is often by appointment.

full costing   An approach to costing which allocates all the costs of production to cost centres to ensure that everything is taken into account.

goodwill   As an accounting concept it is the difference in value between the price for which a business is sold and the value of the assets. It is a reflection of the trading value or reputation of the business.

grants   The provision of finance in a way which does not expect repayments. Grants and charitable institutions often give support in this way.

gross income   Personal income before any deductions. The full amount earned.

gross profit   The profit made on actual trading activities before considering the expenses of running the business. Found by subtracting cost of goods sold from net sales revenue.

growth   The extent to which an economy or a business adds value to itself. In money terms growth means increases in money values which are above the rate of inflation.

health and safety   It is a legal requirement that employers or providers of facilities and services ensure that their premises are a safe and healthy place to work in accordance with the established code of practice. It applies to most activities and institutions as well as places of work, e.g. schools, churches and entertainment places. The main legislation is the Health and Safety at Work Act and the Food Safety Act.

Herzberg, F.   Developed the two factor theory of motivation at work. The development of his work was through job enrichment (see below).

hire purchase   A form of medium-term credit purchase involving a deposit followed by regular monthly payments. The goods are not owned by the purchaser until the last payment is made.

human resource management   Modern term for the personnel function which includes a wide range of activities designed to recruit, train and efficiently use human resources.

hygiene factors   One part of Herzberg's two-factor theory. The hygiene factors are extrinsic to the job and can cause dissatisfaction if they are not adequately provided. Includes salary, work conditions and excessive supervision.

import duties   Taxes levied in this country on goods bought from abroad.

income tax   The tax on personal incomes which is determined each year by the amount of income earned and the budgetary decisions of the Chancellor.

incremental budgeting   Budgeting on the basis of a change (usually an increase) on the budget for the previous period.

indirect costs   Costs which must be covered but which cannot be directly attributed to producing a particular product, process or service.

indirect taxes   Taxes levied through the spending of money, e.g. VAT.

induction   The process of introducing new employees to their place of work, the culture and operational methods of the business, the roles they are meant to adopt and those within which they will work. Poor induction or no induction are often reasons why people leave firms.

industrial marketing   Attempting to find customers among other businesses as opposed to consumer marketing.

inflation   A fall in the value of money. It is a government objective to keep inflation low.

informal groups   Usually arise rather than created. Have no roles defined from outside and membership is determined by the norms of the group. Examples are a friendship group or a group of those who play cards in the lunch hour.

inputs   The resources which are brought together to produce goods and services.

insolvency   The firm is unable to meet its immediate financial commitments.

intangible assets   Those assets which have no physical form but which are of monetary value to the business, e.g. goodwill, copyright and patents.

investment goods   Those goods and services which are bought to enable production. Machines and raw materials are examples.

job description   Details the nature of a job. Often the basis of an advert and usually sent out to potential employees. Should be part of the contract of employment and should be changed whenever an employee's job is changed or redesigned.

job enlargement   Making a job bigger so that it is more complete or more challenging.

job enrichment   Developing the characteristics and requirements of a job so that the job gives greater satisfaction to the worker and hence provides greater motivation.

job production   Producing one unit at a time. This is often customising the product at the same time.

job rotation   Increasing the flexibility of the work force and the variety of the work they do by moving them from one job to another on a regular basis.

joint venture   A co-operative activity between two or more organisations or countries. Concorde and the Channel Tunnel were both produced by joint ventures.

just-in-time   Part of a lean production attitude. It tries to avoid holding stock of any kind. Just-in-time seeks delivery of stock, or work in progress or finished goods just when they are needed and not before.

Kaizen   Continuous improvement rather than improvement in lumps (see diagram on page 244).

labour intensity   The extent to which production depends upon labour as a factor of production. Craft industries, the arts and many of the professions are labour intensive.

labour turnover   The number of people who leave an employment as a proportion of total employed. High labour turnover has substantial costs for a business.

laissez-faire leadership   A leadership style that leaves much of the running and decision making of the business to the workforce. This may be appropriate in research and development departments staffed by skilled specialists that are self-motivated.

leadership   The fact of leading, the role adopted when workers have to be guided towards the achievement of objectives. There are many styles of leadership and the appropriate one must be found for any given situation.

lean production   Not really a method, this is more an attitude of mind or a culture within which the objective is to eliminate waste of all kinds from original stock order through to customer service.

leasing   Renting a service, an asset or a property. It reduces the capital required to use an asset but carries the risks of non-ownership.

legal personality   Conveyed on companies by incorporation it gives them rights and responsibilities, treating them as people in the eyes of the law.

legislation   The means by which new law is brought into being. We are subject to laws made by our regional and national assemblies as well as those made by the EU (see directives above).

lenders   Those who provide funds to a business without rights of ownership. Money borrowed must be repaid and attracts a rate of interest in most cases.

limited liability   Reduces the risks of ownership for

shareholders in companies, to the investment they have made in the company and prevents any claim on their personal assets.

line and staff   Line workers are those who work in a given position in the chain of command of a given department. Staff workers do not work in the line but may be called into it to give support, advice or to maintain a common policy or approach. There is often conflict between the two.

liquidity   The speed with which the current assets of a firm can be converted to cash without a reduction in their book value. The ratios which measure this are the current ratio and the acid-test ratio (see above). The ability of a firm to pay its short-term creditors.

liquidity ratios   Those ratios which measure the ability of a firm to pay its short-term creditors. The main two are the acid test and the current ratio.

McGregor   Author of Theory X and Theory Y (see below).

management accounting   An alternative phrase for decision accounting (see above).

management by objectives   Determining the required outcome and managing the efforts of a worker or workers towards its achievement. The method often sets up individual short-term targets to guide workers more easily towards success.

management style   The approach to management adopted by a single manager or by all within the culture of an organisation.

marginal costing   Costing in terms of the cost of the last unit produced. If 100 units are produced and output is raised to 101 units, the marginal cost is the cost of producing that 101st unit.

mark up   The amount added to the unit cost of products to determine the price at which they will be sold.

market growth   The rate of increase of sales in the whole market for a product.

market orientation   Focusing on the markets and the needs and wants of the consumer.

market positioning   Placing a product within the market in terms of an image, e.g. young and fashionable.

market segment   A part of the market for a good or service which has its own characteristics and which can be identified and targeted. Segmentation can be by any variable, e.g. sex, age, occupation, region.

market share   The percentage of total market sales held by one brand or business.

market standing   The reputation of a firm among its suppliers and customers.

marketing   All the processes and practices which link producers and potential buyers.

marketing mix   The combination of marketing variables which is put together to form a plan or strategy.

marketing objectives   The particular objectives which a marketing team will pursue in order to meet the objectives of the business as a whole, e.g. market penetration or market leadership.

Maslow   Best known for his hierarchy of needs as a basis for pinpointing and satisfying human needs and hence motivating people at work (see diagram page 177).

Mayo, E.   Concluded from experiments at the Hawthorne works that co-operation with, and supportive observation of, people at work can increase their productivity. Also undertook research into the effects of fatigue and boredom.

memorandum of Association   A legal document required before a business can become an incorporated company. It contains the objectives, the amount of authorised share capital and the types of shares to be sold.

motivation   The desire which people have to work well. Not easy to measure except through careful observation of behaviour.

movement   A concept developed by Herzberg. Movement is those processes which take people to work, putting them in a position to do it. People who are at work are not necessarily motivated.

net current assets   Another name for working capital. Measured by subtracting current liabilities from current assets. It indicates the sufficiency of the funds with which the firm is carrying on its day to day transactions.

net income   Personal income after tax and national insurance payments have been made.

net profit   That profit which remains after all the expenses and provisions of running the business have been deducted and any additional incomes have been added in.

niche market   A small segment of the market which a firm can target and hold successfully against competition. Sock Shop is an example of a niche approach.

noise   Any form of disturbance which makes communication difficult.

objectives   The outcomes which a firm or organisation attempts to achieve. Overall objectives normally include survival, profit and growth. There may be others. Departments will develop objectives designed to ensure achievement of corporate ones.

observation   A direct method of research. Has the advantage that what is seen has actually happened.

off-the-job training   Training which takes place away from the job. This often takes place in a firm's own training school or in colleges following appropriate courses.

on-the-job training   For many jobs the only way to train is by doing the job, usually under controlled or observed conditions. Examples are teaching, medicine and bus driving. A great many training programmes are a combination of both on- and off-the-job training.

operating profit   The actual profit earned from what the business does.

opportunity cost   The cost of something in terms of the next-best alternative. Example: if I can buy either a pop disc or a dance ticket but not both, the cost of one can be expressed in terms of the other. The cost of the disc is the ticket I could not have.

organisation   (a) A work unit not necessarily a business one, e.g. a church or a golf club.
(b) The process of structuring work and workers so that activities are efficiently undertaken.

organisation charts   Diagrams which represent the way a firm is organised and define the inter-relationships between workers. The most common form divides and organises work by function, but it is also possible to organise by product, by team, by system or by a matrix approach.

organisational objectives   The pattern of objectives which an organisation decides upon and attempts to fulfil (see Objectives above).

overheads   The costs of running a business over and above those of producing specific products. Overhead costs can be either fixed, e.g. office premises, or variable, e.g. telephone calls.

partnership   A legal form of business organisation in which two or more people – the partners – trade collectively.

paternalistic   This style of leader treats the workforce as a family. Staff may be consulted but decisions are taken by central management.

pay back period   The length of time it takes for an original investment to be paid back by the net inward cash flows involved.

planning   The process of organising how things should be done to achieve a given objective.

price elasticity of demand   The responsiveness of demand to a small change in price. Measured by the percentage change in demand/percentage change in price.

price stability   Keeping prices stable. In part this is a matter of controlling inflation. In part it may be a deliberate policy by businesses or by the State, to avoid price wars.

price wars   Competition by businesses which uses price as a major weapon. Particularly common when there is over-supply of a good or service.

pricing strategy   The plan of action through which a price or prices are determined or changed, normally part of an overall marketing strategy.

primary activity   Business activity in the primary sector using national resources. Fishing, agriculture and mining are examples.

primary information   Often called field research and is collected with specific reference to the matter being investigated.

private limited company An incorporated business that is owned by shareholders but does not have the legal right to offer shares for sale to the public. They are often family-owned businesses.

product development Making the product or the product range more suited to the needs of the market place. Sometimes used to mean the development stages before the production and launch of a new product.

product life cycle The stages through which all products which survive the launch, go through to the end of their natural life (see diagram on page 112).

product orientation Focusing on the design and quality of the product, often made in traditional ways, rather than on using market research to establish the products that are most likely to be successful in the market.

product positioning Places a product in the market in terms of its rivals (see diagram on page 115).

production The process of adding value when inputs are used to create outputs of goods and services.

productivity Not to be confused with production. This is a measure of efficiency. Measurement can be in terms of the use of any of the factors of production and is still commonly expressed in terms of productivity per employee hour. Productivity per £ of capital invested is often more significant.

profit The difference between the total costs and total revenue of a business. The word has no precise meaning on its own.

profit and loss account The account in which the net profit or net loss made by the business in a specific trading period is calculated, part of the final accounts of a business. Has three elements: (i) the calculation of the gross profit often called the Trading A/c, (ii) the calculation of the net profit after tax and interest deductions, (iii) the decision as to how the disposable profit is used or distributed often called the appropriation account.

profitability ratios Ratios which focus on the profits made in relation to assets used. The leading ratio of this kind is the Return on Capital employed (ROCE) which is net profit/capital employed.

promotion strategy Promotion is any activity designed to persuade a successful sale. The strategy is the total approach in line with a given objective.

public limited company An incorporated business that has the legal right to offer shares for sale to the public. Shares of these companies are listed on the Stock Exchange.

published accounts Accounts of companies which are available to shareholders and the general public. They consist primarily of the final accounts of a business. Most businesses now make them available on the Internet.

qualitative information Information of a non-numerate kind, often based on judgments, opinions, attitudes or experiences.

quality Some goods like Thornton's chocolates are meant to be of a high standard of excellence. Others like cheap ballpoint pens are meant to be as cheaply produced as possible as long as they do their job. From this it is clear that quality is a variable standard which once established at a given level, the production line will work to achieve.

quality assurance Giving assurances to the buyer, which may be an internal one, that required specifications have been met.

quality circles Groups of workers involved in different stages of work who meet together at regular intervals with the objective of ensuring or improving the quality of work done.

quality control Sometimes built in and often statistical it seeks to control quality by testing and then rejecting sub-standard goods. Often demotivating where it involves an inspector rejecting and criticising.

quantitative information Information which is collected in numerate form and can be meaningfully aggregated and interpreted.

questionnaires A means, through direct questionning of respondents, of collecting information. Questions may be open or closed.

quota sample When a demographic pattern of the population is known and samples are drawn from it in proportion to the characteristics of the pattern. Example: If 70% of shoppers are women then 70 out of every 100 interviews in a shopping survey should be women.

random sample   When every person in the population being surveyed has the same chance of being selected.

rate of interest   The cost at which money can be borrowed.

ratio analysis   The technique which relates two bits of accounting information so as to enable interpretation of a reported situation.

recruitment   The process of finding the employees needed. Good recruitment is based upon effective workforce planning and carefully designed selection procedures.

recycling   Processing waste products so that they may be used again in some form, now a major industry applying to a wide range of used materials.

redundancy   A worker is redundant when dismissed because there is no longer any work for the worker to do. Dismissal followed by the employment of someone else to do the same job is not redundancy. Under certain circumstances workers receive redundancy payments related to their average weekly wage and their length of service.

research   Discovery activities. Market research looks for market information; technological research looks for new ways of doing things.

resource management   The quality of the management of resources of all kinds, and the extent to which waste can be reduced or eliminated.

retained profit   That part of the disposable profit of a business which is retained by the business. It is sometimes called 'ploughed back' profit and is one of the major sources of finance for companies.

return on capital employed   The relationship between net profit and capital employed (ROCE). Considered the most important profitability ratio.

revenue expenditure   Expenditure incurred to meet the day-to-day expenses of the business. It does not add to asset values, it simply pays for costs which are incurred. Examples are payment of wages and advertising expenditure.

role   An employee's expected function within the total workforce.

role conflict   When two or more roles are such that the proper completion of one makes it difficult or impossible to complete the other.

role reversal   When roles in one situation are the opposite of roles in another. Jennifer may be a Secretary to John at work but she may be his leader as Mayor of a council of which he is a member.

salaries   Payment to staff calculated on an annual basis but usually paid monthly. Offers more security than wages.

sale of assets   The conversion of assets to cash often followed, in the case of fixed assets by lease back. Organisations will sell assets which have come to the end of their useful life. They will also sell as an internal source of finance.

sales turnover   May be expressed in money in which case it is net sales for a period or it may be expressed in volume and is the number of units of product(s) sold.

sampling   The process of collecting information from a population which is either unknown or too large to ask everyone (see definitions of the different kinds of sample).

sales promotion   A promotion strategy which is focused on a sales target. Commonly it sets out to attract the consumer with sales-based promotions, such as 'buy one get one free' or demonstrations.

scientific decision making   The technique of using a logical scientific method to solve business problems and to take decisions. First explained by F.W. Taylor.

secondary activity   Business activity which uses natural resources and other inputs to construct or manufacture.

secondary information   Often called desk research, this is information which already exists and is not specific to the matter being investigated.

semi-variable costs   Costs which have both a fixed and a variable element, e.g. salaries which have an element of commission payment in them, or costs which vary with output but not proportionately, e.g. use of power.

services   Activities which satisfy consumers' needs. Services may be personal, e.g. hairdressing, or financial advice or public, e.g. transport and telephones.

shareholders   People who own shares and hence are part owners of a company.

social costs   Measures the cost to society as a whole of a decision or activity. Examples might be pollution of the atmosphere, the closing of a school or the dumping of waste materials.

social responsibility   Accepting accountability for the social and environmental consequences of a process or a decision, taking into account the objectives and interests of all stakeholders.

sole trader   An individual owning and operating a business on his/her own.

span of control   The number of subordinates for whom a supervisor or manager is responsible. There is no perfect span it varies widely within the circumstances.

specialisation   Concentration on part of a process or activity. Usually increases standards because specialists are good, or become good, at what they do. Businesses may also specialise, e.g. in certain segments of a market.

stakeholders   Those who have an interest in something. Used to indicate all those different groups who have an interest in the activities of a firm. Examples are employees, customers and the State.

stock   Goods held for manufacture or for sale. There are three kinds of stock: (i) the stock of components and raw materials held for manufacture or processing, (ii) the stock of products which go through several stages and which take time to complete or mature (this is work-in-progress), (iii) the stock of finished goods ready for sale.

stock control   Finding a method of controlling stock where it is held. This varies from the completely manually and physically controlled to that which is totally computerised as in supermarkets. Good stock control is crucial where it may deteriorate, or be stolen or simply become rapidly obsolete.

Stock Exchange   The major market for shares in most countries. The shares of all the major companies are quoted and traded on the Stock Exchanges of the world.

stock turnover ratio   Measures the rate at which stock is sold or the number of days it takes to sell average stock. The lower the number of days the more efficiently the firm is using its working capital.

stratified random sample   A population is divided in accordance with the proportions in which its known and relevant characteristics exist. Each of the identified groups is then randomly sampled.

supply   The amount offered for sale at a given price over a given period of time.

suppliers   Those from whom goods and services are obtained.

SWOT analysis   A technique which critically assesses strengths, weaknesses, threats and opportunities in a given situation. It clarifies problems and issues and enables decisions but it does not make them.

tangible assets   Those assets which have a physical form, e.g. all fixed and current assets.

Taylor   Father of the Scientific Approach to management. He used work study to establish what might be expected from workers and how it should be rewarded. Saw production as a combined effort and hence did not see a role for unions.

taxation   The amount drawn from personal and business incomes by the state. This may be through direct taxes or indirect taxes (see above).

team working   A modern approach to business activity which puts the emphasis on workers working together and their responsibility to and for each other within that team, the approach is said to give greater empowerment and satisfaction to workers and hence to be more motivating and productive.

tertiary activity   Business activity which provides services for consumers, retailing and refuse collection are examples.

Theory X and Y   McGregor argued that management attitudes to workers varying from the extremely positive position of Theory Y, in which workers are seen as wanting to work and seeking responsibility, to the extremely negative position, in which they are viewed as disinclined to work without close control and under instruction.

training   Necessary when a firm wishes an employee to undertake something new which cannot be done without increased information, skill or experience. Some training is specific and other training is developmental.

unemployment Applies to all resources but most commonly applies to the workforce and to being economically active but unable to find a job.

unfavourable variance A difference between budgeted and actual costs or revenues which are to the disadvantage of the firm, e.g. lower sales or higher costs than planned for.

unfair dismissal Dismissal which has not followed procedures or which has not treated the worker fairly as compared with other employees. Employees may take the matter to a tribunal if they consider dismissal has been unfair. It is a matter of fact, to be decided by the Tribunal, whether dismissal has been unfair.

unique selling point A feature of a product or service which can be promoted to attract customers for it. Most businesses try to find or develop a USP for their product.

unlimited liability Applies to sole traders and partners. They risk everything they own if a business venture fails.

value added The difference made by production. The difference between the value of inputs and the value of output from them.

value added tax A tax which is paid on the value that is added at each stage of a production process. It is reclaimed at all stages except the final one of sale when the tax is levied on the consumer. Some goods like food are exempt.

variable costs Those costs which vary relatively proportionately with output. Examples are raw material costs and wages paid on piece rates.

variance analysis The technique which enables management accountants to identify cause of differences between budgeted and actual figures for a given period.

watchdog bodies There are three kinds:
(a) Self-created: These are created by organisations themselves. Good examples are the Law Society and the Association of British Travel Agents (ABTA)
(b) Government bodies such as OFTEL and OFSTED
(c) Pressure groups such as the Consumer Association and Greenpeace.

waste The extent to which resources and goods of all kinds are lost. One of the biggest wastages in our society is unemployment.

work in progress Part-finished goods whose value has been assessed. A necessary part of construction industries in particular where completion may extend over two or more financial years.

workforce planning Working out the overall human resource requirement and the way the jobs of the personnel will interact. This is the basis for effective recruitment.

working capital The net current assets of a business. It uses these to transact its day-to-day business in the conversion of stock into products, products into debtors and debtors into cash. It is measured by deducting current liabilities from current assets.

zero budgeting Assumes there is no budget and requires a justification for each expenditure as it is planned or occurs. Prevents the assumption that budgets will rise each year.

zero defects Part of the lean production approach. The assumption is that quality will be tested continuously so that there are no defects and hence no waste of finished or part finished products.

Index

Note: Page references in *italics* refer to Tables and Figures